Quake 4™ Mods For Dummies

Important Console Commands

Command	Function
bind <key> [command]	Assigns a command to a keyboard key
clear	Clears the console
com_allowConsole 0	Allows toggling console with the ~ key
com_showFPS 0	Shows frames rendered per second
com_showMemoryUsage 0	Shows total and per frame memory usage
conDump <filename>	Writes the console to a text file
developer 0	Runs the game as a developer
devmap <mapname>	Loads a map in developer mode
disconnect	Disconnects from a game
editGUIs	Launches the GUI Editor
editor	Launches the level editor Radiant
exit	Exits a game
fs_game path	Returns the loaded mod path
g_showActiveEntities 0	Draws boxes around thinking entities (Dormant is yellow; non-dormant is green.)
g_showEnemies 0	Draws boxes around monsters that have targeted the player
g_showHud 0	Turns the HUD on or off
g_showTriggers 0	Draws trigger entities orange and their targets green
g_spectatorChat 0	Lets spectators talk to everyone during the game
god	Enables god mode
image_usePrecompressedTextures 1	Uses DDS compressed textures when available
killMonsters	Removes all monsters
listCmds	Lists all commands
listCvars	Lists all cvars
modview	Launches the model viewer
r_brightness 1	Changes brightness level
r_fullscreen 1	Switches between fullscreen and windowed modes
r_gamma 1	Changes brightness level
r_multiSamples 0	Number of antialiasing samples
r_showPortals 0	Draws portal outlines
r_showTris 0	Enables wireframe rendering of the world
r_useScissor 1	Hides triangles outside of player's view
trigger <name>	Triggers an entity
vid_restart	Restarts your video

For Dummies: Bestselling Book Series for Beginners

Quake 4™ Mods For Dummies® Cheat Sheet

Mapping Editor Shortcuts

Action	Shortcut
File Open	Ctrl+O
File Save	Ctrl+S
Camera Up	D
Camera Down	C
Camera Forward	↑
Camera Back	↓
Camera Left	←
Camera Right	→
Camera Angle Down	Z
Camera Angle Up	A
Camera Strafe Left	, (Comma)
Camera Strafe Right	. (Period)
Activate Clipper	X
Clip Selected	Enter
Flip Clip	Ctrl+Enter
Split Clip	Shift+Enter
Redo	Ctrl+Y
Undo	Ctrl+Z
Rotate Selection	Shift+Ctrl+R
Duplicate Selection	Spacebar

Action	Shortcut
Delete Selection	Backspace
Hide Selected	H
Show Hidden	Shift+H
Drag Edges	E
Drag Vertices	V
Entity Color	K
Surface Inspector	S
View Textures	T
View Entities	N
View Console	O
Previous Leak Spot	Shift+Ctrl+L
Grid Increase	]
Grid Descrease	[
Set Grid Size	Number keys 1–7
Open Game	F2
Render Mode	F3
Realtime Render Build	F4
Change 2D View	Alt+Tab
Zoom In	Delete
Zoom Out	Insert

Game Dimensions

Game Element	Measurement
Player's height	74 units (1 unit = 1 inch)
Player's crawling height	40 units
Player's width	40 units
Player's maximum step without jumping	16 units
Player's maximum jumping height	48 units
Player's maximum jumping distance	112 units
Player's highest fall without damage	136 units
Steepest angle a player can climb	45 degrees

Wiley, the Wiley Publishing logo, For Dummies, the Dummies Man logo, the For Dummies Bestselling Book Series logo and all related trade dress are trademarks or registered trademarks of John Wiley & Sons, Inc. and/or its affiliates. All other trademarks are property of their respective owners.

Copyright © 2006 Wiley Publishing, Inc. All rights reserved. Item 3746-6.

For more information about Wiley Publishing, call 1-800-762-2974.

For Dummies: Bestselling Book Series for Beginners

Quake 4™ Mods FOR DUMMIES®

Quake 4™ Mods FOR DUMMIES®

by Erik Guilfoyle

Wiley Publishing, Inc.

Quake 4™ Mods For Dummies®

Published by
Wiley Publishing, Inc.
111 River Street
Hoboken, NJ 07030-5774

www.wiley.com

Copyright © 2006 by Wiley Publishing, Inc., Indianapolis, Indiana

Published by Wiley Publishing, Inc., Indianapolis, Indiana

Published simultaneously in Canada

No part of this publication may be reproduced, stored in a retrieval system or transmitted in any form or by any means, electronic, mechanical, photocopying, recording, scanning or otherwise, except as permitted under Sections 107 or 108 of the 1976 United States Copyright Act, without either the prior written permission of the Publisher, or authorization through payment of the appropriate per-copy fee to the Copyright Clearance Center, 222 Rosewood Drive, Danvers, MA 01923, (978) 750-8400, fax (978) 646-8600. Requests to the Publisher for permission should be addressed to the Legal Department, Wiley Publishing, Inc., 10475 Crosspoint Blvd., Indianapolis, IN 46256, (317) 572-3447, fax (317) 572-4355, or online at http://www.wiley.com/go/permissions.

Trademarks: Wiley, the Wiley Publishing logo, For Dummies, the Dummies Man logo, A Reference for the Rest of Us!, The Dummies Way, Dummies Daily, The Fun and Easy Way, Dummies.com, and related trade dress are trademarks or registered trademarks of John Wiley & Sons, Inc. and/or its affiliates in the United States and other countries, and may not be used without written permission. Quake 4 is a trademark of id Software, Inc. All other trademarks are the property of their respective owners. Wiley Publishing, Inc., is not associated with any product or vendor mentioned in this book.

<u>LIMIT OF LIABILITY/DISCLAIMER OF WARRANTY:</u> THE PUBLISHER AND THE AUTHOR MAKE NO REPRESENTATIONS OR WARRANTIES WITH RESPECT TO THE ACCURACY OR COMPLETENESS OF THE CONTENTS OF THIS WORK AND SPECIFICALLY DISCLAIM ALL WARRANTIES, INCLUDING WITHOUT LIMITATION WARRANTIES OF FITNESS FOR A PARTICULAR PURPOSE. NO WARRANTY MAY BE CREATED OR EXTENDED BY SALES OR PROMOTIONAL MATERIALS. THE ADVICE AND STRATEGIES CONTAINED HEREIN MAY NOT BE SUITABLE FOR EVERY SITUATION. THIS WORK IS SOLD WITH THE UNDERSTANDING THAT THE PUBLISHER IS NOT ENGAGED IN RENDERING LEGAL, ACCOUNTING, OR OTHER PROFESSIONAL SERVICES. IF PROFESSIONAL ASSISTANCE IS REQUIRED, THE SERVICES OF A COMPETENT PROFESSIONAL PERSON SHOULD BE SOUGHT. NEITHER THE PUBLISHER NOR THE AUTHOR SHALL BE LIABLE FOR DAMAGES ARISING HEREFROM. THE FACT THAT AN ORGANIZATION OR WEBSITE IS REFERRED TO IN THIS WORK AS A CITATION AND/OR A POTENTIAL SOURCE OF FURTHER INFORMATION DOES NOT MEAN THAT THE AUTHOR OR THE PUBLISHER ENDORSES THE INFORMATION THE ORGANIZATION OR WEBSITE MAY PROVIDE OR RECOMMENDATIONS IT MAY MAKE. FURTHER, READERS SHOULD BE AWARE THAT INTERNET WEBSITES LISTED IN THIS WORK MAY HAVE CHANGED OR DISAPPEARED BETWEEN WHEN THIS WORK WAS WRITTEN AND WHEN IT IS READ.

For general information on our other products and services, please contact our Customer Care Department within the U.S. at 800-762-2974, outside the U.S. at 317-572-3993, or fax 317-572-4002.

For technical support, please visit www.wiley.com/techsupport.

Wiley also publishes its books in a variety of electronic formats. Some content that appears in print may not be available in electronic books.

Library of Congress Control Number: 2006926168

ISBN-13: 978-0-470-03746-1

ISBN-10: 0-470-03746-6

Manufactured in the United States of America

10 9 8 7 6 5 4 3 2 1

1B/RY/QX/QW/IN

About the Author

Erik "foyleman" Guilfoyle joined the game-modding scene shortly after the release of *Half Life* in early 2000 by creating a custom level and supporting material for the game. After that, Erik was hooked on modding games.

Two years and a lot of practice later, *Soldier of Fortune* was released. Erik jumped at the opportunity to map a custom level for this game and was among the first to release a map for the game with custom textures. This led to a flurry of e-mails requesting advice for constructing custom material, and the beginning of a compendium of game modification tutorials.

Not much later, Erik started up his own Web site to host existing and new tutorials. The site grew until he had the largest collection of tutorials on the Internet for *Call of Duty* mapping. Now, Erik is running the www.modsonline.com modding community with the assistance of two other administrators and several friends, covering many games, including *Quake 4*. As new games are released, he starts off the tutorials section with beginner instruction and leads the member forums in preparation for the next up-and-coming game.

Aside from his love for games, Erik is also the vice-president of an established media company, Tres, Inc. His company has been producing 3D models, animations, motion graphics, and Web sites for companies and corporations throughout New Jersey for over five years. Tres, Inc., is now working on an animated short and preparing a game of its own.

Dedication

This book is dedicated to the `www.modsonline.com` modding community.

Author's Acknowledgments

I would like to express my thanks to those that have knowingly and unknowingly helped me to gain the knowledge that I now have in the field of game modding. David Gonzales helped to get me started in the world of modding and gave me time to continue even when we had real work to get done. Discussions with Turbo gave me revelations and insight into game levels that have stuck with me to this day. My wife Kate has allowed me to spend countless hours on the computer rather than with her, without too much complaining, and I must thank her for that. John McNicol, Don McElyea, and Jeff Sale have been there to encourage me onward while offering advice when needed. Also, thanks to Peter and Cathy Guilfoyle, my parents.

What would this book be without the *Quake 4* game itself? id Software, Inc., and Raven Software, Inc., have built an awesome game and have allowed people like me to wreak havoc on the code that makes it all work. Activision, Inc., has helped to put it in the hands of you and me. For this game, the games before it, and the games to come, thank you for making the world that much more fun.

This book would not have been possible if it were not for the kind and talented folks at Wiley. Melody Layne gave me the opportunity to work with Wiley and got me on track with an easy-to-follow format that anyone can read. Christopher Morris, Leah Cameron, Virginia Sanders, and Clint McCarty helped to keep me on that track with insightful and helpful suggestions during editing. As these are only the people I directly dealt with at Wiley; I know there were several others who had a part in helping me put this book together and I extend my thanks to them.

Finally, thanks to all the fine members of `www.modsonline.com`. It is with them that I have learned so much and continue to learn more with each game that comes out. I only hope that all the tutorials, forums, posts, and everything else I do help to one day make games even more outstanding then they are now.

Publisher's Acknowledgments

We're proud of this book; please send us your comments through our online registration form located at www.dummies.com/register/.

Some of the people who helped bring this book to market include the following:

Acquisitions, Editorial, and Media Development

Project Editor: Christopher Morris

Acquisitions Editor: Melody Layne

Copy Editor: Virginia Sanders

Technical Editor: Clint McCarty

Editorial Manager: Kevin Kirschner

Media Development Specialists: Angela Denny, Kate Jenkins, Steven Kudirka, Kit Malone

Media Development Coordinator: Laura Atkinson

Media Project Supervisor: Laura Moss

Media Development Manager: Laura VanWinkle

Editorial Assistant: Amanda Foxworth

Sr. Editorial Assistant: Cherie Case

Cartoons: Rich Tennant (www.the5thwave.com)

Composition Services

Project Coordinator: Tera Knapp

Layout and Graphics: Carl Byers, Joyce Haughey, Stephanie D. Jumper, Barbara Moore, Barry Offringa, Alicia South,

Proofreaders: Leeann Harney, Joe Niesen, Techbooks

Indexer: Techbooks

Publishing and Editorial for Technology Dummies

    Richard Swadley, Vice President and Executive Group Publisher

    Andy Cummings, Vice President and Publisher

    Mary Bednarek, Executive Acquisitions Director

    Mary C. Corder, Editorial Director

Publishing for Consumer Dummies

    Diane Graves Steele, Vice President and Publisher

    Joyce Pepple, Acquisitions Director

Composition Services

    Gerry Fahey, Vice President of Production Services

    Debbie Stailey, Director of Composition Services

Contents at a Glance

Introduction 1

Part I: The ABCs of Modding 7
Chapter 1: Modifying the Game 9
Chapter 2: Getting Familiar with Modding Tools and Techniques 17
Chapter 3: Breaking Down the Game 23

Part II: Making Your Own Maps 31
Chapter 4: Getting Set Up for Mapping 33
Chapter 5: Creating Your First Game Map 49
Chapter 6: Decorating the Scene 67
Chapter 7: Adding Lights and a Player 75
Chapter 8: Putting the Pieces Together 83

Part III: Expanding Your Creation 91
Chapter 9: Expanding Your Map with Additions 93
Chapter 10: Building with Optimization in Mind 109
Chapter 11: Heading to the Great Outdoors 125
Chapter 12: Adding a Few Details 151
Chapter 13: Playing Alone or with Someone Else 185

Part IV: Going Beyond the Basics 219
Chapter 14: Scripting Advanced Actions 221
Chapter 15: Creating Custom Textures 245
Chapter 16: Gaming with GUIs 285
Chapter 17: Separating Your Files 311
Chapter 18: Re-Skinning the Models 319
Chapter 19: Showing the World 345

Part V: The Part of Tens 355
Chapter 20: Ten Great Tips and Tricks 357
Chapter 21: Ten Great Mods 367

Appendix 379

Index 383

Table of Contents

Introduction 1
About This Book 1
Conventions Used in This Book 2
Foolish Assumptions 2
How This Book Is Organized 3
    Part I: The ABCs Of Modding 4
    Part II: Making Your Own Maps 4
    Part III: Expanding Your Creation 4
    Part IV: Going Beyond the Basics 5
    Part V: The Part of Tens 6
Icons Used in This Book 6

Part 1: The ABCs of Modding 7

Chapter 1: Modifying the Game 9
Shoot First, Ask Questions Later 10
Checking Out Quake 4 11
Adding To or Changing the Game 11
    Finding out what you can mod 12
    Knowing what tools you need 13
The Modding Process Goes Something Like This 14
Sharing the Game with Others 15

Chapter 2: Getting Familiar with Modding Tools and Techniques ...17
Gathering the Tools Involved 17
    Writing plain text 18
    Unpacking your luggage 18
    Drawing, painting, and taking pictures 19
Using Best Modding Practices 20
    Following standard naming conventions 20
    Instructing the end user 21
    Including all the files required 21
    Avoiding the overwriting headache 22
    Saving and saving again 22
Differences between Quake and Other Games 22

Quake 4 Mods For Dummies

Chapter 3: Breaking Down the Game 23
Making Maps and Playing Levels 23
Making Your Own Maps 24
   Building blocks of a map 25
   Setting boundaries 25
   Seeing in three dimensions 26
   Measuring in units 27
Toying with Textures 28
   Painting the walls 28
   Building interest 28
Evoking Entities 29
Sorting Out the Scripts 30
Messing with User Interfaces 30

Part II: Making Your Own Maps 31

Chapter 4: Getting Set Up for Mapping 33
Firing Up the System 34
   Creating a shortcut to Quake 4 34
   Customizing your Quake shortcut 35
Adjusting Your Game's Video Settings 36
   Changing from Fullscreen to Windowed mode 37
   Turning off antialiasing 38
   Reducing the brightness 39
Launching the Editor 41
Arranging Your Windows 41
   Adjusting your screen resolution 42
   Adjusting your work environment 43
Working the Windows and Exploring the Interface 45
   Looking at windows 45
   Pressing buttons and working menus 47
   Using shortcuts for success 48
   Avoiding errors 48

Chapter 5: Creating Your First Game Map 49
Selecting a Texture 49
   Loading texture sets 50
   Caulking your map 51
Drawing the First Brush 53
Maneuvering the 2D Window 54
   Counting in power of two 55
   Zooming and moving the view 55
Resizing and Moving Brushes 56

Hollowing Out the Room	58
Maneuvering the CAM Window	60
Fixing Overlapping Issues	60
Leaking Is Not an Option	64
Saving Your Map	64

Chapter 6: Decorating the Scene 67

Loading the Common Walls Texture Set	67
Selecting and Painting Faces on the Walls	68
Inspecting the Surface	70
Painting the Remaining Faces	72

Chapter 7: Adding Lights and a Player 75

Lighting the Way	75
Positioning the entity	78
Adding a bit of color	78
Adding a Place to Start	79
Positioning and providing some direction	80
Playing with properties on the Entity tab	81

Chapter 8: Putting the Pieces Together 83

Leveling the Playing Field	83
Building the BSP	84
Seeing what can be seen	85
Lighting the scene	86
Comparing the old with the new	87
Processing the Pieces	87
Listening to the console	88
Building the puzzle	89
Playing the Result	90
Exiting the game	90

Part III: Expanding Your Creation 91

Chapter 9: Expanding Your Map with Additions 93

Making Copies	93
Joining Rooms	96
Drawing your halls	96
Making room to play	97
Retexturing the Hallway Walls	104
Lighting the Path	105
Running in the Halls	106

Chapter 10: Building with Optimization in Mind 109

Commanding as a developer..110
Outlining your world...111
Mitering for Mappers..112
Fixing those corners 114
Mitering the floor and ceiling?..116
Automatic optimization...117
Creating Portals..118
Can You See Me?...122

Chapter 11: Heading to the Great Outdoors 125

Building Another Addition...125
Multiplying the ground..128
Filling in the useless corner..129
Defining your boundaries..130
Making a Scene...132
Throwing dirt on the ground...132
Fitting the outer building...132
Climbing the roof 133
Walling in the yard and adding sky 134
Getting Outside...136
Clipping out some doors 136
Touching up the textures 138
Fixing a Bottleneck...141
Sliding the Door Open..142
Making that door move 142
Sealing your area 144
Lighting from Above...145
Understanding your real environment 145
Adding a virtual sun...146
Simulating ambient light..149
Testing Your Progress..150

Chapter 12: Adding a Few Details 151

Doing Some Decorating...151
Pulling a ledge...152
Lighting the porch..155
Defining the indoor lights..160
Pairing the Doors 162
Adding Some Crates...163
Creating climbable crates..164
Placing crates for strategy 166
Making crates for other environments 168

Table of Contents

Picking Up on Pickups 170
    Adding armor 170
    Restoring health 172
    Finding weapons 173
    Grabbing ammo 176
    Powering up 179
    Placing a model to decorate the power-up 179
Testing and Having Fun 182

Chapter 13: Playing Alone or with Someone Else 185

Adding Single-Player Enemies 186
    Inserting a Strogg..186
    Inserting a gladiator 192
Adding Multiplayer Opponents 195
    Playing one-on-one 195
    Teaming up with others 197
Playing Multiplayer Levels 204
    Defining your level 204
    Making a custom loading screen 206
    Creating a thumbnail image 211
    Determining the level size 212
Considering Other Game Types 215
    Playing the tourney 215
    Capturing the arena 216

Part IV: Going Beyond the Basics 219

Chapter 14: Scripting Advanced Actions 221

Finding Tools You Already Had 221
Breaking Apart the Script...226
Lifting Sensations 228
    Constructing the platform..229
    Texturing the platform...231
    Creating the track..233
    Turning the platform..234
    Controlling your lift..236
    Scripting the action..239
    Adding the final touches 243

Chapter 15: Creating Custom Textures 245

Slicing Up the Texture 246
Installing Some Tools 247
Bricking Up the Joint 247

Finding the Right Size 248
Tiling on Forever 251
    Shifting the image to expose the seam 252
    Stamping out your seams 255
    Shifting back to ground zero 258
Mapping Your Images 260
    Splashing on some color: The diffuse map 260
    Picking out the highlights: The specular map 261
    Bumping polygons in and out: The normal map 267
    Creating a normal map without the filter 271
    Defining the ups and downs: The height map 272
    Finding the texture: The editor image 276
Making Everything Work Together 281
    Building a shader 281
    Applying your material 283

Chapter 16: Gaming with GUIs 285

Opening Doors 286
    Looking at the wall 286
    Interacting with an entity 288
    Controlling your doors 290
    Working on your own 292
Creating a Custom Interface 293
    Starting the GUI editor 294
    Building your first GUI 294
    Saving your work 307
Applying Your Custom Interface 308
Exploring Deeper into the Game 310

Chapter 17: Separating Your Files 311

Understanding Game-Defined Mods 313
Naming a Mod of Your Own 315

Chapter 18: Re-Skinning the Models 319

Locating the Models and Their Skins 320
Hunting Down Your Mod Files 325
    Searching in materials 325
    Making changes 331
    Compressing to DDS 343
    Viewing the mod 344

Chapter 19: Showing the World 345
Creating the Package 345
    Packaging additions to the game 346
    Packaging mods that alter the game...................... 351
Distributing the Goods 354

Part V: The Part of Tens 355

Chapter 20: Ten Great Tips and Tricks 357
Come Up with Original Ideas 357
Plan Your Build 358
Design Minimally 358
Avoid Errors 359
    Subtracting with CSG 360
    Dragging out a triangle 361
    Super-sizing brushes 361
Follow Examples 362
Use Prefabs 362
Mesh Objects 363
Measure the Player 363
Find More to Mod 364
Look for Help 365

Chapter 21: Ten Great Mods 367
Corpse Stay and Self Shadow 367
    Possible pitfalls 369
Drach-FPS-Mappack 369
    Possible pitfalls 370
Fleischhaus 370
    Possible pitfalls 371
Logo Crosshair 371
    Possible pitfalls 372
Q4GIB 372
    Possible pitfalls 373
Dark Matter Mayhem 373
    Possible pitfalls 374
Quake 4 WOD 374
    Possible pitfalls 376
Q4 X-Battle Battlemod 376
    Possible pitfalls 377

Q4MAX 377
    Possible pitfalls..377
SABot 378
    Possible pitfalls..378

Appendix 379

System Requirements 379
Using the CD with Microsoft Windows 380
What You'll Find on the CD 380
    Author-created material 381
    WinZip 381
    Adobe Photoshop Elements..381
    The Compressonator 381
    Normal Map Generator 381

Index 383

Introduction

If this is your first time venturing into the world of game modding, let me post a warning now. You are entering into something that many people, including myself, have described as addicting, exciting, and frustrating all at the same time. I know of very few people who have started on the path of game modification and found it easy to stop working on their projects for even a few days. If you are experienced in game modification, you already know what you're getting yourself into. Either way, I welcome you to *Quake 4 Mods For Dummies*.

I've led many beginners along the path of game modification, and they all say the same thing. This is an addictive hobby, and it isn't easy to put down even for the night. On several occasions, I've sat down in my computer chair to work on my game, planning to accomplish only a few things. The next thing I know, it's 2 o'clock in the morning, I'm still working, and I have to get up for work in another four hours.

So, heed my warning, but also enjoy what is to come. This book gives you the knowledge and skill to mod on your own. You not only figure out how to create modifications for the *Quake 4* game, but also create content that will have you bragging to your friends and family. Although this book can't tell you every aspect of modding *Quake 4,* it shows you how to continue on your and grow into a master of games.

About This Book

When the first version of *Half-Life* came out, a buddy of mine and I decided to create our own mod for the multiplayer version of the game. From that moment on, I was hooked on modding. There really was no turning back for me, and I just kept on creating more and more content.

Eventually, I moved on to another game to see what kind of things I could create elsewhere. This other game was *Soldier of Fortune*. Quite often I was unable to find assistance online for creating my custom content, so I decided to learn it on my own. Through much trial and error and many discussions with other modders online, I discovered that I was able to help others with their projects. That's when I decided to dedicate my efforts to teaching and guiding others on the how to mod the *Soldier of Fortune* game.

Over the years, I furthered my exploration and tutelage of modding with other games, and here I am now with *Quake 4*. I really enjoy showing others how to make mods for games, and I can do the same for you. All you need to do is read on.

My goal in this book is to show you by example many aspects of modding *Quake 4*. I provide you with an understanding of how things work so that you can take what I show you and further your newly found knowledge on your own. I leave you with not just information, but also something you can play in the game and show off to your friends and family.

Conventions Used in This Book

I lead you into the world of modding *Quake 4* by way of two methods, both of which I feel are equally important. The first and most obvious is by way of example. As I walk you through the different aspects of modding, I show you, step-by-step, the methods to use. I don't leave you guessing as to what needs to be typed, clicked, or done.

For each chapter that has you creating something for the game, I have also supplied an example. On the media in the back of the book, you can find chapter-based files containing all the work that was reviewed. You can use this either for reference of the current chapter or as a starting point for the following chapter, which builds upon the previous.

The second method that I use is that of background. I provide you with all the necessary background for each subject in modding. A statement made to me once a long time ago that I have never forgotten is that "it's easier to drive a car if you know how it works." You can apply the same principle to games. The more you know about how a game works, the easier it is going to be to mod.

Background provides you with understanding. With understanding, you can do more than create. You can also better find out why something doesn't work. There are going to be moments that something doesn't turn out as you expected. With a background of how you got to your issue, you should be able to solve any problems that arise.

Foolish Assumptions

To find a starting ground upon which to write, I had to make a few assumptions. I must first assume that you have a basic understanding of your computer. You must know how to use the keyboard and mouse and how to turn it on.

Because you purchased this book, I assume you know something about games. You should already have a copy of the *Quake 4* game, not just in your hands, but also installed on your computer. Hopefully you installed the game by using the default installation paths. After you installed the game, I assume you got it running and perhaps even played it a little bit. You bought the game, so you should spend a little time enjoying it.

Due to the requirements of the tools that you will be using, I assume that you have a three-button mouse. Although you can following along with a majority of this book without a three-button mouse, there are one or two operations that you won't be able to do without this type of mouse.

Perhaps not so obvious, I assume that you're working on a computer by using the Microsoft Windows operating system. At the time of writing this book, it is possible to modify the *Quake 4* game only on a Windows installation. If you are using a Linux or Mac operating system, I cannot be certain that the chapters contain proper examples.

Because you have a Microsoft Windows operating system, I have taken the liberty of making a few other assumptions. I figure that you know how to open and use Windows File Explorer for browsing folders and files on your computer. I also figure that you have the basic programs that come with Windows, such as Notepad, installed and accessible.

Now, if you don't have a Windows operating system, the contents of this book can still be of great value. Through example and history, the information I provide you can be useful regardless of the game or platform on which you're working. The discussions here help you to understand the modding process for most games out there. You will be ready to mod, even if you can't actively follow my examples right now.

How This Book Is Organized

Although this book is written in a particular order and each chapter builds upon the next, this doesn't mean you can't skip around. If you want to know how to make your own textures, go for it. Head over to Chapter 15 and start on your custom textures. There I show you how to create your own texture from start to finish.

If you'd prefer to better optimize your map, Chapter 10 is the one for you. There you will figure out how to build your map and modify it for smoother play in the game. It will have better speed and rely less on your processor.

As for the chapters that build upon the previous chapters, those are fine to skip around as well. Just load the example files from the previous chapter as found on the media in the back of the book. Then go on your way as if you've accomplished everything I've written about up to that point. If I feel you should reference a previous chapter for clarity, I make sure to mention it.

This book is broken into five parts as follows:

Part I: The ABCs of Modding

Allow me to introduce you the world of modding. In this part, I help you better understand what it means to modify a game. I point out specific aspects of the game and relate them to something you're familiar with: real life. Then, I briefly walk you through the steps involved in modding a game.

After you're familiar with the concept of modding, I introduce you to some of the tools you'll be using and how you can use them. I acquaint you with some important things that you should remember while modding, and I explain why you want to remember them.

Then, I start breaking down the game. You've perhaps already played through *Quake 4,* but I'll bet you haven't seen it the way I'm going to show it to you. I help you look at the game through different eyes.

Part II: Making Your Own Maps

In Part II, I ease you into the modding process of making your own levels. I start you off with the tools required and show you around. When you're familiar with the popular map editor, I get you started on making your first level. It won't be much, but by the end of this part, you will have a level that you can play in the game.

While making your own level, you get all the basics required. From creating a room and painting the walls to adding light, you build a place to start. From there, you convert your level from the editor and load it in the game for some fun.

Part III: Expanding Your Creation

Part III goes beyond the basics of building a simple level for the game. This is where you go from a single room to something you can enjoy with your friends online. This is arguably the best part of making a level for *Quake 4.*

I start you off with simple additions to the level. You expand from creating a single room to creating something a bit bigger. From there, I show you some optimization tricks. These advancements are some of the most valuable because they can perhaps help the novice and advanced alike.

With your small level in hand, you next turn it into a fun single-player and multiplayer level. You add on an outside area with a great sky. Then you introduce some monsters that won't think twice about fighting back. From there, I show you how to set up your level for multiplayer fun by adding more players for deathmatch, team deathmatch, and CTF excitement.

Part IV: Going Beyond the Basics

Making custom levels isn't the only thing you can do to modify the game. In Part IV, I take you on a path that can not only help to improve the level you created in previous chapters, but also separately improve the game.

The trip starts with scripting, where you can discover how to command things in your level with just a few lines of code. You can rise above the rest by running text-based commands from within the game.

Moving on from scripts, I show you the world of textures. Textures are what can take your player from the dunes of Mars to the beaches of Hawaii. From the confines of a dungeon to the vastness of space, you can create the images that line the walls of everything in the game. Not only are the walls covered in this part, but so are the faces and bodies of the players within the game. Textures cover it all.

On track with the visuals in the game, I show you the graphical user interfaces. Not only do these wonderful creations allow you to create interactive screens in the game, but also don the face of the game menus themselves. This is what can turn your modification from simple add-on to a total conversion of the original game.

Closing off this part is what you need to know to get your mod out to the world. I show you what's involved in packing up your level for distribution. Then I guide you through what should be done to get your mod onto the Web sites for all to see. Why not let the world have as much fun as you did with your awesome creation?

Part V: The Part of Tens

Part V puts everything else into perspective. Modding doesn't stop where I left off. There are tons of other things that you can do to customize the game, and I provide you with ideas to get you started. At this point, you have the knowledge to further yourself in the world of modding or to find more help when needed.

I provide you with ideas and examples of modding tips and tricks and where to look for them. Then I provide examples of the different mods currently available online and why I think they're a cut above the rest.

Icons Used in This Book

As you read through the book, you'll find some fun little icons in the margins. These icons alert you to special content that often highlights the topic at hand. Here are the icons you might see and what they mean:

Tips provide helpful information about the subject. Although perhaps not immediately relevant to performing the task, these tips will come in handy at sometime in the future.

Remember icons remind you of an important idea or fact that you should keep in mind as you explore *Quake 4* mods. They might even point you to another chapter for more in-depth information about a topic.

Warnings point out specific actions that you want to keep your eye on. Read each of the warnings as you're going through a chapter to make sure that problems do arise later.

Technical Stuff icons provide further insight into the subject being read. You can skip them if you like, but I find them to be quite informative.

Part I
The ABCs of Modding

The 5th Wave   By Rich Tennant

"Mary-Jo, come here quick! Look at this special effect I learned with the new Quake 4 editing software."

In this part . . .

Games can be a lot of fun to play. They allow your mind to explore a virtual world as someone or something that you've never been before. From your own home to the jungles and deserts of the world to the infinite possibilities of space, you can go anywhere you want. The only limitations you have are those of the people who created the game.

Well, playing games is just where the adventure begins. You can be the one who tells the story of a faraway place. You can create lands and worlds that come from your own imagination. Then, you can be the one who takes your friends on the adventure that you created for them.

Let me take you behind the curtain that is your computer screen. In this part, I show you that there is no limitation to what can be accomplished with games. The fun doesn't stop when you reach the end credits — this is when the fun just begins.

Chapter 1
Modifying the Game

In This Chapter

▶ Looking at the game through a modder's eyes

▶ Finding modding tools that you had all along

▶ Walking through the making of a mod

▶ Going public with your creations

Have you ever been playing a video game and thought, "I would have done it differently" or "I could have done it better"? Perhaps you thought, "Wouldn't it be cool if. . . . " Well, you don't have to just think it. You can make changes to games and you don't have to be a software engineer to do it.

Game modification is the process of changing something in a game and has generally been associated with the first-person shooter and real-time strategy genres. The change could be very small, such as making a player's outfit orange instead of blue, or the change could be very large, such as creating a whole new environment for the player to explore. You could change almost every aspect of a game and make it look and feel like something completely different, or instead of altering an existing part of the game, you could add new elements to it. Anything that in some way modifies a game from what it was when the publisher released it is termed a *mod*.

Game modification is not a new practice. It has been going on for quite some time, but only recently, with the creation of multiplayer shooters for the PC, has it become popular. It was this genre of gaming that gave people the inspiration to show off. At first, players competed to see who was the best first-person shooter (FPS) player. Later, when players realized that they could modify the game, the competition grew to include this aspect of the game and to see who could make the most impressive changes to a game.

Shoot First, Ask Questions Later

The FPS game genre was created in early 1990. You play from the point of view of the in-game character just like that of *Quake 4*. Also, like *Quake 4*, it is id Software, Inc., with the creation of *Doom,* that made this genre popular.

As far as staking claim to being the first FPS game, there is much controversy. It's a toss up between *Spasim* and *Maze War,* which were first developed in 1973. Then, later that year, player versus player game-play was tested between two linked computers playing *Spasim*. The following year, both games were introduced to a network, and multiplayer gaming as you know it was invented. Because both games played from the first-person perspective with weapons, this marked the birth of the FPS.

In 1991, id Software released the game *Hovertank 3D,* which was a simple maze game from the first-person perspective. The environment was very flat, and the enemies were nothing more than 2D graphics. Later that year, *Catacomb 3D* was released as a modified version of this *Hovertank 3D*. *Catacomb 3D* displayed textured walls and showed the player's hand on-screen like you now see in *Quake 4*.

1992 offered the addition of VGA graphics with the release of *Wolfenstein 3D*. This game was a huge hit and inspired more development in the genre. The following year, *Doom* added even more graphical detail. This game offered rooms of various sizes, outdoor environments, and textures on what were previously flat surfaces. However, the most important upgrade to this rising game genre was the ability for anyone connected to a network to enjoy the multiplayer aspect.

The first version of *Quake* was introduced by id Software in 1996. It had highly upgraded graphics as well as networking capabilities and was the first game in the genre to gain widespread fame as a multiplayer Internet game. It broke the bounds of its predecessor, *Doom,* by networking globally. To further its success, *Quake* was the first game that offered developer support for user modifications. This was the beginning of mods created by the consumer rather than the industry.

From that point on, the FPS genre grew. Graphics greatly improved over time as innovations in computer hardware developed. The ability to process more information has increased the number of simultaneous events that can happen during a game. All the while, several new games emerged that attempted to copy the success that id Software started. *Quake* and *Doom* sequels were produced, bringing further enhancements. *Quake 4* is the legacy of a great series of games from a great developer, id Software.

Checking Out Quake 4

Whether you purchase *Quake 4* with or without the intent to modify it, you should begin by playing around with it. Play through a few single-player missions and then move on to the multiplayer games. If you don't want to play online, start multiplayer games of your own. You might be the only one in the game, but you will still enjoy yourself.

After playing the game and enjoying what the developers were able to deliver, play the game again — but this time, instead of running around and shooting everything that moves, take some time to look around. Stop and look out windows and over railings. Walk around the other players in the game and see what they're wearing. Take a closer look at the walls to see the details that were included, and then see what happens when you shoot them with different weapons. Listen to the sounds the weapons make as well as the sounds all around you.

By investigating the details of the game, you will start to see things differently. It will be like looking at a room where you live and thinking about painting the walls a different color or moving the furniture around. It could also be like considering a different outfit for the day as opposed to the same green armor you wear every day. (You're a *Quake 4* marine, remember?)

Adding To or Changing the Game

At first, it can be difficult to see which game elements you can change. However, as you begin to understand the different pieces that make up the game, you will start looking at all games a little differently. You will be able to relate the various elements you see to specific files within the game, and you'll start to know which of those files you can modify.

For instance, look around the physical area in which you are now sitting. Within the area, you see objects like the book you are now holding; a table with some items on it; or if you are outdoors, maybe some trees. In the game world, each different item could be considered a separate object that the game would refer to as an *asset*. Each asset, because it may be used more than once in a game, is defined in files. If you change one of these files so that, say, the book you are holding is a different color, you have just made a modification.

So what does this have to do with mods and modding? Well, if you modify the game so that it's in any way different from when you purchased it, you have created a mod. *Mod* is just a short way of saying *modification.* Then, it stands to reason that the act of modifying could be called *modding.*

The mods you make can be simple or complex. You can make them by adding something new to the game or by changing something that already exists. You could make your changes to provide an improvement to the game, or you could completely change everything and create what is called a *total modification* of the game.

You might be surprised to know that many of the games on the shelves are total modifications of another game. *Quake 4* is essentially a total modification of *Doom 3.* There are quite a few additions to the code of the game, but Raven Software, Inc., based the *Quake 4* game on the *Doom 3* game developed by id Software.

Finding out what you can mod

Games are just groups of files that are read by one master program that displays those files' contents on the screen. When one or more of these files is changed, the change is reflected within the game. Official game updates and expansion kits can perform these changes, but you can, too. So why not include your own changes to the game to create something completely new?

Upon first glance, you might not realize just how much game content you can mod. Everything, all of what you see from the time you double-click the game icon to the moment you close down the game, can be changed. A short list of moddable things in a game would read like this:

- **Loading screens:** The loading screen for the game and the loading screens for each level of the game. You can change all these screens from their original designs. Right now the program's loading screens show a lot of green and the primary *Quake 4* symbol, but you can turn these screens into something else if you want. In Chapter 13, you see how to create a custom loading screen that is displayed while loading your level.

- **User interfaces:** The selection windows before playing the game and the usable computer screens within the game can be modified. You can set up these screens to better meet your needs or to make things look any way you have dreamed. Chapter 16 shows you how you create your own user interface and use it within a level.

- **Textures and images:** Everything that you see while playing any of the levels within *Quake 4* started as an image. Whether it's the bricks on the walls or the face on another player, these are all images that can be added. Chapters 15 and 18 show you how to do exactly this.

- **Levels:** From multiplayer to single player, you can build completely original levels for the game that you and your friends can play. What could be more fun than playing a multiplayer level together with your friends online?

The preceding is just a very short list of what you can mod in this game. As long as you have access to the files that make a game run and you have the tools to change them, you can modify that game as much as you like. You could even turn *Quake 4* into a new version of *Donkey Kong* if that's what you want.

The reason *Quake 4* can be modded so extensively is primarily due to the developers. Luckily, id Software has provided access to the files of the game so that you can modify them. Not all game companies do that.

Knowing what tools you need

There are tools for every job, and game modification is no exception. Some tools are provided for you by the game developers, but others you must obtain. However, you might be surprised to know that most of what you need, if not all, is already installed on your computer. You just need to know which programs you can use to modify each of the different files within the game.

As you dig deeper into modding, you will need to install additional tools that you might not yet have. However, these tools have been supplied for you on the CD-ROM located in the back of the book. For the most part, these tools are for editing images that are used in the game and will not require any foreknowledge of their use. When it comes time to use these tools, you will be instructed on what to do and how to do it.

As modding became popular, game developers started to assist the modification community. They offered words of advice and eventually tools and documentation to make more complicated changes. As the modifications became bigger and better, so did the sales of the original game because more and more people wanted to play the game with these new modifications installed. This inspired more participation from developers and publishers who offered even better tools and documentation.

The Modding Process Goes Something Like This

The most common type of modification is to create a custom level for the game. The process of doing such goes like this:

1. **Plan your custom level with notes and drawings.**

    Write down what you want to include in your custom level and maybe even sketch out how you want things to lay in the game.

2. **Construct the level in a program by building walls.**

    This is a lot like playing with blocks. You create and place your different shaped blocks where you want them in order to create a room, several rooms, or any other structure for the player to roam.

3. **Add some color to the surfaces in the level.**

    Adding color is a simple process of selecting an image and applying it to the wall, floor, or any other surface in the game.

4. **Place additional elements in the game such as lights, monsters, weapons, or other objects.**

    Again, just select elements from a list and place them where you want them. Then you can fine-tune the way they work. (For instance, you can change the color of a light.)

5. **Compile and play the level in the game.**

    Choose a compile command from the editor's menu, and it creates all the files required so that you can play your finished level in the game. Then you just load the level and start having fun.

6. **(Optional) Give your level to the world.**

    This optional step puts all the custom files together into a single file that you can place online for download or on a disc to hand to your friends. This way more people can enjoy the work you put into your custom modification.

As you can see, the process isn't all that complicated. In this book, I show you where you can find the necessary tools, how to use them, and the options that each tool has to offer. With this information, you soon will be on your way to making your own custom game levels.

Sharing the Game with Others

In the list in the preceding section, I mention that the last step of the modification process is optional; however, sharing your creation is most often the purpose of making a mod. I think that it's perhaps the most exciting part. For my part, knowing that many other people out there are getting enjoyment from something that I built motivates me to do more.

In this book, I not only show you how to package all your files together for distribution, but I also show you where to go from there. I offer advice on where to send your files and how to get them out to the public for all to enjoy.

Chapter 2

Getting Familiar with Modding Tools and Techniques

In This Chapter
- Exploring your modding tools
- Writing a README
- Backing up and saving your work
- Comparing *Quake* with other games

*E*very job requires the right tool. If you were working on the engine of your car, you would use a wrench or a screwdriver. Modding games is no different, but the necessary tools come in the form of programs.

Gathering the Tools Involved

Some of the tools you will use to modify the game have already been provided along with the game. These tools are integrated within the game and don't require much additional effort on your part to access. They include:

- A mapping editor
- A graphical user interface (GUI) editor
- A model viewer

However, some tools that you will need don't come with the game. Some tools you already have and just don't know it yet. The remaining tools have been provided on the CD-ROM that accompanies this book. Those tools, discussed in detail next, are

- A plain text editor
- A compression utility

- An image editor
- An image compressor

Each of these additionally supplied tools serves a very specific purpose. You probably are already familiar with most of these tools in some way. However, even though you might have used them previously, you might not have realized how they can be related to modding *Quake 4*.

Writing plain text

The most common tool used in all forms of game modification is the plain text editor. *Plain text* is simply text that is stripped of all formatting. When you use a word-processing program such Microsoft Word, the software introduces unseen formatting to the text. This formatting could be as simple as bold or italics attributes to the more complex font selection. Plain text doesn't have any of this hidden information. The hidden data would only confuse the game when it attempts to read what you've written.

Since you're working with the Microsoft Windows operating system, you already have an excellent plain text editor installed. Notepad comes with your Windows installation and is the tool that I use throughout the chapters of this book. With Notepad, what you see is what you get, and there is no hidden formatting.

Unpacking your luggage

Many of the editable game files installed with the game are contained within compressed files. A *compressed file* is a single file that contains a number of other files that are packed together. During the packing process, the data of the packed files is written in such a way that the size of this single compressed file is smaller than the total sum of the sizes of the packed files.

Now, it isn't important to know that these files were compressed, but it is important to know that these single files contain many files within them. The game has been instructed to look inside these packed files and use the files within them. This means that just a few files can be installed on your computer in less space than would have been required by the many separate files by themselves. These packages of files are named with the file extension `.pk4` and are called *pak files* for short.

You can access these compressed files with a simple utility that you might already have installed. Pak files are nothing more than WinZip files that have been renamed with the `.pk4` extension. So, if you have a compression utility like WinZip, you can use it to open and explore the contents of these files by simply telling WinZip that it can open these files. This is something that you do in Chapter 14.

You can use a number of possible compression utilities to access your pak files. Some people like to use WinRar, and some utilize the compression utility that comes with Windows, the Microsoft Zip utility. However, I've found that WinZip is the simplest utility to use and also the one that results in the fewest complications.

> **TIP:** If you don't have WinZip installed, you should install the trial version now. It's been provided on the CD media in the back of the book. You can also download it from the Web site, `www.winzip.com`.

Drawing, painting, and taking pictures

The *Quake 4* game consists of many images, large and small. Everything you see in the game has some sort of image applied to it. From the walls in a room to the face on a character, everything starts as a picture and is then applied to the corresponding piece in the game.

All the images within the game are either provided in the Targa (`.tga`) image format or started as a Targa image. Those that began as Targas were eventually converted to a different format called DDS. The DDS image is created by using The Compressonator, discussed next.

So, when choosing your image-editing software, it is important that you choose one that can work with Targa images. The `.tga` image format is the image format primarily used with this game.

The most widely used program for working with images is Adobe Photoshop, and a trial version has been supplied on the CD media in the back of the book. I use Photoshop in the examples in this book. Although you could use other software applications for editing images, I recommend that you install and use Adobe Photoshop while following this book. This will help to avoid miscommunication, and you might find that you really like this program.

Another image application that I use in this book is a DDS image converter called The Compressonator. The DDS (DirectDraw Surface) image is a special image used by *Quake 4* that helps to make the game run smoothly. With The Compressonator, you will be able to take your Targa image and convert it into the DDS image for use within the game.

What makes the DDS image so much more efficient for the game is that it's really more than one image compressed into a single file. The DDS image contains several different sizes of the same image within its file. Based on different factors, such as your distance from the object displaying the image or the quality settings of your game, *Quake 4* decides which size to display on-screen. If you were far away from the image, the smaller version would be used because you wouldn't see all the details that larger version provides. And, by displaying the smaller version, the game is saving your computer from the work required to show the highly detailed, bulkier version of that image.

The Compressonator has been supplied on the CD media located in the back of the book. It is freeware, meaning that it won't cost you anything to use, and it is provided by ATI.

Using Best Modding Practices

Modding is still a fairly new activity. There aren't many strict guidelines that you have to follow. However, some very advisable practices are in place. These practices are primarily to avoid conflict with other mods when sharing your final work with others as well as to prevent loss of work because your files weren't properly saved to disk.

Following standard naming conventions

Whether you're creating a single level or a complete modification of the game, naming your work is very important. You want to come up with an original name for your modification, be it a single file or a group of files, that most likely has not been used by someone else. Otherwise, when two mods with the same name are downloaded and installed, files will be overwritten and lost. Try doing a little research on similar mods that are already available on the Internet before coming up with the final name of your work to avoid such issues.

For example, say that I release a custom game level under the name of MyLevel and I name the file `MyLevel.map`. If you decided to name your level the same thing, there could be a conflict. If one person downloads and installs both custom levels of the same name, one of the levels is going to overwrite the other. This problem might seem trivial at first, but it happens quite often and is somewhat avoidable.

Instructing the end user

Always include a README file with your final work. The README file is a text file that contains information about you and your mod. With it, the user knows who to contact for help or kudos, what your mod consists of, and how to properly install and use it with the game.

Don't ever assume that the end-users know what to do with your files. Rather, assume they know nothing other than how to access your README file, and then instruct them with what to do from there. If your reader doesn't know how to install the file and isn't tempted enough to open the README text file and actually read it, at least you've done what you could to inform the end user to the best of your ability. This file is explained in more detail in Chapter 19.

Including all the files required

When making your mod, check to see whether any of the files you used are part of a mod that you previously installed. If you installed a level that comes with custom images, for example, make sure you've included those images with your mod. You don't want to distribute a mod that doesn't have all the required files.

If you do include files that were previously provided via another mod, make sure you give credit to the author of those images. Make mention of where those unoriginal files came from within your README. Then, make sure those files are also included with your distribution in case the user doesn't have the same mods installed.

Avoiding the overwriting headache

In Chapter 17, I introduce you to creating your own mod folders within the game. Primarily, you do this so that you don't overwrite the original game files, thereby destroying the original game. You don't want to make any permanent changes to the game. Instead, create a mod folder of your own and place your altered files in there. This prevents you from having to tell users that they have to reinstall their game to get it back to the way it was before they installed your mod.

Saving and saving again

Game modding is still a young hobby. As such, the available tools are not quite perfect. Errors can occur when using modding tools that can render your files useless. Although I mention ways to avoid the most common errors, some errors will occur seemingly without reason.

To avoid letting these errors ruin the effort you put into your mod, make sure that you save your work regularly. Save it often. Save it under different names for different versions. Then, when you've saved it a number of times after a week or more of work, back it up to another location. Put it on CD, DVD, or other removable media.

One day, you will think back to these few paragraphs about saving your work and you will be thankful. You will be thankful that you have a backup of your work that you can go to after a disaster, however minor your changes between backups may be.

Differences between Quake and Other Games

Games from different developers are created differently. Although modding practices are relatively the same among the various games, some fundamental differences can have a big impact on the way you plan your mod.

When it comes to level design, the *Quake* game series is roughly the same from version 1 to version 4. You create a box and place all your buildings, rooms, halls, models, and everything else inside it. This big box must be made without any gaps because the box defines the boundaries of your level. Without boundaries, the game would crash because it would contain too much information for your computer to process.

You are presented with an empty area like the void of outer space. You create your level by adding to this space blocks such as the walls of your buildings. I like to refer to this process of level creation as *adding to the void.*

However, some other games (such as the *Unreal* series by *Epic Games*) work this process in reverse. They present you with a giant block like a block of clay. You then carve out your level from this solid block.

With *Quake 4,* you add to your environment. I find this a much simpler concept to understand. Just like building a house in the real world, you add a wall, add a room, and add details by building up from nothing.

Chapter 3
Breaking Down the Game

In This Chapter
▶ Making your own maps
▶ Placing textures in the game
▶ Adding interactive elements as entities
▶ Scripting your way to reactive elements
▶ Using graphical user interfaces to make a more interactive world

Quake 4 consists of several elements that all come together to create what you see on the computer. There are sights, sounds, and interactive elements. All these pieces that make up the game can be found within one common location in the game: the game level. However, before it becomes a level, it starts as a map.

Making Maps and Playing Levels

The *level* is the virtual world in which you exist as the player. After you start the game and make a selection from the available menu, be it a single-player or multiplayer game, your player is released into the level. Here you can explore the game environment very much the same way you would explore a local park, school, or other environment in the real world.

Whether you are playing a single-player mission or a multiplayer battle, each environment between loading screens is called a level.

Loading screens appear in both the single-player and multiplayer game types. The multiplayer games make the screen obvious with the display of a loading bar and still image. However, the single-player loading screens are often hidden with short movies called *cut-scenes*. These span the time between the end of one level and the start of another in the hopes of keeping you further submersed in the game play.

> ### Leveling levels
>
> The term *level* most likely came from the predecessor of the shooter gaming genre, the role-playing game. The goal of role-playing games is to increase the level of a player by progressing through the increasingly difficult environments of the game. Therefore, the two terms became synonymous. You would level up your player by progressing through varying levels of difficulty in each environment.

Before an environment becomes a playable level, it starts life as a *map*. The map is named such for a few important reasons:

- As you create a playable environment, you must map out the position of everything within your environment. Thankfully, the mapping editor takes the tediousness out of this task.
- You then save the map with the `.map` extension.

Versions of *Quake* prior to *Quake 4* had no use for the map file other than for the original creation of the level. The map, when completed, would be converted into a file that could be played by the game, and the map file was no longer of any use. The difference between the map and its compiled version has lessened since the development of *Doom 3*. The map file is now one of the files required by the game for play.

Making Your Own Maps

I find that one of the biggest thrills of modding is the ability to make my own maps and then play them in the game. I really enjoy being able to create a virtual environment, make it unique, and then offer it to others to enjoy.

Mapmaking requires more than just the placement of a few buildings. It's more like creating a real building or small community, and then furnishing it. You must place all the walls, ceilings, floors, and other structural elements together to make up the buildings in your game. However, you must also paint the walls, add tables and chairs, and drop in enemies to fight. You must consider every object or feature that is to be represented while playing the game.

I could just jump right into the map-making process with you, but first I think you should have a good understanding of the game environment. To make a good map, you should understand how your placed objects and features are perceived within the game. Don't worry, this doesn't mean you need to go back to school and learn new theories and rules. Because you live in a three-dimensional (3D) world, relating the real world with the virtual one is fairly easy.

Building blocks of a map

Adding walls, ceilings, and other structures to your map is much like playing with blocks or Legos. You lay out each block next to another to create a sealed room where the player can have fun. The blocks can be of various sizes and shapes and placed together in just about any orientation you can think of, allowing limitless possibilities for the construction of your map.

The blocks placed to make up the structures and constraints are called *brushes*. Although brushes can be made into various shapes and sizes, they must be solid in form. This means that they must have at least four sides, like a three-sided pyramid with a floor.

With at least four sides, they can be defined as solid, structural blocks in the game, which is important. The game performs some optimization techniques to help it to run smoothly. Part of this optimization depends on the ability of the game to define what the player can and cannot see. Because the game assumes that the player cannot see through solid brushes, this helps with that optimization.

Another restriction that brushes have is that they must be convex in shape. This means that you can't have a single brush with a concave or U-like shape. This limitation reduces the work required by your processor during game play and, because you can place multiple brushes together to create any shape imaginable, it is a fair compromise to make.

Setting boundaries

Within each map, you must create specific boundaries with the placement of brushes. When creating buildings and other things in your map, you are confined to a single space. You have a large area in which to build; it's kind of like building in outer space. However, if your computer had to calculate a virtual world that went on without boundaries, it would quickly run out of free memory and processing power and crash.

To avoid crashing the game, you must set the boundaries of your map. By creating a large, sealed room around all your other structures and elements, you can define these boundaries. Then, when the game begins putting your 3D world together, it won't lose its cool and crash on you. This game-creation process is known as *rendering*. Rendering is the process of making your data visible on the computer screen. Your computer takes the code that has been written to the map file and turns it into visual data that makes up your game.

Seeing in three dimensions

Earlier, I refer to the environment as a 3D world. What I mean by this is that, just like the world we live in, the game world also as three dimensions called the X, Y, and Z planes. One dimension runs from left to right and, in *Quake 4*, this is called the X plane. Another plane, the Y plane, runs from back to front. Last, the plane that runs from bottom to top is the Z plane. Together, they make up the three planes of the 3D environment. Figure 3-1 helps to illustrate these three planes.

TIP

Those of you with a background in mathematics or modeling might be confused by this configuration of axes. You would be more familiar with a vertical Y axis and a horizontal Z axis. However, in the world of gaming, these axes are reversed. This is because many games such as *Quake 4* use the Cartesian coordinate system, which defines the third axis, the height, as the Z axis.

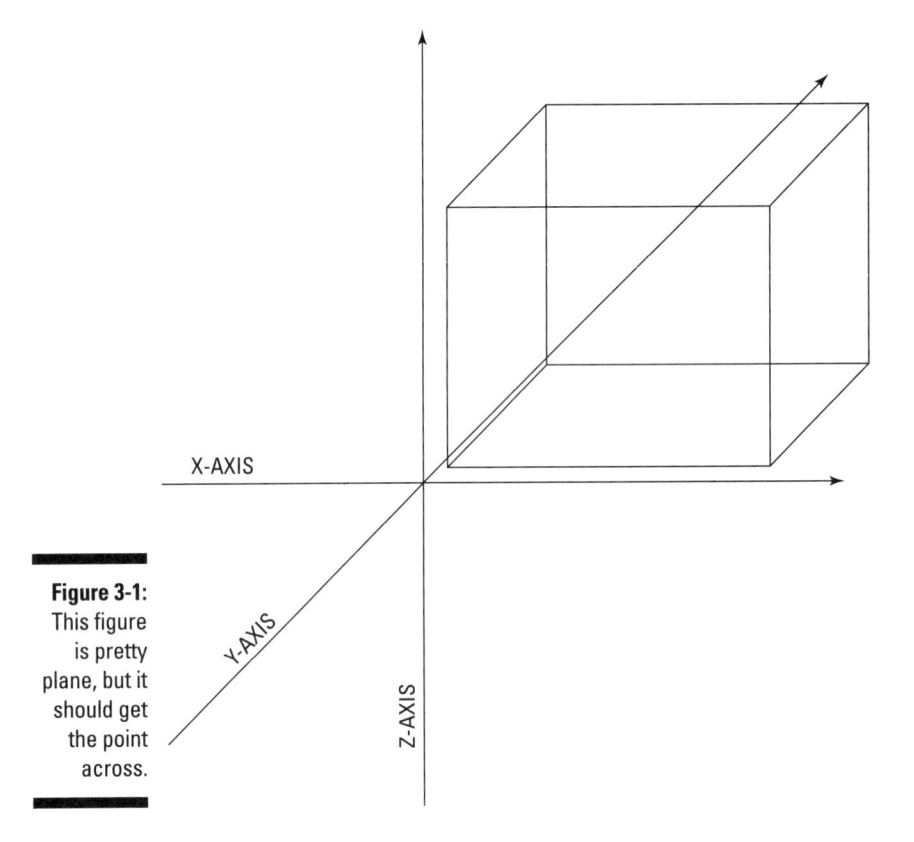

Figure 3-1: This figure is pretty plane, but it should get the point across.

Chapter 3: Breaking Down the Game

If you were to measure a box, like the post office does before shipping, you would have to measure in these three dimensions. The width, length, and height of the box would relate to the X, Y, and Z planes respectively.

Measuring in units

The game world has its own way to express distance. Instead of using inches or centimeters, it uses units. Although it isn't easy to picture how big a unit is in reference to real-world objects, it does relate to another digital medium of measurement: pixels. One unit in the game is equal to one pixel. This might be confusing at first, but after a week of being submersed in the mapping world, it will become second nature to you.

Measuring things this way makes it easy to create images for use within the game, but not everyone likes it. A large number of modders would rather this measurement relate directly to real-life measurements so they can more easily reproduce in the virtual world real-life environments such as their homes or offices. If you are one of these modders, the real-life conversion of units to inches is listed in Chapter 20. There you can also find other helpful measurements for reference when building your maps.

Toying with Textures

The virtual world of games is full of images. I don't just mean the images invoked in your mind of the wonderful things you can do. Everything that you see in the game starts as unpainted objects. The walls begin as just plain boxes, and the players start out lacking in color, definition, and everything else that makes them look like players.

Painting the walls

When the game is being built, the person doing the building puts the color into the game. This is done by placing images on everything, but these are not the same kind of images you can get with your camera. These images have additional features specified within them. These features define how light will bounce off of the image, how the image can convey the appearance of little bumps or scratches and other similar things. Altogether, these images and features make up what is referred to as a *texture*.

Textures carry a very important role in the game. They provide the color and other features that would otherwise be missing. Without textures, everything you see in the game would look flat, colorless, and plain.

Building interest

Textures do a lot more than just add color to a scene. They also define bumps and scratches and other forms of dimension. Sure, color is the primary function of a texture, but it also does quite a bit more.

While you're playing a game, your computer has to render the 3D environment. The more rendering that your computer has to do, the harder it has to work. So, if you had a wall with complex trimming mounted both near the floor and near the ceiling and if you also had wood paneling with more trim along the middle of the wall, all this would add up to a lot of dimension. All the trim would stick out from the surface in different ways and indentation would occur between each of the boards of wood paneling. This level of detail would cause a great deal of rendering.

With textures, you can fake most of this bumping so your computer doesn't have to do it. The less work your computer has to do in creating its environment, the faster it will be able to provide you with an exciting and fun game. This also means the structural part of your wall doesn't have to be so complex. You can create a flat wall and make it look more complex simply with the use of textures.

I show you how to create these textures in Chapter 15. I show you how to go from simple color to the highly detailed bumping and shining that a texture can bring forth in the game.

Evoking Entities

Entities, in very basic terms, are the opposite of structural brushes. Brushes are the building blocks of a map. They help to define what the player can and cannot see within the game.

Entities, on the other hand, don't provide any structure to the game. However, what they do provide is activity and interactivity. If you walk up to a door and

Chapter 3: Breaking Down the Game

that door opens or moves as a result of something that you did, that door is an entity. If you walk up to a control panel or an elevator or anything else that reacts to your action, it is an entity within the game.

That door or control panel is a type of entity known as an *active brush;* however, another type of entity is a *point entity.* A point entity has an effect on the environment in some way, but it isn't quite as interactive. Point entities are small, single points that affect the game environment (for example, a light). A point entity is a non-solid object that exists in a single point (as opposed to the door, which is solid and consists of several points for each of its corners).

Sorting Out the Scripts

Scripts carry a valuable role behind the scenes in the game. Scripts are lines of special text that instruct the game to perform an action or reaction. If you were to walk up to an elevator in the game and press a button to make it move, a script would tell the elevator how to move.

One script example details how an elevator will move when the player steps on it. This is an example that I cover later, in Chapter 14. When the player steps on the elevator, the script tells it to move up. When it reaches a certain height, it then turns to allow the player to exit. A few seconds later, the elevator returns to where it started all by itself. These are just a few of the different steps you can tell the elevator to take during its trip.

Scripts use a lot of terms that you might not be familiar with. These terms sometimes read like words you use every day, but because you aren't used to reading them in this fashion, they can be difficult to understand. In Chapter 14, I show you how to understand scripts. Then, you write your own scripts and create actions within your own games.

Messing with User Interfaces

When you were playing *Quake 4,* you might have come across one of the several different computer-like screens that the player either can read, view, or interact with. These screens are called graphical user interfaces, or GUIs for short, and Figure 3-2 shows a GUI from the game.

Part I: The ABCs of Modging

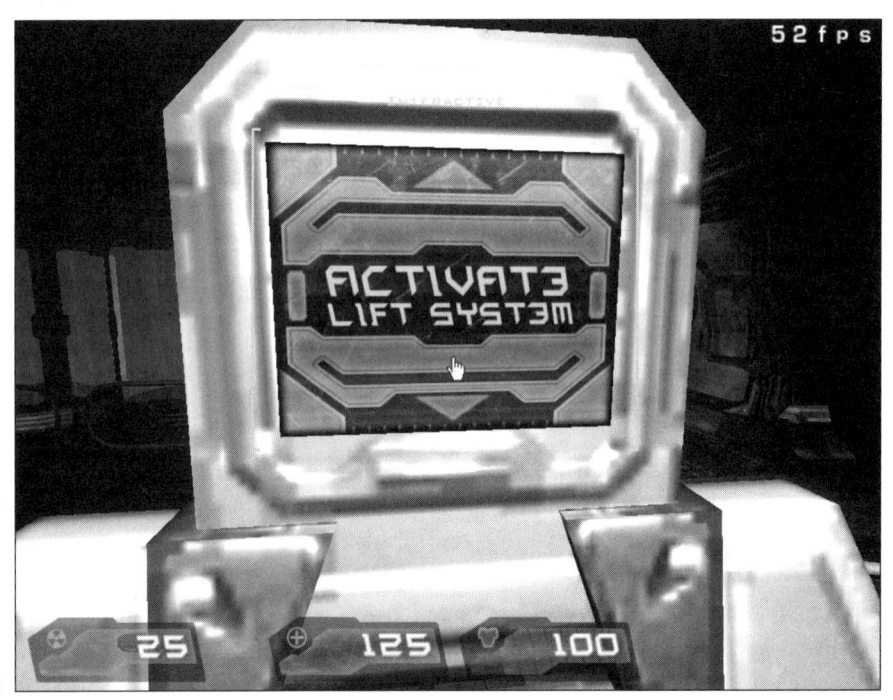

Figure 3-2: One of the many GUIs from within the game.

GUIs allow the user to see fancy visuals that are either moving or static. The most exciting part about these interfaces is that you can make them interactive for the player. This means that you can create an interface that looks like a computer screen. Then you can make certain parts of this screen clickable. Each click can control a different script or entity in the game.

GUIs don't stop at player interfaces. They also encompass the loading screens in the game, the user interfaces for selecting playable levels, and every other screen outside of the actual game play. You can change every single aspect of the game and make it your own modified version of the game for anyone to play. This means that you can make the GUIs interactive for both the player within the game and the player outside of the game.

Part II
Making Your Own Maps

The 5th Wave   By Rich Tennant

It's called the Quake 4 editor. I used it to create this 3D virtual-reality simulation of my own apartment.

You need to dust.

In this part . . .

Game modification is an extremely broad subject. It can span from programming lines of code to creating the cut-scenes that play between each level. However, the most popular mod for almost any game is the one that takes the players someplace they've never been before.

It's time to get set up and into gear. In these chapters, you install some of the tools and start making your first custom game level. By the end of this part, you'll have something to show your friends. You will officially be a modder.

Chapter 4

Getting Set Up for Mapping

In This Chapter

▶ Preparing to launch the game-enabled editor
▶ Making adjustments to the screen
▶ Launching the editor
▶ Getting to know the editor

*i*d Software, Inc., the developer of the *Quake 4* game engine, really made installation of the mapping editor a breeze. id Software not only provided the mapping editor on the disc with the game, but it also installed the editor with the game.

In the past, games built on the *Quake* game engine required that you download and install a program called Radiant. This third-party map editor made you follow specific (and sort of tricky) installation instructions. If you weren't experienced with Radiant from previous *Quake* games, this installation wasn't a trivial process. You had to install the editor in the correct directory, on the same hard drive as the game, and with specific settings. Unless you did everything perfectly, you wouldn't have a working editor.

These difficulties led to a demand for support regarding the editor and its installation. The *Quake* game developers didn't support the editor (because they didn't create it). The editor's developers didn't support it because they were busy just making the editor work (and not working with it in a game situation). The resulting quest for help manifested itself as forum questions, e-mails, and user-created tutorials. It became obvious that users needed more support from the game and editor developers.

I believe it was this outcry that inspired id Software to integrate the popular Radiant editor into the game. This integration reduced the amount of setup and expertise required by the end user to get the editor installed and working. And (I'm sure) it also reduced the number of support requests from those end users. For my part, I know that I certainly don't get as many e-mails asking for help with the editor installation.

If you've installed the full version of *Quake 4,* you've installed Radiant. All that is left is a little setup to make accessing and using Radiant a little easier.

However, if you've installed only the demo version of the game, you need to get crackin' and install the full version before you can proceed. The demo version has reduced functionality and doesn't support many of the game's advanced features — such as the editor.

Firing Up the System

I know that you're anxious to start using the Radiant editor to bring your personal touch to the *Quake* game, but bear with me through a few additional steps that make accessing the editor easier. These steps allow you to reduce the amount of time it takes to load the game, reduce the keystrokes involved in launching the editor, and in general, make modding *Quake* a simpler process.

If you don't make any changes to the game's default installation, you have to sit through the opening introductions — including the seeing-them-once-is-enough animations from id Software, Raven Software, Inc., and Activision. And then after the game actually loads, you must open a console with a series of keystrokes. The *console* enables you to enter commands directly into the game, and I show you how to do this in section "Reducing the brightness," later in this chapter.

For quicker loading: If you make a few adjustments now, you get rid of these obstacles that slow down your play. You can set things up to automatically skip over the opening animations and jump right into the initial starting screen for the game. And you can make accessing the console as easy as pressing one key. These adjustments speed up your ability to get to both the game and the editor.

Creating a shortcut to Quake 4

You know that you can launch programs from within Windows by using the Start menu or a desktop shortcut. I like to customize the desktop shortcut for *Quake 4* with some special commands that take effect when I launch the game.

If you don't already have a shortcut to the *Quake 4* game on your desktop, you first need to create one. Follow these steps to set up your Windows shortcut:

1. **Choose Start**⇨**All Programs**⇨**Quake 4.**
2. **Right-click the Quake 4 menu selection in the Quake 4 folder, and then choose Send To**⇨**Desktop from the resulting pop-up menu.**

You should now have the game's shortcut on your desktop. As shown here, the shortcut icon has the *Quake* insignia with the text *Quake 4* underneath.

Customizing your Quake shortcut

You don't have to use a desktop shortcut just as is; in fact, you can edit some of its properties to make it work the way you want. To run *Quake* with an eye toward modding, you are particularly interested in editing the shortcut's Target field. The Target field contains the link to the game's executable file on your hard drive. By adding some additional text to the end of the target, you can adjust how this file is executed.

The first command, `+set com_allowConsole 1`, tells the game to allow easier access to the console. Without this command, you would have to press a series of keys for console access rather than just one. I explain the console in greater detail later in this chapter.

The second command, `+disconnect`, tells the game to skip over the opening animations and take you right to the first screen in the game. Because you'll be loading the game often, skipping the intros saves you a lot of time otherwise spent waiting for them to play through.

Follow these steps to add these commands to your *Quake* shortcut's Target field:

1. **Right-click your Quake 4 desktop shortcut and choose Properties from the pop-up menu.**

    This launches the Shortcut tab of the Properties dialog box, which contains different properties of the shortcut itself. The Target field looks something like this:

    ```
    "C:\Program Files\id Software\Quake 4\Quake4.exe"
    ```

2. **Place your cursor at the end of the target after the last quotation mark.**

    The space after the last quotation mark is where you start typing those special commands I mention earlier in this section.

3. **Type the commands that you want to execute when you launch *Quake* from your desktop shortcut.**

    In this case, type **+set com_allowConsole 1 +disconnect**. Your new Target field should read like this:

    ```
    "C:\Program Files\id Software\Quake 4\Quake4.exe" +set
         com_allowConsole 1 +disconnect
    ```

    Don't miss the space that's placed after the closing quotation and before the first plus sign. It might not be noticeable in the text here, but failure to include this space will result in an error.

4. **Click Apply at the bottom of the Properties window to apply your changes.**

5. **Click OK to close the window.**

   You're now ready to launch the game with your new, beefed-up shortcut.

Go ahead and double-click the new desktop shortcut to load the game. You'll immediately see how much more quickly the game loads!

Adjusting Your Game's Video Settings

Getting your *Quake* game loaded properly is just a start. To ensure the best view for modifying the game, you need to make some adjustments to the video and display settings in the game itself. Some video settings can cause the editor not to load or display correctly, but I can help you make sure that everything is set properly before loading the editor. In particular, you want to change the settings that affect the following:

- **Display mode:** You can view the *Quake* game in either Fullscreen or Windowed mode. When you want to have access to other windows — like the editor window — while you're playing the game, you must use the Windowed mode.

- **Antialiasing:** The editor cannot be properly displayed with this game feature enabled. Therefore, you must turn it off.

- **Brightness:** Although you might enjoy being able to see into those dark corners of the game without straining your eyes, a high level of brightness will wash out the editor window, making it impossible to use. You must adjust the brightness to make the editor easy on the eyes.

Changing from Fullscreen to Windowed mode

The first thing you need to do is change the display mode from Fullscreen to Windowed mode. This means that your game's graphics will be displayed in a window equal to your screen's resolution settings instead of across the entire screen. Think of it in terms of your browser window's Maximized or Minimized window modes. Figure 4-1 shows how the Maximized window mode, equivalent to Quake's Fullscreen mode, fills the entire screen with the browser window, but the Windowed mode is smaller and can be moved around the screen.

Chapter 4: Getting Set Up for Mapping 37

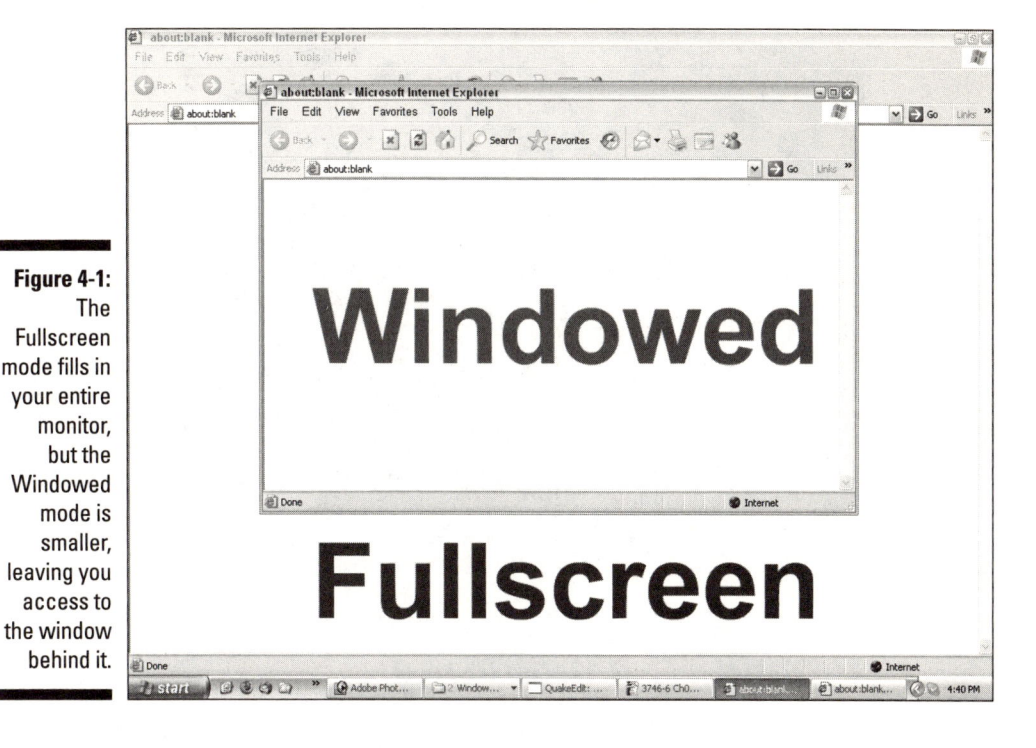

Figure 4-1:
The Fullscreen mode fills in your entire monitor, but the Windowed mode is smaller, leaving you access to the window behind it.

The purpose of turning on Windowed mode is to allow you to leave the game running while working in other programs, such as a text editor. If the game were in Fullscreen mode, you would have to exit the game in order to access that text editor. This benefit becomes apparent later in the book.

To change the display mode to Windowed, click the Settings link found on the first screen presented upon loading the game. Next, click the System link. In the System Settings window, under the Video Settings heading, you can find the option for Fullscreen. Click this setting until it reads No, as in Figure 4-2.

The changes won't take effect right now. You have to restart the video within the game before the settings take effect. I show you how to do that later after making a few more adjustments.

Part II: Making Your Own Maps

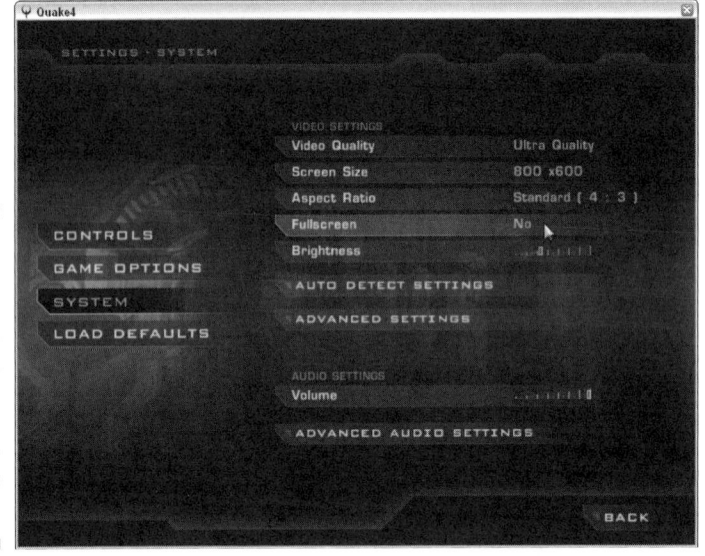

Figure 4-2: From within the System Settings window, click the Fullscreen option to select No as the value.

Turning off antialiasing

The next video setting you want to change is found under the Advanced Settings link, located on the screen shown in Figure 4-2. Click the Advanced Settings link. Next, make sure your Antialiasing setting is set to Off, as in Figure 4-3. If it isn't, click it until it is. After changing this setting, click the Close Advanced Options link.

> *Antialiasing* affects the quality of the images in the game. Basically, this feature smoothes out what can become harsh lines between contrasting images. The result of enabling antialiasing is a better-looking image overall. The problem with this effect is that it doesn't work with the mod tools that come with the game and must be turned off.

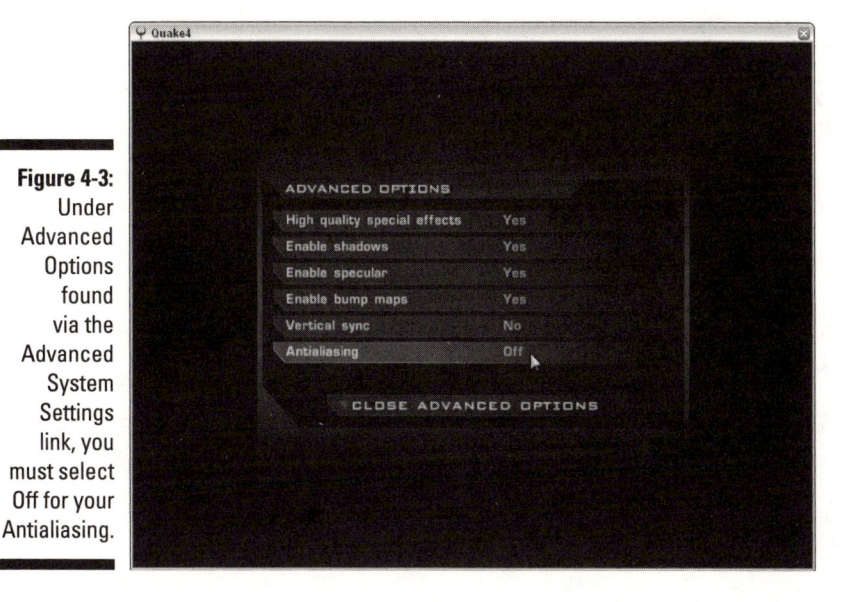

Figure 4-3:
Under Advanced Options found via the Advanced System Settings link, you must select Off for your Antialiasing.

Without changing this setting, the editor won't load correctly: All but one of the editor windows will load empty and white, and the only window displaying information will list a number of errors. This is your indication that the Antialiasing setting is still on.

Reducing the brightness

You need to make one more change, and that's to the brightness level of the game. Before you make this change, you must apply the changes you've already made. Without restarting the video, the changes made have not taken effect and won't take effect until you restart either the game or the video for the game. I show you how to do the latter and assume that you already know how to exit and restart the game.

To restart the video, open the console by pressing the ~ key. This causes the console window to drop down from the top of the screen, as in Figure 4-4. A blinking cursor shows you where you can type text commands directly into the game. The command I want you to type is **vid_restart**. After typing this command, press Enter.

Part II: Making Your Own Maps

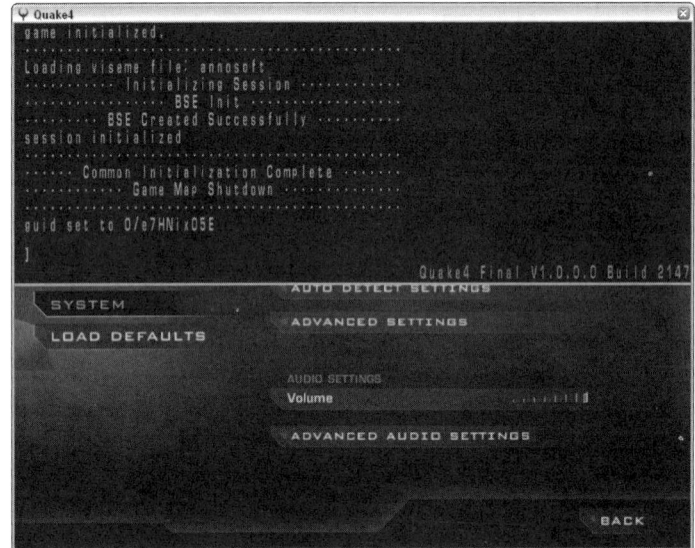

Figure 4-4:
The console window.

When you press Enter, the screen might go black for a few seconds and then return to normal. You should see your game in Windowed mode at this point.

Close the console by pressing the ~ key.

Now you can adjust the Brightness level of the game. This option is located in the System Settings window (shown earlier in Figure 4-2). The game's default Brightness level is often a little brighter than the monitor's normal appearance. The goal is to have the game's Brightness level to be as close as possible to your monitor's normal appearance for editing.

Adjust the Brightness meter while watching the screen around the outside of the game window. Because you are in Windowed mode, you should be able to see your desktop or other open applications behind the game window. Adjust the slider until the background looks normal to you — not too bright and too dark. I like to set mine to just above the third marker, as in Figure 4-5.

That's all the setup you should require in order to access the mapping editor from within the game.

Chapter 4: Getting Set Up for Mapping 41

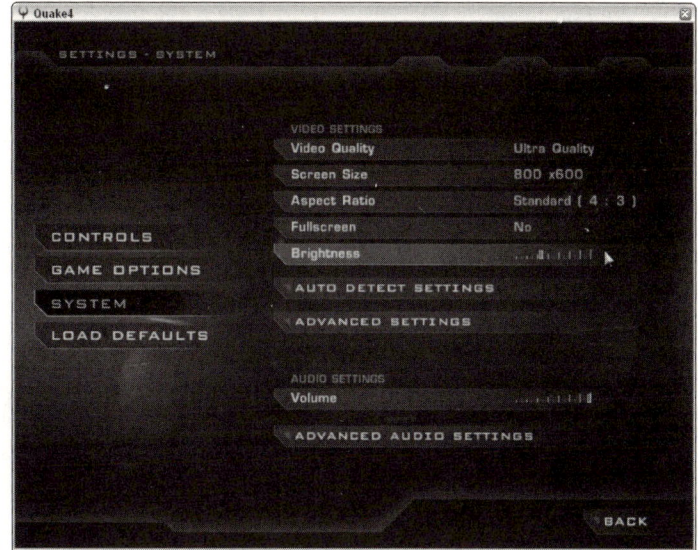

Figure 4-5: Adjust your Brightness level.

Launching the Editor

After you've set up the editor to run properly, you can get it running and start looking around.

Although launching most programs requires only the clicking of a button or link, the editor requires a couple more steps. If you closed the game after setting up, reload it by using your desktop shortcut that you set up earlier in this chapter (see "Customizing your Quake shortcut"); because the customized shortcut skips the opening movies, the game shouldn't take long to load. When the game has loaded, press the ~ key to open the game console. Here, type **editor** and then press Enter. This causes windows on the screen to close and open as the editor is launching. Within a few seconds, the editor loads and displays on the screen. You're now ready to start mapping, but first I show you around your new environment.

Arranging Your Windows

What you see when the editor is loaded depends on what your screen resolution is set to. The editor was designed to be used with a screen resolution of 1280 x 1024 pixels. If your resolution is set as such, then when the editor loads, you see all the smaller windows with the editor nicely arranged and in full view. If this is true, you can skip over this section of the chapter. However, if your windows resolution settings are other than 1280 x 1024 pixels, you will probably want to make some adjustments.

Part II: Making Your Own Maps

If your screen resolution is currently set to 1024 x 768 pixels when you load the editor, you see what is shown in Figure 4-6. Notice that the windows in the editor appear to be leading off the edge of the screen. This must be adjusted so that you can see all four windows in their entirety.

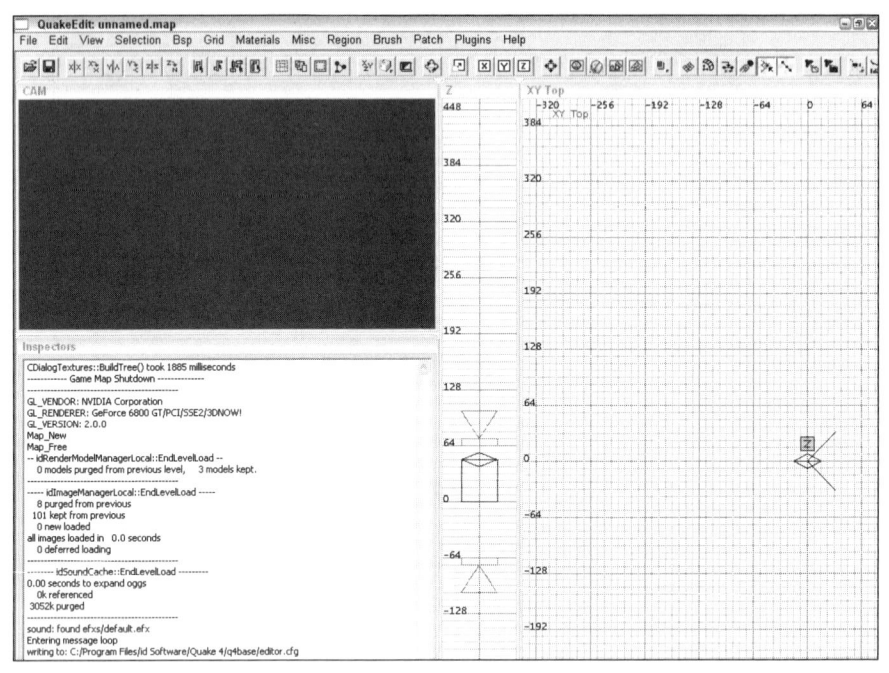

Figure 4-6: With a less-than-ideal screen resolution, the editor's windows won't fit your monitor and will have to be adjusted.

You have two options for adjusting your mapping environment:

 ✓ Adjust your screen settings to the optimal resolution (1280 x 1024 pixels).
 ✓ Adjust the editor's windows to fit your screen.

In the next two sections, I go over the steps for each change. Although I prefer the first solution, you can decide which is best for you.

Adjusting your screen resolution

My preferred way to adjust the environment for the map editor is by adjusting my screen resolution. To adjust this setting on your computer, follow these steps:

 1. **Right-click your desktop and choose Properties from the menu.**
 2. **Click the Settings tab in the Display Properties dialog box.**

Chapter 4: Getting Set Up for Mapping

3. Adjust the slider for your Screen resolution until it reads "1280 by 1024 pixels," as shown in Figure 4-7.
4. Press the Apply button.
5. Press OK to exit the Display Properties dialog box.

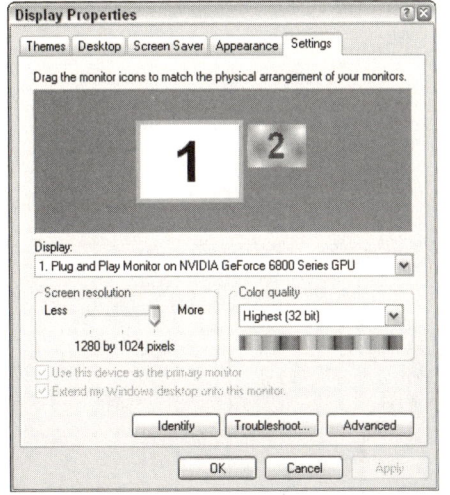

Figure 4-7: Select the screen resolution that reads "1280 by 1024 pixels" for an ideal work environment.

Adjusting your work environment

An alternative to adjusting your screen resolution is adjusting the windows in the editor. The reason I don't think this is an ideal solution is that making the windows smaller within the editor provides you with less space to work. Also, in the event that your video settings are reset for the game, you might have to go back and make these changes again. However, other than these annoyances, this solution works, and the editor will still function properly.

The necessary adjustments are actually quite simple. You just need to move and resize the four visible windows in the editor that is now loaded. Each of these windows can be dragged and sized to your liking and can even be arranged in a different order. However, I must ask you not to change the order of the windows while reading through this book because it might be confusing. If you do rearrange them, I might refer to a window that is no longer on your screen.

To change the size of a window, select its outer edge and drag it to the desired size. Just like when you resize a window in Windows, as you place your cursor over the outer edge of a window, the cursor point changes to two arrows. You can then click and drag that edge in the directions indicated by those arrows.

After sizing a window, you might want to move it. To move the window, click and drag the title bar of that window and move it to its new location.

Part II: Making Your Own Maps

When you're done with your adjustments, the result should look something like Figure 4-8. You don't want to rearrange the windows so that they're in different locations. Rather, you just want to resize them so that they're all in view.

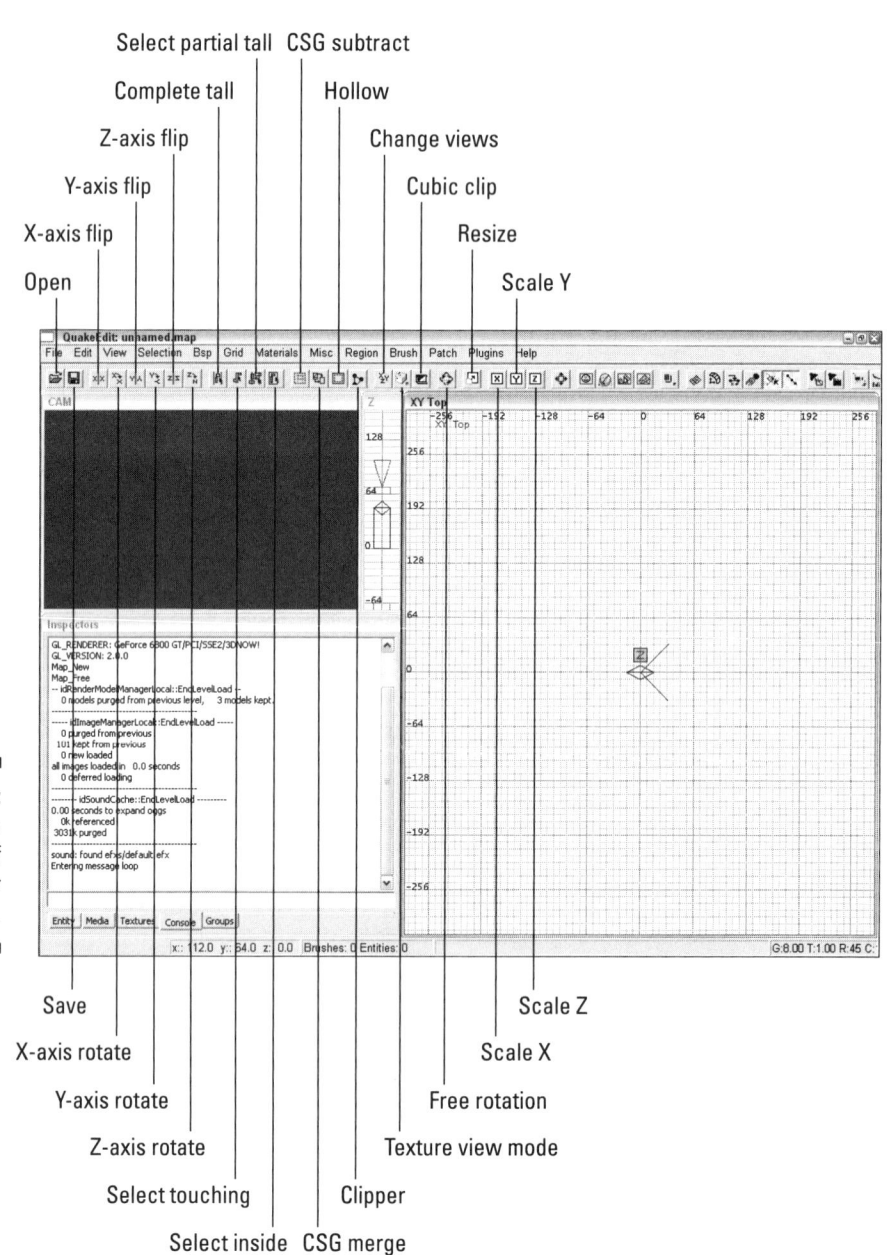

Figure 4-8: Align the windows of your editor like this.

Callouts (clockwise from top):
- Select partial tall
- CSG subtract
- Complete tall
- Hollow
- Z-axis flip
- Change views
- Y-axis flip
- Cubic clip
- X-axis flip
- Resize
- Open
- Scale Y
- Scale Z
- Scale X
- Free rotation
- Texture view mode
- Clipper
- CSG merge
- Select inside
- Select touching
- Z-axis rotate
- Y-axis rotate
- X-axis rotate
- Save

Working the Windows and Exploring the Interface

The editor might look somewhat intimidating when you first see it. It has a number of open windows with unfamiliar names, a string of buttons across the top, and a lot of words that you might not know. Don't let this worry you. By the end of this chapter, you should feel much more comfortable with what's onscreen. You'll also be ready to plunge into the world of mapping — Chapter 5 shows you how to construct your first map.

Looking at windows

Begin by going over the four windows now open on the screen. You can move each of the windows by clicking and dragging the title bars. This might be useful to you later if you want to move them to someplace else on the screen for personal preference. For now, I recommend that you leave them where I've placed them in Figure 4-8 while I show you around. I refer to the windows throughout the book, and they'll be easier to find if you haven't moved them.

CAM window

The window located on the top-left area of the screen is the CAM window. This is your 3D viewport. (Refer to Figure 4-9.) The purpose of the window is to present you with a visual representation of your map. Right now it's empty, but later, when you start working on your map, you will be able to see in this window what you are working on as if you were in the game. The CAM window also makes it a lot easier to select portions of the map that you're working on. I go into this further in the next chapter.

Part II: Making Your Own Maps

Figure 4-9: Each window in the editor has a specific purpose, all of which are very important to editing a map in *Quake 4*.

Callouts (top, left to right):
- Move selection
- Don't select models
- Show primitive bounding box
- Show patches as wireframe
- Redisperse patch points
- Weld patch points
- Show light volumes
- Spline options
- Add curve points
- Delete curve points
- Show sound bounding box

Callouts (bottom, left to right):
- Select only brushes
- Select primitives by bounding box
- Show models as
- Patch bend mode
- Add caps to current patch
- Select drill-down rows/columns
- Light option
- Edit curve points
- Insert curve points
- Show sound volumes
- Launch game for testing

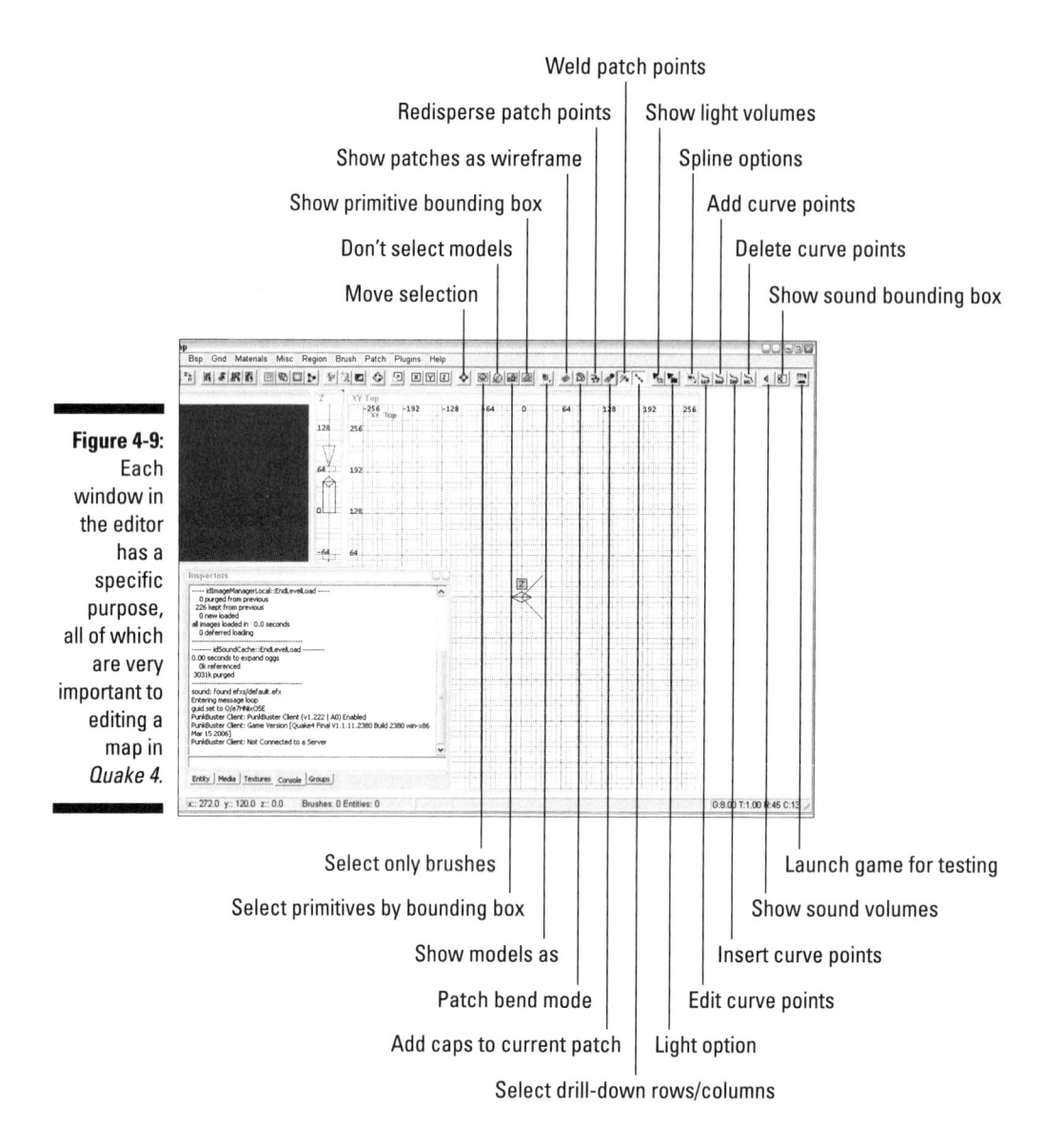

Multi-Purpose window

The window located on the bottom-left of the screen is the Multi-Purpose window. (Refer to Figure 4-8.) This window houses a number of tabbed windows providing details about different parts of your work environment. From here you can edit the properties of different entities in your map, view and select media and textures, refer to the editor console for possible compiling errors, and work with the various grouped objects of your map. Although the title of this window reads as Inspectors in Figure 4-8, the title changes depending on the operations you are performing within the editor. I simply refer to this window as the Multi-Purpose window. You will have a chance to explore each of these tabs while making your first map later.

2D window

The window located on the right of the editor is your 2D (two-dimensional) window. (Refer to Figure 4-8.) It is displayed as a grid and is labeled XY Top in the figures in this chapter. This window is your primary working environment. This is where you will be constructing the pieces of your map.

Although this window is displaying only two dimensions of your three-dimensional world, you construct and edit everything from here. When this is selected as the active window, pressing Ctrl+Tab switches among the three available views: XY Top, XZ Front, and YZ Side. The combination of these windows provides you with a view of all three dimensions.

You will be working in this window of the editor most. Here you can draw the objects in your world, move them around, resize them, add entities, and much more.

Z window

The last window is the one located in the middle of the screen located between the CAM window and the 2D window and labeled only with the letter Z. (Refer to Figure 4-8.) Your Z window refers to the Z axis of your three-dimensional world. When used in conjunction with the XY Top view in the 2D window, you can see a complete three-dimensional view of your map.

Pressing buttons and working menus

The buttons at the top of the window contain the commands most often used. I don't get to all the buttons in this book. Actually, it's my goal that by the end of this book, you won't even need any of the buttons. It's more efficient to know the keyboard shortcuts to all the commands in the editor than to rely on buttons and menu options. But before I go over the essential shortcuts in Chapter 5, let me introduce you to these buttons:

> **TIP**
>
> You might not be able to see all the buttons to the right on your editor. This is because the editor is meant to be used with a wider screen resolution than 1024 pixels. Widen the view of your monitor if you would like to see and use these buttons. However, remember that you have a drop-down menu and shortcuts to use instead.

There is also the menu at the top of the screen. Here you can find all the editor options available. If you don't have the keyboard shortcut memorized or you don't see the button for the operation you want to perform, you can find it in this menu.

Using shortcuts for success

You should get to know the keyboard shortcuts for the editor. There really is no quicker and easier way to work on your map other than when you are using keyboard shortcuts. You might find it difficult to remember them at first, but trust me when I tell you that it's worth the effort. The more you use them, the better you will remember them.

If you forget a keyboard shortcut or want to look for one you haven't yet learned, you can find a list available from the menu. Choose Help➪Command List to get to the complete list of available keyboard shortcuts available for the editor.

As you read through the coming chapters, I introduce important shortcuts. If you're looking for a reference to all the shortcuts, flip over to the Cheat Sheet found behind the front cover of this book.

Avoiding errors

In a perfect world, there would be no errors. Sadly, however, the Radiant editor was not built in a perfect world. There are some buttons and tools that you should avoid (and even the experienced mapper should avoid) in order to prevent errors that can ruin your work.

As you go through the chapters in this book, I make note of certain functions you should either use with caution or avoid altogether. I never enjoy having to tell someone that his or her map is ruined and can no longer be used, especially after he or she has spent countless hours working on it. I recommend that you heed my warnings, or you could find yourself with an unusable map and have to start all over.

Why are these failure-prone options available in the editor? The editor was built to mimic that of a 3D modeling program, such as 3D Studio Max. Back before the Radiant editor was available, modeling programs such as 3D Studio Max were used to create much of the 3D world. These 3D programs are usually free of such errors that can pop up in Radiant, and they should be, considering the amount of money they cost. Then came an open-source alternative to editing called Radiant. This program was available to the public for free and was well maintained by its developers. Over time, Radiant became the editor of choice by mod makers and game developers. As for the errors that can occur with certain tools and operations, I believe the developers of the editor hope to one day fix them. However, until Radiant is perfected, these options are available but should be avoided.

Chapter 5
Creating Your First Game Map

In This Chapter
▶ Selecting the texture for your walls
▶ Zooming and moving the 2D window
▶ Using brushes
▶ Changing your room from solid to hollow
▶ Keeping a seal on your room

*I*t's time to jump right in and start creating your first game map. Your goal is to create a very simple room. It will just be a small area with four walls, a ceiling, and a floor. This might not sound like much, but from this you will be able to create great things.

Whenever I'm starting a map or testing ideas, this is where I start. I create a small room with the basic necessities for playing in the game. Then I build my additions onto this small map. The additions could be an entire city with streets and skyscrapers that stretches on for blocks, or it could be something I want to invent and test, like a fancy door, before adding it into my final piece.

All great things start small, and this chapter is where you begin. In no time, you'll be building onto the small space you create and making something fantastic.

Selecting a Texture

Before you begin creating the walls and parts of your room, you need to select a base texture that will be applied to the things you draw. Textures are really just images that are painted onto the surfaces of what you see within the game. Just like the walls in your house, it's a good idea to start with a *primer,* which is your base texture, and later go back and apply the *final coat,* which is what the player sees in the game. I explain more about the base texture in the next section.

Loading texture sets

Now that the editor is loaded and ready to go, you need to select an initial texture — the base texture — from which to build. While you're creating things within the editor, the selected texture will be automatically applied to it. You can change the selected texture at any time, and you can even go back later and apply different textures, but as your map grows in size and complexity, so does the tediousness of going back and replacing all the textures.

You want to select the Caulk texture. The Caulk texture is used as your base texture because, although it is ignored by the game as a texture, it will create a solid structure. The Caulk texture makes solid walls, thereby making your map self-contained. A map needs to be self-contained so that it cannot leak — as I explain in further detail later in this chapter. And because it is ignored by the game as a texture, the Caulk texture doesn't take up any additional computer memory or processing power.

To select the Caulk texture, you must load the texture set that contains it. Select the Media tab from Multi-Purpose window. This Media tab displays a list of folders that looks a lot like the folder listings in Windows File Explorer, as you can see in Figure 5-1. At this time, you are interested only in the Textures folder listed at the top. This contains the available textures for use within the editor.

Figure 5-1: The Media tab in the Multi-Purpose window is where you can find your Textures folder.

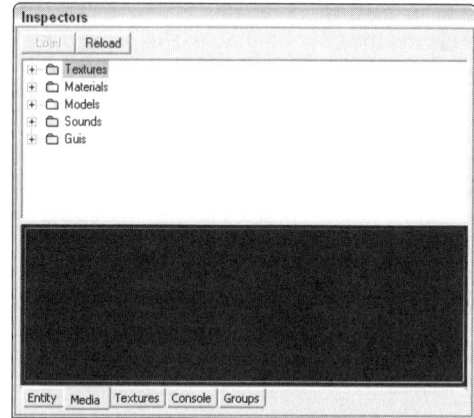

Radiant doesn't have any preloaded textures and therefore has no default texture selected for you. When starting a new map, you must load a texture set and select a texture before you start working in the editor. If you don't select or apply a texture to everything in your map, errors will occur.

Chapter 5: Creating Your First Game Map   51

> **WARNING!** Don't double-click the Textures folder icon! This action will result in loading every available game texture into your computer's memory. This could cause a system crash or slow computer response because all the memory could be used up. If you do accidentally double-click the Textures folder icon, try to press the Cancel button on the small loading dialog box that pops up. If this doesn't work, you might need to close and reload the editor to clear your computer's memory of the loaded textures.

To explore the Textures folder, select the plus icon to the left of the Textures folder icon, as shown in the margin. This opens a list of subfolders, as shown in Figure 5-2, each of which contains a set of textures (which is why they are called *texture sets*).

Figure 5-2: Expanding the Textures folder reveals the list of available texture sets.

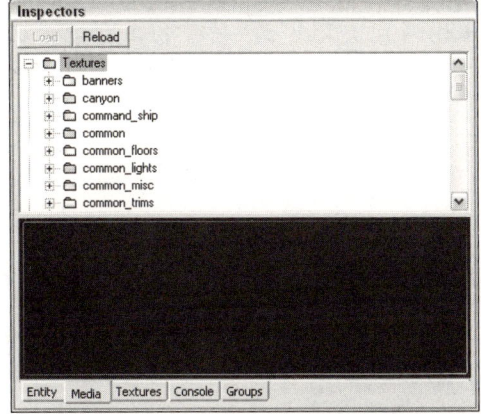

You could explore each of these texture sets and select the individual textures that you want, but there is a much simpler way of doing this. Double-click the texture set folder icon. This loads all the textures in the selected texture set, and loading this smaller group of textures won't overwork your computer.

Caulking your map

You want to load the Common texture set, which you can see in the list of available texture sets in Figure 5-2. This set contains the Caulk texture as well as other textures commonly used when building maps. However, you are currently interested in the Caulk texture only.

To load the Common texture set, double-click the folder icon. This loads into memory every texture available within that set.

The Caulk texture explained

The Caulk texture is ignored by the game even though you can see it in the editor. When applied to a brush face, that brush face is not drawn in the three-dimensional world. Also, because no texture is loaded, Caulk reduces the amount of used memory on the computer when playing, thereby creating a faster, smoother running level in the game. This makes it perfect for places that can't be seen by the player, such as the areas behind walls, between brushes that are butted against each other (see the "Drawing the First Brush" section for an explanation), and so on.

With the new textures in memory, you can select the Textures tab within the Multi-Purpose window. Here, as in Figure 5-3, is displayed a thumbnail list of all the loaded textures and their text titles. Some of them appear very small, and others appear very large. You can now see why this is the simpler method of selecting textures as opposed to going through the Media tab each time you need a new one.

Figure 5-3: Textures that have been loaded can be previewed for selection within the Textures tab.

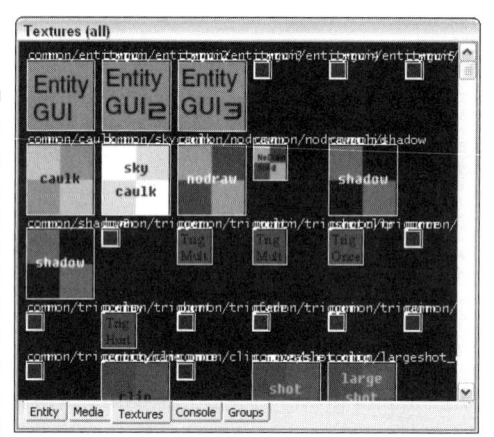

If some of the textures are too small or too large for your screen, you can change their size. To do this, choose Materials⇨Texture Window Scale from the top of the editor, and then select the scale at which you want them to be displayed. The default scale is 50%, which is half the texture's actual size. I recommend changing the scale to 100%, but feel free to adjust this to your liking.

TIP

If you have an older computer and you find that the editor crashes a lot after changing the texture scale, change the scale back to 50% or lower. The larger image size requires your computer to work harder.

Chapter 5: Creating Your First Game Map   **53**

From the list of textures displayed in the Multi-Purpose window, select the Caulk texture. This texture looks like a pink checkerboard with the word *caulk* in the middle. When you select the texture, it is surrounded by a red outline, as shown in Figure 5-4.

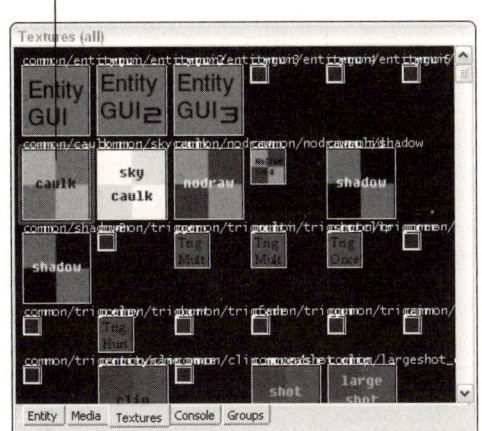

Figure 5-4: Textures that have been selected are indicated by a red outline.

Drawing the First Brush

The world inside 3D games is made up of building blocks called *brushes*. If you think of this world as being a house, every wall, floor, and roof would be made up of one or more of these brushes.

With your texture selected, you are ready to start creating your game world by drawing your first brush. To create a brush, click and drag a rectangular shape into the editor — this act of clicking and dragging a brush is called *drawing*. The following steps show you how to do this:

1. **To draw out your first brush, begin in the 2D window, which should be labeled as XY Top.**

2. **Click anywhere within near the middle of this window and drag the mouse.**

   As you drag, a square with a dashed, red outline appears.

3. **When you've created a medium-sized square on the grid, release the mouse button.**

   You aren't concerned with the size of the brush right now because you'll be going back to resize it shortly. You should have something like what appears in Figure 5-5.

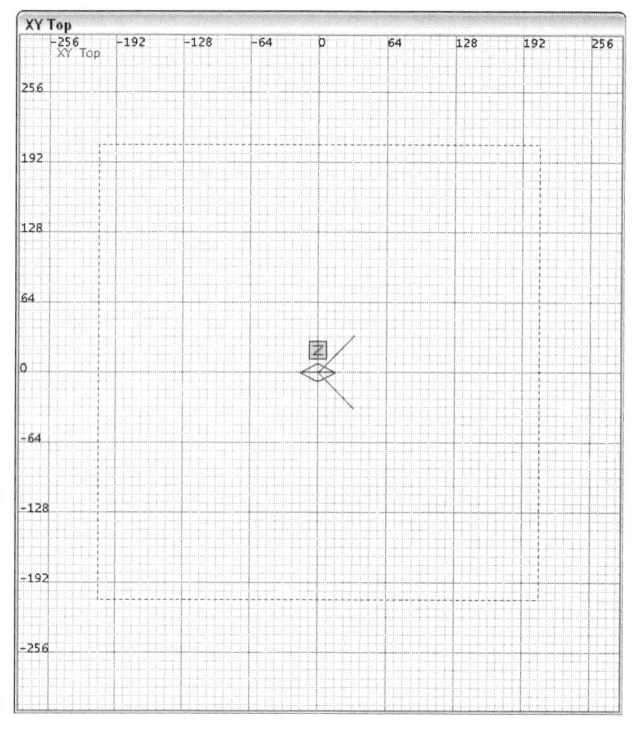

Figure 5-5: Your brush appears outlined with a red, dashed line.

There you have it. You have just started your first map and created your first brush. You can't yet play it in the game and it doesn't look too fancy, but it's the start of something that might be played by thousands of gamers when you're done.

Maneuvering the 2D Window

Before you get back to resizing and building upon your first brush, you should get more familiar with the 2D window. You will be working in this window most of your mapping life, so it's important to understand how it works.

The 2D window contains a series of lines, like the graph paper you might have used in school. These are here as guides to help you line things up as you build the map. Understanding how the lines are spaced will eventually help you to better understand the editor and the maps it builds.

Counting in power of two

The numbers in the world of mapping revolve around the power of two. All textures for a game are sized by using numbers such as 8, 64, 128, 256, 512, or some combination thereof. The reason is that when images are scaled from one size to another, they look best when they are scaled by powers of two.

Textures in many games are created by using a special format that already contains the scaling information for each texture size. So, a texture that is 512 x 512 might already contain the information for the same texture that is 256 x 256, 128 x 128, and so on.

A similar sizing pattern is found in the way the 2D window is laid out. The default setup places the grid lines eight units apart. The darker grid lines are 64 units apart.

Next, note that each unit in the editor is equal to one pixel in a texture. Placing a 64 x 64 texture on a brush face that is 64 units square results in an optimally sized texture-to-brush ratio.

Zooming and moving the view

Maneuvering inside the 2D window is pretty simple; you should be able to master it easily. If you need to move your view to the left, right, up, or down, right-click and drag the grid area as if you were sliding a piece of paper. It moves around quite easily.

When I need to zoom in or out, I find it easiest to use the mouse wheel. However, you also have two other options:

- You can use the keyboard shortcuts Home and Delete. Home zooms out, and Delete zooms in.
- You can press Alt as you right-click and drag to zoom in and out.

If you use the keyboard shortcuts, don't worry about pressing Delete — it won't actually delete anything in your map. That function is reserved for the Backspace key.

If you want to change your grid size to something other than the default 8 units, do one of the following:

- Press [to decrease your grid size or] to increase it.
- Directly select the numbers 1 through 7, 1 being the smallest grid size and 7 being the largest.

Part II: Making Your Own Maps

> **TIP:** Pressing these shortcut keys at this point, without anything within your window to zoom on, you might not see much of a difference. Right now, only the numbers in the lower-right corner of the editor will change. Later, when you have something to zoom on, you will notice the changes that occur by using these shortcuts.

I prefer using the [and] keys. But if you'd like to use the numbers, you can get a better understanding of which number does what by selecting Grid⇨Grid Size, you will find the corresponding shortcut to grid size is listed there.

That's your quick review of the 2D window. In the following sections, you get to practice using it.

Resizing and Moving Brushes

Getting back to your map, you need to finish sizing your medium-size brush that you created in the section, "Drawing the First Brush," earlier in this chapter. You want to size it equal that of the entire room you are making, which is going to be 512 units in width, 512 units in depth, and 128 units in height. The reason I chose 512 units square is because this will create a room large enough to experiment in without making it too large. A room with a height of 128 units makes the player feel comfortable. You could create a room of nearly any size when constructing your map, but for practice purposes here, you should use the dimensions listed.

You already know how to move around in your 2D window, but now you need to understand how to resize and move your brushes as well as change your views from just the XY Top to the other two views: XZ Front and YZ Side.

To resize a brush, all you need to do is click outside the brush on the side you want to change and drag the mouse. This stretches that side of the selected brush in the direction you pull. If you click and drag near the outside corner of a brush, you affect the two closest edges of that brush. You can also use the Z window when sizing and moving brushes; however, this affects only the height of the brush because it affects only the Z plane.

To move a brush around the map, just click inside the brush and drag the mouse. That's all there is to it.

Now resize the brush. Your goal is to create a brush that is 512 units in width, 512 units in depth, and 128 units in height. First resize the width and depth. From within the 2D window, stretch each of the four sides of the brush until they land on –256 and 256 units. (See Figure 5-6.) Use the numbers on the top and on the left of the window to help you adjust the size. Remember that you can zoom in and out of the window's view as well as move the grid around for better control of your brush.

Chapter 5: Creating Your First Game Map   **57**

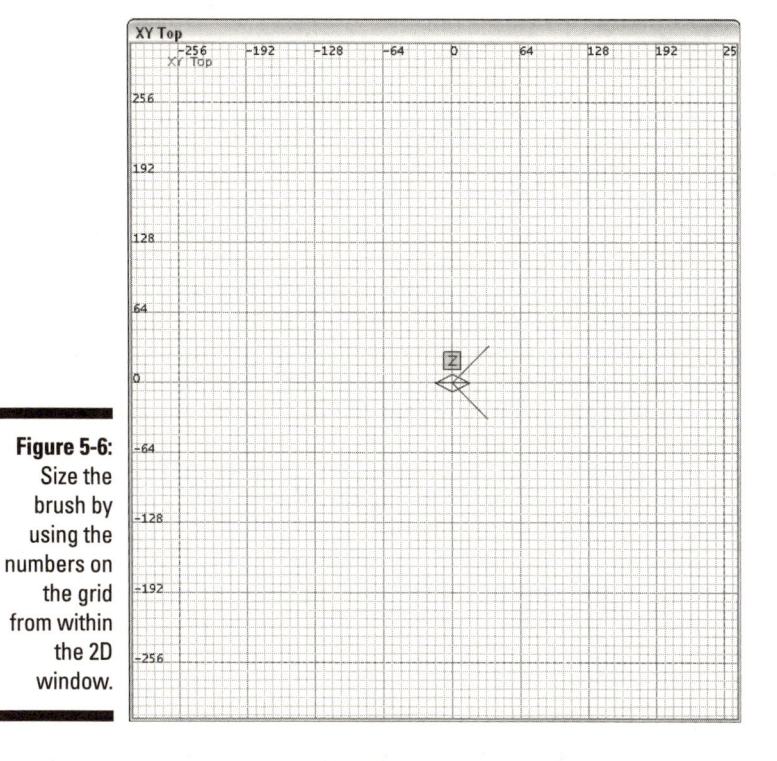

Figure 5-6:
Size the brush by using the numbers on the grid from within the 2D window.

Next, resize the height of the brush from the Z window found between the CAM window and the 2D window. Click and drag upward — starting above the red outlined brush — until the brush reaches the 128-unit mark. The bottom of the brush should already be sitting on the 0-unit mark, but if it isn't, adjust the brush by stretching or moving it accordingly. The resulting Z window should look something like the one shown in Figure 5-7.

Figure 5-7:
Adjust the height of a brush by using the Z window.

Hollowing Out the Room

When your brush is properly sized, you need to hollow it out to make room for your player. Right now, it's a solid block. Your goal is to create an empty room with four walls, a floor, and a ceiling.

Before you hollow, check the grid size selected in the 2D window. When you hollow the brush, the wall thickness changes to a size equal to the grid size. Ideally, wall brushes are created at 8 units thick, so make sure the grid size is set to the default 8 units apart. One way you can check is by looking at the very bottom-right area of the editor and reading the text shown in Figure 5-8. The text should begin with G:8.00, which stands for Grid: 8.00 units. Adjust your grid size if needed, either by using your mouse wheel or by using the shortcuts [and].

Figure 5-8: The bottom-right corner of the editor.

The bottom-right corner of the editor provides you with some information about your editor settings. Reading from left to right, you have the following information displayed:

- **G:** This is the grid size that is actively set in the 2D window. When you load the editor, the default size is 8.00, meaning that the grid is at 8 units apart, or 8 x 8 units.

- **T:** This is the texture scale that has been set in the editor's preferences. This number should always read as 1.00; otherwise, what you see in the editor won't be the same as what you see in the game.

- **R:** This is the default degree of rotation a brush or other selected item in the map will turn when using the rotation shortcut.

- **C:** This defines the viewable distance in the CAM window and is preset during installation. Your distance in the editor is limited so as not to slow down your computer with all the additional processing.

- **L:** This defines your texture lock modes. MR means that your textures will stay locked in place on the brush when you go to move them (M) or rotate them (R).

Chapter 5: Creating Your First Game Map   59

> ### Avoiding file corruption
>
> Even though this editor has been around for a number of years and was updated with improvements after every major game release, there are still options in the editor that you should use with caution or not at all. Using the Hollow tool on more complex shapes is one of these potentially corrupting options. However, you can hollow out simple shapes such as cubes by using the Hollow tool without much worry that doing so will corrupt the map. More information about tools that require warnings can be found in Chapter 20.

REMEMBER: In the Figure 5-8, you can't see the values for C or L. This is because the editor is meant to be used at a larger screen resolution than 1024 x 768. You don't need to see these values. However, if you do want to see them, you will need to adjust the resolution of your monitor accordingly.

Locate the Hollow button at the top of the editor. It's pictured as a red square with red dashed lines inside a square with solid lines, as shown here. (When you hover your mouse over this button, it opens a box labeled Hollow.) Press this button now to hollow the selected brush, which happens to be the brush you were just working with.

You now have something that looks more like a room and less like a solid block. (See Figure 5-9.) Your brush that was once solid is now looking more like a room made of six brushes: one for each side, one for the top, and one for the bottom.

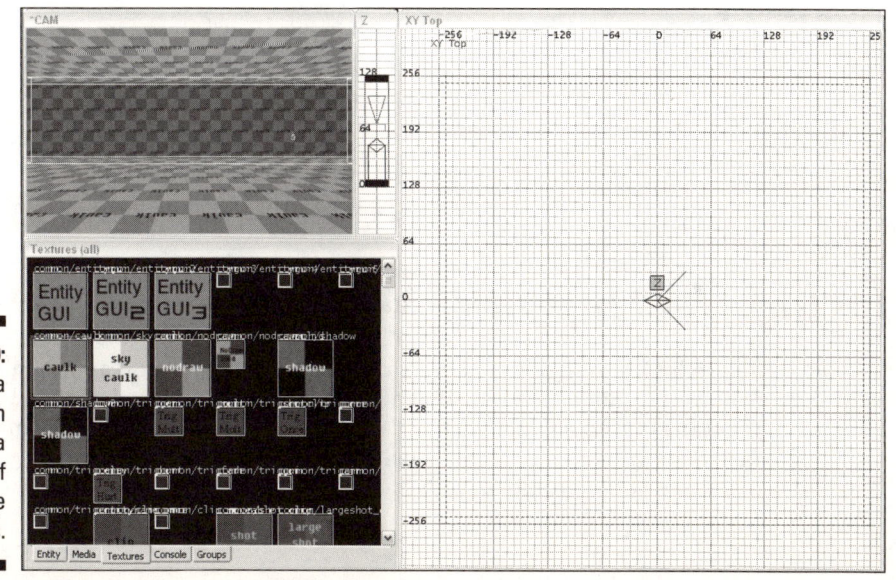

Figure 5-9: Hollowing a solid brush results in a structure of multiple brushes.

Maneuvering the CAM Window

This is a good time for you to start playing with the CAM window. Now that you've hollowed this large brush (check out the preceding section), you should be seeing something new in this window: the inside of your new room. With your map started, you can use this window just as much as the 2D window for previewing and selecting your world.

Right now, all you should be able to see is one of the inner walls of your room. There are a couple of ways to move around in this window, but for this book I stick with the simplest and most accurate method: the keyboard shortcuts. Moving around in this window requires the use of the keys in Table 5-1, shown in order of most frequently used:

Table 5-1	Shortcut Keys Used to Move Around in a Window
Key	**Result**
Up arrow	Move forward
Down arrow	Move backward
Left arrow	Turn left
Right arrow	Turn right
D	Move up
C	Move down
A	Look up
Z	Look down
<	Strafe left
>	Strafe right

Fixing Overlapping Issues

Take a look at one of the corners of the room, like the one shown in Figure 5-10. You're going to notice that after hollowing your brush, instead of leaving the walls butted against each other, they are overlapping. This is an important issue you need to fix after using the Hollow tool. If you don't fix this, you might see some problems with the overlapping textures when they are rendered in the game.

Chapter 5: Creating Your First Game Map **61**

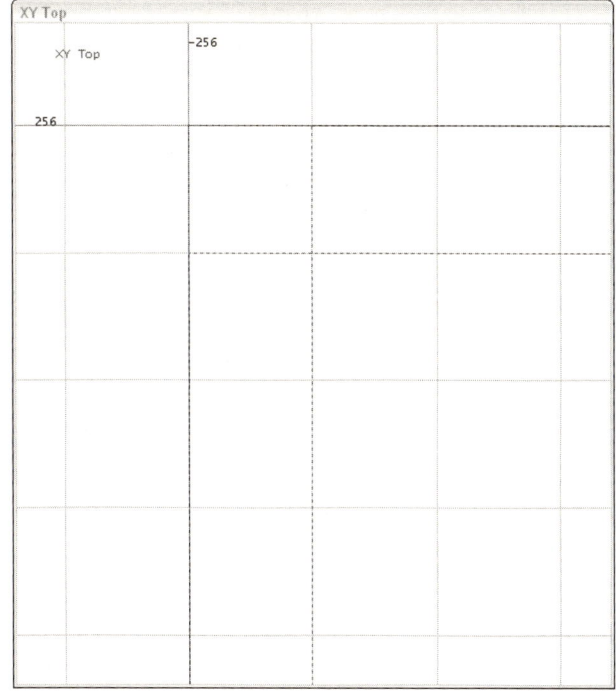

Figure 5-10: After using the Hollow tool, you must go back to fix overlapping brushes.

To fix the overlapping, you're going to move some of the brushes around. You do this in the same way that you resize a brush before hollowing it out. (See the section, "Resizing and Moving Brushes," earlier in this chapter.)

Start with the ceiling and floor brushes. You are going to move the ceiling up and the floor down, but first you make sure you won't accidentally mess up the work you have done by moving more than you plan. Here's how:

1. **Press Esc to deselect everything in your map.**

   I press Esc to deselect everything quite often so I don't mistakenly manipulate the wrong object. Then I select the one object or multiple objects I want to adjust. Reselecting your brushes is easier than finding and fixing what was messed up during a previous operation.

2. **With everything deselected, select the ceiling brush in the room. Do this from the CAM window by pressing Shift+click on that brush.**

   When you select the brush, it will be colored with a shade of red and have a white outline. This way you can see what is selected and what is not.

Part II: Making Your Own Maps

> ### Selecting brushes from the CAM window
>
> You might be asking yourself why you don't just select your brushes from the 2D window. In the case of the ceiling brush, you could do just that by using the same shortcuts. However, if you can select the ceiling brush, how do you select the floor brush? In answering this question, it is understood why you wouldn't select the floor brush from the 2D window. When you use the 2D window, only the uppermost brush is selected. This is why you use the CAM window when selecting brushes.

 3. **Move the brush up 8 units so it sits on the top of the wall brushes and is no longer overlapping.**

    You can do this from the Z window or the 2D window by clicking anywhere within the selected brush and dragging it up. However, if you use the 2D window for this, make sure you change your viewpoint.

    I show you how to use the 2D window to move the brush. Here's what you do:

    a. Press Ctrl+Tab to change your view from XY Top to either the XZ Front view or the YZ Side view.

    b. Move the window around by right-clicking and dragging, and then zoom in by pressing Delete or using the scroll wheel on the mouse so you have a good view of the brush you're going to move.

    c. Click and drag the brush up.

    If you want to make sure you move the brush only in one direction, press and hold the Shift key after clicking the brush, and then drag it up. (Just be aware that accidentally pressing Shift *before* clicking selects or deselects different brushes in the map.)

 4. **After moving the brush up, make sure you didn't accidentally move it to the side.**

    You need to make sure you moved the brush only upward and not in any other direction; otherwise, you get errors later when you go to compile your map. Use your keyboard shortcuts along with your CAM window or 2D window to confirm it is in place.

 5. **With the ceiling in place, move the floor down 8 units and into place:**

    a. Press Esc to deselect everything.

    b. Shift+click the floor brush in the CAM window.

    c. With the floor brush selected, move it down 8 units so it sits just under the wall brushes.

    Remember to check that the brush was moved only downward and not to either side.

Chapter 5: Creating Your First Game Map 63

Next up are the walls. To save a little time, you resize two opposing walls at the same time rather than each one separately. You shrink them to fit inside the other two wall brushes.

6. **Switch your 2D window view to XY Top by using Ctrl+Tab.**

7. **Press Esc to deselect everything, and then select two opposing walls.**

   It isn't important which two walls you select as long as they aren't next to each other. In the examples provided in this section, I have selected the Northern and Southern walls, as displayed in the 2D window.

8. **Place your mouse outside of the selected brushes on the edge you want to adjust. Then click and drag them so they fit inside the other two walls.**

   You can adjust multiple brushes at the same time this way. Just be careful not to adjust the thickness of the selected walls by dragging the mouse too far in the wrong direction.

9. **Inspect the resulting fit to make sure the walls are touching but no longer overlapping.**

   Again, it's very important that they touch and that you haven't moved them too far.

10. **Adjust the other side of the same selected walls to fit between the touching walls by using the same method as outlined in Steps 8–9.**

    The result should look like Figure 5-11.

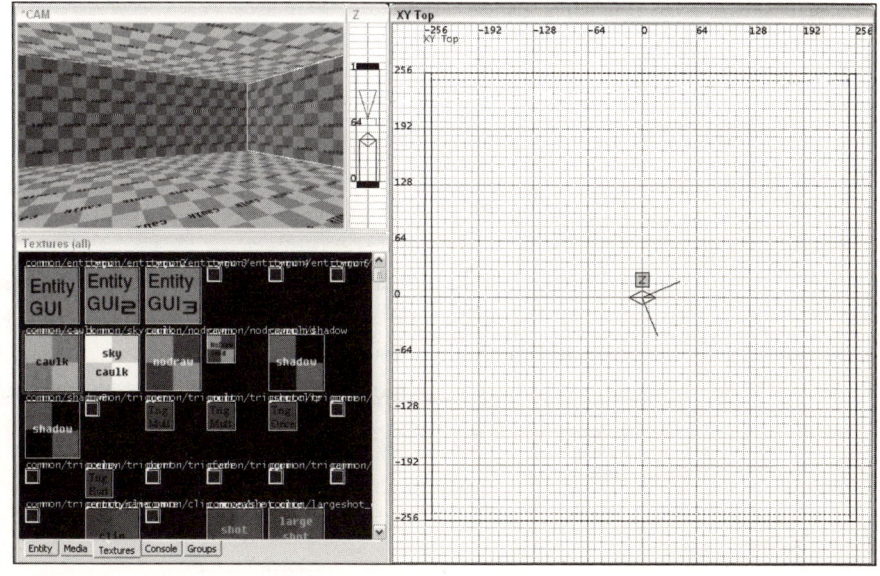

Figure 5-11: Adjust your brushes to remove any overlap after using the Hollow function.

Leaking Is Not an Option

Making sure that your map has a good seal is crucial. You will be adding entities that create light or are interpreted as objects that can create light. If you allow this light to escape into the void outside your map, which I describe in Chapter 2, you create what is known as a *leak*.

The game engine doesn't like leaks because they present too much information for it to process. When you take your map and compile the information into a playable level, the process must also calculate how light acts and reacts in the environment. Some textures reflect light like a mirror, and that reflected light can in turn reflect off of another surface. This bouncing effect is perhaps the most intensive process for your computer to calculate during the compile process. If you allow the light to go beyond the confines of your playable area, your computer will foresee an endless amount of calculating for the light that is bouncing into the void, and the computer reports back that a leak has occurred.

So before you save your map, go back and check for potential leaks. Make sure there are no visible gaps between your brushes. Look in the corners for holes, and if there are any, adjust the brushes to close them before you continue.

That's it for the structure of your room, and this is a good time to save your work before you continue.

Saving Your Map

If this is your first time saving a map, you must create a folder on your hard drive to save your new file. The folder location can't be just anywhere; it has to be someplace specific that is recognized by the game and the editor. To do this, follow these steps:

1. **Open Windows File Explorer and open the folder** `C:\Program Files\id Software\Quake 4\q4base`.

   Here you need to create a new folder called `maps`.

2. **Right-click an empty area in Windows File Explorer and choose New⇨Folder from the pop-up menu.**

3. **Name the new folder** `maps`.

Chapter 5: Creating Your First Game Map

4. **Open that new folder and create another new folder called** game.

   You should now have a new folder path that reads `C:\Program Files\id Software\Quake 4\q4base\maps\game`. This is where you should save your maps because this is where the game will look for them.

To save the map, you have several options:

- You can click the save icon, as shown here, from the top of the editor.
- You can choose Save⇨Save or Save⇨Save As.
- You can use the keyboard shortcut Ctrl+S.

When naming your map, make sure to use only alpha-numeric characters and no spaces. Any other characters result in errors when you go to compile and play your map. For example, instead of naming your map `my room.map`, use `my_room.map`. This saves you a headache later.

Because you're working on Chapter 5 of this book, save it under a name that makes it easy to reference later. Name it `chapter5.map`.

Chapter 6

Decorating the Scene

In This Chapter
▶ Grabbing new textures
▶ Covering the caulk with fresh paint
▶ Adjusting textures

The stage is set, but what about the scene? Right now, the walls in your `chapter5.map` file are just covered in the Caulk texture. This texture is great for keeping the processing power required by the game to a minimum, but is quite unsuitable for your game play. Your player cannot see this texture in the game, so you should dress things up with some textures.

Textures are really just pictures painted on the sides of the brushes in your map. (A side of a brush is called a *face*. Texturing the side of a brush is known as *painting a brush face*.) These pictures are often designed to look like concrete, brick, metal, wood, or other materials you commonly find in the real world. Most of the time, these pictures are created in small squares that can be stacked on top and next to each other endlessly and saved in an image format that the game can recognize. These are called *tileable images* because the image is applied like tiles on the floor.

Your objective is to place some of the textures onto the brush faces of your map. You can put down a concrete texture on the floor, a metal texture on the walls, and a decorative tile on the ceiling. All the textures that you need are available in the editor; they're based on the levels already created for the game. If you see a texture in the game, you can use it in the editor for your map, as well.

Loading the Common Walls Texture Set

In Chapter 5, I show you how to load the Common texture set, which is where you can find the Caulk texture that you use while building a room. You are now going to load another texture set, and this one is called Common Walls. Here's how:

Part II: Making Your Own Maps

1. Open the Media tab within the Multi-Purpose window.
2. Expand the root Textures folder if it isn't already expanded.
3. Double-click the Common Walls texture set to load the textures into memory.
4. When they have finished loading, open the Textures tab within the Multi-Purpose window so that you can preview and choose your next texture.

It is on this Textures tab that you will find a thumbnail list of all the textures within the Common Walls set.

Selecting and Painting Faces on the Walls

Before you select the new texture you want to apply, you must select the brush face of one of your walls. This distinction (the brush *face,* not the brush) is important because you don't want to apply the texture to the entire brush on each of the walls. This would defeat the purpose of using the Caulk texture when constructing the room.

First, make sure everything is deselected by pressing Esc. Then in the CAM window, select just one face of that brush by pressing Shift+Ctrl+click on that brush face. The brush face now has the same red coloring that the entire brush has when you select it, but the coloring is present only on the specific brush face, and it isn't outlined in white. (See Figure 6-1.)

With your brush face selected, you can now apply a new texture. Because this is just a basic room, you don't need to get too fancy selecting a texture. Apply the first available texture in the list of textures you just loaded, `common_walls/ba_wall1_5c`, to the selected brush face. (See Figure 6-2.) Clicking this texture applies it to whatever faces you have selected. Because you have only the one brush face selected, only one face will receive the new texture.

Figure 6-1: Press Shift+Ctrl+click to select just one face of a brush.

Chapter 6: Decorating the Scene 69

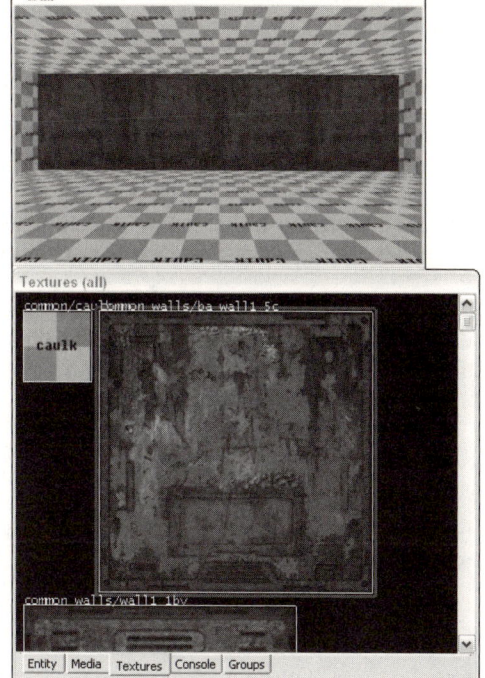

Figure 6-2:
Selecting a texture from the Textures tab applies it to the selected brush face.

Next, apply this texture to the remaining three walls in the room. You could do this by individually selecting each brush face as you did before and then applying the new texture by selecting it from the list. However, an easier way is to copy the texture you just applied to the other faces, provided you have a middle mouse button.

With your first textured brush face still selected, press Shift+Ctrl+middle-click on the wall next to the previous brush face. This copies the texture that has been applied to the selected brush face and pastes it onto the newly clicked brush face.

> **REMEMBER:** When you're copying textures from one brush face to another, make sure to use the Shift+Ctrl+middle-click combination. Just like when you're selecting brushes, pressing only the Shift key while clicking applies your texture to the entire brush, but pressing both the Shift and Ctrl keys while clicking affects only one brush face.

Continue to apply the texture to the remaining walls on the inside of your room until they all have been textured. Use the CAM window to move your camera around and select each brush face.

Inspecting the Surface

You aren't limited to simply applying a texture to a brush face. Sometimes the texture might be too tall or too short, too wide or too narrow, or just not line up the way you had planned. You can adjust all these measurements to your liking.

Center your camera on one of the textured walls. In this section, I take you through some of the ways you can adjust a texture after you've applied it.

Select the brush face that you are now facing. When it's selected, press S to bring up the Surface Inspector dialog box shown in Figure 6-3. This dialog box allows you to adjust a number of settings now present in your texture, such as its position and rotation.

Figure 6-3:
The Surface Inspector allows you to adjust the finer points of a texture.

The first field in this dialog box is the Material field. This is the location and name of your selected texture. You could manually enter the texture you want displayed on the brush face, but it's easier to select it from the Media and Textures tabs in the Multi-Purpose window.

Changing the values in the Shift Horizontally or Shift Vertically fields moves your brush in the specified direction by those numbers of pixels. If you place a negative value in either of those boxes, the texture flips in that direction. Sometimes this is necessary if there is text on the texture you chose and the text is displaying backwards. Another way to shift your texture is by using

Chapter 6: Decorating the Scene

keyboard shortcuts. With this Surface Inspector window closed, you can shift your textures by pressing Shift and the arrow key for the direction in which you want it to move.

The Scale values allow you to set the width and height of your texture. If you want your texture to be twice as wide, then enter a value of 2 in the horizontal scaling box. By selecting the Absolute check box, your scaling adjustments are made in correlation to the textures current size. So, if you had scaled your texture ten times in either direction, when you select the Absolute check box and scale again at a value of 1, nothing will change. This is because you are already at a scale of 1 in correlation with your texture's current size.

Use the Fit button in correlation with the Width and Height values to the right. When these values are each set to 1, pressing the Fit button stretches the texture so that it is equal to 1 times the width of the brush face and 1 times the height of the brush face. You can change the values of the width and height based on your needs.

The CAP button is only used for aligning textures on capped patches. Patches are complex brushes that resemble models. I don't get into Patches in this book because they aren't a required part of modding. However, you are welcome to play with the Patch options at your leisure.

The Natural Button is great for resetting your texture scaling and rotation values. Its function is to restore the texture to its natural state.

The Flip X and Flip Y buttons do just as the name implies. They flip your texture on the horizontal X axis or the vertical Y axis when pressed.

As for the Subdivide Patch option and those other options located near it, they won't be necessary tools in this book. They are used to increase the detail of a brush. The cost of using this option is that it can lower the performance of the game without much of a gain in quality. I recommend experimenting with this in your spare time only if you think your map needs a boost in quality.

Feel free to experiment with the texture settings I describe here. When you're done, you can re-apply the texture by selecting it from the list in the Multi-Purpose window or by copying it from another wall. The values will be reset based on your selection.

Painting the Remaining Faces

The last two brush faces left to paint are the ceiling and floor. In this section, I how you how to select and apply different textures to each, starting with the floor. Here's how:

Part II: Making Your Own Maps

1. **Load the texture set Common Misc from the Media tab.**

   The Common Floors texture set is good, too, but I wanted to apply a concrete texture found in Common Misc.

2. **Before selecting a new texture from this set, make sure you press Esc to deselect everything.**

3. **Shift+Ctrl+click the floor brush face to select it.**

4. **Then select the texture** `common_misc/concrete05`.

   You'll find it about a third of the way down the list, and it will look like what is shown in Figure 6-4.

Figure 6-4: Applying the concrete05 texture to the floor of your room.

For the ceiling, you are going to select a texture from the Common Floors texture set. Load this texture set, deselect everything, and select the ceiling brush face. Select the `common_floors/floor5_1` texture from the list, as shown in Figure 6-5.

Chapter 6: Decorating the Scene 73

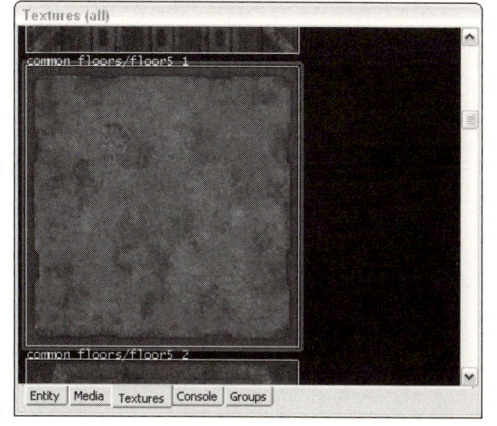

Figure 6-5: Applying the floor5_1 texture to the ceiling of your room.

Figure 6-6 is an example of what you should see in your CAM window. The walls, floor, and ceiling have been textured and are ready for your player to enjoy, and you are ready to move on.

Figure 6-6: All the walls in your room should be textured with something other than the Caulk texture.

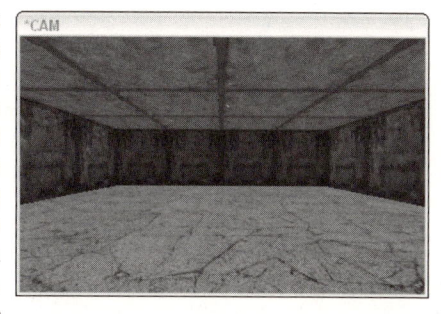

Choose File➪Save As and save your map as `chapter6.map`. You don't want to lose the work you've done up to this point, and it's good practice to save your map under progressing names as you go along, such as `mymap1.map`, `mymap2.map`, and so on.

Chapter 7

Adding Lights and a Player

In This Chapter

▶ Adding light to the room

▶ Coloring a light with the Color Picker

▶ Creating a player spawn point

▶ Adjusting spawn point properties from the Entity tab

After you create a room for your player as you did in the preceding chapter, you need to add two important things: light and a player spawn point.

You need light to see. Without the light, everything is black. Sometimes you want the player to rely on his or her flashlight or other resources to see where he or she is headed, but generally you want to provide some source of light.

Next you need to define where your player will *spawn* (start) in the level. Without the spawn point, the game won't know where to put the player when the game starts. Although, later you will want to add multiple spawn points for many players, for now, you need just one so you can spawn into your level for testing.

Lighting the Way

Adding light to a map is quite important and really simple. Without the light, the player can't see in the game. Although it's true that sometimes you want a dark area in the level — it can provide a place to hide something like a *pickup* (such as a weapon, armor, or health pack), an enemy, or the player — you probably won't want the entire map to be completely dark. If the player can't see where he or she is going, he or she will become frustrated. So, you should provide at least one dim light within your level.

Part II: Making Your Own Maps

To add light to your level, you must add what is called an *entity* to your map. Entities are active or interactive elements of a game such as a light, a door, or a pickup. Here's how to add one to your map:

1. **Press Esc to make sure nothing is selected in the map.**

   If anything is selected, you run the risk of turning that item into the entity you are placing.

   TIP: If you do forget to deselect everything before adding the light entity, just stop and reload your saved map. Then go back and add the light after making sure everything has been deselected. (*Note:* This Tip works only if you saved your map before starting Step 1.)

2. **Right-click the 2D window in the location where you want the light to be placed.**

   You don't have to place it in an exact location. You can move it around later.

   TIP: When adding entities, I find it easiest to place them from the XY Top view in the 2D window. This view allows you to place your entities and adjust their positions without getting lost in the map.

   When you right-click in the window, a pop-up menu appears and displays a list of entities. Most of the entities are grouped to make it easier to find what you're looking for. The entity you're interested in right now, Light, is in the first list.

3. **Choose Light from the pop-up menu.**

You now have a light entity in your map, and it looks like a small red square with a red dot in the middle. (See Figure 7-1). Surrounding this small red square is a much larger pink square. The small red square is the actual entity. The red dot in the middle is the entity's center point. The much larger pink square is the light radius. This represents how far out the light reaches in the darkness.

If you move around in the CAM window, you can see a white, diamond-shaped object like the one in Figure 7-2. This represents your light in the editor. Don't worry about this strange object being seen by the player in the game — the light entity is a *point entity* because it is not a direct interactive element in the game, but rather it is an active element that produces the action of providing light from a single point. The player cannot see point entities directly.

Chapter 7: Adding Lights and a Player 77

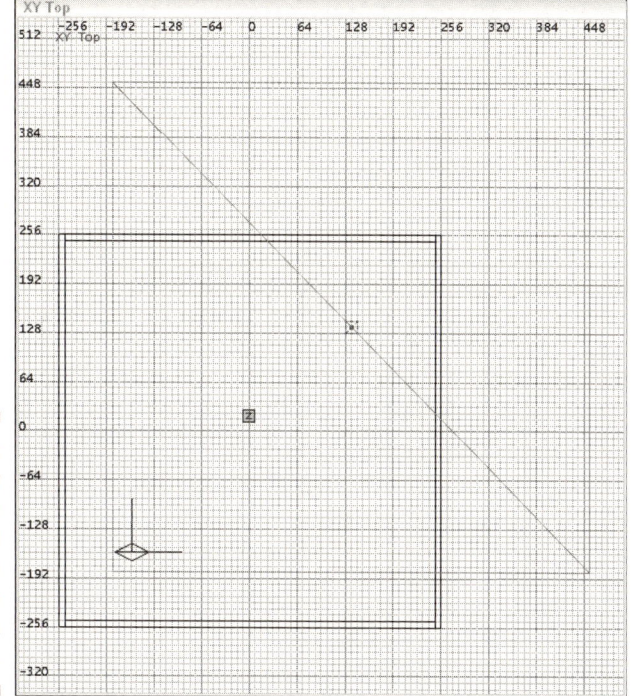

Figure 7-1: A light entity looks like a small red square with a large pink box around it.

Figure 7-2: From within the CAM window, the light entity has a diamond shape with a square outline.

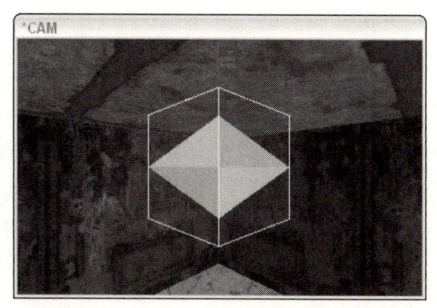

The following sections tell you how to position and color the light. I show you how to dress them up to look nicer in Chapter 12.

Positioning the entity

The light entity should be positioned in a way that will make sense to the player. It wouldn't make a lot of sense if the light came from the center of the floor or a bottom corner of the room (that is, unless you put something else there that looks like it should create this light). Instead, the player is going to expect the light to come from the ceiling as if from a light fixture.

From within the 2D window, click and drag the light entity toward a corner in the room and place it similarly to the entity shown in Figure 7-1. Also, you can move the light toward the ceiling either by adjusting the Z window or by changing your view in the 2D window. Although you don't have to click inside this entity to move it, it is bad practice to click outside anything with the editor to move it. If you do this, some entities might stretch, like the walls or other brushes in your room, and result in something you didn't want.

For now, leave this light in the corner so you can see the difference of light and dark within the game when you test the compiled map.

Adding a bit of color

The diamond-shaped entity in the CAM window is white because that is the default light color in any map. However, sometimes you might want to choose a different color depending on the environment you're trying to simulate. A change of color can make a huge difference in the look of your level.

As an example, try changing the color of the light to red so that you can see the difference it provides in the game. Here's how:

1. **With the light entity selected, press K.**

   This opens the Color Picker dialog box, where you can select or define the exact color you want for the light. (See Figure 7-3.)

2. **Select a red color from either of the color selector options in the window or simply type the values (such as 255, 0, and 0 for Red, Green, and Blue, respectively) in the RGB Values area.**

3. **Press OK to apply the color change and close the dialog box.**

   The once-white light entity in the CAM window has now turned a red color so that you can see what color the light is from within the editor.

That's enough with the light in this map. You'll finish up your lights in Chapter 12. Now it's time to move on to creating the player spawn point.

Figure 7-3: Pressing K opens the Color Picker dialog box, where you can define the color of your light.

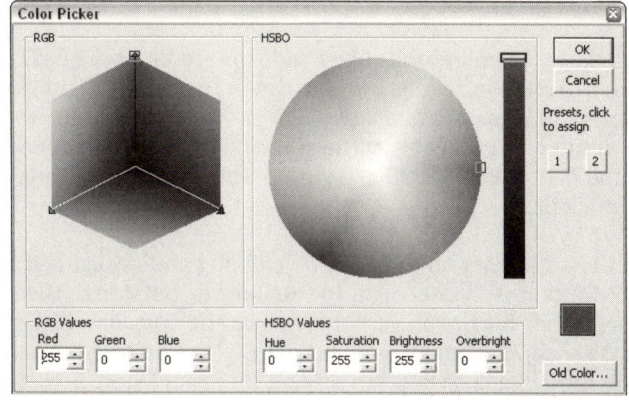

Adding a Place to Start

The *player spawn point* is the location where the player starts within the game. A player spawn point is also an entity. You can define the location as well as the direction the player is facing when he or she spawns. Here's how:

1. **Press Esc to make sure nothing is selected within the map.**

    If you forget to deselect the previously placed light entity with the Esc key before adding the spawn point, don't worry. Rather than loading the saved map and starting over, press Backspace to delete the light. Then go back, re-add the light, and start again with Step 1 for adding a spawn point. Because forgetting to deselect just a light is a minor oversight, it's easier to replace it than start over.

2. **Make a decision as to where you would like the player to spawn within your map.**

    You can move the spawn point entity around after you place it, so you don't have to get it exactly placed right now. For now, I recommend placing the entity in the corner of the room, opposite that of the light you place earlier in this chapter.

3. **Right-click and choose info⇨info_player_start from the pop-up menu that appears.**

    This is the single player spawn point; it's the simplest and easiest entity to use when testing your maps. Regardless of the type of map you're making — CTF, deathmatch, or any other — you can create the single player spawn point and test your map before adding the other spawn points.

Positioning and providing some direction

A newly added spawn point looks like a tall, square block. The 2D window displays it as a dashed red square with a dot in the middle, and the CAM window displays it as a solid block of black and red. Move your view around in the CAM window so you can see the spawn point. (If the last entity you placed was the light in the section "Lighting the Way," the new player entity is most likely stuck in the ceiling.)

Move the entity so it rests on the floor by clicking and dragging it in the 2D window. Make sure it isn't sticking into the floor or outside of the room; this creates errors either for the player when he or she spawns or for the compiler when you compile your completed map. The resulting placement of your entity in the 2D and Z windows should look like Figure 7-4.

Looking at the entity in the CAM window, you should notice a white arrow attached to one side of the spawn point. This represents the direction the spawn point is facing and defines which way the player faces when he or she spawns into the game. The next section shows you how to change that direction any way you like.

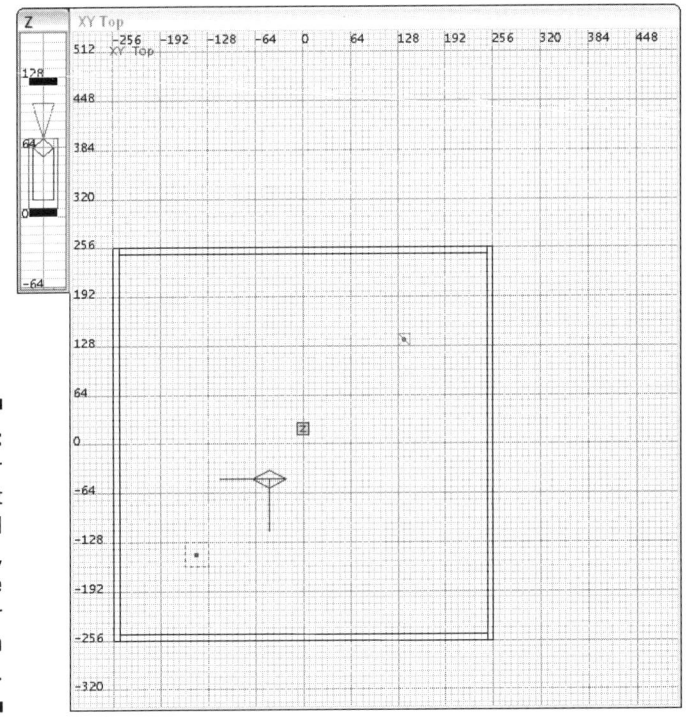

Figure 7-4:
Your player entity must be placed on the floor, not outside the map or hanging in the air.

Playing with properties on the Entity tab

As you define where the player spawn point is placed within the map, you've probably got a picture in your mind about what the spawning would look like in the game. This picture in your mind probably doesn't start with the player facing the wall, but instead toward the open area of the room. This orientation is something you can adjust.

It would be ideal to have the player face the light when he or she spawns into the game. So, with the spawn point selected, press N to open the Entity tab in the Multi-Purpose window. (You can also get there by clicking the Entity tab at the bottom of the Multi-Purpose window.) The Entity tab is where you can define the direction the player is facing when he or she spawns into the level. (See Figure 7-5.)

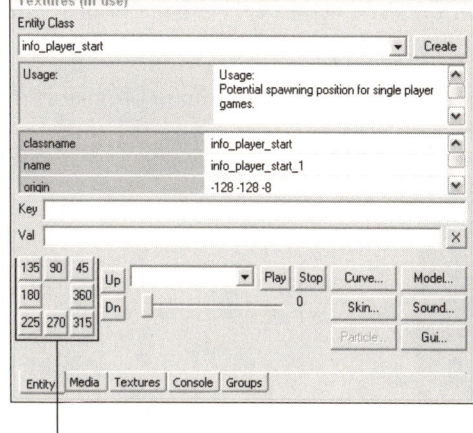

Figure 7-5: The Entity tab in the Multi-Purpose window.

Numbered direction buttons

This window displays most of the information about the selected entity. The top portion contains useful information provided by the developers of the editor. In this case, the `info_player_start` entity is defined under Usage. Other special features listed here that could be defined for the entity are useEffect and skin and can be viewed by scrolling that area which begins with *Usage*. Some information on how to enter this is listed for you to the right of its name, but all you're concerned with at this time is the direction the player is facing. The middle portion of the window displays the current settings. The *classname* is the name of the entity. The *name* is the user-defined name of the entity (in case you need to rename it). The *origin* is the point within the map where this entity is located. The bottom portion of the window provides you with shortcuts to commonly used operations. One of those operations is defining the direction. Here's how to do it:

1. **Look at the direction you want your player to face in the map as positioned in the 2D window in the XY Top view.**

2. **From the group of numbered buttons in the bottom-left corner of the Entity tab shown in Figure 7-5, select the direction you want the player to face.**

   These numbers represent degrees of rotation. If you want the player to face to the right, select 360. If you want the player to face left, press 180. Because I want my player to face the light in the upper-right corner of the 2D window and my player is positioned in the bottom-left corner, I press 45. That is a 45-degree rotation of the entity.

Because you have defined an angle, a couple things showed up in the editor, as shown in Figure 7-6. In the Multi-Purpose window, you see a new definition for the entity listed titled Angle. The value listed is 45. In the 2D window, if you look closely, an arrow emanates from the center point of the `info_player_spawn` entity. This arrow is pointing to the 45-degree angle. This arrow is also visible within the CAM window. These features are here to help you more easily identify what is occurring within the map.

All right, this is another good point to save your map. Choose File⇨Save As and save your map as `chapter7.map`.

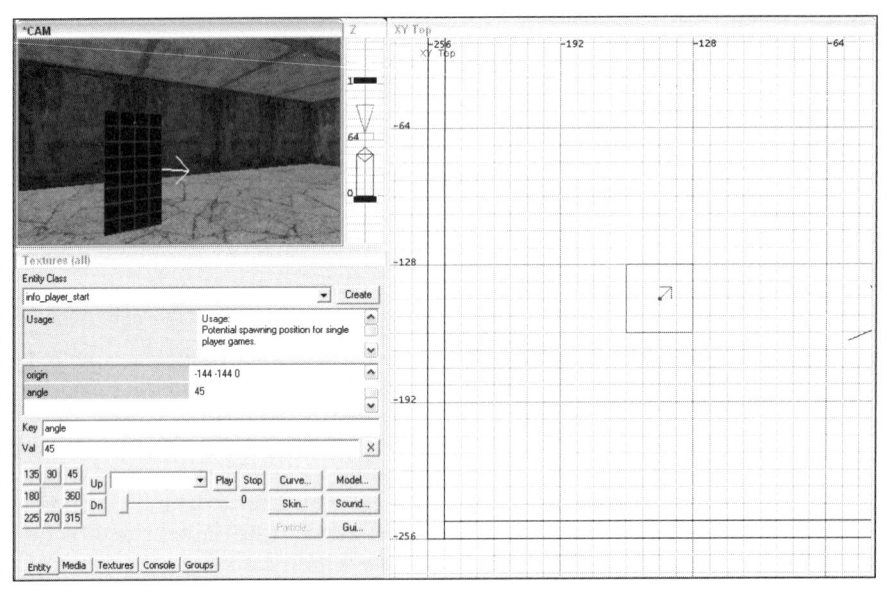

Figure 7-6: The angle of the entity is also represented by an arrow in the 2D and CAM windows.

Chapter 8

Putting the Pieces Together

In This Chapter

▶ Understanding the compile process of the map
▶ Turning your map into a playable level
▶ Playing your custom level in the game

*I*f you've gone through the preceding chapters, you have constructed all the pieces of your map. You created a basic room for your player to start the game. You dressed things up by placing textures on all the walls. You added some colorful light to the area and gave a player a place to spawn. These are all the elements you need to create your map, but before you can play it, you need to turn it into a level.

There is an important difference between maps and levels. The map is where you put all the pieces together to make up the world for your game. However, a level is what the player can load and play in the game. A *level* is a map file that has been read, converted, and saved into a file or group of files that is read by the game and interpreted as the playable field.

Leveling the Playing Field

Before you go through compiling your map into a playable level for the game, let me explain how the process works. A buddy of mine who now works for a popular game developer once said to me, "It's easier to drive a car when you know how it works." From that point on, I started to look at a game engine the same way a mechanic looks at the engine under the hood of a car. I studied the mechanics of the map files, their conversion process, and the result as seen in the game. Now, when something goes wrong with a map I'm building, I know where to start looking for the problem, or at the very least, I know where not to look. This is because I know what's going on under the hood.

Part II: Making Your Own Maps

The compile process takes a map file and turns it into a playable level for a game. This process, as it turns out, happens to be very similar for most of the games on the market today. There are three stages in the compile process, and each one does its part to turn the map file into a playable part of the game. This process is easier to understand for the previous *Quake* games, but it's extremely similar in the new *Quake 4* game. In the following sections, I explain here the three steps as they occur for the *Quake* games 1 through 3, and then I show you how this relates to the new *Quake 4*.

Building the BSP

The first process the map goes through is the Binary Space Partitioning (BSP) process. Here, the map file is read and picked apart and creates only the basic compiled level, excluding lights. Each brush face is located in the map file and then checked in relation to how it interacts with the other brush faces in the map. If it touches another brush face, that brush face is split where they touch.

Take a look at Figure 8-1. Here you look down on a simple map from the top. It's a rectangular room with two walls placed within. This is what the map looks like from above before it goes through the BSP process.

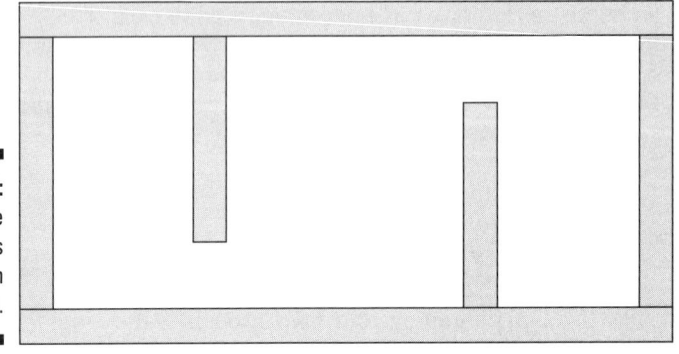

Figure 8-1: A simple map as seen from the top.

Now look at Figure 8-2. This illustration shows what happens after the BSP process. Each dashed line represents where the floor and ceiling of the room were split as a result of where other brush faces — such as the walls within the map — were touching them. The split starts where the walls touch the floor and continue until either the end of the brush or to the next split.

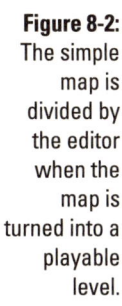

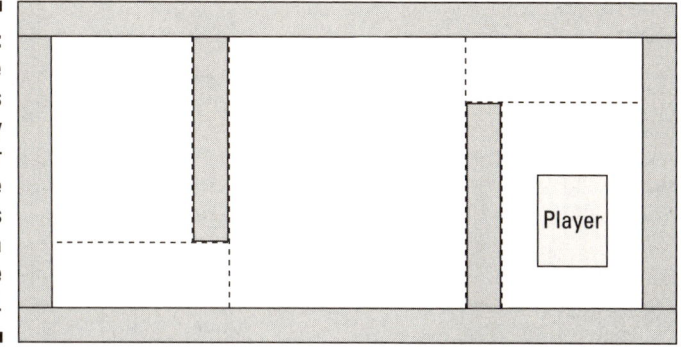

Figure 8-2: The simple map is divided by the editor when the map is turned into a playable level.

Seeing what can be seen

The second process of compiling the map is the Visibility (VIS) process. This is the process during which player visibility is determined to assist the game in maximizing the rendering of what you see. The map is checked to define what the player can and cannot see from any point within the level by dividing it up into smaller blocks. These smaller blocks have gone by many names for different games, but id Software, Inc., has referred to them as both *areas* and *portals* in *Quake 4*. I call them areas in this chapter and define them as a combination of the splits created in the BSP process (see the preceding section), predefined algorithms, and *portal brushes,* which I explore further in Chapter 10.

When the game reads this area data during the game, it determines which areas can be seen by the player, and it three-dimensionally re-creates only those areas for the player during the game. This re-creation is called *rendering*. The computer renders the visuals within the level by determining which areas can "see" each other.

In Figure 8-3, you can see a possible scenario of how a map might be divided into areas. As the player looks across the splits in Area 1, you notice that he can see Areas 2 and 3. Therefore, everything contained within these areas is re-created and drawn within the game because it's assumed that if Area 1 can see these areas, the player can, too. The other areas in the level, because they cannot be seen by Area 1, are not drawn in the game at this time. Area 2 cannot see Area 5, and therefore when the player steps into Area 2, all areas except Area 5 would be drawn. Only when the player steps into Area 3 will the game re-create the entire level because only that area can see all other areas. The places at which these areas split from one another are called *portals* because they act as a viewing portal from one area into another.

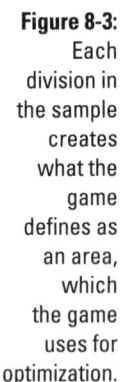

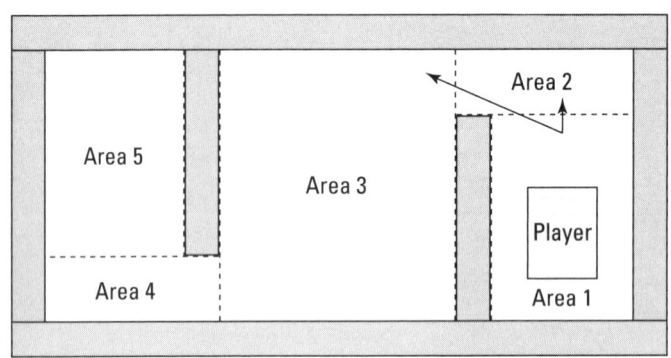

Figure 8-3: Each division in the sample creates what the game defines as an area, which the game uses for optimization.

Why is this important to know? Well, now that you know how this works, you can prevent problems that can occur with the game. For example, if the game were to try to render the entire level all at once, there would be too much information for the computer to handle. This would result in the game running ridiculously slowly or crashing. You'll often notice this slowdown in the form of lag on some custom maps. You can prevent this by either properly positioning your brushes during the design of your map or by adding special brushes called Hint or Portal brushes that can help you force the splitting where you want them. This is discussed in detail in Chapter 10.

Lighting the scene

The third and final process of compiling the map is the lighting process. It's been called QRAD, for Quake Radiance, and called Flare by some other games, but the meaning is the same. This stage is when the light is properly added to the map, and it's often the most time consuming of the three stages. Light comes from the sky, light entities, and some other entities, as well. Other map objects such as walls might cast shadows, but that doesn't mean the light just stops at those objects. In many cases, light bounces off of them like the sunlight bouncing off of a pond or a piece of paper. The calculations go on for a default value of five bounces, which is the effect of light bouncing off of five surfaces. Considering the number of surfaces that could be in a map and the amount of open space the light is traveling through, it's understandable why this process can take so long.

Comparing the old with the new

Although the BSP process is the first of the three stages in compiling your map, the compile process as a whole is called the BSP process. For the previous

Chapter 8: Putting the Pieces Together

Quake games, the result of compiling a map would be a single `.bsp` file that would load into your game as a playable level. So, if you were compiling a map file by the name of, say, `chapter8.map`, the result would be a new file, `chapter8.bsp`. For *Quake 4,* the process is the same; however, the resulting files are different.

When you compile your map for *Quake 4,* you end up with seven new files. All seven of these new files, which do not include the `.map` file, make up the contents of your level and are each required for the game to play properly. See the section, "Building the puzzle," later in this chapter, for a complete description of these files.

Processing the Pieces

Now it's time for you to compile your custom map. If don't have your last saved map file open in the editor, open it now. If you are following along with the book, the map file you need is `chapter7.map`. When the editor is running, you can open your map file from the menu by choosing File⇨Open and selecting your `chapter7.map` file.

Because you are now in Chapter 8 of this book, resave this map as `chapter8.map`.

The compile process is really quite simple. If you look in the Bsp menu, you can find a list of options that you can choose from. Most of those options are there for testing purposes, but you don't need to test compile this small map; it wouldn't save you any time. Choose Bsp⇨bsp. When you do, a small window pops up, and a lot of text begins filling the console tab in the Multi-Purpose window of the editor.

> **TIP:** Actually, when it comes to compiling my maps, I don't use any Bsp option other than the first, complete Bsp selection found in the list. The other selections have been less reliable in the past, and I don't trust that they will compile a map properly. Stick with the main Bsp option and you will avoid any mistakes or unexplained occurrences.

Listening to the console

When the compile process is complete, the first thing you want to do is look at what is printed in the console window. This information tells you whether any errors require your attention. The most important error would be a leak. I mention in Chapter 5 that you need to be careful not to leave any gaps between the walls; doing so creates leaks and stops the compile process from finishing. Scroll through the text in the console looking for an error that looks like this:

Part II: Making Your Own Maps

```
***********************
WARNING: ******* leaked *******
***********************
```

In the event that you see this text in the console, you need to locate the leak and seal it up. Sometimes, when working on very large maps, it's nearly impossible to find a leak without any guidance. Well, not to worry, because the editor will actually show you the way. In Figure 8-4, a solid red line comes out of the player spawn point in the 2D window, makes a few turns, and stops outside of the map. You can also see this red line from within the CAM window. Using these two windows, you can follow the path of the red line to the source of your leak and patch it by adjusting your brushes to close the gap. When you're done patching, run the bsp command again until the map has compiled successfully without any errors.

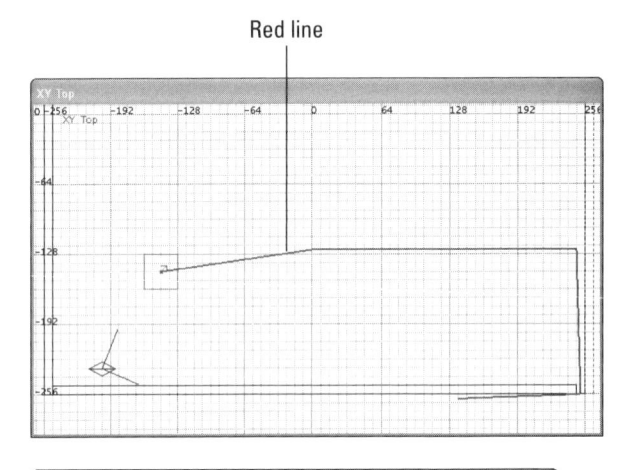

Figure 8-4: When the map leaks, you can follow a red line to the hole that created the leak.

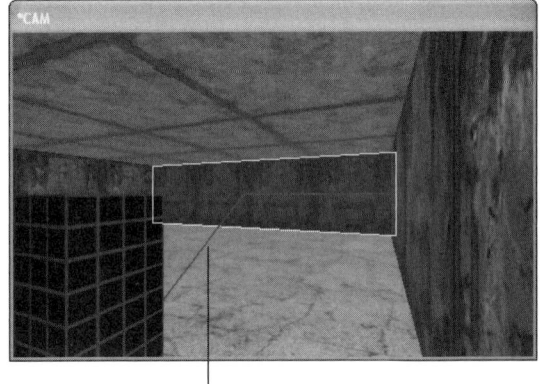

Leaks are the most common errors that you will run into and most likely won't even occur if you have followed the advices given with this book. Any other reportable errors won't come up until you are at a professional level of modding. At that time, you will be able to solve whatever error that comes up either by experience or further research online.

Building the puzzle

With the compiling of your map complete, you should have seven files for your game. In this section, I help you make sure they are where they need to be.

Open Windows File Explorer. Go to the folder `C:\Program Files\id Software\Quake 4\q4base\maps\game` (or something similar if your game was installed in a different location). This is the maps folder you created to save your map file (see Chapter 5) and where `chapter8.map` is now saved. The following seven files should be located within this folder:

- `chapter8.aas128`: All the .aas files are Area Awareness files used to help the AI within the game navigate within your level. Each file breaks down the playable areas in your level into sizes to be referenced by the different sized enemies in the game. Smaller enemies can fit into the smaller and larger sized areas, but larger enemies can fit only into larger sized areas.
- `chapter8.aas250`
- `chapter8.aas32`
- `chapter8.aas48`
- `chapter8.aas96`
- `chapter8.cm`: The collision geometry, or .cm, file, defines the physics of your level such as the walls you bump into and cannot cross.
- `chapter8.proc`: The .proc file is very similar to the .map file except that all the information here is preprocessed to assist in rendering the level during game play. For instance, it helps to produce the shadows made by lighting beforehand to reduce the strain on your computer's processor during the game.

If you don't see these files, the compile process did not complete correctly. Look at the console tab in the Multi-Purpose window of the editor and read through the text for anything related to errors. This provides you with the reason why your map didn't compile correctly. Fix the error and recompile the map.

With everything compiled properly, you're ready to load the level into the game and start playing.

Playing the Result

Finally, it's time to take your playable level and load it into the game. Here's where you get a chance to see the results of your hard work.

Start the game so that you can load your level. You actually have two options for launching the game:

- You can close your editor and launch the game from your desktop shortcut.
- You can launch the game from the editor by using a shortcut.

If you're loading a map that isn't overly complicated (like `chapter8.map`), you should probably launch the game from the editor. If your map is large and more complex, you're better off running the game without the editor open in the background. The open editor uses system memory that might be better spent in the game.

To launch the game from the editor, just press F2. This opens the game as it was before you launched the editor. If you prefer to use the other method, close the map editor and load the game from your desktop shortcut.

With the game open, you're ready to load the level. Press the ~ key to open the game console. To load the map you named `chapter8`, type **devmap game/chapter8** and press Enter. The level loads, and your player spawns in the level.

Take a few moments to look around at your handiwork.

Exiting the game

If you launched the game from the editor and you want to close the game window, you can't simply exit the game. If you do, the game reports an error that it cannot close while Radiant is running. Instead, open the console by pressing the ~ key, and then click outside of the game window. This brings you back to the editor and closes the currently running game.

Part III
Expanding Your Creation

The 5th Wave   By Rich Tennant

> Jeez — that's impressive! Let's fire that dark matter gun again.

In this part . . .

You've got the knowledge to make your own map, but now it's time to become an artist. Take that one-room level and turn it into something you can take online and play with your friends. In this part, you step outdoors for the first time, and I show you the door that leads to a bigger, better level that plays with ease for any number of players.

Chapter 9

Expanding Your Map with Additions

In This Chapter
▶ Duplicating selections
▶ Joining rooms with halls
▶ Adding doors
▶ Texturing and lighting the hall
▶ Play-testing the new map

*I*n the previous chapters, you put together a very simple room — really just a box with a light where you can play. In this chapter, I help you expand on this creation and make it more interesting. I show you how to add another room to your map, placed diagonally from your current structure. Then you connect the two with an L-shaped hallway.

If you don't already have the map from the last chapter loaded in the editor, do so now by choosing File⇨Open and opening `chapter8.map`. I show you how to build your additions onto this already constructed map.

Making Copies

You could go through the same steps outlined in Chapter 5 to create your second room, but instead I show you another option. Because the goal is to create a room just like your first room, you can just duplicate the existing structure. Then you can move your copy diagonally in your 2D window to create the second room.

Part III: Expanding Your Creation

1. **Make sure you have selected all the brushes and objects that make up your first room.**

   Do this from the CAM window. Move around the CAM window by using the arrow keys. Select the walls, ceiling, and floor by pressing Shift+click from within the CAM window. Also select the light that is in this room. Don't select the player spawn point; you do not want to make a duplicate of this entity. Finally, with everything selected, change your 2D window view to XY Top (if it isn't already).

2. **With everything selected that you want to duplicate, press the spacebar.**

   Press this key only once because another duplicate is created every time you press it.

   The duplicate appears very close in proximity to the original, and it might not be obvious that a copy has been made. The copy is also selected within the editor, and your original brushes from which you made the copy are no longer selected. The result looks something like Figure 9-1.

   Notice how the duplication was made within the editor. In the 2D window, you can see it was created one grid line to the right and one grid line down from the original. This off-center reproduction occurs only in the 2D window; nothing happens in the Z window.

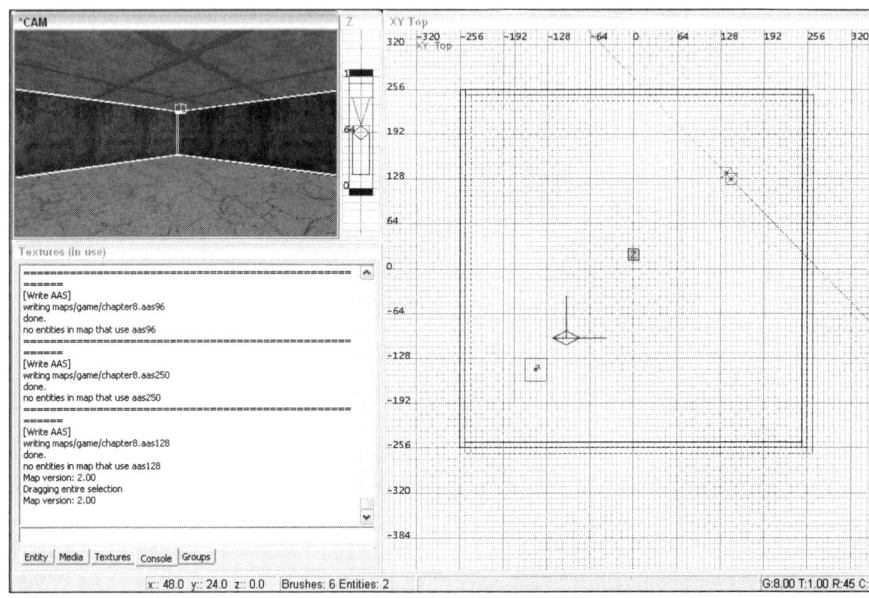

Figure 9-1: Duplicated map objects are placed one grid line down and to the right in your 2D window.

Chapter 9: Expanding Your Map with Additions

3. **Zoom out so you can see more of your map.**

   Right now the window is probably zoomed in on your original room. By zooming out, you will be better able to move the copy to another location. Use either the mouse wheel or press Home to zoom out.

4. **Move your copy by clicking anywhere within the current selection and dragging it up and to the left diagonally. Drag them until they have one 64-unit block between them, as shown in Figure 9-2.**

   Clicking outside of your selection results in stretching the selected brushes; the damage done by this is difficult to fix. If you do accidentally stretch them out of place, you might want to delete them by pressing Backspace. Then you can make a new copy.

5. **With your duplicate room in place, press Esc to deselect everything.**

Now you have two identical rooms. To make your new room different, change the color of the light. The light in the original room is red, so make the light in the new room blue:

1. **Move your camera in the CAM window into the new room.**

   Right now, it's still located in the original room, and you want to leave that light as it is. Move your view in the CAM window using the arrow, D and C keys as was done in Chapter 4.

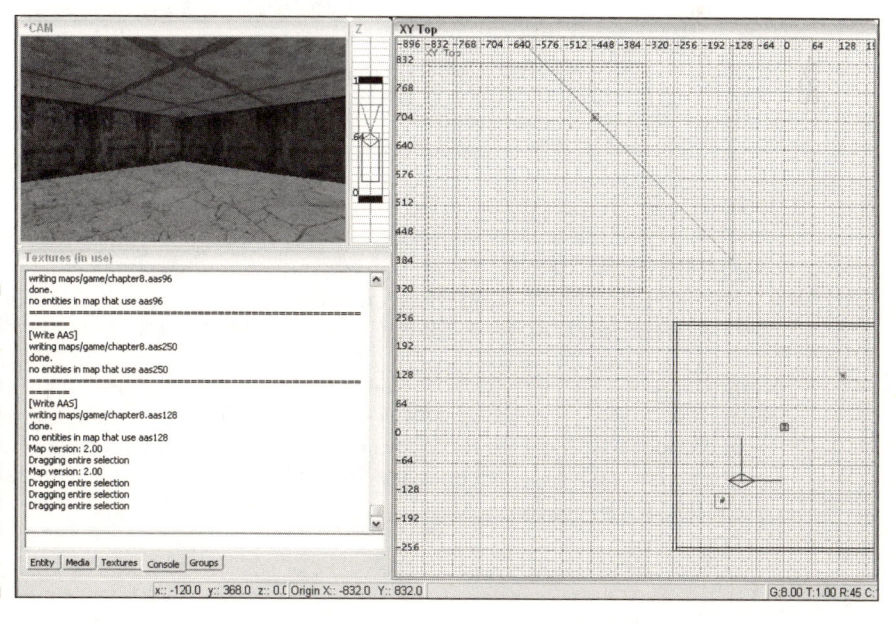

Figure 9-2: Drag your duplicate up and to the left of the original to create two separate rooms.

2. From within the new room and the CAM window, select the light entity.

3. Press K to open the Color Picker and select a deep blue color for your light.

4. When you have the color selected, press OK to apply the color change and to close the Color Picker.

5. Save your map as chapter9.map by choosing File➪Save As, entering the new name, and pressing Save.

Joining Rooms

You now have two rooms in your map, but no way to move between them as a player. To solve this, you need to add a hallway connecting the two rooms. In this section, I show you how to create an L-shaped hall below your new room and to the left of your original room. The halls will connect to the center of a wall on each of your rooms.

Drawing your halls

How wide should the hall be? How tall? Determining the width and height of structures such as hallways is something that comes with experience. There is no set number that you must use when constructing different areas of a map, but there are ideal numbers. The hall you are creating will be 128 units wide, and the height will be equal to that of your rooms. A width of 128 units makes your player feel comfortable and also allows multiple players to pass each other in the same hall without having to squeeze through.

After making sure that everything is deselected, you need to select the Caulk texture. This is the texture you should use to build all your structures before applying decoration. Begin by drawing out a solid brush for your first hallway. Use the same method that you use when creating a room by drawing a solid brush and hollowing it out. (Refer to Chapter 5 for more on how to do this.) Use the 2D window to draw the brush. Remember that you can change your view in this window by pressing Ctrl+Tab. You can use either the 2D window or the Z window to adjust the height. The new brush should be touching the wall of one room and reach to where the next hallway will meet with it. The result should look like Figure 9-3. In the figure, I've shaded in the brush you are adding.

Chapter 9: Expanding Your Map with Additions 97

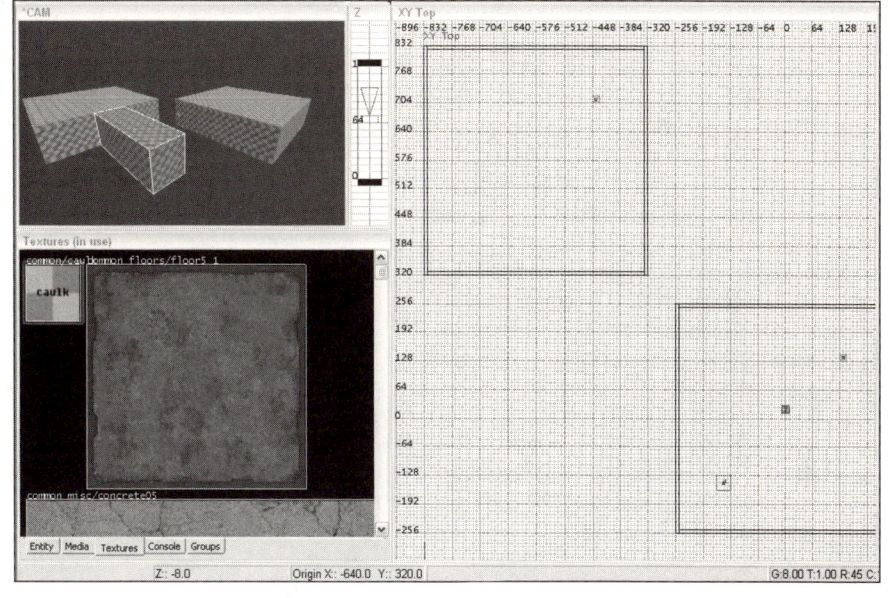

Figure 9-3: Create the first leg of the hallway perpendicular to one room.

Before you hollow this brush, you need to draw the next one, the second part of the L-shaped hallway. This way you can be certain that both parts are the correct size. You can do this either by pressing Esc and then drawing a new brush, or by pressing the spacebar to copy your current brush and then resizing it by dragging its outer edges to its new location. I chose the latter after setting my 2D window to XY Top to make sure the height is correct. Then click and drag the side of the brush you wish to resize. Remember, when you make copies, the copy doesn't move on the Z axis, but only in the two directions shown in the 2D window.

After the second brush is in place, the soon-to-be hallway has its L shape, as shown in Figure 9-4.

Making room to play

It's time to hollow these two brushes, one at a time. You should hollow each of these brushes separately so that you don't create errors with the map structure. With one brush selected, press the Hollow button from the icon menu to hollow the brush. When that's done, deselect everything (by pressing Esc), reselect the other hallway brush, and then hollow that one the same way.

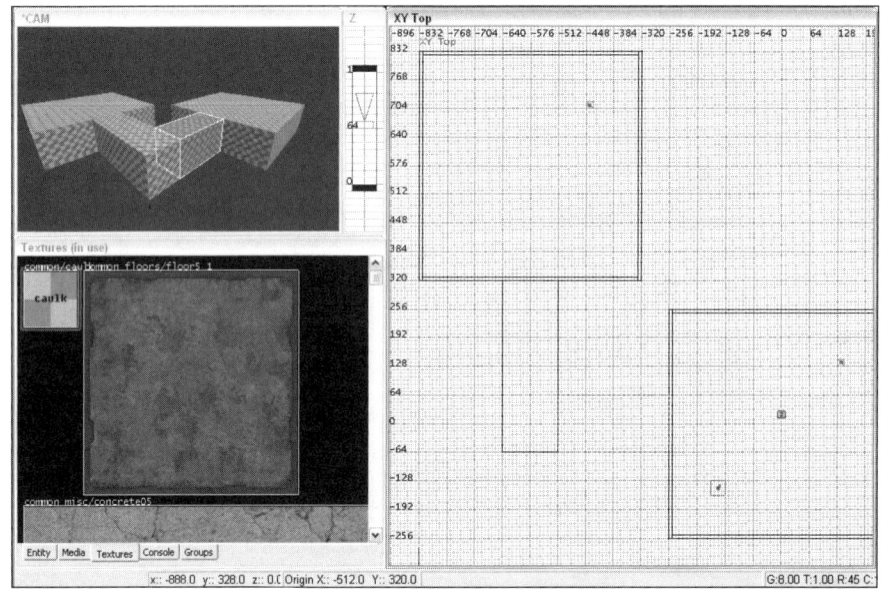

Figure 9-4: The second leg of the hallway should complete the L shape for the entire hall.

When you use the hollow function to create a room (refer to Chapter 5), you have to go back and fix the overlapping brushes. You're going to have to do the same here, as well as delete and move other brushes around. The idea is to create a single hallway from your two hollowed brushes.

To start, delete what you don't need. You don't need the four brushes located at the ends of each of your halls. In Figure 9-5, I've highlighted the four you need to delete. Use your CAM window to locate and select each of the brushes. To delete them, press Backspace.

Figure 9-5: Select and delete the end brushes of each of the hallowed halls.

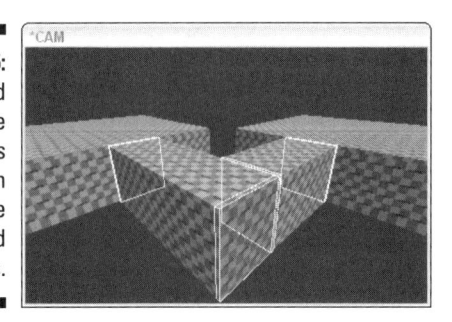

Next, resize the walls of your hallway so that they fit between your ceiling and floor. Right now they are overlapping, and you need to fix this. Using the CAM window, select each of the four remaining walls by pressing Shift+click on the brushes you wish to select. Then click outside of that brush from

Chapter 9: Expanding Your Map with Additions

within the 2D window and drag it to resize it properly. Deselect that brush by pressing Esc and repeat this process with the next brush you wish to adjust. You can select all four brushes together by pressing Shift+click in the CAM window on each of those brushes and resize them at the same time if you want. I do this to make sure I size them all equally. Then use the Z window to fit them properly. Figure 9-6 shows you the results after resizing the walls.

Figure 9-6: Resize the height of the walls in your hallway so that they do not overlap the ceiling and floor brushes.

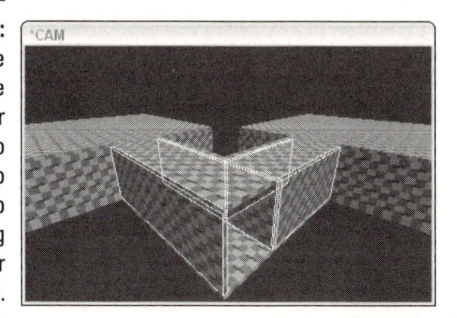

Next you need to resize one of the four walls in length (to cover the hole you created when deleting one of the end brushes) and shorten another wall to create an opening that joins the two halls into one. Leaving two walls in place of one clutters up your map and can make it run less smoothly during game play. You need to adjust these brushes separately. Figure 9-7 shows you what the walls should look like after you resize them.

Figure 9-7: Resize two of the walls in the hallway.

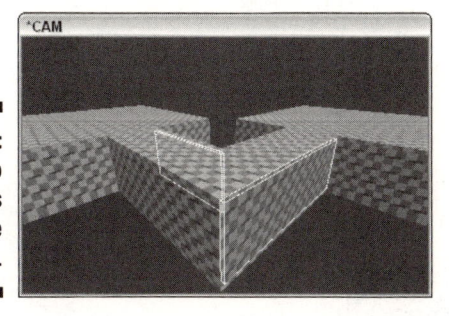

You now have two rooms and a hallway between them. However, you don't yet have access to your new hallway. What you need to do is cut in some doorways. I show you two methods to accomplish this task:

Building brush by brush

Starting with the room on the lower-right side of the map, you need to make a doorway for the player to get into the hall. Here's how:

1. **From within the CAM window, select the wall that is against the hall.**

    You may need to move your view in the CAM window to see the wall in the hall. To do so, use your arrow, D, and C keyboard shortcuts as shown in Chapter 4.

2. **Resize the wall until it rests to one side of the hall as in Figure 9-8.**

    Click outside of the wall's edge from within the 2D window and drag it to resize it. When you're done, the wall in the hall and the wall in the room should create a corner where they meet.

Figure 9-8: Stretch the wall of the first room to make an entrance to the connected hallway.

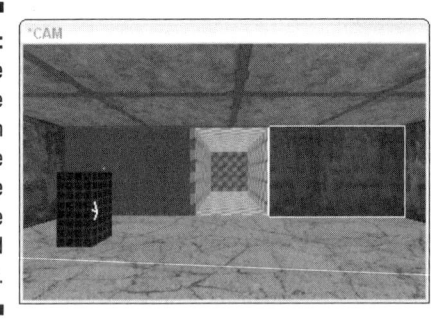

3. **For the other side of the wall, add a new brush.**

    There's an easy way to do this: press the spacebar to create a duplicate wall, and then move that duplicate to the other side of the hall entrance. The result should look something like Figure 9-9.

Figure 9-9: Duplicate the selected half of the wall and move it to the other side of the hall to complete the wall in the room.

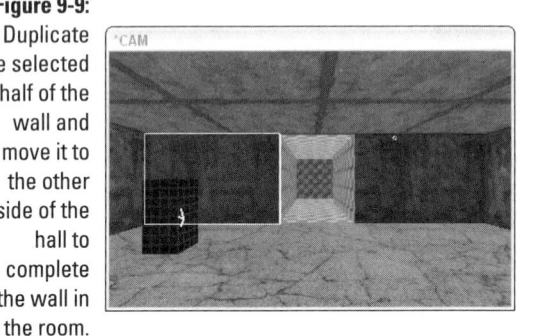

Chapter 9: Expanding Your Map with Additions

4. **Adjust the texture on the wall that you just duplicated.**

   Because the texture currently is an exact copy of the first wall, the texture does not align as it did previously. You can choose to ignore this because the two walls are no longer next to each other you can choose to adjust these textures.

   To resolve this inconsistency, select the brush face from the first wall. Then, copy this texture onto the new wall by pressing Shift+Ctrl+middle-click on the new brush face. The result is a perfect copy of the other texture and a wall that looks consistent and without seams.

   If you do not have a three-button mouse, then you will have to attempt to line up the texture by sight using the methods from Chapter 6 or just re-apply the texture to both walls. There is no other way to copy the texture and apply it to another wall.

That completes the hallway entrance for one room. For the next entrance, I show you another method.

Clipping brushes

Move the camera in the CAM window into the other room so that it faces the wall you want to cut. You are now going to cut an entrance into the wall of this room.

Instead of stretching and copying walls, you are going to use another tool, called the Clipper. Here's how:

1. **Select the wall you want to edit, then select the Clipper tool by pressing X.**

   Alternatively, you can select the tool from the menu by choosing Selection⇨Clipper⇨Toggle Clipper or you can select it by pressing the icon button at the top of the editor, as shown here.

2. **Before using the Clipper tool, move your 2D window view so that you're looking at the long side of the wall brush.**

   Change the view in the 2D window by pressing Ctrl+Tab until you are looking at the XZ Front view. Then center your view on the hallway, as shown in Figure 9-10. What you're going to do is split this brush in half and then just adjust each half to fit properly. It's necessary for you to see the area you want to split.

   To use the Clipper, you're going to plot two points in the 2D window. The line created by these two points is where your brush will be split in two.

3. **Place one point above the wall where you want it to split by clicking within the 2D window.**

   When you click, you see a blue dot with the number 1 next to it.

102 Part III: Expanding Your Creation

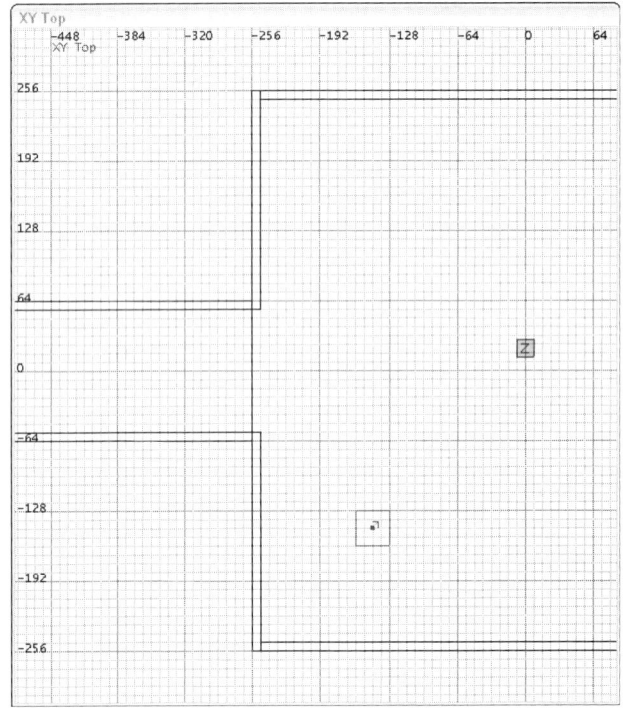

Figure 9-10: Select the wall in the second room in preparation for making a hallway entrance.

4. **Place another clipping point under the wall on the same Y axis line, creating a straight line down the wall.**

   When you do, you will see a blue dot with the number two, and half of the wall will disappear. This is normal. Figure 9-11 shows how it appears in the editor.

   The Clipper tool actually has more than one function. In this case, you've used this tool to split your wall into two. Another option would be to cut or clip off part of your wall, hence the name *Clipper* for this tool.

   If you accidentally click the screen more than twice or if you want to change your selection, press Esc to deselect the Clipper tool and start again.

5. **To split your brush, press Shift+Enter.**

   The result should look like Figure 9-12. The Shift+Enter command splits the brush; pressing only Enter clips it. If you didn't hold down the Shift key, you can either press Ctrl+Z to undo the operation or continue creating the hall entrance as you did in the preceding section.

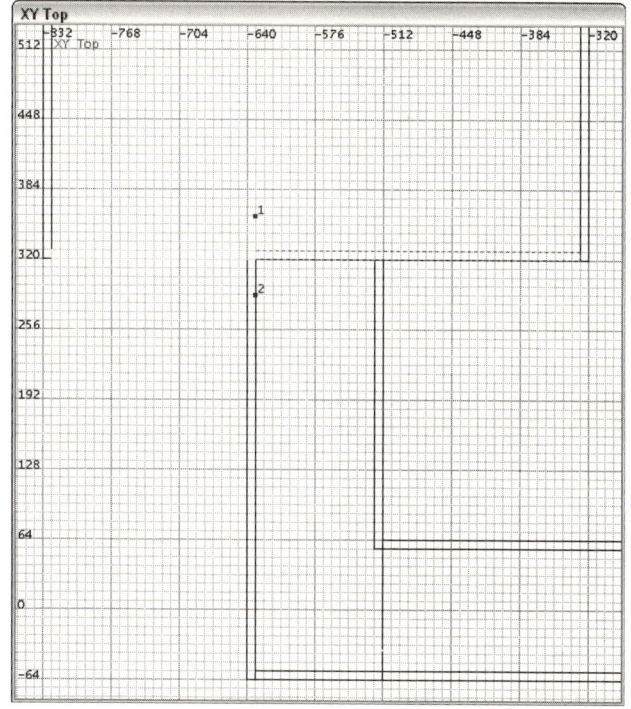

Figure 9-11: With the Clipping tool selected, plot two points across the wall you want to split to create the slicing point.

When that's done, make sure you deactivate the Clipper tool by either pressing the Clipper tool menu icon or pressing X to deactivate it. Then remember to save the map.

Now that you have two halves of your wall, adjust them to fit around the hall entrance. After splitting the brush, both halves of the wall will be selected. You can deselect a brush the same way you select one: by press Shift+click within the CAM window on the brush you want to deselect. Then you can resize the other wall into position. (Because you split your brush, you don't need to move it.)

Using the Clipper tool means you don't have to readjust the textures like you did by using the duplication method as on the first entrance. Because you're splitting the wall, the textures remain in place as they should be.

When you're done, the result should look very similar to Figure 9-13.

Figure 9-12: Press Shift+Enter to split the wall in two.

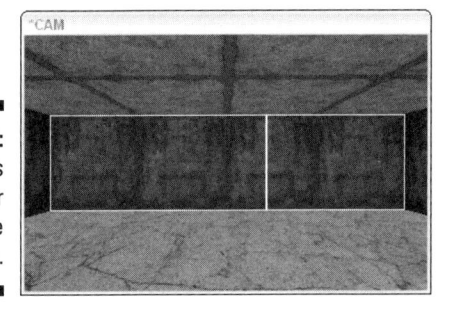

Figure 9-13: Resize the split walls to create an entrance into the hall and to complete the wall.

Retexturing the Hallway Walls

Now you need to texture the walls in your hall. They should still be textured with the Caulk base texture, which won't do you any good in the game. You can apply the same textures that you have in the rooms to the walls in the hall.

To copy a texture from a selected brush face onto another brush face, you pressed Shift+Ctrl+middle-click. Do this to all the player-visible surfaces in the hall, selecting the textures from the ceiling, walls, and floor from one of the rooms and applying that to the ceiling, walls, and floor of the hall. Remember to add texture to any thin strips of wall edge, as shown in Figure 9-14, which occur whenever a wall edge is left uncovered.

The thin corner strips are here at the moment because you haven't done any mitering yet. For now, go ahead and texture them. In Chapter 10, you find out how to miter corners, eliminating the thin corner strips.

When you're done with applying all the textures, save the map again.

Figure 9-14: Remember to apply a texture to the small strips of wall at the corners of the hall.

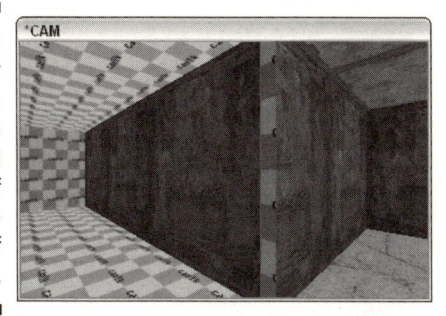

Lighting the Path

Your structures are complete. However, when the player enters the hallway, he is not going to see much because there isn't much light there. You need to add some more lights to your map.

Start by adding more light to one of your rooms and its adjoined hallway leg. Here's how:

1. **Select one of the lights within one of the rooms.**
2. **Press the spacebar to duplicate the light.**
3. **Move the copied light to another corner in the room.**

   Repeat this process until you have a light in three of the four corners of the room. Leave one of the corners a little dark so you can hide yourself or something else in it later.

4. **Make one more copy of this light and place it in the middle of the hallway closest to the room.**

   Using the same light color used in the room, this lights the hallway enough for the player.

Now, repeat this process within the other room. The result is a level that has half blue light and half red light. Your 2D map will look something like Figure 9-15.

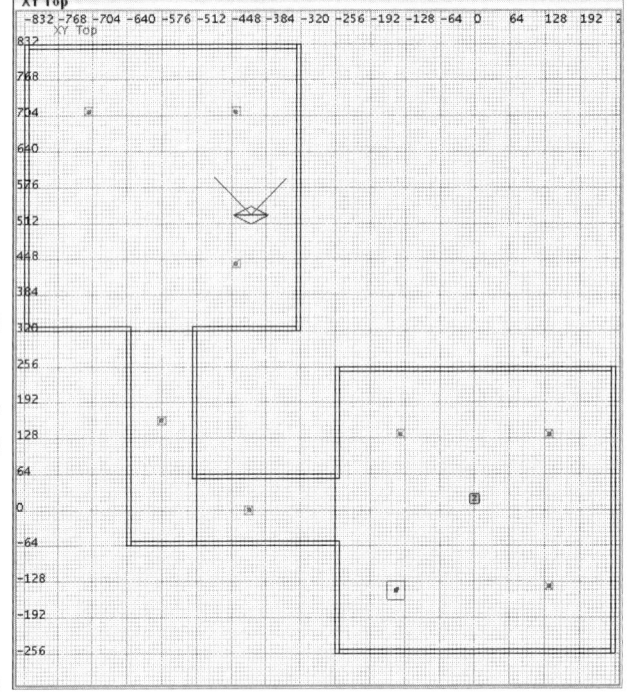

Figure 9-15: Make copies of the light entities in each of the rooms and distribute them like lights in a house.

Running in the Halls

With your changes complete save your map so you don't lose any of the hard work just completed. Then you are ready to test it in the game. Go ahead and compile the map again to create your playable level. To do so, choose Bsp⇨bsp from the editor menu. When the compiling is complete, review the text in the console and make sure there weren't any errors reported. If a leak was reported, be sure to go back and fix your holes (as I discuss in further detail in Chapter 8).

Now it's time to load the level in the game and take a look at the beautiful work you've completed thus far. Press F2 to launch the game from the editor. Open the game console by pressing the ~ key. Because you saved your last map under the name of chapter9.map, type **devmap game/chapter9** into the console and press Enter.

With your new map loaded, you should see something that looks like Figure 9-16.

Chapter 9: Expanding Your Map with Additions   107

Have fun playing your new map, but if the game runs too choppy for you, close everything down, including the editor. Restart the game from your desktop shortcut and load the level from here without launching the editor.

Figure 9-16: The final result of your map will look awesome in the game once compiled and loaded.

While looking around, take notice of your textures and brushes. Make sure your textures line up. You don't want to see any seams in the middle of the wall that make the wall look broken. Make sure all your corners are straight and nothing is sticking out or too far in. Most importantly, feel proud that you just completed this map and you can now have fun playing in it.

Chapter 10
Building with Optimization in Mind

In This Chapter
▶ Looking at your level as a developer
▶ Mitering corners
▶ Dividing the map into areas
▶ Viewing the map from a new perspective

The map you have built in the preceding chapters is pretty small: just two rooms and an L-shaped hallway. If it were four or more times larger, optimization would be an important concern. When you play-test your new level within a game window that you launch from the editor, you might notice that the game plays in a choppy manner. Player movement isn't smooth at all, and it feels as though the game is lagging. With a poorly optimized map, this will actually happen during a real game even when the editor isn't loaded in the background. Your map might end up being unplayable.

When you experience these slow downs or jittery issues, it's your computer's way of asking for help. There is too much information, and your computer can't handle it all. Think of all the game elements it must load, display, and keep track of, including all the textures, the brush faces, and even the other players running around the map. These elements make your computer work very hard.

This is where optimization techniques come into play. The methods listed in this chapter should be employed when you're building a map. Now that you know how to build a map, it's a good time to explore these methods. Afterwards, I walk you through some testing methods that help you to find and fix trouble spots in your map.

No matter how small your map is, optimizing it is always a good idea.

Most problems that occur in maps are caused by allowing the player to see too much of the map all at once. In Chapter 8, I explain the compiling process and how the level is rendered within the game based on areas and portals. In the following sections, I cover methods of displaying the onscreen images in the manner that the game has rendered them. Understanding what the game is doing to create your visuals is the best way to understand how to control it with your mapping technique.

Commanding as a developer

Before you can understand the hows of optimizing, it's important to know the whys. When your game is lagging and your computer is struggling to keep up, you can enter a few commands into the console of the game to find out what your computer is working so hard at. These commands show you what is being rendered within the game regardless of where the player is located in your level.

When you can see what is being done in the game, you'll know what needs improvement. If your player can't physically see around the corner of your hallway but the computer is drawing the room that's over there anyway, something needs to be done to stop this. There is no reason the game should think the player can see around corners he or she actually cannot see around. Fixing this is one example of optimization. Here's how you do it:

1. **Load the last saved version of your map and resave it under a new name.**

   The last version was `chapter9.map`, so open this file and then save it as `chapter10.map`.

2. **Compile this map by using the BSP process.**

   I explain the BSP process in Chapter 8.

3. **When the map has been compiled successfully, close the editor.**

4. **With the editor closed, load the game.**

5. **Load your new map by typing** `devmap game/chapter10` **in the console and pressing Enter.**

6. **Open the console again while the map is running and type the following three commands, pressing Enter after each:**

   - `r_showTris 2`: *Tris* is short for triangles, a term used to describe the polygons that are rendered in the game world. As with most games, when *Quake 4* compiles your map, it converts each of your brushes into polygons and then triples them, resulting in only three-sided polygons. The `showTris` command draws an outline around every triangle seen by the player within your level.

- `r_useScissor 0`: A *scissor* prevents any triangles outside your immediate visibility from being drawn by your video card. You can think of this as a command to cut out what you don't need to see. This doesn't mean that the game isn't using up your processor and memory resources trying to draw them, but that your video card is smart enough to ignore what can't be seen. You set a scissor to a value of 0 to turn it off and cut out what isn't in plain view, providing you with a true visual of what the computer is attempting to show.

- `r_showPortals 1`: Showing the portals allows you to see where the game is splitting up the map to create the *areas* discussed in Chapter 8. Although you're going to place specially textured brushes to define where these portals are located, it's good to see where they are within the map.

Don't worry about these settings affecting your game play later. These settings reset themselves to their default values when you shut everything down and restart. However, as long as you don't close the editor and restart, the settings remain in the game. If you do close the editor, you will have to re-enter the commands from Step 6 to see these special developer tools within the game.

Outlining your world

With the settings from the preceding section in place, close the console by pressing ~ again. What you now see are white lines all over your map like in Figure 10-1. These white lines represent the outlines of the polygons that the game renders for the player. The more polygons your player can see, the harder your computer has to work to render the level on your screen. Your goal is to reduce the total number of polygons rendered in the level so your computer doesn't have to work so hard.

Figure 10-1 also shows you that you can see the entire level regardless of where you stand as the player. It doesn't make sense that the room the player can't physically see is being rendered. This is one of the things you can fix through optimization.

Close the game window and load the map in the editor. It's time to optimize.

112 Part III: Expanding Your Creation

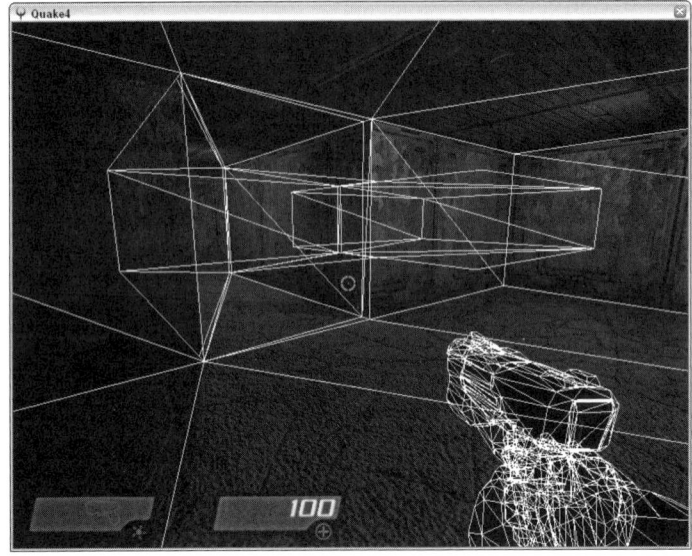

Figure 10-1:
The white outlines of the polygons in your map.

Mitering for Mappers

Mitering is not just a word for carpenters and woodworkers. It's also an important part of mapping. When carpenters miter the joint between two pieces of wood, they bevel the edges of both pieces at a 45-degree angle to form a 90-degree corner. In Figure 10-2, there are two corners as seen from the mapping editor. The corner on the left has not been mitered; a player looking at it from within the game will see three brush faces because the thin edge of one wall is exposed. The corner on the right has been mitered; a player looking at it will see only two brush faces.

This nonmitered edge creates additional geometry within the game. It increases the number of brush faces, resulting in additional polygons, and also more splits to surrounding surfaces. Figure 10-3 is an example of this additional geometry. Sure, this won't have an impact on a small, two-room level, but if this were a larger map with more corners, problems during game play would arise.

When you create maps, you should perform all the mitering work to the walls and other brushes as you go along. It's easy to miss some of the corners if you wait until the map is big and complicated.

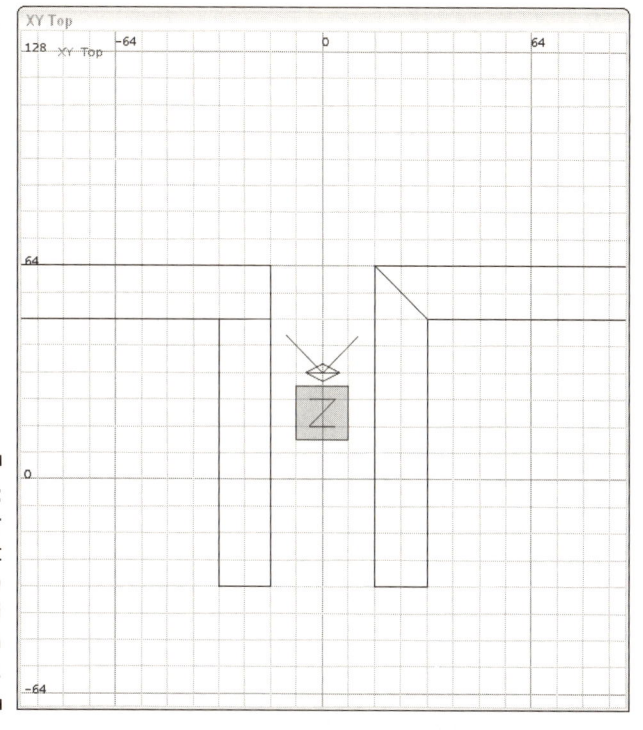

Chapter 10: Building with Optimization in Mind   **113**

Figure 10-2: The corner on the right has been optimized through mitering.

Figure 10-3: Failing to miter corners creates additional geometry.

Fixing those corners

Now, in the editor, go back to your map (`chapter10.map`) to fix those corners. In this section, I show you how to miter your corners by moving the edges of your brushes. Because the outside of the map is never seen, you aren't concerned about the outside corners. Instead, there are five inner corners that need your attention. In Figure 10-4, I have circled each of the five corners for your reference.

To understand what a brush edge is, think of what makes up a rectangular brush. There are six sides in a rectangle, and an edge is where each side meets another. So, when you're looking at the flat side of a brush like that of Figure 10-5, the corner at which one side meets another is its edges. These edges can be manipulated to allow you to turn that rectangle into a trapezoid or any other shape.

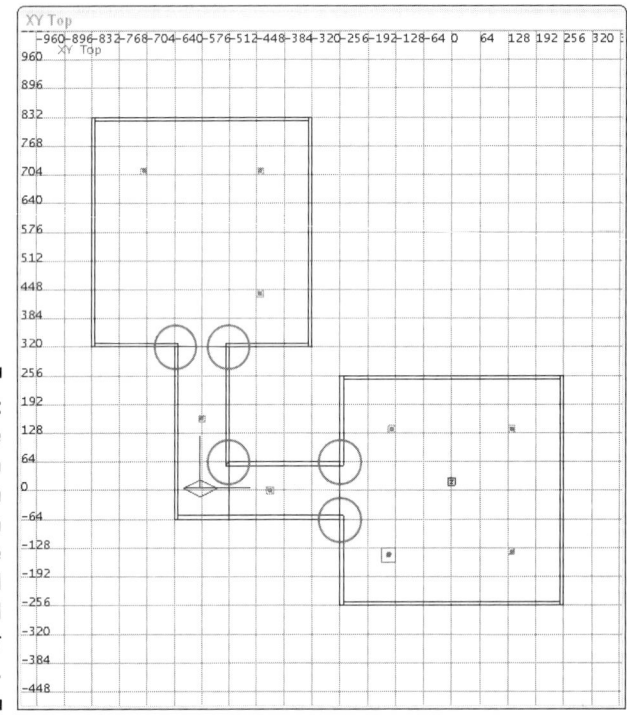

Figure 10-4: These five corners can be seen from within the game and should be mitered for optimization.

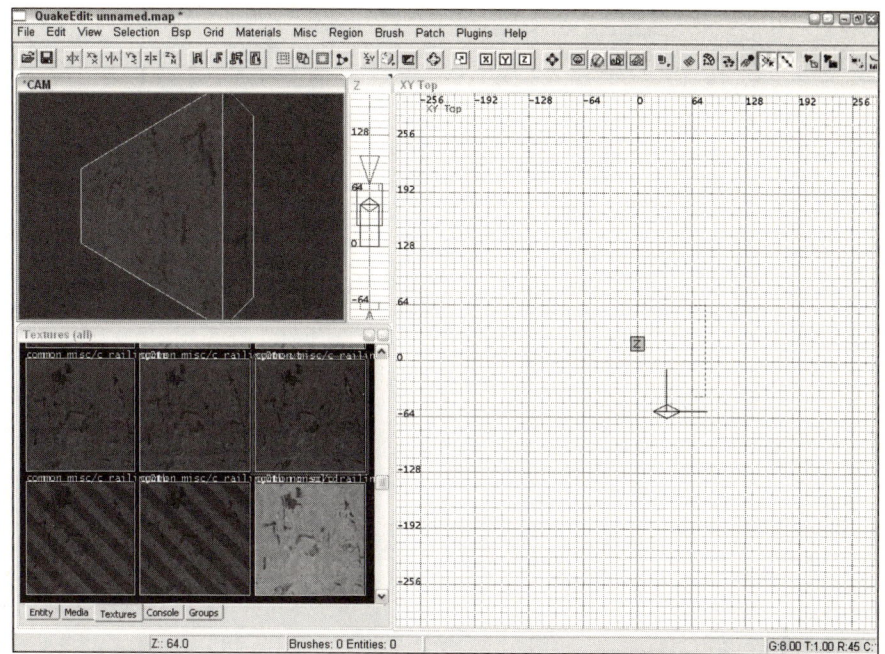

Chapter 10: Building with Optimization in Mind *115*

Figure 10-5:
An edge is where two brush faces meet.

To create your mitered corner, follow these steps:

1. **Zoom in close to the corner that you want to miter so you can get a good view.**

   I started with the corner in the middle of the hall.

2. **From the CAM window, select one of the two walls.**

   What you want to do is move one of the corners of the selected brush to create your 45-degree bevel.

3. **Press E to activate edges.**

   A blue dot, representing each edge of the brush, appears in both CAM window and the 2D window.

4. **Click and drag the brush corner that you want to move until you have a 45-degree angle like the one I have in Figure 10-6.**

5. **With one wall completed, deselect everything and do the same for the wall next to it.**

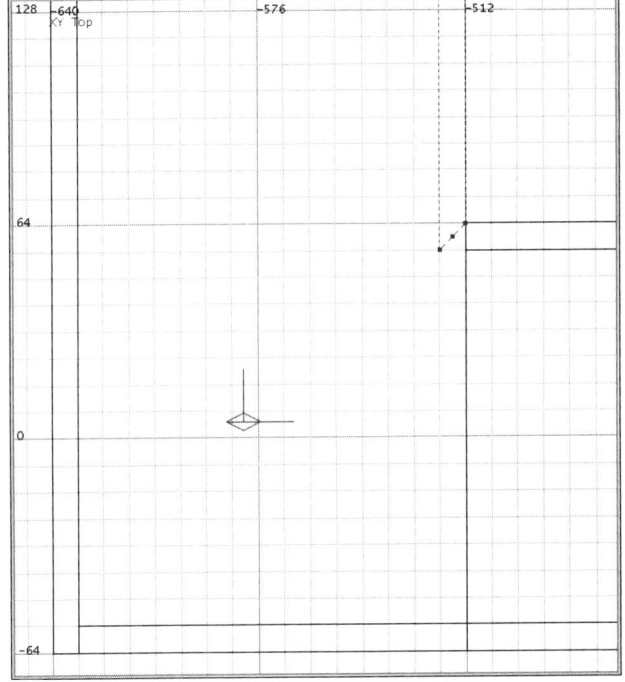

Figure 10-6: Drag the brush corner until you have a 45-degree angle.

When you're done, you will have two mitered brushes that meet up perfectly with each other and will look like Figure 10-7. You have effectively reduced the number of polygons and splits within your level.

Continue with this method until all the corners within the playable area of your map are mitered.

Mitering the floor and ceiling?

You've now mitered the visible corners in your map. But, what about the corners that you can't see such as those on the floor, the ceiling, and outside of your map?

Because the player never sees these areas of the map, there is no need to optimize them. You only need to worry about what the player will see; everything else is simply ignored by the game.

Chapter 10: Building with Optimization in Mind

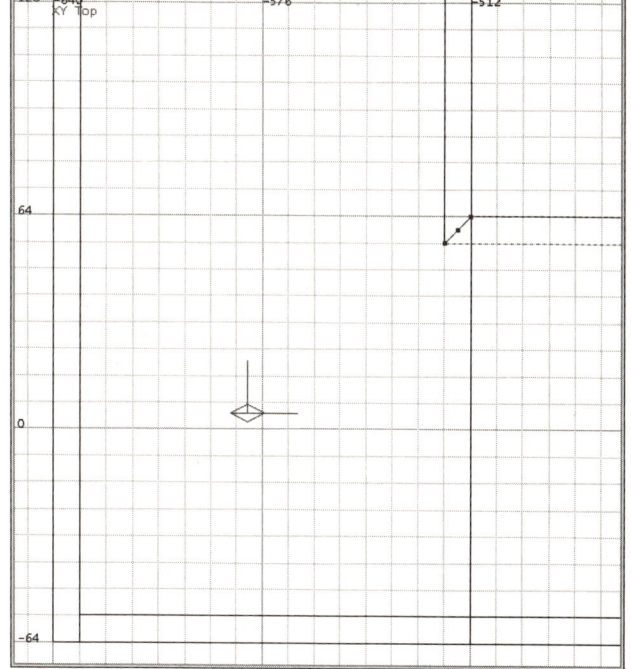

Figure 10-7: After you miter your corner, you will have fewer visible brush faces.

Automatic optimization

Although the compile process is capable of optimizing some of these brushes for you, you shouldn't rely on it.

The compile process is capable of automatically reducing the brush face count and will attempt to do so regardless of any settings. When the compiler looks at two adjacent brush faces, it also looks at the textures applied to them. If the texture values are exactly the same, as with a continuous texture, it merges the two brush faces.

If you copy and paste the same texture throughout the level (as you did for the map in this book), the compiler automatically merges your brushes for you. However, if later you decide to make any changes, such as texturing the hallway differently, you will have to go back and test the results in the game as you may need to make some adjustments for better optimization in the editor.

Luckily, when you test your map later with the developer commands (see the earlier section, "Commanding as a developer"), you will see whether there is an issue that needs your attention. All the splits in the brushes will be outlined.

For now, save the map over the existing file, `chapter10.map`.

Creating Portals

Mitering corners reduces polygons, and that helps with optimization. However, you still have to solve the issue of too much area being rendered within the game. You are in one room and you can't see the other room, so why should your computer work at rendering the other room's contents? To fix this, you must add some portals.

As I discuss in Chapter 8, portals define areas within the map. This affects what the game thinks the player can and cannot see. You are going to create a couple portals in your map. In the example map, these portals will split the map into three areas so that the outer two areas, the two large rooms, cannot see each other. Because they can't see each other, the game won't render the contents of the room you aren't located in.

Figure 10-8 shows how you can divide the room in such a way that the two outer rooms cannot see each other. Creating a portal on this diagonal will effectively split your map into three separate areas where Area 1 cannot see Area 3, and vice versa. You do this by splitting the one large area into three smaller areas with an angled portal brush. I show you how to put this idea into action, and then you can see the benefit of such practice.

To create a portal, you need to add a brush that completely fills in your opening from wall to wall and floor to ceiling. Then you must texture this brush on one side with the portal texture and on the other sides with the no-draw texture. The no-draw texture will be ignored by the game, and the portal texture will divide your map into separate areas.

TIP

Make sure that your portal brush creates a tight seal between the walls it is touching. If you don't slice all the way through, you don't have two separate pieces. You need to create two separate areas with your portal.

The most difficult part of this operation is creating the three-sided brush with a diagonal face. To do this, use the Clipper to slice a square brush in half on that diagonal. The process is similar to the one used for splitting the wall for the hall, as I discuss earlier in this chapter, except that you do it on a diagonal.

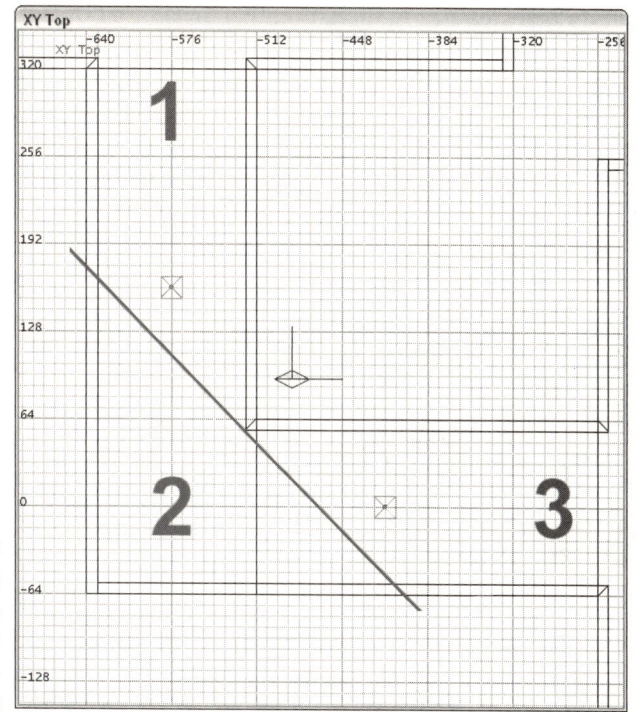

Chapter 10: Building with Optimization in Mind *119*

Figure 10-8:
Splitting one large area into three.

Before you draw your brush, you should locate and select the Nodraw texture. Because all but one side of the brush is going to be textured with the Nodraw texture, it makes sense to start with this one. To find it, load up the Common texture set. This is where you will find the Nodraw texture. It looks like a darker version of the Caulk texture except that it has the word Nodraw written on it, as shown in Figure 10-9.

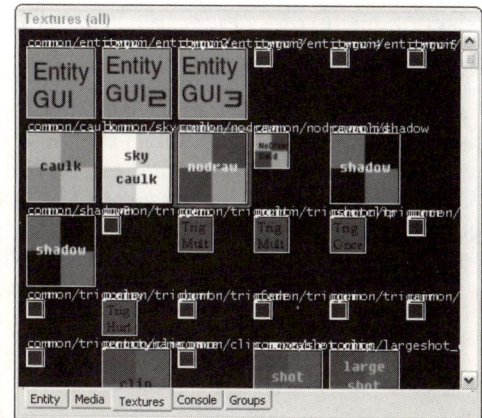

Figure 10-9:
The Nodraw texture is completely ignored by the game.

1. **With the Nodraw texture loaded, create a brush that fits into the hallway corner.**

   This brush needs to be large enough to cover the area you plan to split, so in the example map you need to drag out the brush to 192, –384 on the X,Y axis, as in Figure 10-10. Also, make sure that it meets up with your ceiling and floor. This brush needs to meet all four walls of the hallway and create a seal.

   Figure 10-10: Create an oversized brush to clip on the diagonal for your portal brush.

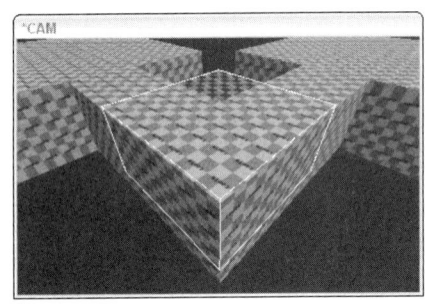

2. **Split the brush on a diagonal by using the Clipper tool.**

   Press X to turn on the Clipper, and then place two cutting points over your portal brush. The easiest way to do this is to place your first point on the tip of the inner corner in the hallway and the other point one grid line down and to the right on the diagonal, as shown in Figure 10-11.

   TIP: In Figure 10-10, you might be surprised that the second point wasn't even placed outside of the brush you're clipping. The clipping line will be created along the points regardless of where you place them. Placing the two points so close together makes it easier to create a 45-degree cut.

   TIP: If you find that you're cutting off the wrong half of the brush, then before pressing Enter to activate the cut, press Ctrl+Enter to flip your selection.

   With your clipping selection made, press Enter to cut the brush.

3. **Texture the portal side of the brush with the Visportal texture.**

   Deselect everything, and then load the Editor texture set. Select the angled brush face that you just clipped. Then select the Visportal texture. The Visportal texture is colored with two shades of green in the same pattern as the Caulk texture, and it has the words *vis portal* written on it, as shown in Figure 10-12. The result will be a brush that has the Visportal texture on one side and the Nodraw texture on all other sides.

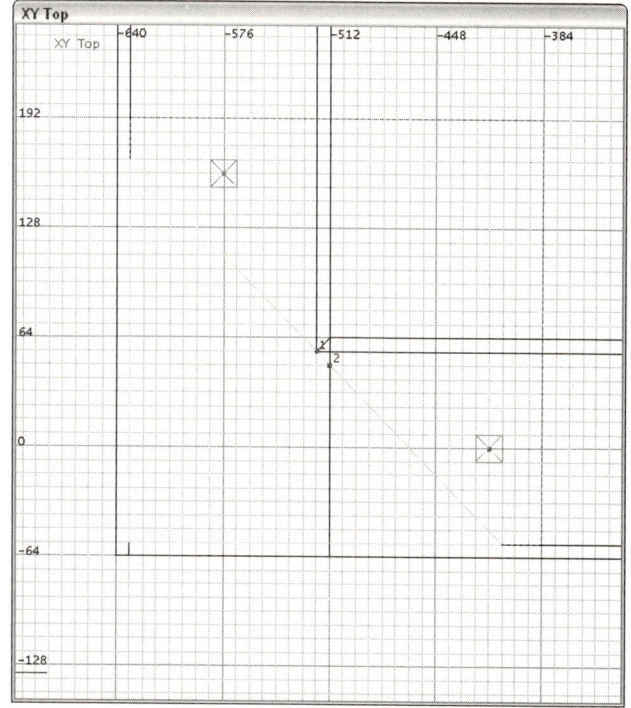

Chapter 10: Building with Optimization in Mind 121

Figure 10-11: Your cutting points can be placed anywhere in your map to create the clipping plane.

That's it for your portal. Because this portal creates a complete seal around all walls and splits the map into three separate areas, you have effectively created two portals: one portal in each hallway.

Make sure to save the map at this time.

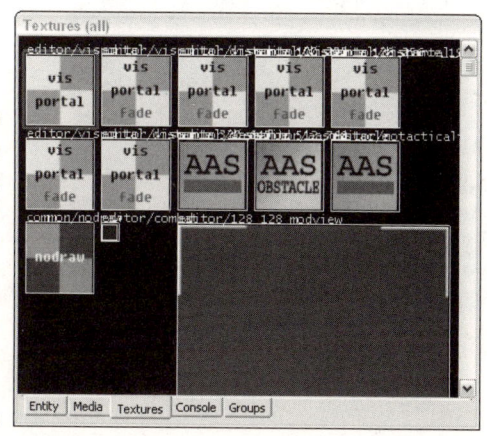

Figure 10-12: A portal is created when you texture a brush face with the Visportal texture.

Can You See Me?

After you have better optimized your map, take a look at the benefits. Compile the map and run the BSP command by selecting Bsp⇨bsp. After the map is compiled, launch the game by pressing F2. Run the level from the console by typing **devmap game/chapter10** and pressing Enter. (`chapter10` is the name of your most recently saved and compiled map.)

When the level is loaded and playing, you should notice the outlines around all the polygons. The result should be something similar to what you see in Figure 10-13. If you don't see these lines, refer to the section, "Commanding as a developer," earlier in this chapter, for the console commands that must be entered to fix this problem.

Now that you've optimized the map, you can see that all your prior problems have been solved. The first noticeable difference is that you can't see the other room until you walk into the next area of the map. This means your portals were created correctly. The next thing you see is that you don't have any unnecessary polygons. Previously, such spots as the entrances to the hallway had additional splits in the wall, which are now gone. Finally, you see that the floor and ceiling in the hallway are indeed properly splitting. This tells you that the texture values throughout these brushes are exactly the same and that the compiler was able to merge them as expected.

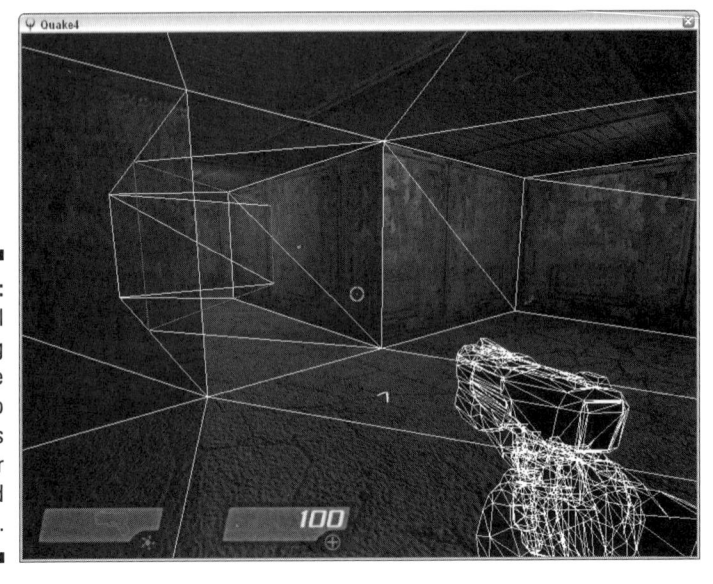

Figure 10-13: The portal brush doing its job. The game no longer has to render the second room.

TIP

If you do see additional splits in the hallway of your level, you need to go back and fix them. Rather than moving brushes around, just copy and paste the textures again to make sure that the texture values are the same throughout. This trick solves the problem.

If you can see the outlines in the second room from the first, you need to check your portal brush. The portal brush must be completely sealed around the walls, ceiling, and floor. Without a complete seal, the portal will leak, and the game will render the other room. Look for the leak within the editor and either move the portal brush around to fix it or delete and reinsert your portal brush.

Chapter 11
Heading to the Great Outdoors

In This Chapter
- Adding an outdoor area
- Texturing the outdoors
- Creating doors between areas
- Using special lighting techniques
- Setting up the doors to move for the player

The preceding chapters help you get a well-optimized indoor map well underway with a couple rooms and a hallway connecting them. However, this map is still pretty small. Now you should continue the expansion, but instead of adding rooms and halls, in this chapter I show you how to head outdoors and work on a different type of environment.

In this chapter, you build your outdoor environment like an addition to the structures in your current map. From there, you apply special textures to make the addition look like the outside world. Then you add some special lighting effects to complete the feel of your map. You need a way to get inside and out, so you install a doorway and an actual door for your player to interact with.

Building Another Addition

Building an outdoor addition is structurally the same as working indoors. You need to create a sealed area that extends from your current work. You need walls, a floor, and a ceiling. However, instead of using concrete or brick, textures on this outside area, you must apply textures that display a sky, dirt, and other outdoor ambiance.

Although the process of building an outdoor environment is simple, you need to plan out a few important details before you begin. Structurally, an outdoor area is a box with a texture on the floor resembling grass or dirt and the rest of the brushes textured with a sky texture. However, when the player approaches the edge of the box, nothing will visually signal the edge of the map. The player will just find himself on the brink of nothing, and he will be unable to move forward. Figure 11-1 is an example of what a map looks like when the player can see over its edge. Because this can be confusing, you need something here that tells the player, "You can't go beyond this point."

Figure 11-1:
The edge of the map where sky meets structure.

To define the edge of the map, you need to add a tall wall. The wall will extend all the way around and be tall enough that the player can't see over the edge. The rest of the box will be textured with the sky texture.

When building your sky, its height needs some consideration. You need the sky to be tall enough that whatever is thrown at it — such as a grenade, body, or whatever — doesn't hit and bounce off the ceiling of your sky box. That would look bad in the game. However, building the area larger than it needs to be is a waste of compile time. In Chapter 8, I explain the compile process and how the third process of compiling is that of light. The more area the light covers, the more processing time the map requires. Perhaps in your small map the extra processing time won't make too much of a difference, but if you start considering it now, you'll be in good shape for larger maps.

Chapter 11: Heading to the Great Outdoors

It's time to start on the outside area in the map. Here's what you need to do:

1. **Load `chapter10.map` in the editor.**
2. **Make sure to have the Caulk texture selected as your base texture.**
3. **Draw a large brush that positions the current structure in the lower-left corner, as shown in Figure 11-2.**

   I've drawn one that starts from –264, –840 on the X,Y axis and stops at 1216, 640 on the X,Y axis. This creates an area large enough to feel like it's outdoors and to encompass the current structure. Also, there is enough room to account for the 8-unit walls that will be created when the brush is hollowed. As for the height, start at the same floor height as the buildings, which is –8, and drag it up to the 320 mark on the Z axis. This should be tall enough. You now have the basic shape that you can work from, but not the final box.

4. **Use the Hollow function to make the solid brush into a room for your player.**

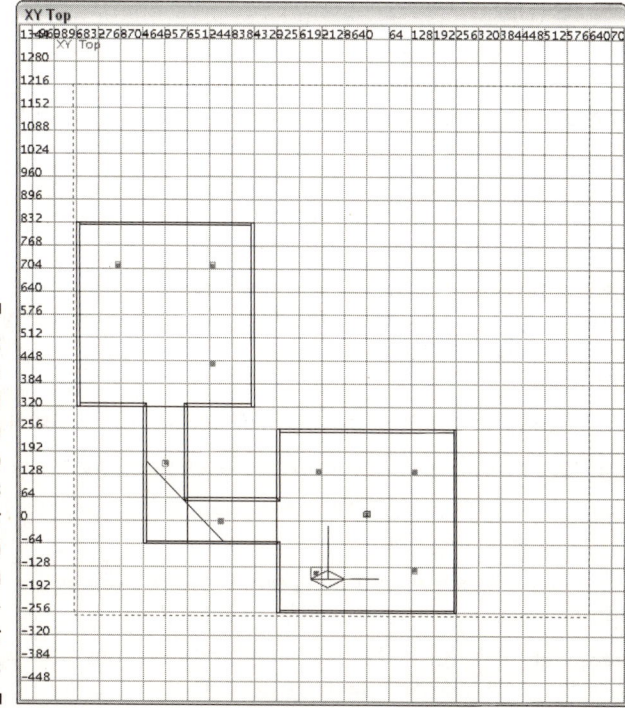

Figure 11-2: The outside area should be large enough to encompass your indoor area, which will rest in the lower-left corner of the map.

5. **Adjust the wall brushes of this new box to fit inside the top and bottom brushes to remove the overlapping.**

    You made this sort of adjustment in Chapter 5 when you built your rooms.

 6. **After it's hollowed, go back and fix the overlapping of the wall brushes, too. You don't want any of the brushes to overlap:**

    a. Select the four walls and shrink them to fit under the top brush and over the bottom brush.

    b. Select two opposing walls, the north and south walls, and shrink them to fit between the other two walls.

    The result is a hollow box that does not have any overlapping brushes.

Multiplying the ground

As it sits now, the ground brush is overlapping the floors of your building. You need to fix that, or the game will display errors as it tries to figure out which texture it should display. The best solution is to split the floor into pieces that fit the area you need to cover:

 1. **Select the ground brush and adjust it to fit in the upper-right corner of the map between the buildings.**

    Remember that the brush must extend under the walls to keep the seal you have in your map, but must butt up against the brushes in your building so as not to overlap.

 2. **From the XY Top view in the 2D window, use the Duplicate function to fill the missing pieces of ground by duplicating the currently selected brush and moving or stretching it.**

    You're welcome to simply draw new brushes for each of the ground pieces, but I find the Duplicate function easier to use in this situation.

 3. **Copy the currently selected ground brush by pressing the spacebar.**

    When using the Copy function, the brush height will remain the same size and in the same location.

 4. **Adjust that copy, which is now selected, to fit into one of the gaps in the ground.**

    Continue doing this until you have completed the ground for your map. Use Figure 11-3 as a guide to placing those brushes.

Figure 11-3: Adjust the ground brush so that it does not overlap the floor brushes. Use duplicates to fill in the missing ground.

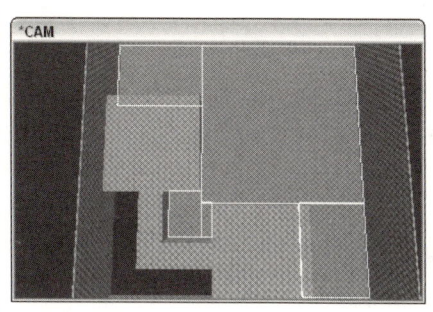

Filling in the useless corner

Looking at the top view of the map, you see a nice, large, outdoor area for your players. However, you also see a small area in the bottom-left that isn't exactly playable. This small area is blocked by the L-shaped hallway connecting your two rooms. Because you won't be using this area in your map, you should exclude it by adjusting the brushes in the map and filling in that corner as detailed in the next few steps.

To start, the two walls that meet in the lower-left corner need to be shortened. In the event that your players are able to see the tops of your buildings, you should leave those tops inside the map. So, what you want to do is remove only the empty space from that corner.

Stretch the brushes of the walls so that they meet up with the backs of the buildings. When you're done, it should look something like Figure 11-4. In this figure, you are looking at the hallway from within the outside area. Notice how the two walls on the left and right (representing the lower and left walls in the 2D window of the editor) extend to the length of the buildings and then stop. Later, when you're done manipulating the ground brush, you will fill in that corner.

TIP: As for the hole you now have in the corner, you could draw in a few more wall brushes to close the gap, but there is a way to save yourself some work. Instead, draw two larger blocks that completely fill in that corner. Each new block needs to touch the ceiling brush of the sky and extend only to about 8 units below the tops of your buildings. (There's no point in extending the brushes below the tops of your inner rooms because the player cannot access this area and you have created the necessary seal.) The result looks something like Figure 11-5.

Figure 11-4: Adjust the brushes in the lower-left corner of the outside area in preparation of closing off that corner.

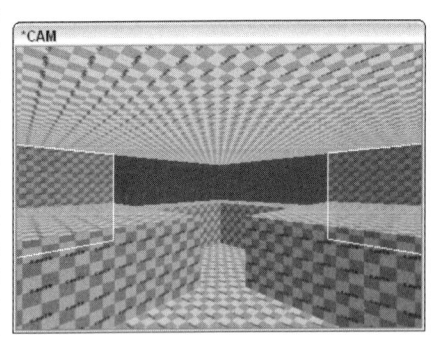

Using a solid brush in this case doesn't hurt your map in any way. Because it's solid, there are no light calculations within it. The compiler sees it only as a fat brush that seals the inside of your level and prevents leaking.

Figure 11-5: Fill in the hole in the lower-left corner with two large, solid brushes.

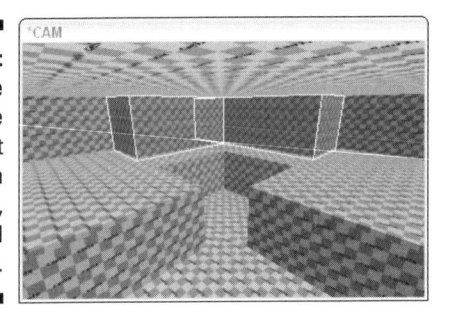

Defining your boundaries

You want to apply two different textures to the outside walls to complete your scene. You want to texture half of the outer brush faces with something that looks like a solid containment wall. This gives the player a sense that the level stops here. The rest of the outside area should be textured with a sky texture.

Resolve this by splitting the walls, the top half being sky and the bottom half being solid wall. Select all the brushes that make up the surrounding wall. Remember to select those blocks in the southwest corner of the map because your solid wall will reach above that point. You'll be making the wall 160 units tall, which is slightly higher than your buildings, and between the 128 and 192

Chapter 11: Heading to the Great Outdoors

Z-axis grid marks. A wall that's 160 units is a good height; it's tall enough that your player won't be able to see over the top when playing in the game.

With all those brushes selected, use the Clipper tool to split them all at once at the 160-unit line on the Z axis, as follows:

1. **Make sure you are viewing your map in the XZ Front view within the 2D window. Press X to turn on the Clipper tool.**
2. **Click within the 2D window to place the first clipping point on the 160 Z axis and anywhere on the X axis.**
3. **Within the same window, click and place the second clipping point on the 160 Z axis and anywhere on the X axis. This displays a horizontal line representing your clipping line.**
4. **Press Shift+Enter to split your selection leaving you with top and bottom halves of your walls.**

The result should look similar to Figure 11-6.

Figure 11-6: Split the walls of your outside area along the 160-unit Z axis to define where the outside walls meet up with the sky.

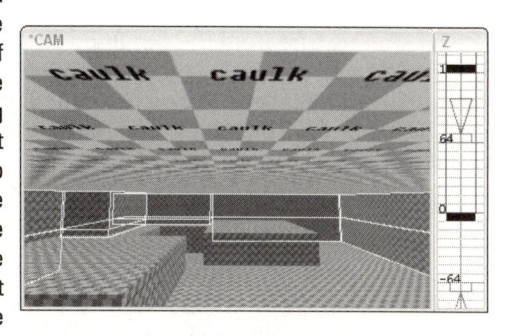

Making a Scene

It would be nice to test your map and see how it plays in the game. However, you still have some very important brush faces to texture. You haven't textured your outside walls and sky. Without it, the map will leak during the compile process, and you won't be able to load it in the game. Presently, everything in your outside area is covered with the Caulk texture. So, it's time to dress things up with some proper textures, starting with the ground.

Throwing dirt on the ground

Because this is an outdoor area, you should select an appropriate texture for your ground. Here's how:

1. **Deselect everything and then load the Rock texture set.**

    This set contains a good group of textures suitable for your ground.

2. **Select one of the brush faces on the top of your ground brush and select the texture `rock/sand01`, as shown in Figure 11-7.**

3. **With that same brush face still selected, go around and copy that texture to the other brush faces on the ground by pressing Ctrl+Shift+middle-click.**

Fitting the outer building

With your ground taken care of, it's time to move onto the exterior of the buildings. Because the interior of the buildings have a metal texture, you should select something similar for the outside.

You originally got your interior wall texture from the Common Walls texture set, so load that again. Deselect everything and select one of the brush faces on the exterior of the building. Then select the `common_walls/outdoor_wall1_1` texture, shown in Figure 11-8, to apply this texture to the selected brush face as well as the other walls of the exterior of the buildings.

While you apply your texture to the exterior walls, you will come across some corners that appear to be in need of mitering. You mitered a few of the interior corners in Chapter 10, but you didn't miter the exterior corners because they weren't accessible to the player at that point. You could go ahead and miter these corners, but you really don't need to. As long as you copy the texture and apply it to all the brush faces on that wall, the compiler will do the work for you. This was also described in Chapter 10. The compiler merges brush faces that have the same texture and values.

Figure 11-7: Apply texture to the ground of your outdoor area.

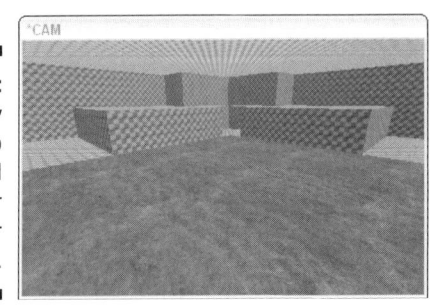

Chapter 11: Heading to the Great Outdoors *133*

Figure 11-8: Apply texture to the exterior of the buildings.

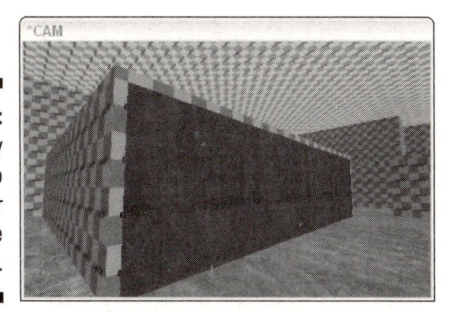

If the texture you applied doesn't look like it fits properly, feel free to adjust it. Sometimes the texture will be too short or too long and doesn't look like it fits the brush face it's applied to. You can move the texture around by pressing Shift and the arrow key for the direction you want to move it, or you can use the surface inspector. Press S to open the surface inspector and choose from the options listed there. (I cover the options in this window in Chapter 5.)

Finally, go through the rest of the level and continue to apply this wall texture. Remember to apply it to all the wall surfaces of the building, including the thin strip at the top of the wall.

Climbing the roof

Now that the walls are done, you need to texture the roof tops. Your player won't be accessing this spot in the map, so the texture you use isn't important. However, because there is a possibility of it being seen when the player jumps, select something that fits the scene. Select and apply the common_walls/outdoor_wall1_1a texture shown in Figure 11-9. Make sure to apply it to all of the rooftop surfaces.

Figure 11-9: Apply texture to the rooftops of the buildings.

Walling in the yard and adding sky

Now you can move on to the outer wall.

1. **Select one of the lower brush faces on the wall.**
2. **Apply the texture common_walls/c_ribwall, as shown in Figure 11-10.**

   When you apply this texture, it begins to repeat itself at the top because the brush is taller than the texture. Don't worry about this repetition. The texture doesn't have to fit, and you will be able to work the overlap into the scene later.

3. **Continue to apply this texture around the outside perimeter until you have what looks like a wall around the outside map area.**

With the solid walls covered, move onto the sky.

Figure 11-10: Apply texture to the walls surrounding the outdoor area.

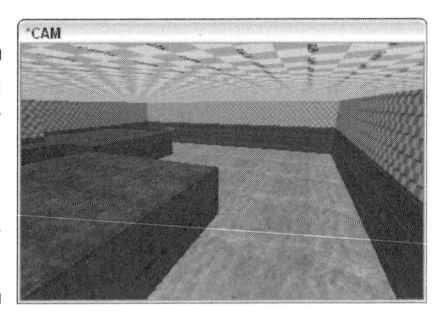

Adding a sky that looks like it stretches into infinity is really a lot easier than you might think. It's nothing more than applying the right texture to the brushes. The game does the rest of the work for you.

1. **Load the Skies texture set and then apply one of the sky brush faces in the map.**
2. **Look through the textures and select the skies/canyonclouds_sky texture, which looks like Figure 11-11.**

   This is a large texture with odd-looking lines streaking across, but it looks fine when loaded in the game. The game will take care of the rest.

3. **Work your way around the map and apply this texture to everything else that should look like sky.**

   When you're done, you should no longer be able to see any Caulk texture from inside the playable area.

Save what you have so far under a new name. Name this chapter11.map. It's good to know you have another version of your map to fall back on if a problem arises later due to an unexpected mistake or error.

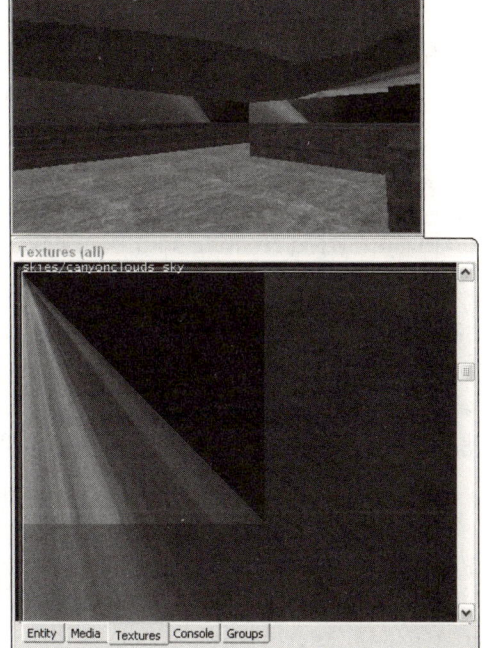

Figure 11-11: The sky texture looks strange, but it creates the illusion of a big sky.

Getting Outside

You have added a great set of brushes for your outdoor scene, but how do you get to it? Right now, your player will spawn inside one of the rooms but can't get beyond the two rooms and the hallway. What you need to do is cut in a set of doors for your player to use. In the next few sections, though, rather than just cut one set of doors, you make two.

You have a number of ways to cut in your first set of doors.

- You can create an entrance by stretching and duplicating brushes (just as you do to the ground of your outdoor area earlier, in the section "Multiplying the ground").
- You can stretch the existing walls and draw in new ones to replace the missing pieces.
- You can use the Clipper tool to split the existing brushes, thereby making a doorway.

136   Part III: Expanding Your Creation

The last option of splitting your wall brush is the simplest method because it won't affect the texturing you already have applied to the interior and exterior of the rooms. If you move brushes around, the textures won't line up as they did before, which creates a visual seam where the walls are joined as well as added geometry.

Clipping out some doors

Here's what you need to do to get started creating your doorways. Use the Clipper tool with Figure 11-12 as a guide:

1. **Begin by selecting the East wall on the lowermost room in the map.**

2. **Change your view in the 2D window to YZ Side so that you're looking at the front of the wall.**

3. **Press X to turn on the Clipper and start clipping the wall for a door.**

4. **Make the first cut to the height of the wall on the Z axis on the 64-unit grid line.**

   When clipping, remember that you want to split the brushes, and the shortcut for that is Shift+Enter.

5. **Make the next cut on the –64-unit grid line.**

   This makes for a pretty large door, but that's okay. You are going to turn these into double doors. The next cut you're going to make will define the height of the door. A good door height in this game is about 96 units.

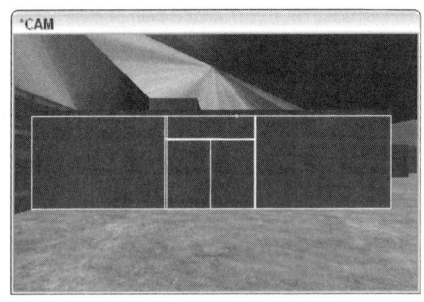

Figure 11-12: Use the Clipper to create the brushes for your doors and doorway.

6. **Deselect the outermost currently-selected brushes so that only the middle one is still selected. Then split the selected brush on the Y axis on the 96-unit grid line.**

7. **Deselect the top brush so that only the door brush is selected and split it down the center to create the two doors.**

Chapter 11: Heading to the Great Outdoors   **137**

With these two doors still selected, you need to do something to make them look more like doors rather than part of the wall, and you can do so by making the doors more narrow than the adjoining walls. This action also helps with the functionality of the doors. Because these will be sliding doors, it makes sense that they are thinner than the walls they are going to be sliding into.

8. **Switch to the top view again in the 2D window and center it on the selected brushes.**

9. **Change the grid size and make it two sizes smaller, equal to 2 units.**

   You can do this by pressing [twice or by choosing Grid➪Grid2.

10. **Now stretch both brushes simultaneously so that they are equally 2 units thinner on each side, as shown in Figure 11-13.**

Figure 11-13: Changing the thickness of the doors makes them stand out to the player and look more like sliding doors.

When stretching the two doors at the same time, make sure that you don't drag the mouse in any direction other than the direction you want it to move, or you could end up changing the shape of the doors by mistake.

11. **Return the grid size back to 8 units (Grid8) by pressing] twice.**

Touching up the textures

With your door brushes created, you might have noticed some of the brush faces around the doors show up as Caulk or some other texture you hadn't planned. You need to touch up the brush faces that you just made visible.

Right now, the doors you created are in your way. You could try to work around them to apply the textures where they're needed, but there's an easier way. Instead, temporarily hide the doors so that you can texture what you need, and then unhide them when you're done.

1. **Select your two doors.**
2. **Choose View➪Hide/Show➪Hide Selected or use the shortcut by pressing H.**

   This hides your selected brushes from view so they're out of your way.
3. **For the inner edges of your doorway, find and select a flat, metal texture.**
4. **Load the Terminal texture set.**
5. **From here, select one of your doorway brush faces and apply the `terminal/t1_metal2` texture, as shown in Figure 11-14.**
6. **Continue to apply this texture around the door until it is fully textured.**
7. **Now, unhide your door brushes by choosing View➪Hide/Show➪Show Hidden or pressing Shift+H.**

The current texture is a bad choice for the doors; it blends in too closely with the surrounding walls. So next, you can touch up the doors:

1. **Load the texture set `mptextures`.**
2. **Select a door brush face and apply the texture `mptextures/vertical_5_new`.**

Figure 11-14: Select a flat, metal texture to apply on the inner doorway of the building.

3. **Adjust the texture to fit the door.**

   Open the Surface Inspector by pressing S. Fit the texture 1x1 to the selected door brush face by pressing the Fit button.
4. **Apply the same texture to the front of the other door.**

   Make sure the texture fits and you should have something that looks like Figure 11-15.

Chapter 11: Heading to the Great Outdoors   139

> **TIP**
>
> When applying textures across multiple faces, you don't have to select a texture that fits the door properly. You can apply a larger texture across more than one brush face to complete the look of what you're trying to portray to the player.

 5. **With the outer brush face of the door still selected, apply the texture to the inner door faces.**

    Move your camera to the inside of the building and press Shift+Ctrl+ click to apply the select texture and its properties to the inside of the door. The result should look something like Figure 11-16.

That leaves you with two more brush faces to complete the doors: the inner edges. You must not forget that when these doors are opened by the player in the game, the inner edges of the doors are visible.

Figure 11-15: Apply the vertical_5_ new texture to the door brush faces.

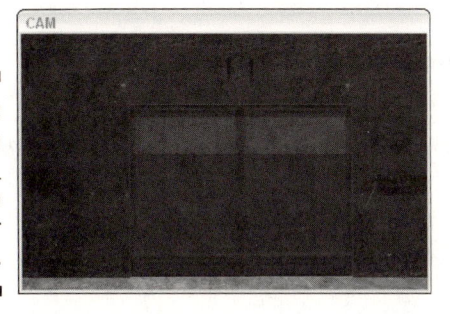

Figure 11-16: Copy the texture from the outside of the doors to the inside, along with the texture adjustments you made.

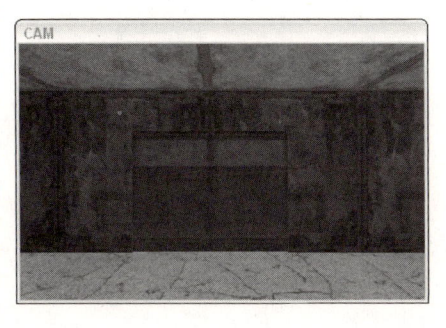

Rather than hiding brushes, the easier method to get to the inner door brushes is to move the door into a more accessible place in the map. Here you make your changes, and then you move the door back where it belongs.

Copying textures

If you select a brush face and adjust its texture properties, the update won't always be included when you go to copy it. Instead, the original texture values will be copied. This is a fault in the editor. To copy this updated information, deselect and reselect the texture you want to copy for the new values to register.

1. **Move one of the doors to where you can access the inner brush face where the two doors meet, as I have done in Figure 11-17.**
2. **Apply the same texture that was used on the inside of the doorway, `terminal/t1_metal2`.**
3. **Move the door back into place.**
4. **Do the same for the second door.**

    When you're done, remember to save your work so as not to lose it.

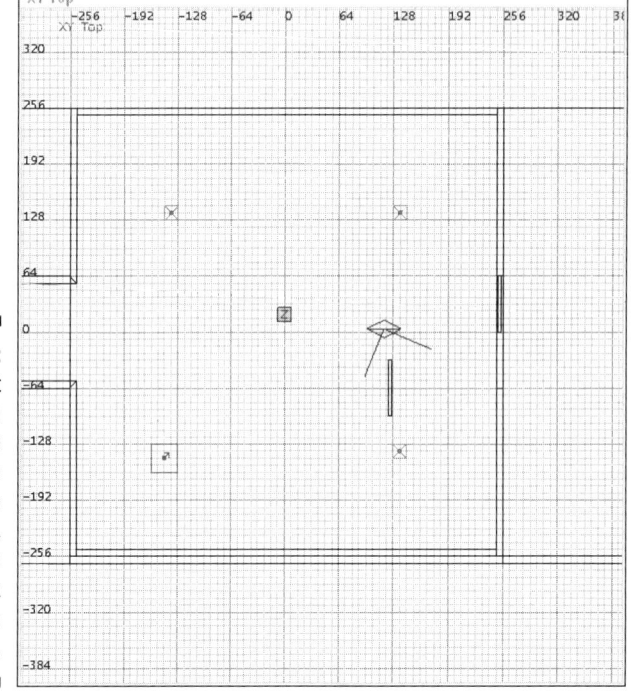

Figure 11-17: If you can't access a brush face easily, move it to where you can, and then move it back when you're done.

Chapter 11: Heading to the Great Outdoors **141**

Fixing a Bottleneck

Having multiple players in two areas divided by a single, small door can cause problems. If they all try to run through that door at the same time, they will get stuck. In addition, the volume and predictability of players moving through this area can make the game predictable. This is known as a *bottleneck*. To solve this issue, you either need to make the door larger or create a second door. The latter suggestion usually makes for a more interesting level in the game.

Right now, your map has two major areas divided by a bottleneck. You have an indoor area and an outdoor area split by a single doorway. To make the level flow better and to create more player options, you would be better off placing a second set of doors in the map in a different location.

To avoid having a bottleneck situation in your map, add a second set of doors to the north wall of the north room. This makes it easier for your players to run between the inner and outer areas of the level, and the additional choice allows for more strategy by the players.

Select the north wall of the second room. Follow steps 1 through 11 in the earlier section, "Clipping out some doors." After you create your second set of doors, texture the brush faces by following the instructions in the section "Touching up the textures." You should end up with what you see in Figure 11-18.

Figure 11-18: Create a second, identical set of doors on the northern wall of the north room.

TIP
When you go to apply the door textures to this second set, you don't have to reload the entire texture set from where they came. Because you have already used them in your map, select Material➪Show In Use to filter your list of textures to include only those currently in use in your map.

Sliding the Door Open

What's missing from your map at this point is a way to get through your doors. Right now, they are just solid brushes. The only difference between them and the walls around them are the textures. The doors should open for the players. Because these are going to be interactive elements of the game, you need to turn them into entities. In this case, door entities will suffice.

Making that door move

Here's what you need to do to get the doors to move:

1. **Move the camera over to one of the door sets in the map.**
2. **Select one of the two doors in the set.**
3. **Right-click the 2D Window work area to open the menu, and then choose func⇨func_door from the list.**

   This is a function door that slides open and closed when a player approaches it.

   You have to make sure that you have only one door selected when you apply this entity function. If you select more than one brush, the editor will turn all the selected brushes into a single door entity that acts as one door. This is great if your door is made up of several pieces. However, because you want the two doors to work independently, you need to apply the entity function to each one separately.

4. **With the door still selected, open the Entity tab.**

   You now want to tell the game which way the door should slide when it opens. In the case of Figure 11-19, you want the door to slide up. Up is represented as the 90 button in the Entity tab because it represents a direction of 90 degrees.

5. **Select the 90-degree button to apply the correct move direction to the door.**

   This key and value are then entered for you into the entity's information as `movedir 90`. Your entity information should look like Figure 11-19.

   While you're looking at the entity options for doors, look through the other options you could assign to the door. The options are shown in the top list of the Entity tab. You can use the scroll bar to look through the list. All the options are fairly well explained thanks to the programmer notes.

6. **Repeat these steps for the next door.**

   You want to follow the same steps as with the first door, except that you will use a different move direction. Select the door brush. Turn it into a `func_door` entity. Assign it a `movedir` of 270.

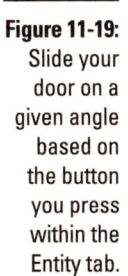

Figure 11-19: Slide your door on a given angle based on the button you press within the Entity tab.

In Chapter 12, I'll show you how to pair the doors together. Right now, they open individually, and pairing them will make them work in unison.

That completes one set doors. Now go ahead and apply the same principles to the second set of doors. Remember to assign the correct move direction so that the doors slide into the wall.

Sealing your area

Now that you have turned part of the wall into an entity, you have created a hole in the sealed area of that room. In Chapter 10, you create a portal brush in the hallway to split the map into three areas. This way, only one room would be rendered in the game while the player was in it, and the other room would be ignored. By creating a hole (by way of the doors) in one of the rooms, the area is leaking into the rest of the map and rendering everything again.

Thankfully, the solution to sealing up this hole is simple. By adding a portal brush inside the doors that fits the entire doorway hole, you can effectively redefine the room as its own area and seal it up again. The area will remain sealed until the doors open and will seal again when the doors close.

To create this doorway portal, follow these steps:

1. **Select the Nodraw texture and draw a brush that fits snugly into one of your doorways.**

2. **Texture the inner brush face with the Visportal texture to create a portal brush in your doorway. Then stretch the brush to make it thinner, placing the Visportal textured face inside the doors.**

   In Figure 11-20, I have removed one of the doors so you can see how it fits inside.

Part III: Expanding Your Creation

> **TIP:** When creating a portal brush for your door, make sure that the portal side of the brush is inside the door brushes. If they are outside the door brushes, the portal will be created in front of the door, causing a visual error in the game.

3. **Create another portal brush for the other set of doors in your map.**

   Make sure that the portal side of the brush is inside the doors and that the brush creates a tight fit around the doorway.

When completed, save your map again.

Figure 11-20: Placing a portal brush inside of a func_door creates a sealed area for better optimization.

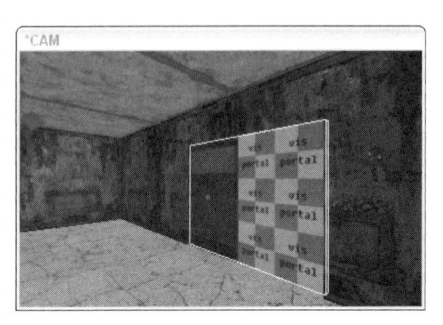

Lighting from Above

For players to be able to see inside your building, you had to add light entities. Right now, if players go into the outdoor area, they won't be able to see anything because there is no light. So again, you must add light entities. However, in the case of your outdoor area, instead of just adding a light bulb to the ceiling, your goal is to replicate something that resembles the sun. This is going to require you to fool the player with some tricky entity placement and settings.

To figure out the best placement for your outdoor light entities, you need a brief understanding of how the earth is lit from the sun.

Understanding your real environment

The light coming from the sky might begin its path from the sun as a single beam of light, but by the time it reaches you on the earth, there is a lot more than a single beam at play. Light shines down through atmosphere, which contains all sorts of particles and elements. Although you can't see it with your naked eye, the light is bouncing off of these particles and shining back to you as if from another source.

Chapter 11: Heading to the Great Outdoors

If you ever saw a rainbow after a rain shower, it is a perfect example of how water breaks up light. The sunlight is split up as it passes through the drops of water in the sky. Sometimes it splits like a prism, sending different colors back through the water, but more often it combines again into a white light.

Now, droplets of water in the sky aren't flat like the mirror in the bathroom. They're round, which means that light doesn't just get reflected back in one direction. Rather, it gets reflected in several directions, some light to you and some light to other droplets of water, where the light-splitting effect happens again.

Looking at Figure 11-21, you can see an example of how the light reaches the ground from the sun. The light starts from the sun. Some of it shines directly down on you as it passes through the atmosphere. Anything that stands between this light and the ground creates a shadow. Other beams of light get caught and are reflected by the atmosphere. Eventually, some of that reflected light makes it way back down to the ground in the form of ambient light. The ambient light doesn't necessarily come from the direction of the sun, but instead it comes from all directions and will fill in that shadow with a less-bright light.

Figure 11-21: As sunlight passes through the atmosphere, it is bounced around and comes to you in the form of ambient light.

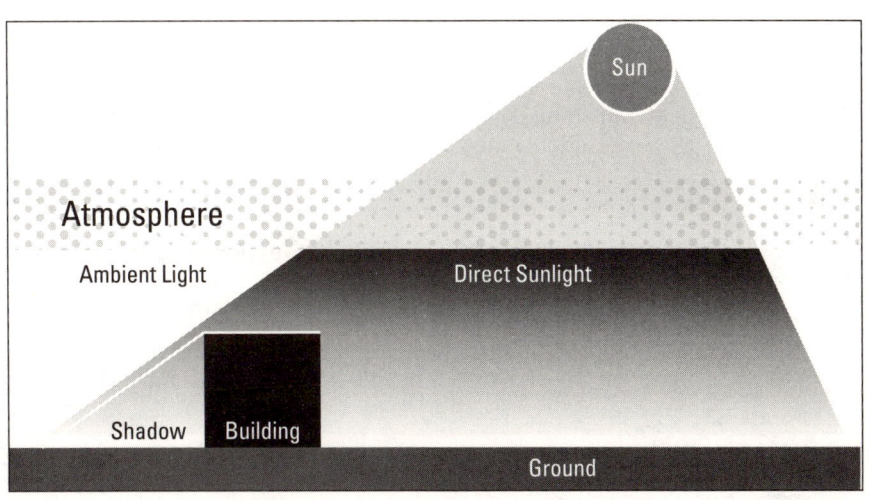

To reproduce this effect that occurs in the atmosphere, you must use more than one light. One light is created and represents the direct light from the sun. It casts shadows and shines on the world. A second light is created on the opposite side of the map. This second light isn't as bright and doesn't cast any shadows or affect the surrounding world in any other way other than to produce the ambient light effect.

You could get further involved by adding even more lights for more effect, but it isn't necessary. Two lights will be enough for most maps to create the effect you're looking for.

Adding a virtual sun

Before you start adjusting the light, set up the CAM window to see how the changes are affecting the level. Press F3 and F4 to activate the Realtime and Render modes in the CAM window, respectively. Render mode displays the level in a way that resembles the game itself. Realtime mode updates the rendering in real time so that as you make adjustments to the light, you will see how the adjustments change your level. At the moment, the picture in the CAM window might look a little bit dark, but that's about to change.

Here's what you need to do to create a simulated sun:

1. **Start by adding a light entity as you did in Chapter 7 to the northeast quadrant of the map, using Figure 11-22 as a guide.**

   Move the light near the top of the sky, where you will pretend your sun is sitting.

   By default, the light isn't strong enough to shine onto the ground of your map from such a distance. You could drag out the distance that your light can shine by enlarging the pink box that surrounds the light entity. However, such a method would create problems with larger maps. You would have to stretch out the box for more than twice the radius of the level itself.

   Instead, you can apply a special texture to the light. *Light textures* are really just combinations of images and short scripts that tell the light how to behave. Light textures are already available in the Light Editor window.

2. **Drag out the size of the light's falloff level to fully encompass your level.**

   This larger, pink box surrounds your light. Make sure the pink lines reach just outside your map in all three directions like you see in Figure 11-23.

3. **Press J to open the Light Editor.**

   The Light Editor, shown in Figure 11-24, allows you to fine-tune the light to meet your needs. Rather than having to remember all the Keys and Values for the light that can be manually entered into the Entity Editor, you can use this window.

Chapter 11: Heading to the Great Outdoors 147

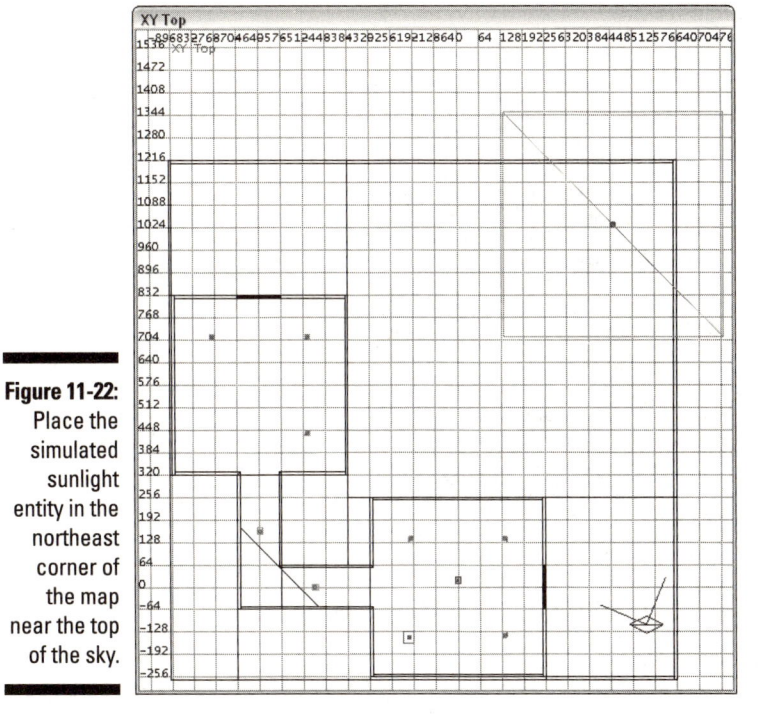

Figure 11-22: Place the simulated sunlight entity in the northeast corner of the map near the top of the sky.

Figure 11-23: Drag the falloff level to fully encompass your map in all directions.

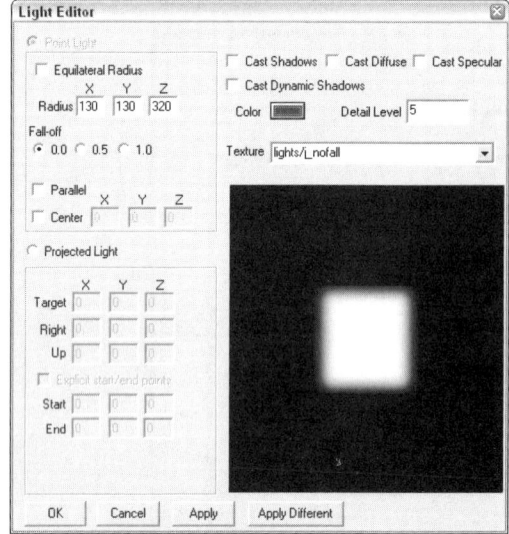

Figure 11-24: The Light Editor window, where you can fine-tune your light properties.

4. **In the Light Editor, change the Texture setting.**

   Pull down the list of available textures. Locate and select `lights/i_nofall`. When selected, the area under the list displays the texture. Click the Apply button and take a look at the CAM window. You should now see light shining in the outside area of your map.

Simulating ambient light

That takes care of your simulated sun, but you still need to add your ambient light.

1. **Copy the light you just added and move the copy to the opposite corner of the map, as shown in Figure 11-25.**

   Placing it in the direct opposite location creates the ambient effect you're looking for, although you still need to adjust this light's options.

2. **Open the Light Editor for the light you just created by pressing J.**

   Because the editor doesn't allow you to change the brightness level of the light, to simulate the lower lever you instead need to change the color of the light. Your first light is white by default, so you want to select something darker.

Chapter 11: Heading to the Great Outdoors   **149**

3. **Click the color swatch located to the right of the word** *Color.*

   This opens the familiar-looking color selector. Because you want a darker color, you need to select a dark gray. Try manually entering 70, 70, and 70 as RGB Values. Press OK when you have the color selected.

4. **Deselect Cast Shadows, Cast Diffuse, Cast Specular, and Cast Dynamic Shadows.**

   Because your ambient light is meant to fill in the dark spots of the map without creating more, you want to deselect all the Cast options found above the Color selector.

5. **Change the Details Level from 10 to 5.**

   You don't need a high level of ambient light detail, and leaving it at 10 is really just a waste of resources. If this were a larger map, compile time would be significantly reduced by this adjustment.

   After pressing the Apply button, the result of the Light Editor window and your CAM window should look like Figure 11-26.

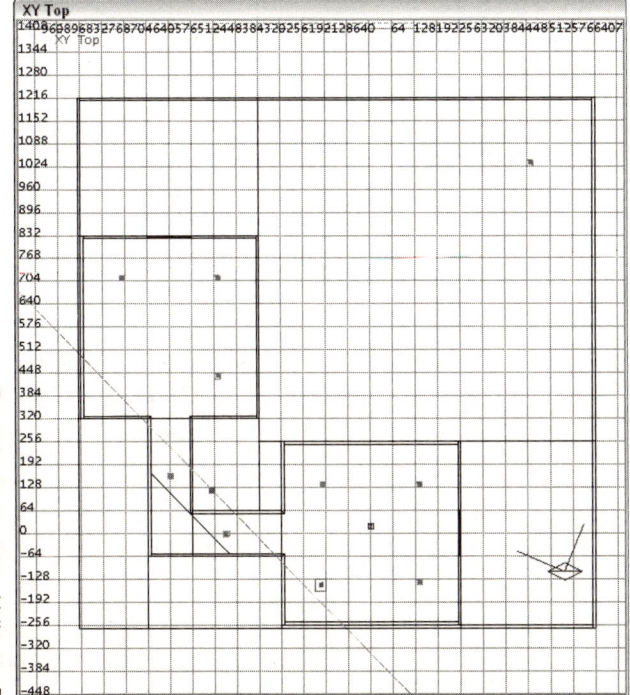

Figure 11-25: Copy your simulated sunlight and move the copy to the adjacent corner of the map.

Figure 11-26:
The fake ambient light has filled in the darker areas of the level to soften the shadows and make the map more realistic.

Testing Your Progress

Finally, after all the work you just put in, you can see how your new outdoor area looks in the game.

Compile the map by running it through the BSP process (which I discuss in Chapter 8). When complete, make sure to review the output in the Console tab. Make sure there are no reports of leaks or other errors that could have stopped the compile process. If you do encounter a leak, follow the red line in your map to the hole and seal it up. If you find an error you don't know how to solve, you might be better off going back to a previously saved version of the map and rebuilding it from that point.

Now that the map has been compiled into a level, load it in the game. Press F2 to open the game window. Open the console and type **devmap game/ chapter11**. Then launch the game when prompted and have fun.

Chapter 12

Adding a Few Details

In This Chapter
▶ Adding a few brushes for detail
▶ Teaming doors to work in unison
▶ Dropping crates in honor of the FPS
▶ Placing pickups for the players

A lot of work has gone into making your first map for Quake 4. In the preceding chapters, you created two interior rooms connected by a hallway. With sliding doors, you extended the play area to go outdoors with a sky and outdoor lighting. With all the work you put into this map, you could call it a second home. However, what is a home without a little decoration? If your home had no furniture, no rugs, no details to make things interesting, it wouldn't be a fun place to hang out.

What's needed are a few details in the playing area. Some details are small and won't be noticed by the player, but others will make a huge difference in the game play of the level. However, all details, no matter the size, add to the overall feel of a map and make it worth playing over and over again.

Doing Some Decorating

To start off, I show you how to add some minor details to the layout. These minor things might not ever be recognized by the other player but will really add depth and character to the environment.

First, I show you how to enhance the outside walls. Even though the texturing helps to make them interesting, extra depth created with the addition of just a few brushes gives your walls the look of strength and security.

Part III: Expanding Your Creation

Pulling a ledge

Here you add a ledge to the top of the wall. A ledge makes the top look and feel more prominent when the light casts a shadow. It makes the walls feel deep. The change doesn't need to be big, but it should be noticeable.

You draw a ledge around the entire outer wall at the top where your current texture is starting to repeat itself. The brush should be 32 units tall and 8 units deep. This size is big enough to give the desired effect without be so big that it takes over the scene.

1. **Deselect all brushes and select the Caulk texture.**
2. **Starting in the southeast corner of the map, draw your first brush in the direction of your building to 32 units tall and 8 units deep. When you get to the edge of the building, stop.**

   The result should look like Figure 12-1.

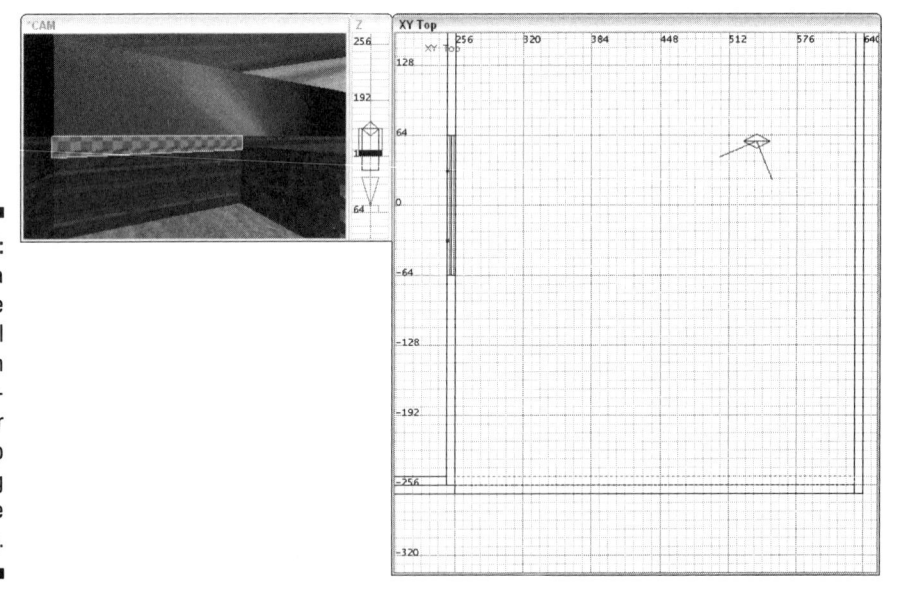

Figure 12-1: Create a ledge on the wall beginning in the lower-left corner of the map and working toward the building.

Note that I stopped at the edge of the building. You don't want to overlap your brush with that of the building, so you need to stop the first brush and then draw a new brush that fits over the building.

3. **Continue along the south wall with the ledge that is now 24 units tall to avoid any overlapping of the building. Stop when you reach the back corner of the map, as shown in Figure 12-2.**

Chapter 12: Adding a Few Details **153**

This is where you can stop with your ledge because adding one over the backs of the buildings would go unnoticed by the player. Instead, texture it later with the texture you choose for the ledge when the construction is complete.

 4. **Move your view back to the southeast corner and continue the ledge brush on the eastern wall.**

    You can afford to make this into one, long brush. The only spots that might cause you trouble are the corners. You need to miter them as you go along, just as you did in Chapter 10.

Figure 12-2:
Rather than overlapping your ledge brush with the building, stop and start a new brush for the ledge that doesn't overlap.

 5. **Start the mitering with the southeast corner and miter each corner as you go along with your ledge.**

    It should look like Figure 12-3 when you're done.

 6. **Continue adding the ledge brush around the wall until it is complete, making sure that the ledge wraps around the enclosed area and stops at the southwest corner.**

When you've added all the ledge brushes, it's time to texture these new brushes. You want to add something that doesn't completely blend in with the current wall but doesn't look out of place.

 1. **Load the mptextures texture set.**

 2. **Apply the texture `mptextures/trim_h5` to the top, front, and bottom brush faces of the trim brush.**

    This texture complements the wall texture that is currently there. However, on some faces, the texture will be incorrectly oriented on the top and bottom brush face, like in Figure 12-4.

Part III: Expanding Your Creation

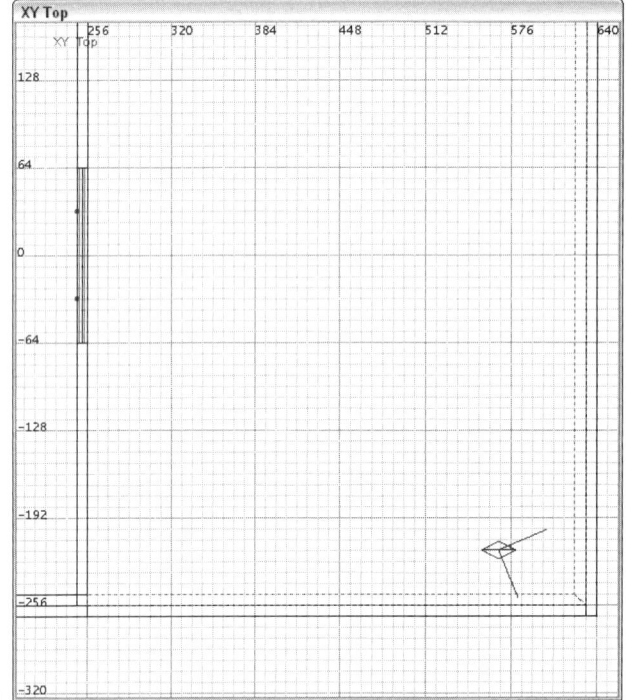

Figure 12-3: Bevel the corners to reduce splitting your geometry.

Figure 12-4: When texturing the tops of the ledges, some of the textures might need to be rotated in order to line up.

 3. To fix this problem, select the texture that needs adjusting.
 4. Rotate the texture until it looks like it lines up with the brush. Press Shift+Page Down to rotate the selected texture clockwise or press Shift+Page Up to rotate it counter-clockwise.

Chapter 12: Adding a Few Details   155

If you need to shift the texture up or down, press Shift+↑ or Shift+↓ to move it in those respective directions.

With the texture properly positioned, all the features of the texture should line up with the brush and texture next to it. The result should look like Figure 12-5.

TIP: If you need help lining up your texture, use the Render mode in the CAM window to view the texture with more detail as it would be seen in the game. You activate Render mode by pressing F3.

5. **Continue to apply the textures as you did here to the rest of the ledge brushes.**

   Remember to apply and adjust the texture underneath the ledge and make sure to texture all visible sides of the brush. You don't want it to leak when you compile it later.

Figure 12-5: This is what your ledge should look like when you're done. The textures are lined up, and the corners are beveled.

When you get to the back corner of the map where you didn't create the additional ledge brush, simply copy the texture to that wall as if it were the ledge. It should look seamless along the back, and the player will never know that it doesn't stick out from the wall.

6. **Save the map under a new name. Name it `chapter12.map`.**

Lighting the porch

Something else that adds a lot of detail to a level is lighting. I don't mean just the general lighting that makes it possible for the players to see where they're going. I'm referring to the lights that accent points in the game such as entrance ways.

Part III: Expanding Your Creation

In this section, you add a light over top of each pair of doors. This makes the doorways more obvious to the player and makes them more interesting at the same time.

1. **With everything deselected, select the Caulk texture and move the camera around and in front of a set of doors, viewing it from the exterior.**

2. **Draw a brush that is 32 x 16 x 16 units (X, Y, Z) in size and place it 8 units above the center of the two doors so that it looks something like Figure 12-6.**

   This brush is the light's basic structure, but you need to shape it so it doesn't look quite so boxy.

3. **Switch your view in the 2D window so that you're looking at the side of the light.**

4. **Reduce your grid size to Grid4 by pressing 4, and then press E to show the brush edges.**

5. **Drag the top-front brush edge down so that the top of the light fixture is sloped downward but there is still a 4-unit lip in the front.**

   Be careful not to drag the edge and create a three-sided brush because this type of brush manipulation will create an error during the compile process. The result should look like Figure 12-7.

Figure 12-6: To start the light structure over the door, draw a box with the Caulk texture.

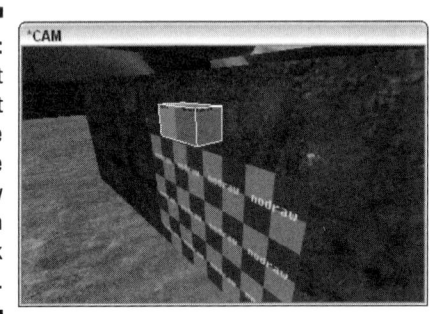

That completes the light fixture structure. Now you need to texture it.

1. **Load the Common Lights texture set.**

   There are a lot of nice accent lights here for you to play with.

2. **Select the bottom brush face of the light, which is where you will place the light texture.**

Chapter 12: Adding a Few Details *157*

3. **Apply the texture `common_lights/rect_light6`.**

   If you're working on the light attached to the red room, your texture will need to be rotated before it lines up properly. After you've rotated it and checked that the edges of the texture line up with the edges of the brush, you will see something like Figure 12-8. If needed, you can also use the Surface Inspector to fit the texture to the brush face.

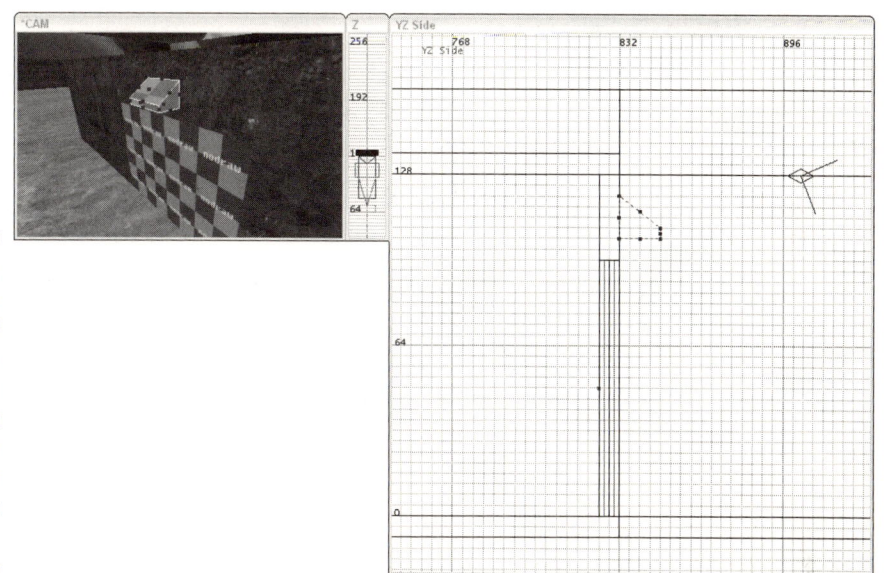

Figure 12-7: Move the edges of your brush to create a shape that looks more appropriate for a light box.

4. **As for the remainder of the light fixture, texture it with a basic steel texture.**

   TIP

   Using the same texture that you used on the inner doorway edges would be great. To find it easily, choose Materials⇨Show In Use to filter your loaded textures in the Textures tab. Then apply `terminal/t1_metal2`, as was done in Figure 12-9.

Figure 12-8: Great light textures are available to you in the editor.

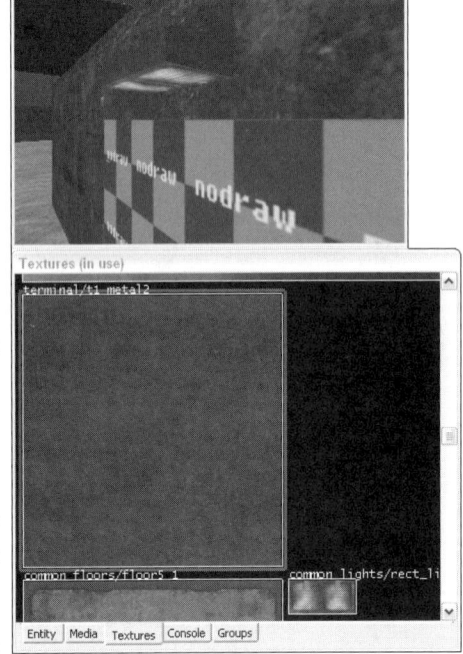

Figure 12-9: Apply a generic metal texture to the sides of the light box to complete the look.

Optimizing the light fixture

In the preceding section, you completed the creation and texturing of the light, but doing so really hurt the map's optimization. In Chapter 10, which discussed optimization, you had a chance to see how your map was being split up into multiple polygons in the game. Every place two brushes met, they created a split.

If you were to take a look at your current map in the game, you would see multiple splits occurring around the light structure that you just made. All this added geometry will start slowing down your map, especially as you add more detail to the level.

To solve this problem, you must define your brush as an entity, not as a structural brush. Only then will it be calculated during the BSP process as something that doesn't create all these splits. You want to turn it into a `func_static` entity. This entity is meant for converting regular brushes into simple entities.

1. **Select the brush.**
2. **Right click the 2D window and select func➪func_static.**

    This converts your brush into the entity that will save your map from a horrible fate: slowness.

Adding a light entity to your light fixture

So, the light fixture looks complete as a structure, but this won't shine light on the area under the door. To shine a little light on things, you need to add a light entity:

1. **Deselect everything and right-click the area near the light fixture in the 2D window.**
2. **From the drop-down menu, select the Light option.**
3. **Position the light entity so that it sits directly under the brush you just created, as shown in Figure 12-10.**

   The light will look good here, but you should adjust the color. To dim the intensity, select a darker color. You want the light to fit the scene and not stand out too much.

4. **Press K to open the Color Picker.**
5. **Set the color and close the window.**

   A dark-orange color with an RGB value of 173 95 0 should work well for you here.

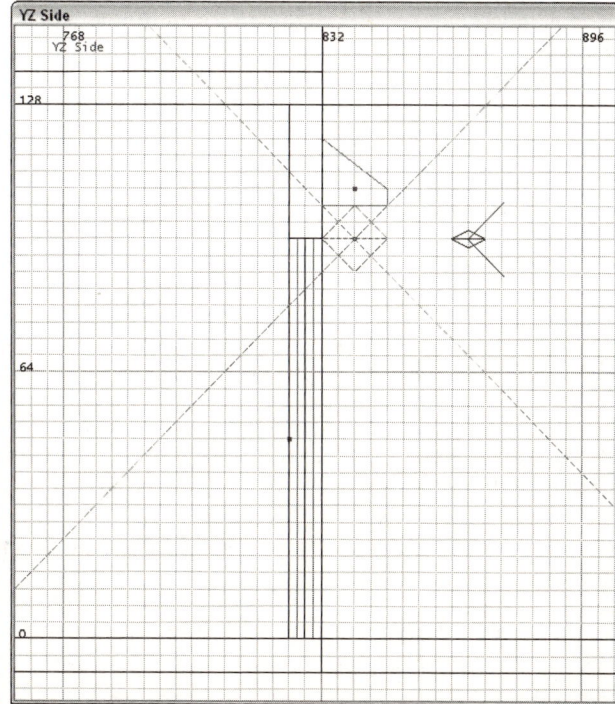

Figure 12-10: Place a light entity directly under the light box to produce the light that will shine down over the doors.

> ### Detail brushes
>
> In previous versions of *Quake,* you were able to turn a structural brush into a detail brush. This reduced the geometry in the same manner as with the `func_static` entity in the section "Optimizing the light fixture." However, id Software removed this option from the game during the creation of *Doom 3,* which was carried over to *Quake 4.* Although you might see this Make Detail option available in the editor, it does nothing to your map and doesn't help you in any way.

Duplicating your light fixture

After you've completed your light fixture, you can duplicate what you have done for the other set of doors, rather than remaking everything. To copy what you have already created, follow these steps:

1. **Select the brush and light and press the spacebar to make a duplicate.**

2. **Move the duplicate near the other set of doors, and then press the z_axis Rotate button, as shown in the margin.**

    This button is located at the top of the editor until the light is properly oriented. Each press of this button rotates the selected objects 45 degrees clockwise. The textures and everything will remain locked to the faces of the brush so you won't have to worry about making any other adjustments.

3. **Move the selection into place over the door.**

    It should look just like the original light over the door, as shown in Figure 12-11.

Defining the indoor lights

For the outdoor lights, you created a brush and textured it with something that looks like the casing for a light structure. When the player notices the light over the door in the game, it's obvious that this is where the light is emanating from. However, you didn't do this for the lights inside the rooms. The lights indoors just seem to magically appear; they should be defined by a source.

1. **Using the Caulk texture, draw a brush 16 units square and 4 units tall inside one of the rooms.**

2. **Position the brush over top of one of the existing lights in the room.**

Chapter 12: Adding a Few Details   *161*

You have to adjust the grid in your 2D window to a smaller size so that you can size the height of the brush to 4 units. The result should look like the brush in Figure 12-12.

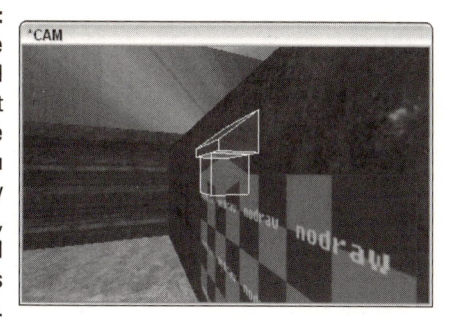

Figure 12-11: For the second light, just duplicate what you already constructed, rotate it, and position it as needed.

3. **Texture the four sides of your light box with the same gray texture used to surround your outdoor lights, `terminal/t1_metal2`.**

4. **To texture the underside of the brush, select the `common_lights/small_light4` texture.**

   This fits a square brush and looks good indoors, as you can see in Figure 12-13.

   After the structure is created and textured, you need to turn this brush into a `func_static` entity, just like you did with the outside lights in the section "Optimizing the light fixture," earlier in this chapter.

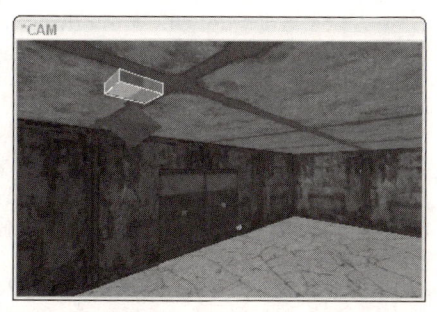

Figure 12-12: Creating a light box over each of the lights inside of your building provides a logical source for the light.

Figure 12-13: Texture the light box appropriately with a new light texture and generic metal.

5. **Select the brush, right-click the 2D window to open the entity list, and select func↪func_static.**

   This keeps the geometry in the game to a minimum and keeps your level running smoothly.

6. **Move the light up to sit closely underneath the brush.**

7. **Copy the light structure (but not the light itself) and place it above each of the light sources within the indoor areas of your map. Make sure to move all the lights up close to the structures.**

Now the players will understand that this is the source of light when they walk inside the building and rooms.

Pairing the Doors

In Chapter 11, you created two sets of doors. Both sets offer a way to move between the indoor and outdoor areas in the map. In testing your map, you might have noticed that it was possible to walk up to a set of doors and make only one of the two open. In some cases, this might be something that you want. However, in this map, it would make more sense to have both doors open simultaneously regardless of the angle at which the player approaches them.

You can tell the game that a group of doors are to work in tandem. The method is to define the doors as a team. So, when one door opens or closes, all doors of the same team will open and close at the same time.

1. **From within the map editor, select the pair of doors connected to the room with red lights in the lower portion of the 2D window.**

   You are going to define these two doors as a team so that they work in tandem. The definition will be to label them in the Entity tab as both having the same team name, and you can do this to both doors at the same time.

Chapter 12: Adding a Few Details

2. **With both doors selected, open the Entity tab.**
3. **In the Key field, enter** team. **In the Val field, enter** doors_red. **Then press Enter to set the Key/Val pair for the entity.**

   Figure 12-14 shows the Key and Val fields with the values entered.

   Make sure not to make any other adjustments to the entity. Any changes you make affect both doors because they are both selected.

4. **When you're done, deselect your doors so as not to accidentally make any other changes.**

Figure 12-14: To make two or more doors work together, simply team them in the Entity tab.

Do the same for the pair of doors connected to the room with blue lights in the upper portion of the map. However, rather than using the same team name for these doors, enter the name doors_blue. If you enter the same team name that you used for the first set of doors, the game will group all four doors together, and that isn't the goal here.

Adding Some Crates

What's a first-person shooter game without a few crates? I can count on one hand the number of first-person shooters that don't have crates. Crates provide players with a place to hide, climb, or change the strategy of game play. They also add to the environment of the level so it doesn't look barren.

I show you how to build a crate for *Quake 4*. Then you will place some crates in the map, using logic behind the placement. I start by showing you how to place crates inside rooms, and then I show you how to place them outside.

You can place your crates anywhere in the map that you want, however some places make more sense then others, and you can use your crates to alter how the map is played. Here are a few ways you can use crates in your map:

- Restrict access to an area.
- Guide the players to follow a certain path.
- Offer places to hide weapons or players.
- Provide a means of climbing up to an otherwise inaccessible location.
- Create a safer place for the player to spawn into the map without being immediately spotted.

Creating climbable crates

A crate really isn't anything more than a textured box. There isn't a lot of work involved in creating the structure; it's the placement that can make the level more fun during play. You start with indoor crates small enough for the player to climb over.

1. **Select the Caulk brush.**

2. **Create a cube 48 units in size in each direction and place the brush in the red room near the lower-right corner.**

   This is a great place to start with your crates because it's near the door and in a darker corner.

   Making the box 48 units in size means that the player can jump high enough to get on top of it. Also, a player needs at least 40 units of space to fit between brushes, so space your boxes at least this distance from the wall to allow access.

3. **Now load the Canyon texture set.**

   This texture set has an ideal texture for *Quake 4* crates.

4. **Select one of the sides of your crate for the new texture.**

5. **Locate and select the texture `canyon/crate_a_front`, as shown in Figure 12-15.**

6. **Open the Surface Inspector by pressing S and fit the texture by pressing the Fit button so that it is sized to fit the brush face perfectly.**

7. **Apply this texture to the other three sides of the box, leaving only the top without a texture.**

Chapter 12: Adding a Few Details **165**

8. **Select the top of the box.**

    Another texture in the Canyon set suits the top of your crate and completes the look of the crate you're building.

Figure 12-15:
Texture your crate with a crate texture and fit the texture to the side of your brush.

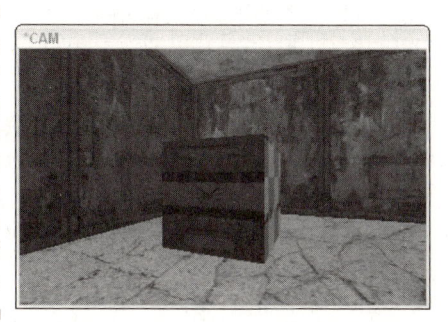

9. **Locate and apply the texture `canyon/crate_a_top`, as shown in Figure 12-16. Use the Fit button in the Surface Inspector to size the texture to fit the brush face.**

Figure 12-16: Texture the top with a separate texture to add variety to the structure.

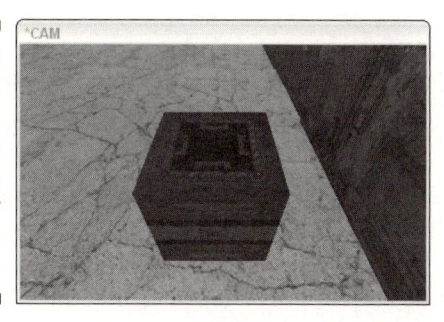

The box is now constructed, but you need to convert it into a detail brush. To keep the geometry in the game to a minimum, turn this brush into a `func_static` entity just like you did with the outside lights in the section "Optimizing the light fixture," earlier in this chapter:

10. **Select the box, right-click the 2D window to open the entity list, and choose func⇨func_static.**

Placing crates for strategy

You've got your first crate built and ready for placement. Now it's time to add opportunities for strategy in the game. Without the additional obstacles in the game, your players have little to hide behind and plan out their attack or retreat. It's your job to add elements to the level that give players choices. That is one of the functions of the crate.

1. **Place your first crate near the bottom-right corner of the red-lit room. Leave just enough room — 40 units — for the player to squeeze through between the crate and the walls.**

2. **Make a duplicate of the crate you just placed. Move this to the left of the first crate.**

   Rather than leave this new crate flush and parallel to the first one, you are going to rotate it to add some variety and whimsy to the placement of the crates in the corner.

3. **With the second crate selected, press R to turn on free rotation.**

   This function allows you to spin the box on the third axis of the 2D window. So, if your view of the 2D window is XY Top, free rotation allows you to spin the box on the Z axis.

4. **Click and drag outside of the box in this window to rotate it. When you have it rotated to the desired angle, press R to turn the function off.**

   Use Figure 12-17 as an example of how I have placed the crates in this room.

5. **Make another duplicate of the first crate and place it flush against the wall and to the left of the second crate.**

   Placing it here means the player can't run into the corner from this side. However, you did make the crates short enough so that the player can jump over them, thereby adding another element of strategy to this corner. This slows the player down a little bit while the other side is open for the player to simply run through.

6. **Place a couple more crates in this corner, but rather than setting them on the floor, place them on top of the existing crates.**

   This creates a really good hiding place or trap for the player. In Figure 12-18, I've not only placed duplicate crates on top of the others, but I've also rotated them slightly to make it more interesting. You should do the same.

   TIP: When moving the crate on top of the others, you might notice that there is no texture on the bottom of the crate. This is easily remedied by copying the texture from the top to the bottom.

7. **Go through the rest of the indoor area of your map and place a few more crates around.**

Chapter 12: Adding a Few Details *167*

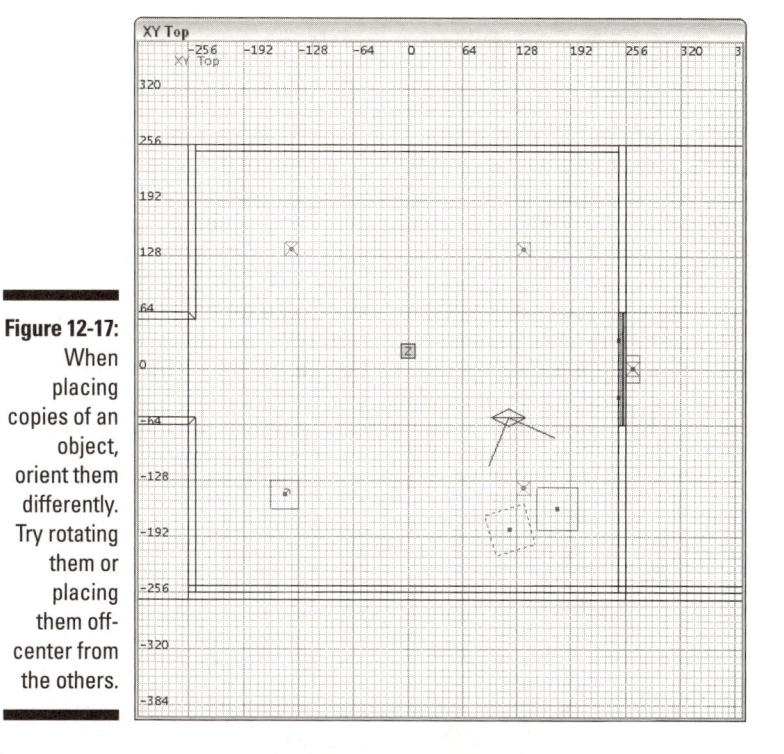

Figure 12-17: When placing copies of an object, orient them differently. Try rotating them or placing them off-center from the others.

Figure 12-18: When stacking your crates, remember to texture the underside.

Try to build some strategic areas for the players, but don't allow the placement to interrupt the flow of the game. Placing a crate in the middle of the hallway would passage through the hall difficult and possibly less fun. However, placing a few crates at the sides of some rooms may make play more interesting and provide places to hide. Use Figure 12-19 if you need some ideas on how to place your crates.

Making crates for other environments

In most cases, you could say that crates are crates, no matter where they are placed. However, when you consider how the player will be interacting with them within the game, crates become much more than just crates. The crates inside the rooms of your building not only provide something for the player to hide behind, but also something to climb over. They become part of a player's strategy.

However, when you take the crates outside, you should be careful. You don't want the players climbing the crates to be able to see "behind the curtain." You don't want them to know that there isn't anything behind the wall or allow them to walk along the roof of the building. Think carefully about all the possibilities as you build and place crates in the outside area of your level.

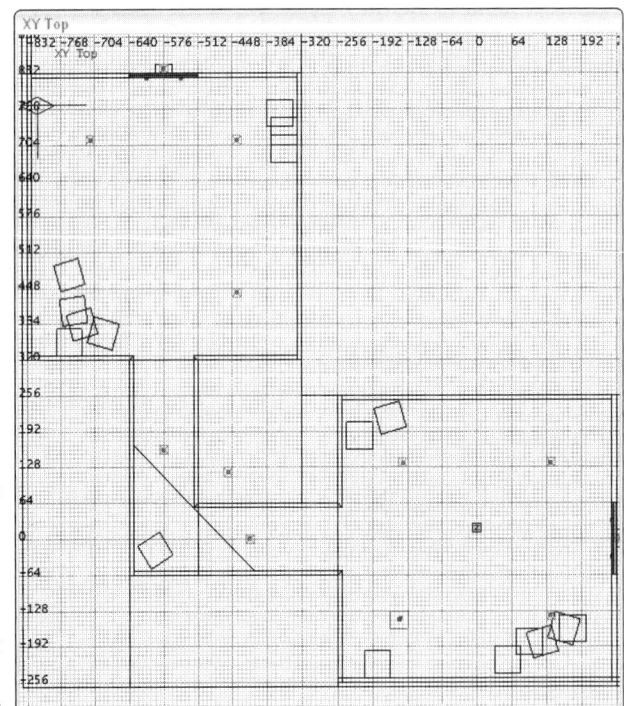

Figure 12-19: Continue placing crates throughout your level.

Chapter 12: Adding a Few Details

So, although crates are allowed outside of the building, they must provide limitations to the player. Such limitations can be made simply by making the crates larger.

1. **In the outside area, create another boxy brush, but this time make it 96 units in size in each direction, resulting in a larger cube.**
2. **Texture the sides and the top just as you did the crates within the rooms in the section "Creating climbable crates," earlier in this chapter.**
3. **Complete the crate by turning it into a `func_static` entity, as explained in "Creating climbable crates."**

Because you are working with such a large crate, you won't need as many of them. When placing them in the outside area, don't crowd the yard, but place enough of them to make things interesting. Also, consider strategy here by placing it far enough from some walls that the player can run behind them. In Figure 12-20, you can see that I have placed a group of them in the middle of the map. They are spaced far enough apart that the player can run between them. They are also placed inexactly to add to the reality and the interest of the scene.

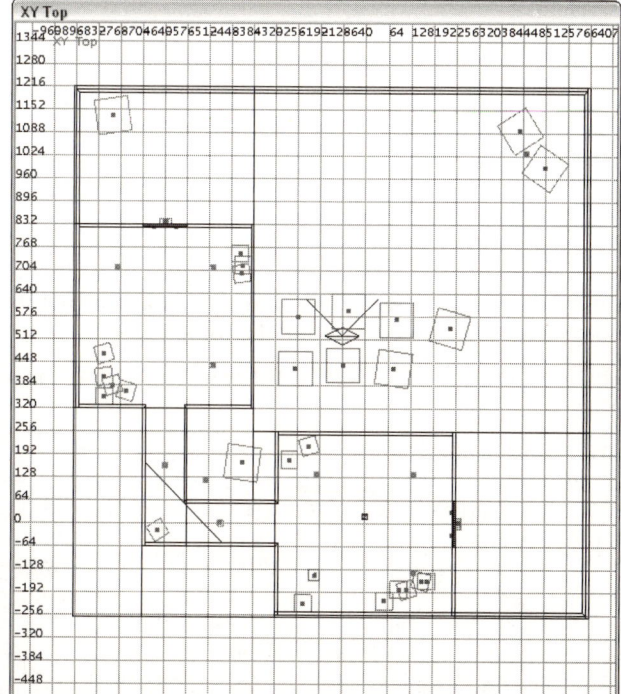

Figure 12-20: Crates placed in the outside area of the map should be larger than the ones indoors.

Picking Up on Pickups

You run around the corner in your level while playing against someone else online. As you emerge, your opponent shoots several rounds into your player, and you escape with only a sliver of health left showing on your health bar. The next thing on your mind as a player is "Where can I find a health pickup to recuperate and get back in the game?"

Pickups are an important part of the game. They range from health and armor to weapons and ammo. In a multiplayer game, pickups are your only means of supplying the player with additional weapons.

Placing these items is very simple. They are entities, and all you need to do to place them in your map is to right-click the 2D window and choose them from the menu.

Selecting a place for your pickups is simply a matter of choice. However, you should consider their placement as you did with the crates. Pickups can be used as lures to encourage players to access different areas of the map and to make players more vulnerable to attack.

Adding armor

Start by placing some armor in the hall between the two rooms. Give players a reason to run though the halls by placing a row of three armor-shard pickups in each elbow of the hall.

1. **Right-click the 2D window.**
2. **Choose pickup⇨item⇨item_armor_shard.**
3. **Move the object to the center of the hall and make sure it's positioned on the floor and not above or under the floor.**
4. **Duplicate and place another five of these pickups in a row along each hall.**

   See Figure 12-21 for placement.

In the case of the hall running north and south in your map, the pickups are not facing an ideal direction. They are sitting long-ways, which makes it difficult for the player to see them. To resolve this, you should change the angle at which these entities are facing. I use the term *angle* because it's better to change the entity angle than it is to rotate an entity. Some entities won't respond in the game to the same rotation action that you performed on the crates earlier in this chapter. Pickups are point entities as described in Chapter 3, and these types of entities require angle settings to tell them which direction to face.

Chapter 12: Adding a Few Details *171*

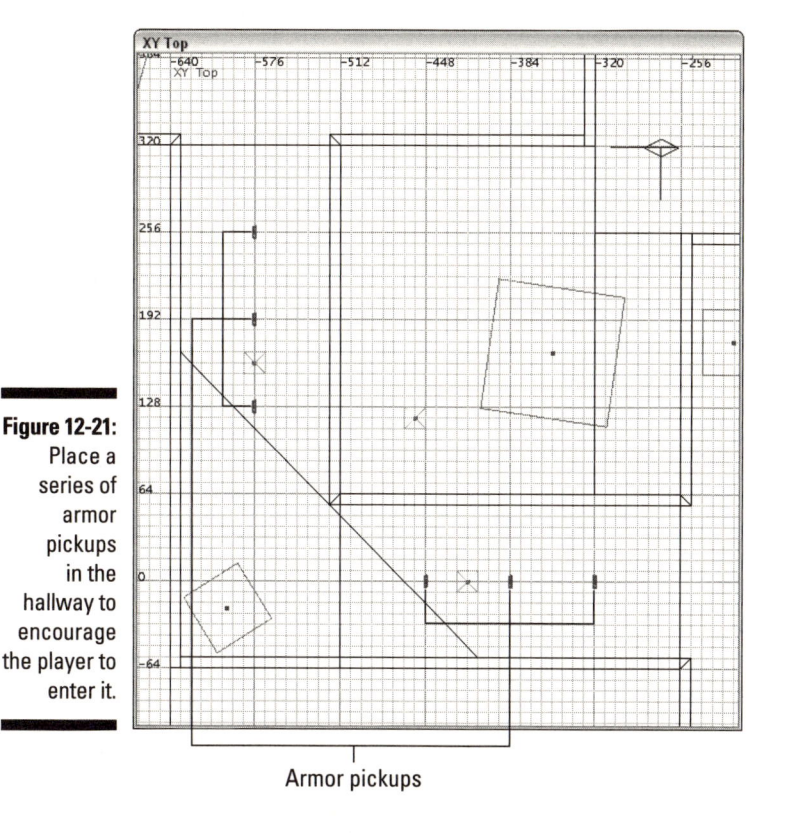

Figure 12-21: Place a series of armor pickups in the hallway to encourage the player to enter it.

Armor pickups

To set the angle of your entity, follow these steps:

1. **Select the pickup that you want to rotate.**
2. **Open the Entity tab.**
3. **Press the 90 button to rotate the entity 90 degrees.**

   This reorients the pickup so it's easier for the player to spot, as you can see in Figure 12-22.

Now that the players have a reason to run through the halls, you are creating a flow for the level. The players have a reason to run from one end of the map to the other end. This encourages interaction between opposing teams and makes for a more enjoyable game. By placing a pickup that restores only partial armor to the players, you are giving them a reason to return for more later when that pickup respawns. In multi-player games, pickups respawn after a few seconds. In single-player games, pickups do not respawn.

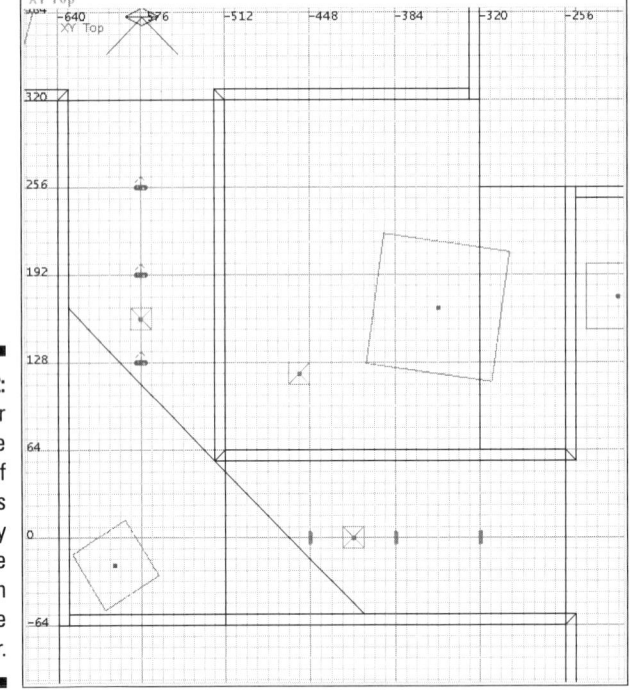

Figure 12-22: Remember to set the angle of your entities so that they can be easily seen by the player.

Restoring health

You should place some health in the map. The health pickup would do well in a separate location than that of the armor. This means that the players are going to have to choose between grabbing armor or health when they need it, and options like these open up the level to more interaction between the players and the level.

1. **Place one health pickup in the upper-left corner of the map behind the crate in the outside area by right-clicking in the 2D window choosing pickup⇨item⇨item_health_small.**

2. **On the Entity tab, change the angle of the entity to 270 so that it faces outside of its hiding spot for the player to see.**

   Figure 12-23 shows you the placement.

One health pickup is rarely enough. Another good location for a health pickup is behind the crates in the upper-left corner of the red room, as shown in Figure 12-24. Now you are encouraging the player to explore the level for more goodies. Placing them in plain sight is sometimes too easy.

Chapter 12: Adding a Few Details   *173*

Figure 12-23: Place health in some of the hidden areas of the map to encourage the player to look around.

Health pickup

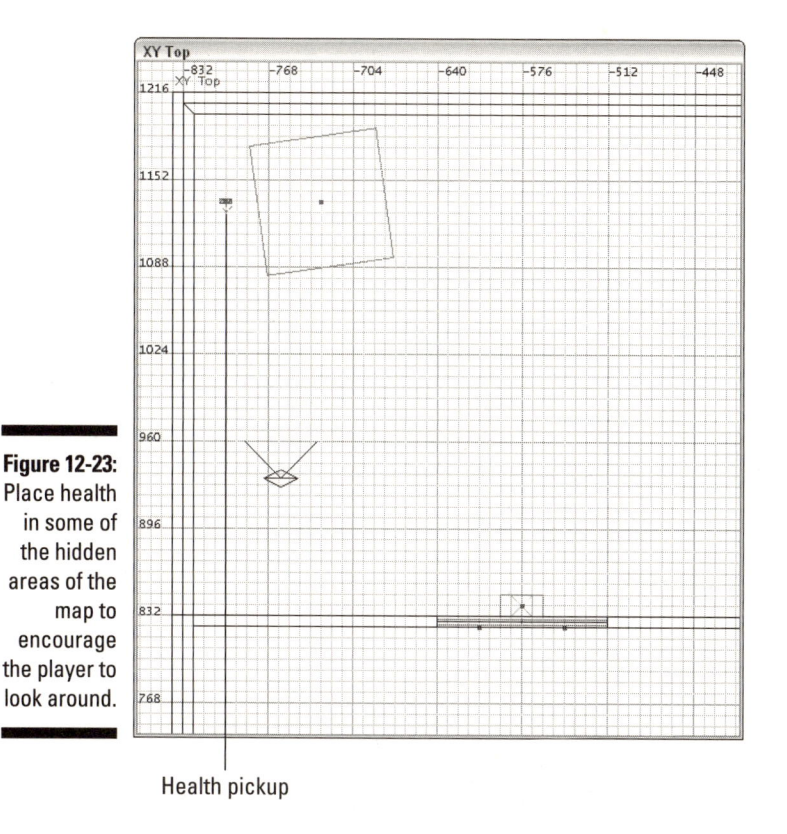

In many games, especially multiplayer games, health is the most important pickup. This is particularly the case in smaller maps because the players are forced to run into each other more often. Placing a few more shards of health will benefit this small map, so place some between the stacks of crates in the outside area. You can refer to Figure 12-25 for placement.

Finding weapons

What is a deathmatch without weapons? Unless you're planning on using your level as a picnic area, you need some weapons pickups.

When placing weapons in a map, consider the proximity at which the players will be fighting. In smaller maps, close-range weapons such as the shotgun become much more valuable to a player than long-range weapons such as a rocket launcher.

Figure 12-24:
You can even hide some health somewhere as a prize.

Health pickup

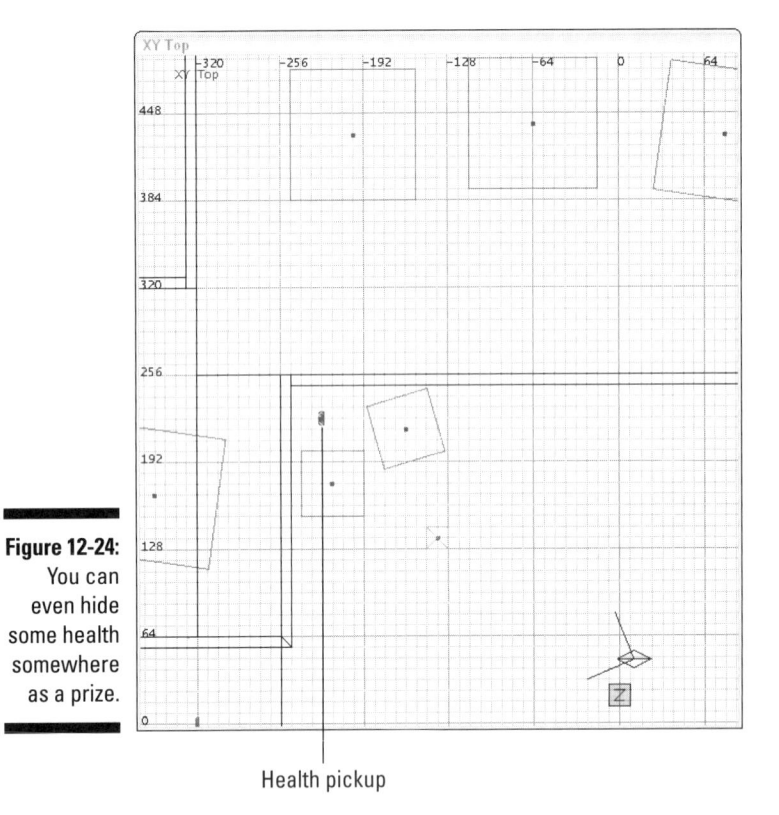

Here's how to add them to your map:

 1. **Place the first weapon pickup by right-clicking the outside nook between the halls (see Figure 12-26) in the 2D menu and choosing pickup➪weapon➪weapon_shotgun.**

    This corner is a good place to draw players and provide them with a close-range weapon such as the shotgun because they might need it to get out of this tight space.

 2. **Place the rail gun in the lower-right corner of the map, as shown in Figure 12-27.**

 3. **On the Entity tab, set the angle of the entity to 135 to make it more visible.**

    This is a place visible to all players, but it's also a place of vulnerability. To get the pickup, the players will have to run out in the open where they can be shot, and although the rail gun is powerful, it doesn't immediately respond. This adds to some of the strategy of the level.

Chapter 12: Adding a Few Details 175

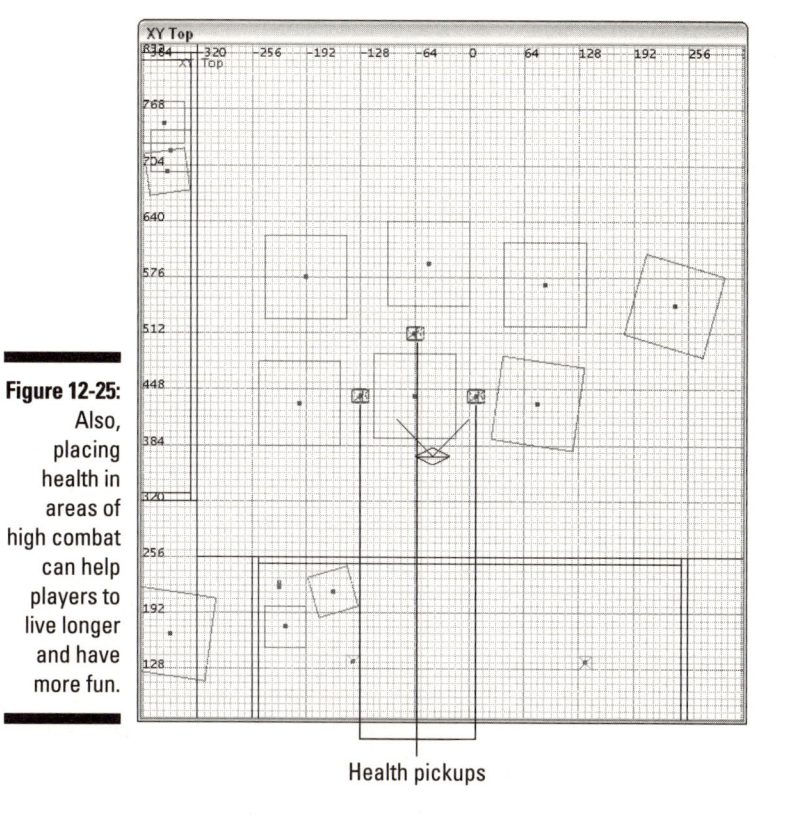

Figure 12-25: Also, placing health in areas of high combat can help players to live longer and have more fun.

Health pickups

Figure 12-26: Place weapons in your map that fit the playability, such as close-range weapons in close-combat areas.

Part III: Expanding Your Creation

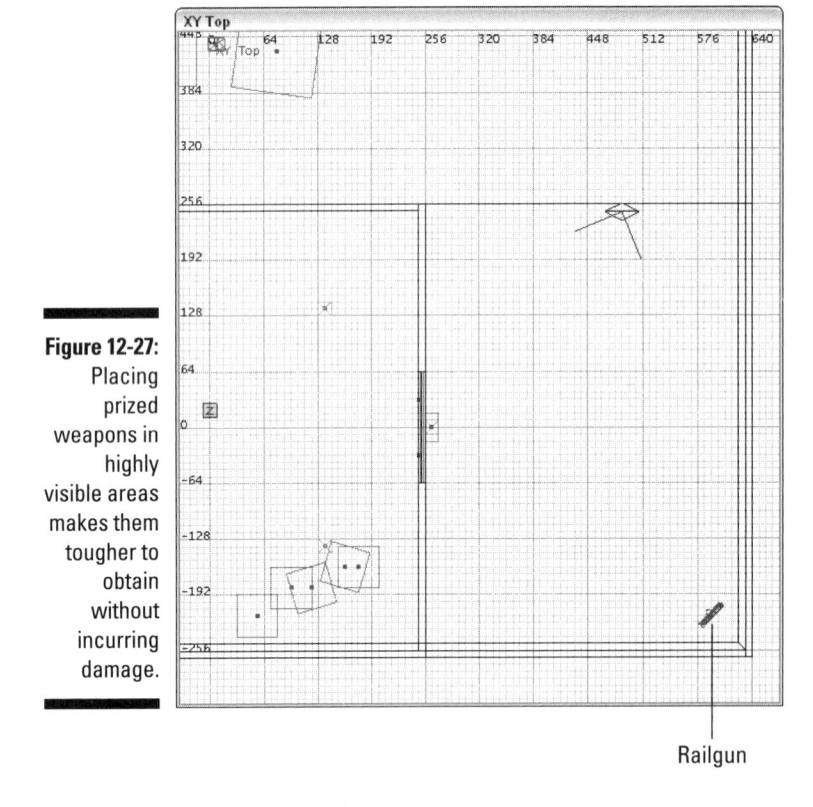

Figure 12-27: Placing prized weapons in highly visible areas makes them tougher to obtain without incurring damage.

Railgun

Now place one more weapon in this small map: the machine gun. Place the machine gun in the upper-right corner of the blue room. Position it so that it's somewhat hidden behind a crate, but not so much that it will go unnoticed (see Figure 12-28). This entity also needs to be rotated to better fit into this tighter spot as well as make it more visible to the player.

Grabbing ammo

Now move on to adding some ammo pickups in the map. Without ammo, the weapons are of no use to the players. Ammo is important. You should place ammo in slightly more visible locations to the players to keep the game going and avoid frustrating the player.

So far, all the pickups you've added have been on the floor. This implies that if players are looking for a pickup, they need to look for it on the floor. You want to change that and get players to investigate the level more fully by placing the next pickup on one of the smaller crates.

Chapter 12: Adding a Few Details *177*

Figure 12-28: It's often more fun to hunt for your pickups than to have them placed out in the open.

Machine gun

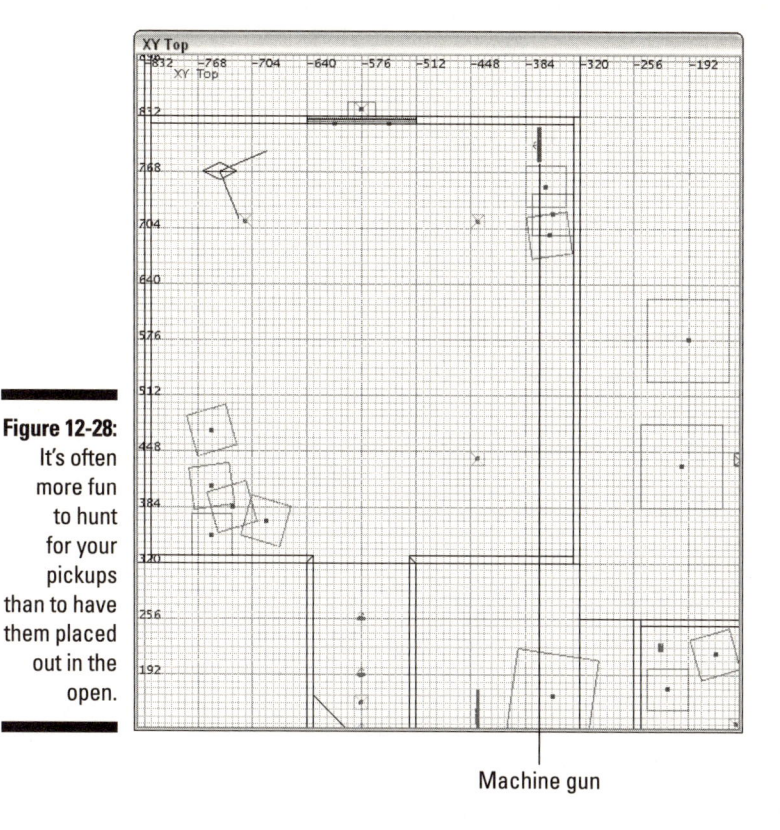

1. **Place some shotgun ammo on the edge of one of the crates in the blue room in the lower-left corner, as shown in Figure 12-29. Right-click in the 2D window and choose pickup⇨ammo⇨ammo_shotgun.**

   By placing the shotgun ammo far away from the shotgun itself, you force the player to go elsewhere in the level to restock. This also helps the players in case they run out while on the run. Make sure the ammo is sitting on top of the crate near the edge so that it's easier for them to pick it up as they run by.

2. **Place some machine gun ammo on the crate in the lower-left corner of the red room. Right-click in the 2D window and choose pickup⇨ammo⇨ammo_machinegun.**

   This is another place that could use some player action, and adding ammo here helps with that goal.

   When you place the ammo, make sure you move it toward the edge of the crate so the player doesn't have to reach for it in the game. Figure 12-30 shows how I placed it.

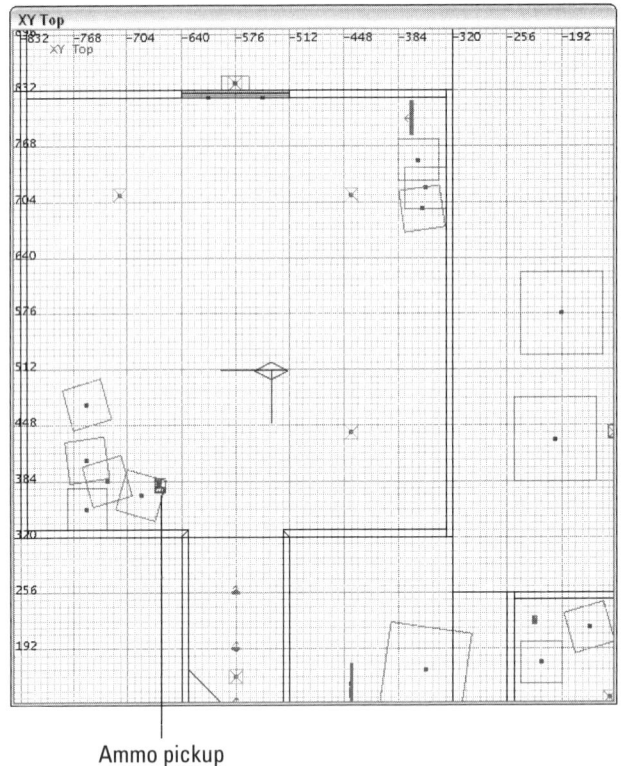

Figure 12-29: Placing ammo or other pickups at different heights encourages the player to look up rather than at the floor all the time.

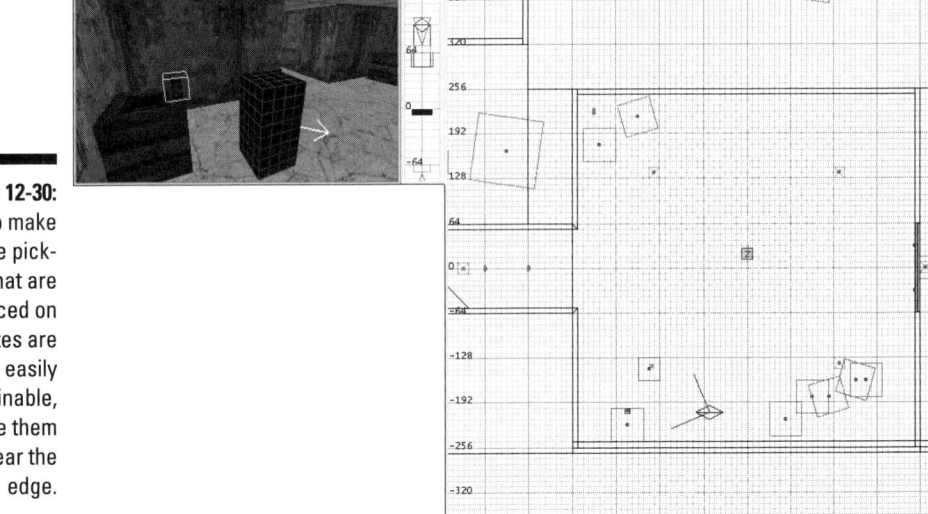

Ammo pickup

Figure 12-30: To make sure pickups that are placed on crates are easily obtainable, place them near the edge.

3. **Place some rail gun ammo in the upper-left corner of the blue room like in Figure 12-31. Right-click in the 2D window and choose pickup⇨ammo⇨ammo_railgun.**

      After you've placed it on the floor, angle the entity toward the center of the room for better visibility. Again, this is far away from the location of the rail gun and might also spark some interest in a player to go looking for the weapon.

Powering up

Because you're building a *Quake 4* multiplayer level, you need to add a *power pickup* (also called a *power-up*). Power pickups are one of the game's signature items. This type of pickup gives the player special abilities such as super-strength (xquad damage), super-speed (haste), or invisibility (invisibility).

For this map, the best power-up is *haste*. Any other power-up would give one player too much of an advantage over the others in this small level. Add this entity to the most visible spot in the map in the upper-right quadrant, as shown in Figure 12-32. Here it will get the most visibility from players so they know either where to get it or where someone else will be coming to get it. To place the haste, right-click in the 2D window and choose pickup⇨powerup⇨powerup_haste.

When you place this item, don't place it directly on the ground just yet. Before you do that, there is something else that you will be adding to the map to make this pickup even more special. However, for now, set the entity's angle to 225 so that it faces the center of the map.

Placing a model to decorate the power-up

The power-up by itself will look great in this level. However, there is more you can do to dress up its presentation. Instead of leaving the power-up on the ground, place it on a platform. And, instead of building a platform from brushes, place a platform that has been already built as a model by the developers of the game.

> **TIP** Some of what you see in the game is actually constructed as a *model*. These models are built in separate programs such as Lightwave or 3D Studio Max. The models are then exported in a special format that is recognized by the game.

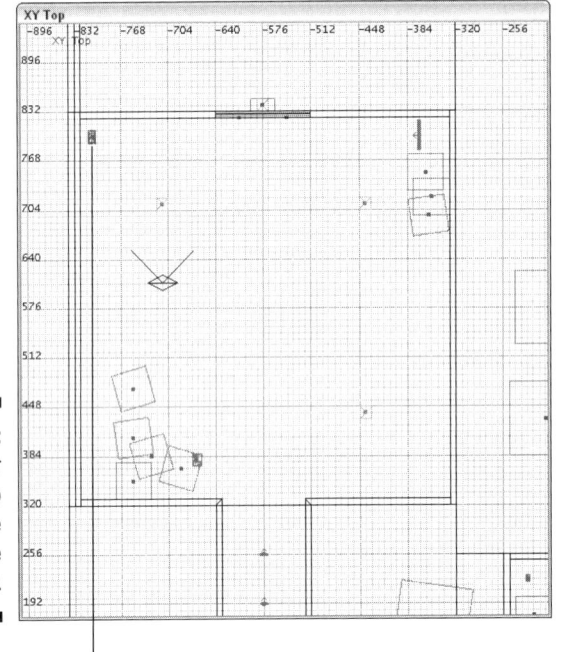

Figure 12-31: Orient your pickups so that they are visible to the player.

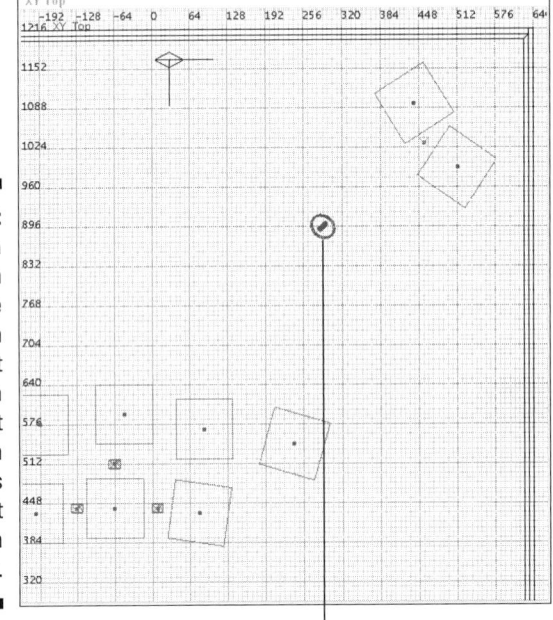

Ammo pickup

Figure 12-32: Place a power-up in the middle of the open area. It could be a great addition to a player's arsenal or it could be a great trap.

Power-up

Chapter 12: Adding a Few Details   181

To place a model in your map, follow these steps:

1. **Right-click your 2D window in the area where you want the object to be placed. From the menu, choose New Model.**

   This opens a dialog box. Within it, you find a single folder icon named base, a black window below it, and a comment box to the right, as shown in Figure 12-33. This is where you can locate and select the model to be placed in your map.

   After it opens, the model's dialog box sometimes takes a few moments before it displays anything for you. This is because when you press the button, the editor must load the list of models available for you to select. This delay is normal.

2. **Expand the base folder and subsequent folders by pressing the plus icon next to it. Use this method to choose base⇨models⇨mapobjects⇨ multiplayer⇨mpbase_hard_edges.lwo.**

   When you select your model, an image is displayed in the black window below the list. This is a preview of the model, as shown in Figure 12-34. Although your preview is small and difficult to see now, the following commands allow you to inspect the model more closely:

   - Rotate Model: Left-click and drag in the dialog box.
   - Move Model: Right-click and drag in the dialog box.
   - Zoom Model: Alt+right-click and drag in the dialog box.

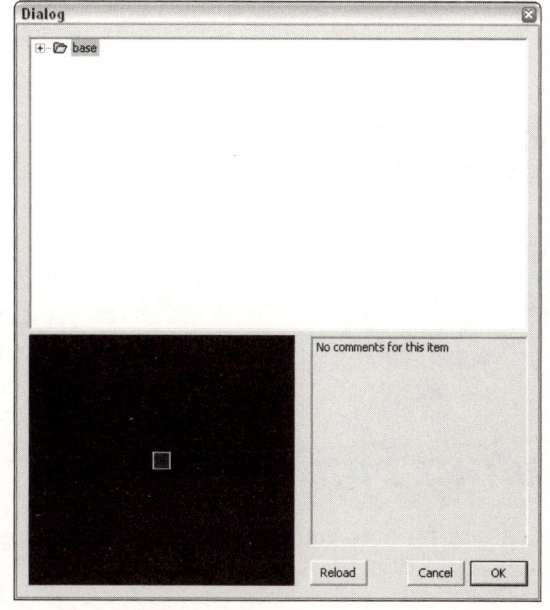

Figure 12-33: Adding a model to your map is as easy as adding an entity.

Part III: Expanding Your Creation

3. **With the `mpbase_hard_edges.lwo` model selected, press OK.**

    This inserts your model into the map as a `func_static` entity.

4. **Move the model onto the ground and under the power-up.**

    When you're done, it should look like Figure 12-35.

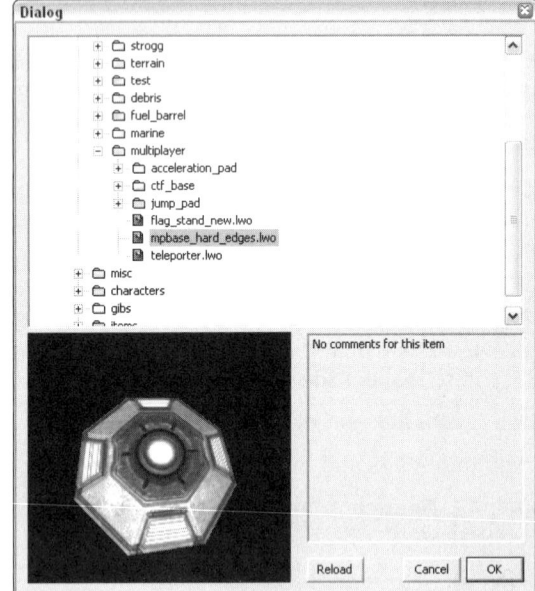

Figure 12-34: Placing this model under a power-up alerts a player to where its spawning point is in the map.

Figure 12-35: As you can see, this model adds to the validity of the power-up.

Testing and Having Fun

That takes care of your map for now. You add more to it in the subsequent chapters.

Chapter 12: Adding a Few Details 183

Compile your map by running the BSP command. Then load it in the game and check it out as a player. It might feel like everything is running slower than normal, but that's because you're still testing in single-player mode. That's going to change in the next chapter, where you add the multiplayer spawn points.

One more thing you might be interested in checking out with your new level is its optimization. When you were placing many of the detailed brushes, such as the crates, light fixtures, and so forth, you turned the brushes into `func_static` entities. You made this change to avoid splitting your geometry, which would slow down your level. As I discuss in Chapter 10, you can enter the console commands to view how the game is rendering the level. The commands are

- `r_showtris 2`
- `r_usescissor 0`
- `r_showportals 1`

After you enter these commands into the console, your map should display the outlines of everything it is rendering for the player. The results should look like Figure 12-36 with simple geometry and not too much of the level being drawn all at once.

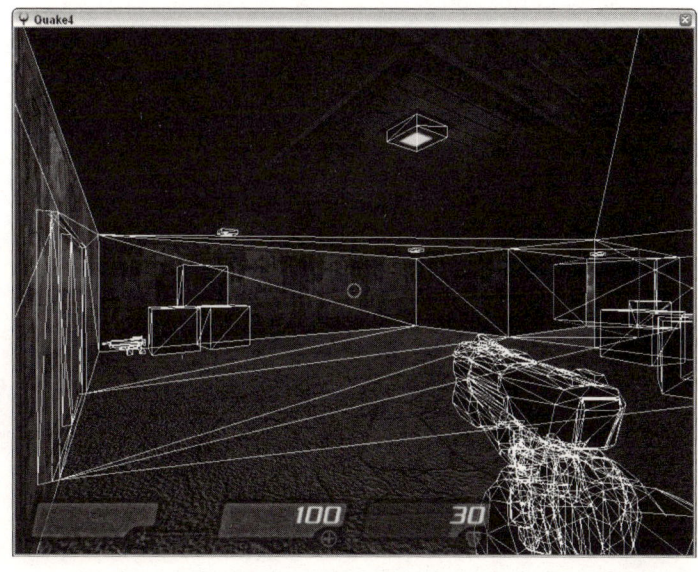

Figure 12-36: Your func_static entities don't split your other brushes, and you retain a well-optimized level.

Chapter 13

Playing Alone or with Someone Else

In This Chapter
▸ Inserting single-player and mutliplayer opponents
▸ Constructing a map for all game types
▸ Making a definition file so the game can find your map
▸ Creating a custom loading screen for your map

*Q*uake games have always focused on player-versus-player action. Some games can put you in the position of solving puzzles, which doesn't require interaction with another player, alive or virtual, but that has never been the focus of the *Quake* franchise. Instead, the *Quake* player's objective is to be on the winning team or to be the last man standing.

Opponents can be broken down into two main classes. For single-player games, the opponents are the Strogg aliens. In multiplayers games, the opponents are other players connected to the game server. Players in multiplayer games can play for themselves (in *deathmatches*) or be organized into teams (for *team deathmatches, capture-the-flag,* or *arena capture-the-flag* play), depending on the game type specified by the server.

In the earlier chapters, your focus was on building a multiplayer level. However, I don't want to completely ignore the single-player aspect of the game. In this chapter, I first show you how to add enemies to your single-player map and then move into the multiplayer game types. Feel free to skip ahead to your section of choice.

Adding Single-Player Enemies

Although the focus of this book has been on creating a multiplayer map, you have been play-testing the compiled levels in single-player mode. The primary difference between single-player and multiplayer levels is the type of spawn points inserted into the map. If you have only a single-player spawn point in your map (as the map `chapter12.map` does), it can be played only in single-player mode.

What's missing from this map are enemies for your player to battle. The enemies could be any of the many classes of Strogg or even the huge mechanical monsters that you might remember from the game. I show you how to add these virtual players to your map.

Inserting a Strogg

Load the map from the last chapter into the radiant editor. This map currently has a single-player spawn point for your player. So, you can spawn into the level, but enemies can't; there are no entities defining where the enemy will spawn. This is what you will add now.

I show you how to add one Strogg enemy inside the building of your level and then add another, larger enemy to the outside area. You add them as entities. Then you will adjust the properties of these entities so that they aren't active until you tell them to be active — otherwise, they will start hunting you down from the moment you start your game.

1. **Focus your editor on the blue room of the map.**

    This is where you will add the first Strogg enemy for your player to encounter.

2. **Right-click the 2D window and add the entity by choosing monster⇨ monster_strogg_marine.**

3. **Adjust the entity's position so that it is resting on or slightly above the floor but not sticking inside of any of the other brushes. Then move this entity so that it is behind the boxes in the lower-left corner of the room, as shown in Figure 13-1.**

    This is a good hiding place for the enemy to emerge from when the player gets close.

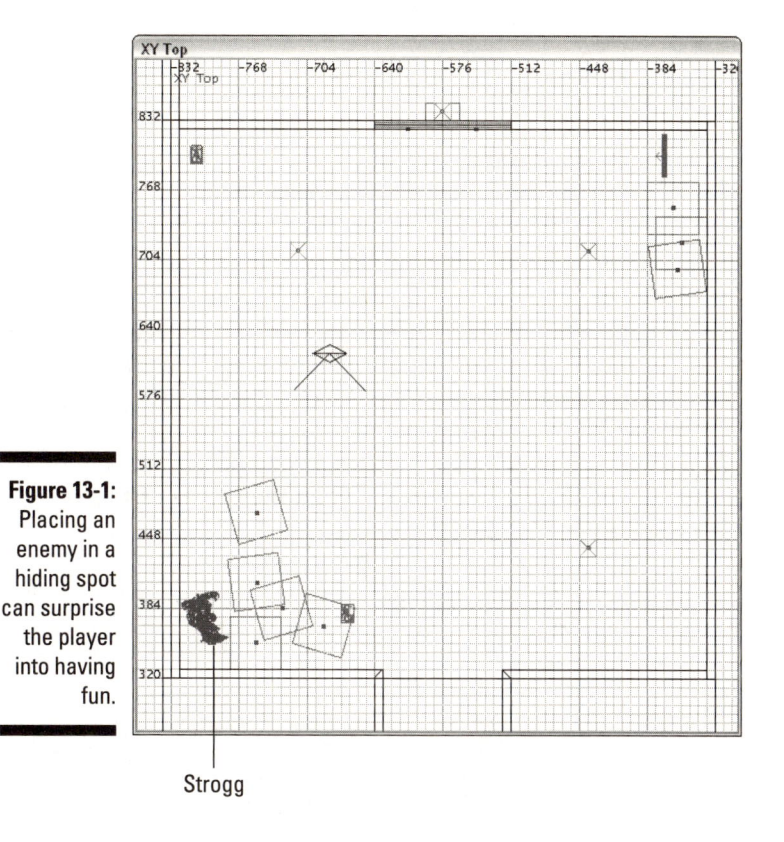

Chapter 13: Playing Alone or with Someone Else 187

Figure 13-1: Placing an enemy in a hiding spot can surprise the player into having fun.

Strogg

If you play-test this level in the game, you'll be able to fight this enemy. However, you won't have to approach the enemy first. Rather, you will be close enough when you spawn in the game that the Strogg will sense your location and come looking for you. I also show you how to add a trigger that tells the enemies *when* to come looking for you. This adds to the level of surprise. *Triggers* are entities that you create in much the same way you create a door in a map. You create a brush that acts as the trigger, apply a special trigger texture, and then turn it into a trigger entity.

The enemy entities are set up to respond to a trigger if one is specified. The trigger in this case is an entity that is activated when the player walks through it. Other triggers could be based on the action or reaction of any entity in the game (like a door or enemy) or based on scripting commands like those covered in Chapter 14. If you add this trigger entity to the level and specify the trigger's name in the enemy's entity, the enemy will come to life only when the player walks through this trigger.

Because there are two ways into this room, you need to add two triggers. This ensures that the enemy is made active regardless of the path the player takes to get into this room.

To create the first trigger, follow these steps:

1. **Load the Common texture set to find the trigger texture.**

2. **Deselect everything in your map and then select the texture common/trigonce.**

    This texture allows you to create a trigger that works only once. Because your enemy has moved after you trigger it in the game, there is no reason to keep triggering it to come after you every time you pass through the trigger.

3. **Draw a brush in the middle of the hallway closest to the room with the enemy. Make the brush large enough that the player can't get around it, as I've done in Figure 13-2.**

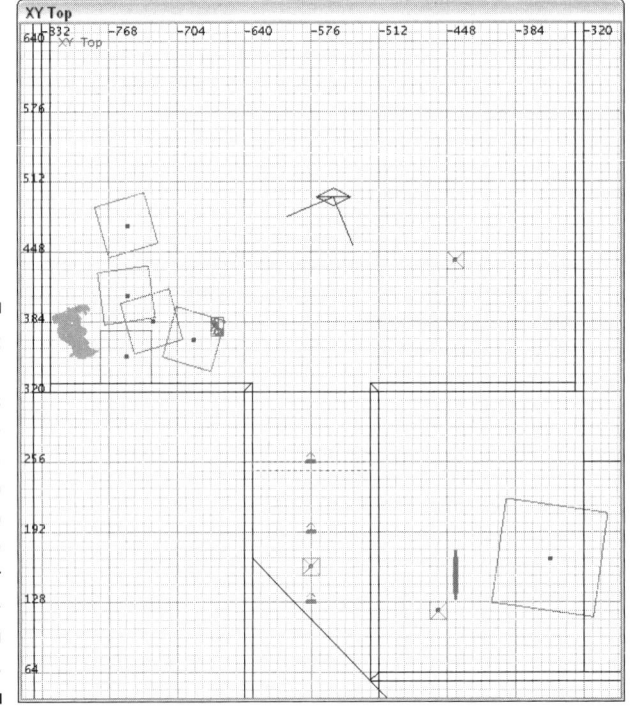

Figure 13-2: Creating triggers for the monsters in your map can help you to time their appearances in your level.

Chapter 13: Playing Alone or with Someone Else 189

You don't want the player to be able to jump over, crawl under, or squeeze by this trigger so that he leaves the enemy standing still in the other room. Yes, triggers can't be seen by the player, but it doesn't mean they can't attempt to avoid them.

4. **With the trigger brush selected, right-click the 2D window to open the entity list.**
5. **Choose trigger**⇨**trigger_once.**
6. **With the trigger entity still selected, select the enemy you are going to activate with your trigger.**

   This enemy is called the *target* because you are targeting it with your trigger.

7. **Press Ctrl+K to target the entity with the trigger.**

   Proof of such targeting will be an orange line drawn between the two entities along with an arrow indicating the direction of targeting, like shown in Figure 13-3.

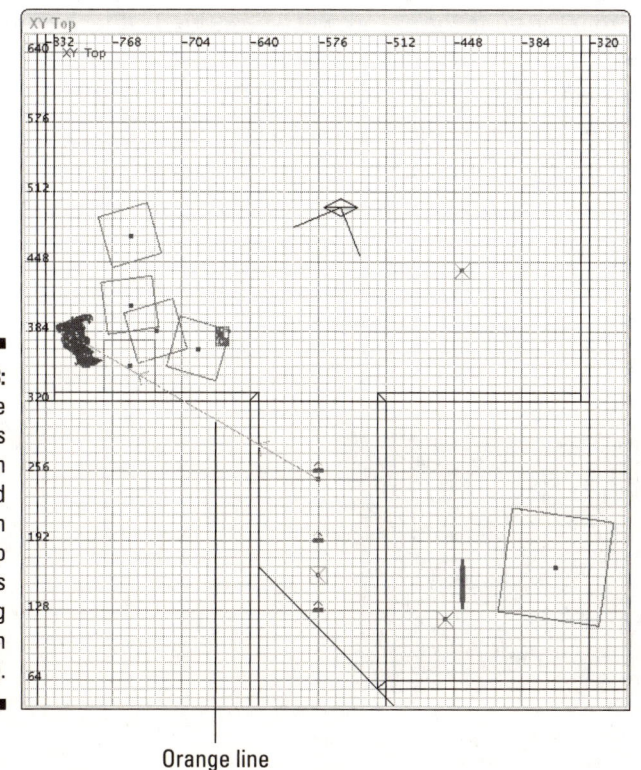

Figure 13-3: An orange line appears between targeted entities in your map with arrows indicating the direction of targeting.

Orange line

Another way you could have defined the target would have been to enter it manually into the entity tab for that trigger. To see what I mean, open the entity editor for the trigger entity and scroll through the list of keys and values that have been defined. One of the values listed after having created a target link with the shortcut is `monster_strogg_marine_1`. This happens to be the entity name of the enemy that you targeted. This key and value combination could have been typed into the Key and Val fields of the entity editor rather than having used the shortcut.

That takes care of one trigger entity. Now you need to create a second one in front and outside of the door leading into this room.

1. **Deselect everything and reselect the `common/trigonce` texture.**

2. **Draw another trigger brush along the doors on the outside of the room. Size the brush so that the player cannot get through the doors without passing through this brush. Also, stretch this brush about 32 units from the door entrance, as you see in Figure 13-4.**

   As you might have noticed, the doors open as the player approaches them rather than when the player touches them. By making the trigger extend from the door, the enemy will be triggered either before or as the doors open.

3. **With this new trigger brush selected, right-click the 2D window and choose trigger⇨trigger_once.**

4. **Select the enemy entity and press Ctrl+K to target it.**

   The result should be a second target line leading from the new trigger entity and landing on the enemy entity, as in Figure 13-5.

Figure 13-4: When placing triggers near doors, make them large enough to activate the trigger before or at the time of the doors opening.

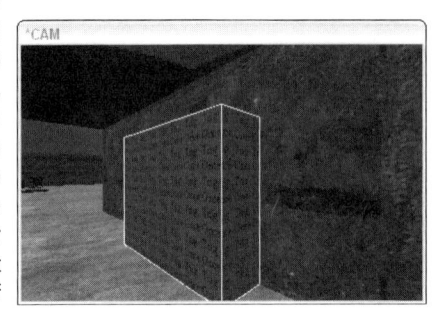

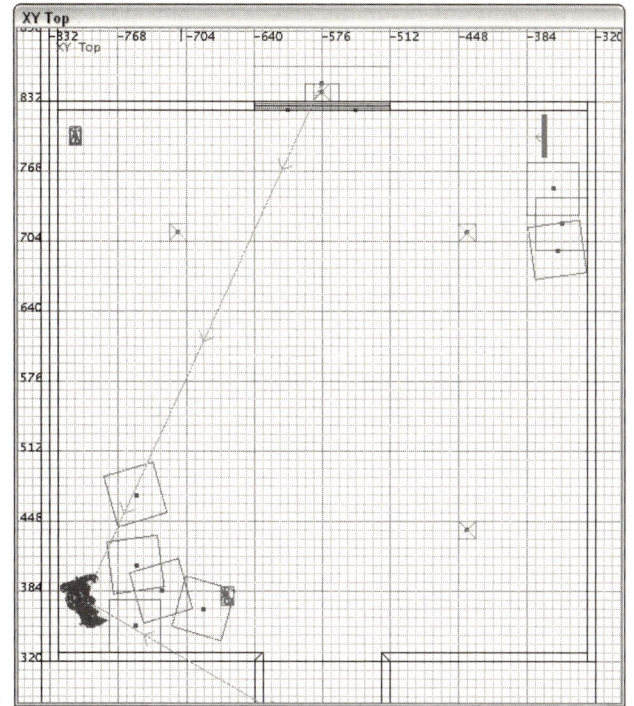

Chapter 13: Playing Alone or with Someone Else *191*

Figure 13-5:
An entity can have multiple triggers.

The last step in setting this enemy to activate based on a trigger is to define it in the enemy's entity properties.

 5. **Select only the enemy entity and open the Entity tab.**

 6. **Enter** target **into the Key field and enter 1 into the Val field, like in Figure 13-6. Then press Enter.**

    This step turns on the property that this entity is not to be activated until it is triggered.

 7. **Enter** hide **into the Key field and enter 1 into the Val field, like in Figure 13-6. Then press Enter.**

    This step hides the monster until it is triggered.

    It isn't necessary to hide the monster entity when it's triggered. However, if you don't hide the monster at all, the game will report an error when it loads your map, but it will still allow you to play the level regardless of the error. Hiding the monster prevents the error from coming up in the console.

Part III: Expanding Your Creation

Now when you go to play the level, the enemy remains dormant while you explore the area. When you cross over either of the two triggers, however, the enemy comes to life and attacks you.

Figure 13-6: Setting the target to 1 instructs the monster to wait until it is triggered.

Inserting a gladiator

Because the outside area is larger and provides more cover for the player, a more formidable enemy should be placed there. The gladiator is a good choice for this location. This is a large enemy for a large area.

1. **In the outside area, near where the power-up has been placed, insert a `monster_gladiator` by right-clicking the 2D window and choosing monster➪monster_gladiator from the list of entities.**

2. **Position this monster in the open area of this corner and make sure that it isn't inside of any brushes, but that it is placed on top of the ground, as in Figure 13-7.**

Figure 13-7: Larger areas call for larger monsters, such as this gladiator.

3. **Adjust the angle of the entity from within the Entity tab so that it is facing the center of the map. The buttons in the Entity tab are positioned in a way that indicates the angle the entity points to. So, to make your enemy face the center of the map, press the 225-angle button.**

The second enemy is now placed. Next, you must add the triggers so that this enemy doesn't hunt you down before you're ready. Because there are two ways out of your spawn location, you need to place two triggers.

Create the first trigger next to the door inside the red room. Here's how:

1. **Deselect everything, select the `common/trigonce` texture, and draw a trigger brush next to the door inside the red room where the player spawns.**

   Make sure the trigger is large enough to cover the door entrance and thick enough that the trigger is activated before or as the door opens. A good thickness is 32 units, as in Figure 13-8.

Figure 13-8: There are multiple ways to get to the gladiator, so remember to set up triggers at each of them.

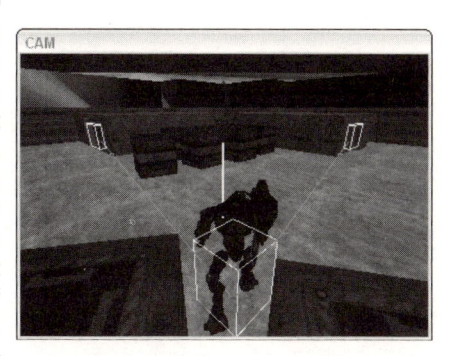

2. **With the trigger brush created, turn it into a `trigger_once` entity by right-clicking the 2D window and choose trigger⇨trigger_once.**

3. **While the trigger entity is still selected, select the monster you want to trigger and press Ctrl+K to define the target.**

For the second trigger, you are going to use this same process. However, this trigger will be placed on the inside of the doors located in the blue room.

1. **Draw your `common/trigonce` textured brush alongside the doors on the inside of the blue room.**

2. **Turn it in to a `trigger_once` entity.**

Part III: Expanding Your Creation

   3. **Target the gladiator with this entity by selecting the gladiator entity after the trigger entity and then pressing Ctrl+K.**

      The result looks like Figure 13-9.

Finally, you must set the properties in the monster so that it will become active only upon being triggered.

   1. **Select only the `monster_gladiator` entity and open the Entity tab.**
   2. **Enter** trigger **in the Key field of and 1 in the Val field. Then press Enter.**
   3. **Enter** hide **in the Key field and 1 in the Val field. Then press Enter.**

Save this map under a new name, `chapter13_sp.map`. Next in this chapter, you add multiplayer components to your map, so naming this current map with `_sp` will help you to later differentiate between your single-player and multiplayer maps.

Now compile the map by using the BSP function, explained in Chapter 8. You're ready to test it in the game.

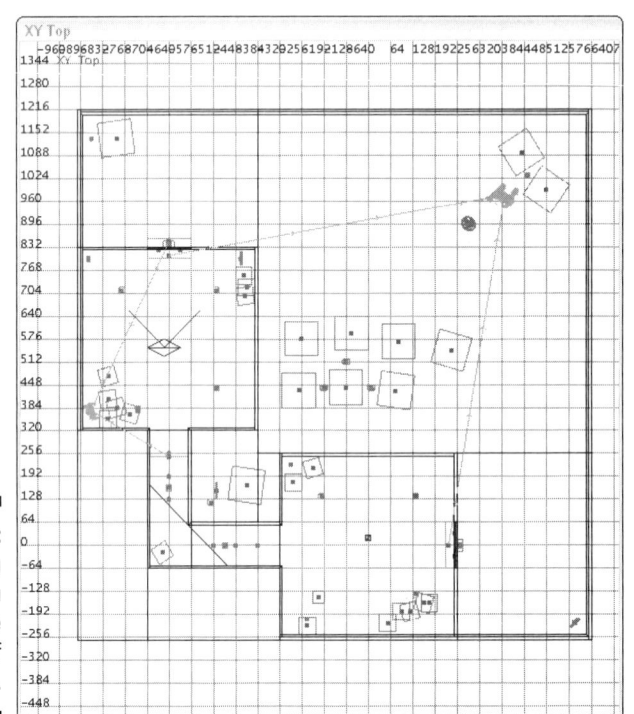

Figure 13-9:
Targeting helps you visualize the actions of your map.

Adding Multiplayer Opponents

In a multiplayer game, you aren't concerned with adding the monster entities that you add in the single-player games. These monsters are not available in the multiplayer game. Instead, you place either deathmatch or team deathmatch spawn points. Whichever one you place depends on the type of game you want. I go over the two types because they are quite similar. Their availability in the game depends only on the type of game that the server started.

> **TIP:** Although you can make only one type of multiplayer map, you can also make a single-player map with multiplayer capabilities. Just add the player spawn entities, and the game will use them appropriately for the game type that is being played.

Generally, however, a single-player level is not used in a multiplayer game. For the following additions and changes, load a previously saved version of the map that doesn't contain the single-player monsters. The map `chapter12.map` should be the one you want to work with.

Playing one-on-one

A *deathmatch* game is a player-versus-player game type. It's a take-no-prisoners, every-man-for-himself kind of game. It's also the most popular type of game found online for *Quake 4*.

The type of map that has been designed up to this point has been for a deathmatch game. It's too small for players to team up and it's been designed so that the players can basically run in a circle either away from their opponent or toward them. This design is going to make it easy to place the spawn points for the deathmatch game type.

A great location for the first deathmatch spawn point is the upper-right corner of the map. Behind that crate, the player can spawn in without being immediately seen by another player, allowing him to figure out where he is before jumping into battle. Here's how to add this spawn point:

1. In the 2D window, right-click the location to bring down the list of entities.
2. Choose info⇨info_player_deathmatch from the list.
3. Make sure the entity is on the surface of the ground and not sticking in any other brushes or entities.

How many spawn points should you use?

The maximum number of players allowed in a *Quake 4* game is 16. In larger maps, I recommend that you place at least 16 spawn points in the event that 16 players try to spawn in at the same time. (Hey, it's possible.) However, you're allowed to place any number that you want, and the game will use what it has available.

4. **Open the Entity tab.**
5. **Select the angle you want the player to be facing when he spawns into the game. Click the 270 button so that the player is facing southwest. The result looks like Figure 13-10.**

    This step is important because you don't want the spawned player to be facing the wall or some other place because this might disorient the player, leading to confusion or frustration.

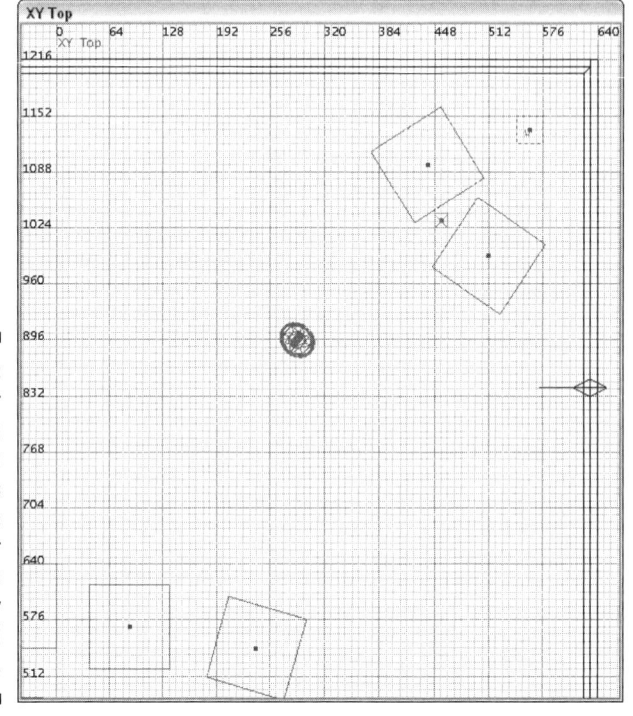

Figure 13-10: Place player spawn points in places where the player won't be immediately spotted and killed.

Chapter 13: Playing Alone or with Someone Else 197

Repeat the process by placing more spawn points around the map. Place them in somewhat hidden locations and make sure they are facing a direction that helps the player orient quickly and begin or continue the fight. Place a total of six deathmatch spawn points in the map and refer to Figure 13-11 for placement ideas within the map. Because the map is so small, it most likely won't be used by more than that number of players, so six would be fine.

When you're done, save this map as `chapter13_mp.map`. Because this is your multiplayer map version, adding `_mp` to the end of the name helps differentiate this map from your single-player version.

Figure 13-11: Here you can see that all these spawn points are well spread out, creating many options for spawning into the game.

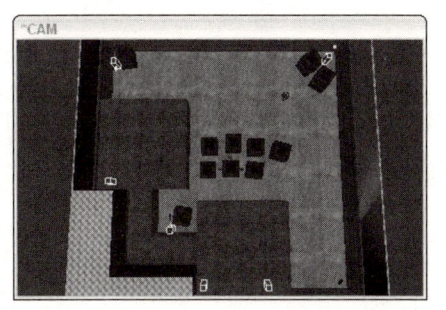

Teaming up with others

Team-based game play is used in a few different game types in *Quake 4*. It's used in team deathmatch, capture the flag (CTF), and arena CTF. In contrast to a player-versus-player environment, you play on one of two teams and fight against the other team of players for domination of either the entire game or a location within the game. Here's a breakdown of these game types:

- **Team Deathmatch:** Two teams fight against each other for the greatest number of kills.
- **Tourney:** Short for *tournament,* this is a game type with one-on-one combat. The winner of each tournament stays for the following round to play against the next player in line while the loser is eliminated. When all players waiting in the tournament line are eliminated, the player remaining wins the tournament.

- **Capture the Flag:** Like team deathmatch except that the object of the game is not to score the most kills but to capture the other team's flag and return it to where your team's flag is located. Each time you capture the opposing team's flag, you receive points, and the team with the most points wins.
- **Arena CTF:** This game plays out the same as Capture the Flag. However, when power-ups are acquired, they remain with the player until the player's death. Only after the player is dead does the power-up respawn where it started.

The most common game type for team play is CTF, so I show you how to place your player spawn points in this fashion. The method for placing spawn points is the same for all team-oriented game types. The only difference is that you have to add an entity that places the team flag used for capture.

Because you have two rooms in your map and they have different color light, you'll use these rooms as bases for your teams. It's important to consider a central location for spawning teams to keep the odds of winning equal between them. In *Quake 4*, the two available teams are Strogg and Marine, so use the red room for the Strogg team and the blue room for the Marine team.

When placing game-type-specific spawn points, you don't have to start a new map or remove anything. Continue working with the same map that you saved with the deathmatch spawn points, `chapter13_mp.map`. Later, you instruct the game how to use this level.

Splitting the map

To use the rooms in your map for team play, it would probably be wise to seal off the hallway. Being able to access the opposing team's base so easily wouldn't be much fun. Using a stack of crates would create an ideal blockade without drastically changing the map. The problem with this idea is that when playing a deathmatch game, the crates will interrupt the flow of the game. This too can be solved after adding your crates.

1. **Create some duplicates of the crates you now have within the rooms and create an impassable blockage in the corner of the hall. If possible, arrange the crates so that each team can see the opposing room, but will be unable to pass through.**

    Figure 13-12 shows an example of how you can do this with four crates. Placing two crates on top of another two crates makes your hallway impassable.

    To solve the problem of the crates being in the way during a deathmatch game, you can instruct the game when to display them and when to hide them. For you to specify these crates with these special properties, they must be entities. Luckily, because you have already made them `func_static` for optimization reasons in Chapter 12, you're already ahead of the game.

Figure 13-12: Divide the map for team games to even the odds of winning and to add fun.

2. **To define when these crates are present in the game, select all three of them.**

   I say three crates because one of them, the one furthest in the corner, can stay where it was and remain visible. This crate doesn't get in the way and makes the hall more interesting.

3. **Open the Entity tab.**

4. **Because you want these crates to show up only during CTF and Arena CTF games, enter the following Keys and Vals:**

Key	Val
filter_CTF	1
filter_Arena CTF	1

   These values tell the game to show these entities only during the filtered game types. So, if you were playing a CTF game, the crates would be there. On the other hand, if you were playing a deathmatch game, the crates wouldn't be there in the players' way. Just make sure that you enter the key exactly as shown or this trick won't work.

   Other available keys for filtering game types are `filter_DM`, `filter_Team DM`, and `filter_Tourney`.

Placing team spawns

Now place some team spawn points around the edges of each room. Place them so that they cannot be seen by players on the other side of the crates within the hallway. Here's how:

1. **In the 2D window, right-click the area you want to place the spawn point and choose info⇨info_player_team.**

2. **Adjust the angle so that the player isn't facing the wall when he spawns into the game and also make sure the player will spawn on the floor.**

The maximum number of players allowed in a *Quake 4* game is 16. So, place eight team spawn points in each room just as you placed the first one. Take a look at Figure 13-13 for placement.

TIP

You can overlap your deathmatch spawn points with your team spawn points. Because each is used only in its specific game type, it doesn't matter whether these entities are overlapping. However, when they overlap, it is not possible to select one entity over the other in the editor without separating them.

Figure 13-13: Place an even number of team spawn points in your map so that their placement ensures some survivability.

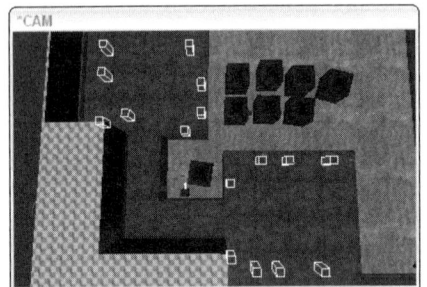

3. **Select all the team player spawn points in the blue room and open the Entity tab.**

   You are now going to define the team to which these players belong. By selecting them all at the same time, any changes made in the Entity tab will be made to all the selected entities at once.

4. **In the Key field, type** team, **and in the Val field, type** marine. **Press Enter when you have finished to apply this setting.**

   This assigns these players to the Marine team.

5. **Deselect these players and select those in the red room.**

6. **In the entity tab in the Key field, type** team, **and in the Val field, type** strogg. **Then press Enter.**

   This assigns these players to the Strogg team.

For a team deathmatch game type, you would be done at this point. You could save, compile, and play the level with your friends. To make it playable as a CTF game type as well, continue with the following sections.

Raising the flags

For a CTF game type, you need to add the flags for capturing.

To add the CTF flag for the two teams, follow these steps:

1. **Focus your editor on the red room. In the center of the room, right-click and choose mp⇨mp_ctf_strogg_flag from the list of entities.**

   When you select the strogg_flag entity, you will see a flat, red marker as in Figure 13-14. Surrounding it, since it is selected, is a white box.

2. **Place the entity so that it rests on the floor and is centered in the room. Once placed, make sure the angle of the flag is set so that anyone running through the doors can see it, which, in this case, is an angle of 360.**

   This angle makes the flag look its best to anyone running into the room. That's it for this flag, now for the other.

3. **Move your focus over to the blue room. Right-click and choose mp⇨mp_ctf_marine_flag.**

4. **Make sure the entity is in the center of the room, but don't worry about it being on the floor at this time. Then set the angle to face the doors in that room, which, in this case, is 90 degrees.**

You have to add one more thing to each room before you're done.

Figure 13-14: Place a CTF flag in each of the rooms, one for each team.

Planting the flags

If you were to play the game as it is in CTF mode, everything would work. However, if the flag were taken, there wouldn't be any marking as to where it used to be placed. If you have played the CTF game type before, you would know that to capture a flag and score a point, you must run your opponent's flag back to the location where your flag is kept. If when you get there your flag is gone and there is nothing marking where the flag used to be, you might not know where to take the opponent's flag to score a point. So, to resolve this issue, all you need to do is place something on the ground under the flag that makes this location more obvious.

In the same location as each of the two flags, place a new model. Here's how:

1. **Right-click the 2D window and choose New Model.**
2. **From the dialog box, choose base⇨models⇨mapobjects⇨multiplayer⇨flag_stand_new.lwo, as shown in Figure 13-15. Press OK when selected to insert it into your map.**

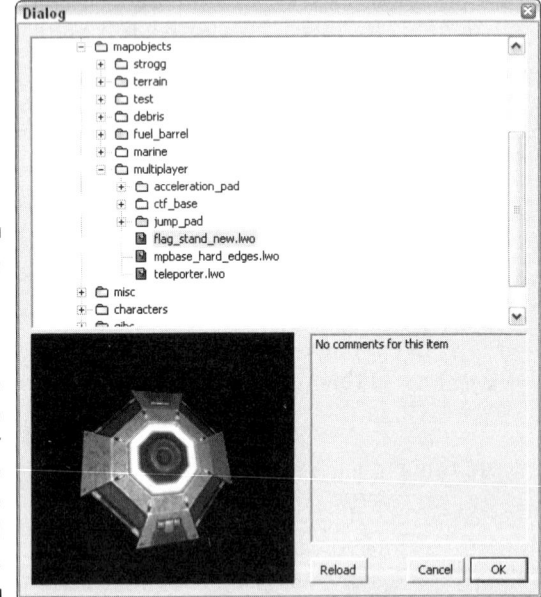

Figure 13-15: Under each flag, place a flag stand model to indicate to the player where the flags are supposed to be.

3. **Place your new model on the ground. Then move the flag up so that it sits on top of the model rather than inside of it.**

   The flag shouldn't be hovering too high over the model, and it shouldn't be overlapping the new model you just inserted. See Figure 13-16 for how it should look.

   That takes care of one flag. Now you need another flag model under the other flag. Rather than going through the process of adding a new model, simply duplicate and move the one you have.

4. **Select only the new model, `flag_stand_new.lwo`.**
5. **Press the spacebar to duplicate it and then move it into position under the other flag. Once placed, move the flag to sit on top of the model.**

Chapter 13: Playing Alone or with Someone Else

Now, you need to do one more thing before you're done fiddling with these new models under the flags. Just like the crates in the hall, you need to hide these models in deathmatch games. Having these flag-base models in a deathmatch game won't make sense because there are no flags. So, hide them by filtering them from the deathmatch games.

1. **Select both models at the same time.**

    Because the same properties are being added to them both, you can make the same changes to them both at the same time.

Figure 13-16: Make sure your models are on the ground and that the flags are on top and not inside the models they sit upon.

2. **Open the Entity tab.**
3. **Enter** filter_CTF **in the Key field and 1 in the Val field, and then press Enter.**
4. **Enter** filter_Arena CTF **in the Key field and 1 in the Val field, and then press Enter.**

    Your Entity tab looks like Figure 13-17. The resulting two models are displayed in the game only during the arena CTF and regular CTF games.

Save this map over the existing one as `chapter13_mp.map`. You now have another game type complete.

> **TIP:** If you decide to compile and play-test your new map in a multiplayer mode, you must completely exit and close the game before going back to the editor. If you don't close down the game before making changes to your level, the new changes won't be saved. This is because the game is protecting what it believes to be an open map file after running in the game.

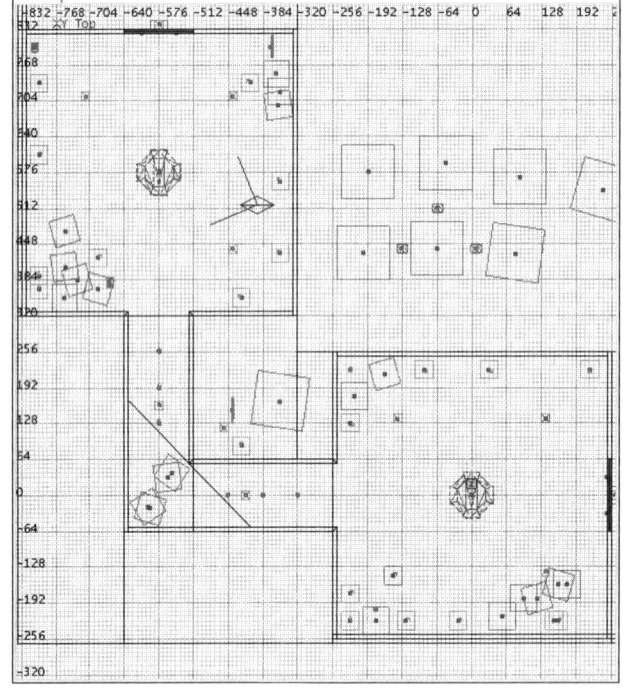

Figure 13-17: Even placement of the flags and spawn points makes for even game play.

Playing Multiplayer Levels

When testing your new multiplayer level in the game, don't bother looking for the new level in the list provided by the game's interface; you won't find it there. The game doesn't yet know where your new level is located, so it isn't listed as being available for play. To solve this, you need to create a definition file for your new level.

Defining your level

A *definition file* is just a text file that defines the different features offered by your level. When the game loads, it loads all the definition files and presents the loaded information to the player. In the case of your level, it presents the information provided in your definition file within the list of available maps that you can load in a multiplayer game.

Chapter 13: Playing Alone or with Someone Else 205

To create a definition file for your two new game types, run a simple text editor application such as Notepad. You can find this program in your list of program for Windows by opening the Start menu and choosing All Programs➪Accessories➪Notepad.

In Notepad, type the following lines of code:

```
mapDef game/chapter13_mp {
    "name"                          "Chapter 13"
    "DM"                            "1"
    "Team DM"                       "1"
    "Tourney"                       "0"
    "CTF"                           "1"
    "Arena CTF"                     "0"
    "Gametype_Deathmatch"           "1"
    "Gametype_TeamDeathmatch"       "1"
    "Gametype_Tournament"           "0"
    "Gametype_CaptureTheFlag"       "1"
    "Gametype_ArenaCaptureTheFlag"  "0"
    "loadimage"                     ""
    "mp_thumb"                      ""
    "size0"                         "0"
    "size1"                         "0"
    "size2"                         "0"
    "size3"                         "0"
}
```

The first line tells the game that this is a map definition and that the name of the map under which it was saved is `game/chapter13_mp`. This is the same name that you would load when testing the level within the game, and the name of this definition must match. To highlight the lines of code that you must enter to make this a valid definition, follow this list:

- name: This is the name of the map you want displayed in the list. You can name this any way that you want, but try to avoid using a long name.

- DM and `Gametype_Deathmatch`: Set this value to 1 if the map can be used as a deathmatch game type or 0 if it cannot.

- `Team DM` and `Gametype_TeamDeathmatch`: Set this value to 1 if it can be used as a team deathmatch game type or 0 if it cannot. Because this level has been created to work as a deathmatch game type, it is set with a value of 1.

- `Tourney` and `Gametype_Tournament`: Set this value to 1 if it can be used as a tournament game type or 0 if it cannot.

- ✓ `CTF` and `Gametype_CaptureTheFlag`: Set this value to 1 if it can be used as a CTF game type or 0 if it cannot. Because this level has been created to work as a CTF game type as well as a deathmatch, it is set with a value of 1.
- ✓ `Arena CTF` and `Gametype_ArenaCaptureTheFlag`: Set this value to 1 if it can be used as an arena CTF game type or 0 if it cannot.
- ✓ `loadimage`: This is a specially formatted image that is displayed while the level is loading. Leave this value blank for now.
- ✓ `mp_thumb`: This is a specially formatted image that is displayed when the level is selected to be loaded. Leave this value blank for now.
- ✓ `size0-3`: This is the amount of information that is loaded by the game, and it influences how the load bar is displayed while the level is loading. Leave this value at 0 for now.

With your definition file created, you need to save it to a location where the game will find it.

1. **Choose File**⇨**Save in Notepad.**
2. **In the Save As dialog box, navigate the folders until you reach `C:\Program Files\id Software\Quake 4\q4base`.**
3. **Here, create a new folder called def, and then open this new folder.**
4. **Save your file in the def folder under the same name as your level but with a `.def` extension. Because your level is named `chapter13_mp`, save your file as `chapter13_mp.def`.**
5. **To see your level listed in the game, close the game and editor if they are open. Then launch the game again.**
6. **Select MULTIPLAYER and then CREATE SERVER.**

   Here, at the end of the list of available maps, you will now find your map listed.

   Because you did not define a thumbnail image to be displayed, the default *Quake 4* image will be shown when you select your new level. When loading the level, no image will be displayed, and the loading bar won't change. None of these additional features are required by the game, but I explore them in the following sections because you may want to include them on your own.

Making a custom loading screen

As you might have noticed, when you load your new multiplayer level from within the game, you don't have a loading image. Instead, you just see a *Quake 4* logo on the screen where the image would display, as is the case in Figure 13-18.

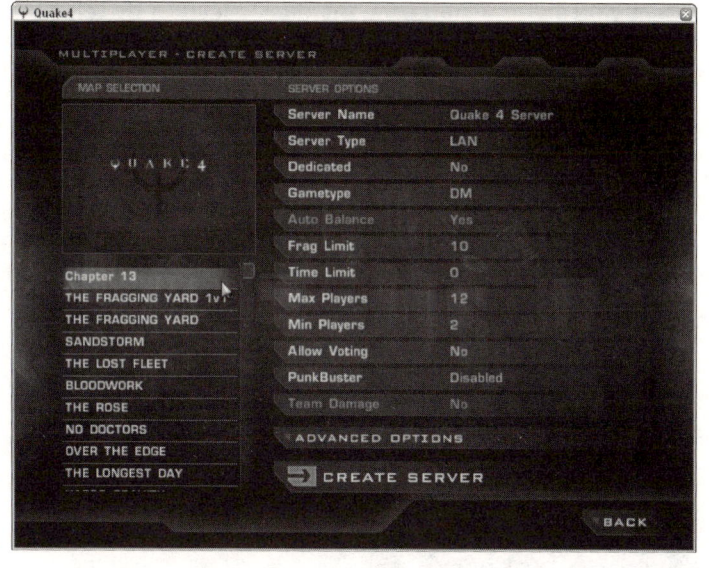

Figure 13-18: The default *Quake 4* logo is used when you don't have a thumbnail image displayed for your level.

I show you how you can create a custom image that is displayed in this area. To keep things simple, the loading image will use a screenshot of your custom level and have the name of the level written in text across the image.

To start, you need to take a screenshot of your level from within the game. A *screenshot* is a picture of what you see on your screen. The game allows you to take screenshots automatically saved in TGA image format in a folder on your computer. By default, the game has set F12 as your screenshot shortcut key. This can be changed from within the game's control settings. If F12 is no longer your screenshot command, check your game options to see what the new command is. You can do this by pressing Esc to get to the game menu, choosing Settings➪Game Controls, and then selecting the Attack/Look tab. This screen displays your keyboard command for screenshots. To take this shot, close the editor, if it's open, and start the game. When it's loaded, follow these steps:

1. **Select MULTIPLAYER.**
2. **Select CREATE SERVER.**
3. **On the right side of the screen, select**
   - Server Type: LAN
   - Dedicated: No
   - Gametype: CTF

4. **Select your custom map from the map selection by selecting it from the list on the left.**

 5. **Click CREATE SERVER to start the game.**

 6. **Now that you are in your game, press F7 to change to Spectator mode.**

    From this mode, you can often find a better angle to take your screenshot.

 7. **Move about your level by using your standard keyboard controls, looking for the picture you want to use in your custom loading screen. When you're ready, press F12 (or whatever your assigned keyboard shortcut is) to take a screenshot, as I have in Figure 13-19.**

Figure 13-19: Position yourself for the most interesting screenshot of your level.

After you've taken your screenshot, close the game. It's now time to edit the image and save it in a format that the game can recognize.

 1. **Load your favorite image-editing program.**

    I recommend using Adobe Photoshop because you need to use a program that can edit TGA image files.

 2. **From within the image program, load the screenshot file that was taken within the game. You will find it in the folder `C:\Program Files\id Software\Quake 4\q4base\screenshots`.**

    Only game screenshots are stored in this folder, so you should be able to find it easily. Because I have only one screenshot in my folder, the file I will open is `shot00001.tga`.

Chapter 13: Playing Alone or with Someone Else 209

3. **Using a text tool, dress up the image by adding some text.**

    This step isn't necessary, but it's a good place to promote not only the level name, but also you as the author. Add the level name and your name and anything else you would like to include. You can look at Figure 13-20 for an idea of what to write.

TIP

To make it easier for you to place text on your screenshot, use the Adobe Photoshop PSD file named `loadscreen_Template.psd`, provided on the attached CD-ROM. When the level is loaded (as shown in Figure 13-21), the game adds a border that might cover over the text or other edits you have planned. To make adding text easier, just replace my screenshot with yours in the provided file, make your changes, hide the *Quake 4 borders* layer by clicking on the eye icon to the left of the layer in the Layers tab, and then continue with sizing and saving your final image.

Figure 13-20: Edit the screenshot in any way that you choose. You can promote yourself and your mapping skills by signing your level here.

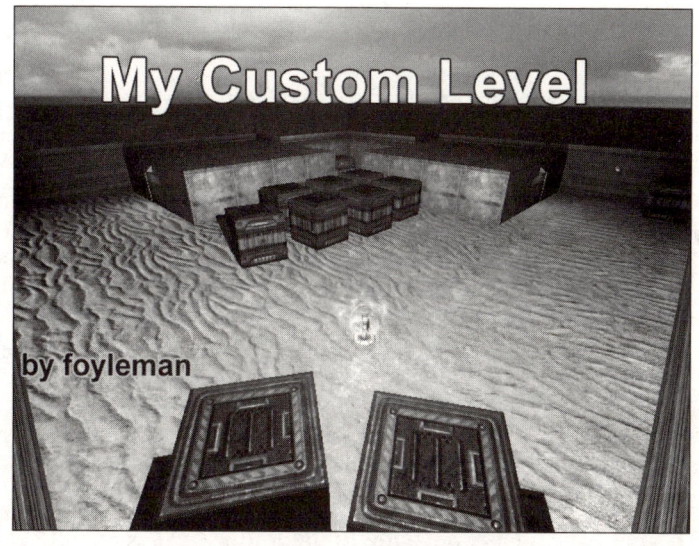

When you have the image you want, you need to resize it for the game. The image size required for the loading screen is 512 x 512 pixels, and your screenshot is currently equal to the resolution for your game. If your game was set to 1024 x 768, the screenshot size will be the same.

Now, what many people fail to remember is that the loading-screen image is stretched by the game back to its current resolution. This means that the image you save as 512 x 512 is resized back to 1024 x 768. This resizing can create stretching and make it look unnatural. To fix this problem, simply resize your image without cropping it. Don't cut the image down to the required size but rather resize it.

> **Hiding the HUD**
>
> If you want to hide the text and other things showing up on the screen, you need to hide the HUD (Heads Up Display) by using a console command. Open the console and type **g_showHud 0**. Press Enter and close the console, and you will have the perfect screen for taking pictures.
>
> If you reopen the game after hiding the HUD, the HUD might not be there. The HUD will return when you completely close the game and editor and restart the game. Or, you can open the console and type **g_showHud 1** to unhide the HUD.

If you're using Adobe Photoshop, the correct process to resize your image while retaining its quality is as follows:

1. **Flatten the image by choosing Layer⇨Flatten Image from the program menu.**

   In Photoshop, layers are used to make editing an image simple. However, if you applied any special filters to the text in your image, such as a shadow effect, the filter will distort the final image when you resize it.

2. **Resize the image to 512 x 512 pixels. You can do this by choosing Image⇨Image Size. To obtain the correct proportions, deselect the Constrain Proportion check box in the image resize box. Enter 512 pixels as the width and 512 pixels as the height. Then press OK to apply the changes.**

   The image is now properly sized for the game even though it might look a little bit squished. It's time to save it to a specific folder.

   The folder you need to save the image in doesn't yet exist on your hard drive, so you need to create the new folder. You can create this folder while saving your image from the Save Image dialog box.

3. **To save your image, navigate to the folder `C:\Program Files\id Software\Quake 4\q4base`.**

   This will probably be one folder up from where you were prompted to save because you had originally opened this file from the screenshots folder `C:\Program Files\id Software\Quake 4\q4base\screenshots`.

4. **From within the q4base folder, create a new folder called gfx and then enter that folder. From the gfx folder, create a new folder called guis and then enter that folder. Then, from the guis folder, create one more folder called loadscreens.**

5. **Enter the loadscreens folder and save your TGA image file as `chapter13_mp.tga`. If you are prompted to select a resolution for your TGA image, select 24bits/pixel.**

   The result should be a TGA image file located at `C:\Program Files\id Software\Quake 4\q4base\gfx\guis\loadscreens\chapter13_mp.tga`.

   Finally, to make this image show on the screen during the loading of your level, you must define the `loadimage` value in your definition file.

6. **Open the definition file you created earlier for this level in Notepad. In the empty value for `loadimage`, enter** gfx/guis/loadscreens/chapter13_mp.

   Take note that instead of using backslashes as Windows does in File Explorer, the image location has been entered with forward slashes. Also, the image file extension has been left off because it isn't required by the game.

Now, when you're loading your level in the game, you will be greeted with a picture of your level, as you see in Figure 13-21.

Creating a thumbnail image

Because you've just completed the loading screen image, making the level thumbnail is a snap. All you need to do is resize the image in your image editor to 256 x 256 pixels square.

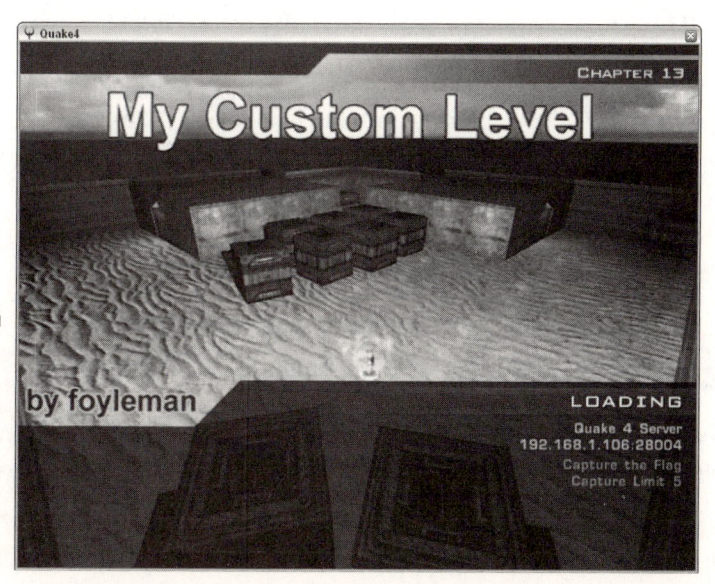

Figure 13-21: Now, when the game loads, your screenshot will be displayed.

1. **Open the image you want to use as a thumbnail, and if you're using Adobe Photoshop, choose Image⇨Image Size.**

    You can use the same image that you used to create the custom loading screen.

 2. **Enter** 256 **as the new width and** 256 **as the new height.**

    Press OK to apply the changes, and the image is ready to be saved. Again, saving the image requires the creation of another folder in the *Quake 4* game folder structure.

 3. **Navigate to the folder** `C:\Program Files\id Software\Quake 4\q4base\gfx\guis`**. Create a new folder here called mainmenu and open it.**

    This is where you save your new image under the same name as your map, `chapter13_mp.tga`. If you are prompted to select a resolution for your TGA image, select 24bits/pixel. The result should be a TGA image file located at `C:\Program Files\id Software\Quake 4\q4base\gfx\guis\mainmenu\chapter13_mp.tga`.

    Although your loading-screen image doesn't have to be named the same as your map name, the thumbnail image must be. If it is named anything other than the same name as your map, it won't display in the game.

    Next, to make this image show when your level is selected from the list, you must to define the `mp_thumb` value in your definition file.

 4. **Open the definition file.**

    You created and saved this file in the *Quake 4 def* folder, `C:\Program Files\id Software\Quake 4\def\chapter13_mp.def`.

 5. **In the empty value for** `mp_thumb` **enter** gfx/guis/mainmenu/chapter13_mp**.**

    Again, instead of using backslashes as Windows does in File Explorer, the image location must be entered with forward slashes. Also, the image file extension has been left off because it isn't required by the game.

Next time you select your map to run in another multiplayer game type, you will see this smaller image as shown in Figure 13-22.

Determining the level size

Size values are used during the loading of the game for proper performance optimization. Currently, your definition file has `size0` through `size3` valued at 0. This means that right now your definition file doesn't specify at all the size of the level file being loaded.

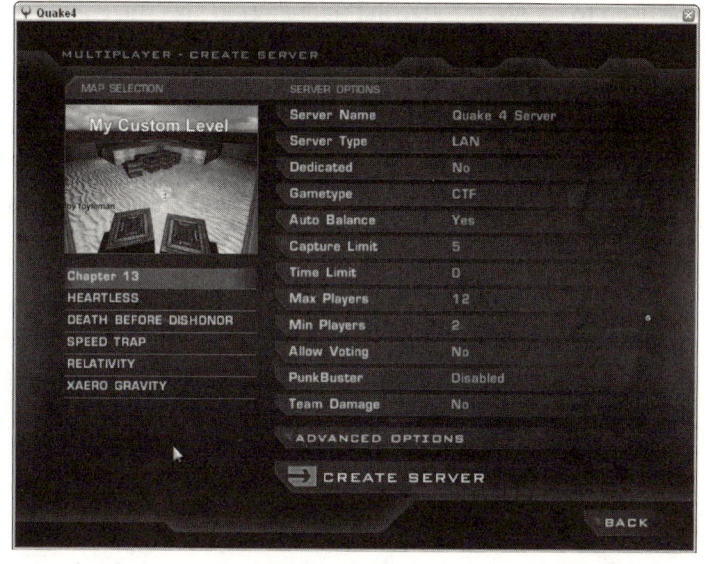

Figure 13-22: With the changes made, your custom thumbnail image is displayed when you select the associated level.

To fill in the missing values, you can force the game to write the correct size into your definition file for you. It's all done with a simple command from the console of the game. Each size in the definition file relates to the video quality your game has been set to. In *Quake 4,* there are four qualities of video a player can choose from: Low, Medium, High, and Ultra.

Although getting the game to update this size information for you is quite simple, you would have to do it four times after adjusting your video settings for each run-through. Instead, it's easier to create a batch file to run through each of these settings for you. The batch file would load the game, change the video settings, load the level, and quit the game four times, once for each of the settings. Here is how to do this.

1. **Open Notepad again and type the following four lines of code:**

   ```
   quake4.exe +bind F10 quit +com_updateLoadSize 1 +com_machineSpec 0 +si_map
              game\chapter13_mp +si_pure 0 +spawnserver
   quake4.exe +bind F10 quit +com_updateLoadSize 1 +com_machineSpec 1 +si_map
              game\chapter13_mp +si_pure 0 +spawnserver
   quake4.exe +bind F10 quit +com_updateLoadSize 1 +com_machineSpec 2 +si_map
              game\chapter13_mp +si_pure 0 +spawnserver
   quake4.exe +bind F10 quit +com_updateLoadSize 1 +com_machineSpec 3 +si_map
              game\chapter13_mp +si_pure 0 +spawnserver
   ```

   Each of these four lines of code in the batch file loads the game in a different quality mode. They represent the four quality modes for which you need to record the size in the definition file. The commands in each of the lines of code are as follows:

- `quake4.exe`: This command loads the *Quake 4* game.
- `+bind F10 quit`: Here you define that pressing the key F10 will immediately quit the game.
- `+com_updateLoadSize 1`: This tells the game that it is to update the definition file with the correct size automatically.
- `+com_machineSpec 0-3`: This defines the video quality of the game that is loading. You need to go through each of the four video qualities to update the four missing sizes in the definition file.
- `+si_map game\chapter13_mp`: This is loading your new level named `chapter13_mp`.
- `+si_pure 0`: To run special commands, you must turn off the Pure server setting, and that's what this command does.
- `+spawnserver`: This command starts up the deathmatch server.

2. **Save this file in the root game folder `C:\Program Files\id Software\Quake 4`. Name the file `resize.bat`.**

   The name isn't important, but it's good to name it something you will recognize later.

   Now you can launch this file.

3. **Make sure the game and editor is closed. Open Windows File Explorer and go to the games root folder, `C:\Program Files\id Software\ Quake 4`. Double-click the file to launch it.**

As it runs, it launches the *Quake 4* game and loads the map specified in the file, `chapter13_mp`. When the map finishes loading, press F10 to quit the game. This process will happen four times, once for each of the four lines in your batch file, and it'll stop after the fourth time. When complete, your original game settings will remain as they were, and you won't have to worry about changes in anything such as your video settings. The batch file was able to run the new settings without making any permanent changes.

Most importantly, if you take a look at the old definition file for your level, you will notice that the size information has been updated accordingly. The definition file now reads as

```
mapDef game/chapter13_mp {
    "name"                                      "Chapter 13"
    "DM"                                                 "1"
    "Team DM"                                            "1"
    "Tourney"                                            "0"
    "CTF"                                                "1"
    "Arena CTF"                                          "0"
```

```
"Gametype_Deathmatch"                              "1"
"Gametype_TeamDeathmatch"                          "1"
"Gametype_Tournament"                              "0"
"Gametype_CaptureTheFlag"                          "1"
"Gametype_ArenaCaptureTheFlag"                     "0"
"loadimage"            "gfx/guis/loadscreens/chapter13_mp"
"mp_thumb"             "gfx/guis/mainmenu/chapter13_mp"
"size0"                                    "118468043"
"size1"                                    "118468043"
"size2"                                    "118468043"
"size3"                                    "118468043"
}
```

TIP: If your definition file doesn't update the size information, check to make sure that your file is not set to Read Only by Windows. The file must be editable by the game in order for the changes to take effect.

Considering Other Game Types

There are two more game types that I haven't discussed.

When you were creating and editing the definition files for your levels, you might have noticed that it is possible to specify a level as being capable of more than one game type. All you had to do was enter a value of 1 for each of the game types, but is it possible for the game to use the same map in this manner?

Yes, you can create a single map and place all the necessary spawn points and related game type entities into it. Save and compile the map and distribute it under the premise that it can be played in all available game types. When the game loads the level, it utilizes what it needs and ignores CTF flags, Arena flags, or the team versus deathmatch spawn points, as needed.

Playing the tourney

Another game type that is quick and painless to add is the tournament, or *tourney*, game type. A *Quake 4* Tournament is a game in which two players fight one-on-one, as in a deathmatch. The winner gets to stay for the following game, but the loser is kicked out of the lineup.

The tourney game type utilizes the deathmatch spawn points in the game. Because you have a regular deathmatch level set up, this map is ready for tournament play. To run a tourney, all that remains is to complete the level's definition file.

1. **Open the definition file for your level in Notepad.**

   It is located at `C:\Program Files\id Software\Quake 4\q4base\def` and named `chapter13_mp.def`.

2. **In this file, you need to edit two lines. The first line is `Tourney`, which should have the value of 0 changed to 1. The second line is `Gametype_Tournament`, which should also have the value of 0 changed to 1.**

3. **Save this definition file, and you're done.**

Next time you start a server by using the tourney game type, your map will be listed.

Capturing the arena

The arena CTF game type works very much like the regular CTF game, except that some of the power-ups available in the entity list are made specifically for it. These special power-ups are team-specific, which means that the other team is unable to use them even though they can see them. Also, when a player picks up one of these power-ups, the effects do not wear off until that player dies.

These special power-ups include

- **Scout:** This allows you to move faster in the game and also to fire your weapon at a faster rate.
- **Guard:** When picked up, this power-up regenerates your health and increases your armor to 200 points. This is double the armor that's available to everyone else.
- **Doubler:** Similar to Quad Damage, this power-up doubles the amount of damage your weapon can inflict.
- **Ammo-Regen:** This slowly increases your ammo count on all of the weapons in your inventory. With this power-up, you never have to pick up ammo again.

When using these power-ups, they should be made available to only this game type. They were not designed to be used in the regular CTF and other game types and therefore should be unavailable to players when those game types are played.

To make them unavailable in other game types, filter them out just like you did with the crates in the hall and the flag bases in the rooms. On the Entity tab, enter a **filter_Arena CTF** in the Key field, enter **1** in the Val field, and then press Enter. Follow these steps for each of the power-ups, and you will be set.

Part IV
Going Beyond the Basics

The 5th Wave — By Rich Tennant

"Dennis! Dennis!! Where are you?! I'm being attacked! I know, I know, but you're the groom. Tell them to just postpone the wedding a few minutes."

In this part . . .

Mapping might be a popular type of mod, but that isn't where modding stops. What you can't do with the mapping editor you *can* do with scripting. In this part, you create custom images to paste throughout the game, find ways to make your games interactive with user interfaces, and turn a player into a virtual version of yourself. Here you put everything you've created into a package and get it out to the world.

Chapter 14
Scripting Advanced Actions

In This Chapter
- Using tools and finding information
- Understanding what makes up a script
- Scripting a lift in your game

A lot of people are intimidated by the thought of scripting for a game. Well, those people just don't know how simple it really is. *Scripting* has been turned into a word with inflated meaning by programmers and hackers who want you to be scared. I'm here to tell you that if you can read and write, you can script.

There's a distinct difference between scripting and coding. *Coding,* or *programming,* is what you do when you edit or hack the lines of code that make the game work. Coding is what id Software and Raven Software, the makers of Quake, did to provide you with such an awesome game. The creators wrote their code; compiled it (in much the same manner you compile your levels) into something the computer can execute; and then released it to us, the users.

Scripting, on the other hand, is nothing more than creating lines of text that instruct the game on how to behave. There might be some words that you don't recognize, but thanks to id Software, you already have a glossary of these terms saved on your computer. When you can't remember a term or you want to look for something new, you can just open up the glossary file and search for some help.

Let me introduce you to the tools you'll need to start scripting.

Finding Tools You Already Had

I'm willing to bet that you already have all the tools you need to start scripting. Here are the essentials:

✔ **A text editor:** For writing, you need a text editor.

 ✔ **A file-compression utility:** To access the glossary, you need a file-compression utility.

These tools come with Microsoft Windows, which is most likely the operating system you're already running.

Writing in plain text

A script is made up of lines of text that instruct the game to do something. Being lines of text, all you need to write your own script is a text editor. You can use Notepad, ConText, UltraEdit, or any other plain text editor you feel comfortable with. However, it must be able to save your writing as plain text. This is very important.

Microsoft Word, WordPerfect, or other word processing programs often interject formatting that is invisible to the reader, but instruct the text to appear bold, italic, or formatted in some other way. This hidden code makes your script unusable by the game, so Word and WordPerfect make bad for scripting.

In this book, I use Notepad. Notepad comes free with every copy of Windows and can be found under your Start menu by choosing Start➪All Programs➪Accessories➪Notepad. This program is a very basic text editor, as shown in Figure 14-1.

Reading the glossary

A glossary of scripting terms is already available to you. All you need to do is extract it from the game files.

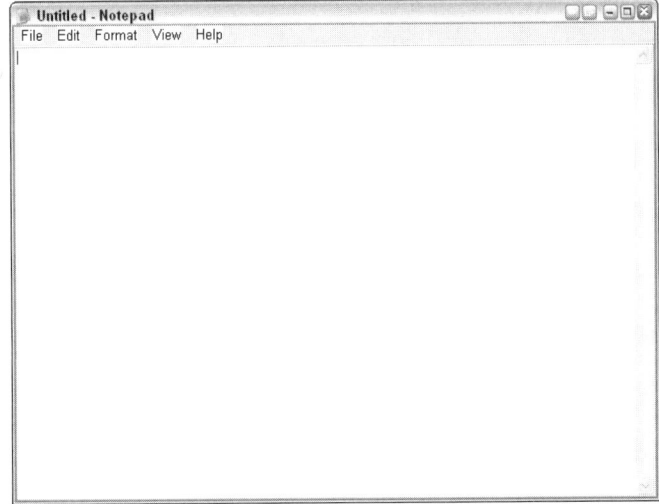

Figure 14-1: Notepad is a plain text editor that comes with every Windows installation.

Chapter 14: Scripting Advanced Actions

Although you could use the file-compression utility that comes with Windows XP, I recommend using WinZip. This program is available at `www.winzip.com` and comes with a 30-day trial period. (It's also available on the attached CD-ROM.) Through my years of modding games, I've always found this program useful, and I highly recommend it. I refer to this program within the examples of this book.

Cracking your game files

The glossary of terms is currently locked away in one of the package files that were installed with your game. You can open these package files with WinZip, but first you need to tell WinZip that it's allowed to open these files. Here's how:

1. **Open Windows File Explorer by choosing Start**⇨**All Programs**⇨**Accessories**⇨**Windows Explorer.**

2. **Navigate to the *Quake 4* base folder found through `C:\Program Files\id Software\Quake 4\q4base`.**

   Here you can see a number of files named with the `.pk4` file extension. These are your game package files, which are commonly referred to as "pak" files. To open these package files with WinZip, you need to tell your computer that all files of this type should be opened with WinZip.

3. **Right-click the file `pak010.pk4` and choose Open With from the contextual menu.**

   If you don't see the Open With option, as might occur in some cases, choose Open from the menu. Either choice launches a dialog box alerting you that `Windows cannot open this file`, as in Figure 14-2. This is because Windows hasn't yet associated these files with WinZip as you are about to do.

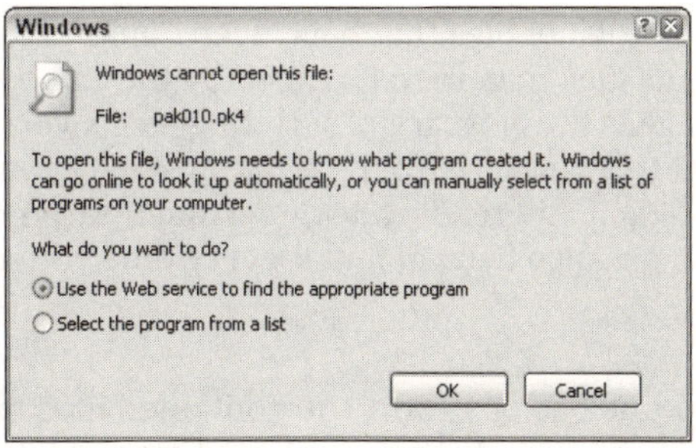

Figure 14-2: pk4 files can be opened with WinZip. All you have to do is tell your computer to use this program with all pk4 files.

4. **Select the Select the Program from a List option and then click OK.**

    This opens a dialog box in which you can select the program that opens this file.

 5. **Select WinZip from the list of programs, and then select the check box that reads Always Use the Selected Program to Open This Kind of File, as shown in Figure 14-3, and then click OK.**

    The file opens. Don't close Windows File Explorer; you will come back to it shortly.

> **TIP**
>
> If WinZip isn't in your list of programs to choose, you must browse your computer for it. Click the Browse button and locate the file `C:\Program Files\WinZip\WINZIP32.EXE` yourself, and then select and open it.

Figure 14-3: Either select WinZip from the available list or browse your hard drive for it to associate it with pk4 files.

When WinZip opens, you see a list of files that have been compressed inside this package file. These are all files that are referenced by the game. Contained within this particular package is the glossary of scripting terms you need. What you're going to do is extract this glossary from the package file to your hard drive. After you do this, finding it and reading it will be much easier because you won't have to open this package file and find it every time you need it.

Extracting the glossary

To find the glossary, it might be easier to sort the contained files by name. Do this by clicking the word *Name* located at the top of the rightmost column, as shown in Figure 14-4. When you click this column heading, the files will sort themselves in ascending or descending order.

Figure 14-4: Sorting the contents of your Zip file makes it easier to locate the file you want.

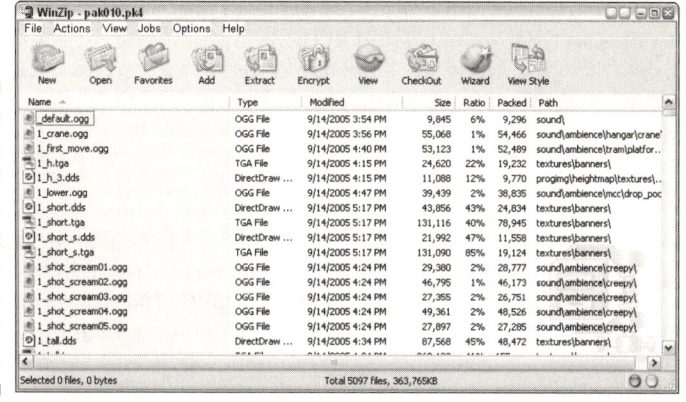

Now that they're sorted, it is easier to locate the file, which is called `events.script`. Here's how you extract it:

1. **Locate the `events.script` file and select it by clicking it once.**
2. **Click the Extract button at the top of the application window.**

   This opens a dialog box in which you can select the location where it will extract.

3. **Within the Extract window, select the folder `C:\Program Files\id Software\Quake 4\q4base`, which is where you found the file that is now open in WinZip, `pk010.pk4`.**
4. **Make sure the Use Folder Names check box is selected, as in Figure 14-5, and then click the Extract button.**

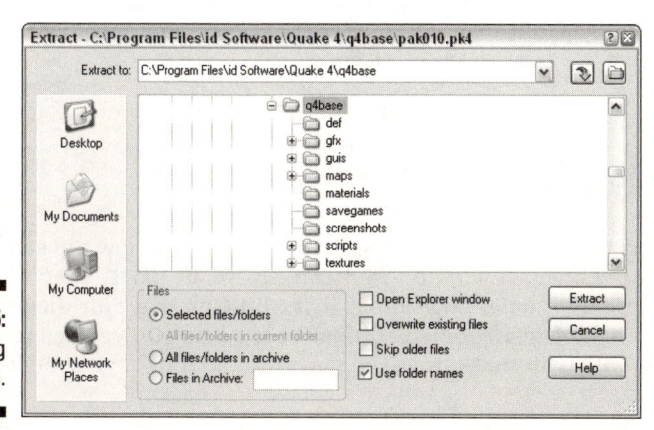

Figure 14-5: Extracting files.

Make sure to select the Use Folder Names check box when extracting your files so they are extracted to the relevant folder on your hard drive. This extracts the file to the selected folder, `C:\Program Files\id Software\Quake 4\q4base`. After the file has been extracted, you can close the `pak010.pk4` file, which is open in WinZip.

Opening scripts

With Windows File Explorer still open to the `q4base` folder, you can see a new folder available in your file list titled `scripts`. Because the Use Folder Names check box in WinZip was selected when you extracted your file, `events.script` was extracted to the same location that it was compressed to by the package file. So, from this folder, now open the folder `scripts` to find your `events.script` file.

I mention earlier that scripts are just text files you can write and read with plain text editors such as Notepad. Well, just as you must tell your computer to open `pk4` files with WinZip, you need to tell your computer to open script files with Notepad:

1. **Right-click the script file and select Open or Open With from the context menu.**

2. **Select the Select the Program from a List option and press OK.**

3. **Select Notepad from the list of programs, select the Always Use the Selected Program to Open This Kind of File check box, and then press OK.**

If Notepad isn't in your list of programs to choose, you have to browse your computer for it. Click the Browse button and locate the file `C:\WINDOWS\NOTEPAD.EXE` yourself, and then select and open it.

The `events.script` file now opens, and you have the glossary of scripting terms at your disposal. I get into more detail later about this file. For now, just know that it's here for your reference.

Breaking Apart the Script

It's time to get down to the scripting. To start, I explain how the game interprets a script. I break down the script and explain its parts. Then you write your own script — something simple, just a little message for the server. Then you can implement some additions to the map you've been working on, starting with a lift that brings the player to the roof of your building.

Chapter 14: Scripting Advanced Actions

A script is comprised of lines of text that are understood by the game. These lines are grouped into functions that can be called by the map when it loads, by entities within your map, or by other functions.

Say you want to create a script that prints a line of text in the console when the level is loaded. For this example, the line of text you are going to print out is going to say, "Hello World!" To do this, you need to start by creating a function that can be run by the game when it's started.

1. **Open Notepad.**

    This is the plain text editor that you're going to use to create your script.

2. **In Notepad, type the following lines of code:**

    ```
    void main() {
        sys.println("Hello World.");
    }
    ```

    What does this script mean? The script starts with a function named `main()`. By naming it `main()`, you know that this function runs automatically when the game starts. You start the line with the word `void` to indicate that what follows is a function. Then, everything between the curly brackets is considered the scripting that is run with the function.

    Within `main()`, the line of code between the curly brackets instructs the game system to print the enclosed line of text to the console. So, `sys.println()` stands for *system: print line*. The text between the quotation marks is what gets printed. The ending semicolon indicates the end of the script line.

    Now, this script isn't going to run itself. You have to indicate to the game that it must load and run this script when it loads and runs your level. Of course, that's what the rest of this step list is for.

3. **Choose File⇨Save As within Notepad.**

4. **For the location to save your new script file, select the folder that contains the map you want the script to run with.**

    In this case, you want to run this script with the single-player map from Chapter 13. Therefore, you save the script in the same place as the `chapter13_sp.map` file; that is, in `C:\Program Files\id Software\Quake 4\q4base\maps\game`.

5. **Give the script the same name as the map it should run with, but give the script the file extension `.script`. Click Save.**

    Because your single-player map from Chapter 13 was titled `chapter13_sp.map`, you should name your script `chapter13_sp.script`.

Part IV: Going Beyond the Basics

> **REMEMBER:** When saving files from Notepad with a `.script` extension, make sure that the file is saved with the name that you indicated. Sometimes Notepad adds `.txt` to the end of your filename. Simply check the file from within Windows File Explorer to make sure that the file was named correctly.

To see the script run, load the game, and then open the console. Launch your single-player level by typing **devmap game/chapter13_sp**. When the game has started, open the console again. There, about three lines up, you can see the line of text you added, as shown in Figure 14-6.

Figure 14-6: Your script has run, as is apparent by the text "Hello World!" a few lines up in the game's console.

Lifting Sensations

After you master scripting, you can implement something for your players to enjoy while playing your custom level. Expanding on `chapter13_sp.map`, you are going to add a lifting platform for the player to access the roof of the building. Because a basic lift that just goes up and down can be done easier with `func_plat` entity, you're going to get fancy. The lift is located in the outside area, and this is how it works:

1. When the player steps up to the lift, it raises him or her up to the roof.

2. When it reaches the roof, it swings around so that the platform is resting on the roof.

Chapter 14: Scripting Advanced Actions 229

3. Here, the platform pauses a few seconds to let the player get off.

4. Then it reverses its path back to the ground again.

Constructing the platform

Before you can write a script for the platform to move, you need to build the platform in the game. Here's how:

1. **Load the map `chapter13_sp.map` in the mapping editor.**

2. **Choose File⇨Save As, make sure you are in the same folder as the original map, and rename it `chapter14.map`.**

   By saving the map under a new name, you ensure that you can't harm the work you've already done.

3. **Focus your editor on the north wall of the red room and select the Caulk texture.**

4. **For the platform, draw a brush that is large enough to hold the player and short enough that the player can step up onto it without having to jump.**

   A good size would be 128, 64, and 8 units in size on the X, Y, and Z planes of the 2D window, respectively, as shown in Figure 14-7.

Figure 14-7: The first brush for your platform is drawn in place.

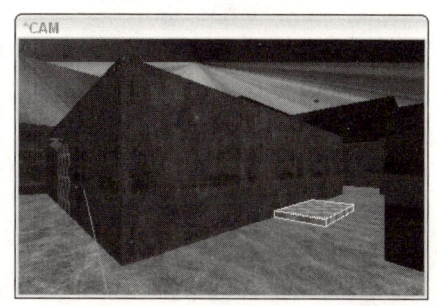

Next, you add some detail to this platform to make it look more like a lift. Adding a beveled edge around the outside of this brush makes it look better in the game.

5. **Draw three more brushes around the exposed sides of the platform, as shown in Figure 14-8.**

   Notice that I also mitered the corners of the brushes where they meet to reduce the amount of splitting that occurs after compiling the map.

Part IV: Going Beyond the Basics

Figure 14-8: Create a three-brush frame around the platform's base and bevel the joints.

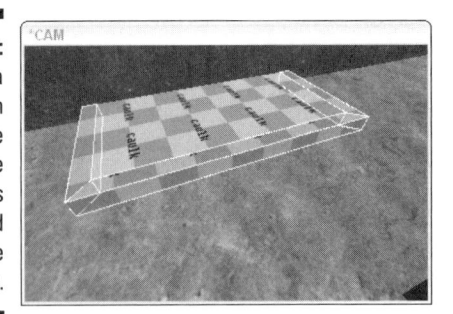

6. **Change your view in the 2D window so you can see the side view of your brushes.**

   In Figure 14-9, the camera is looking down the side of the front brush on the lift.

7. **Deselect all but the one brush you want to bevel and select the Clipper tool by pressing X.**

8. **Clip your brush on the diagonal so that you have a beveled edge that looks like a little ramp on the front of your platform, as shown in Figure 14-9.**

   Clipping, first detailed in Chapter 9, in this case allows you to clip off part of the brush to create a three-sided brush.

9. **Repeat Step 8 for the two sides of your platform.**

   Change your view and select one of the brushes you want to clip. Activate the Clipper and clip the brush on the diagonal. Do the same for the third brush, and the result should look like Figure 14-10.

Figure 14-9: Clip the first brush so that it creates an angle in front of the platform.

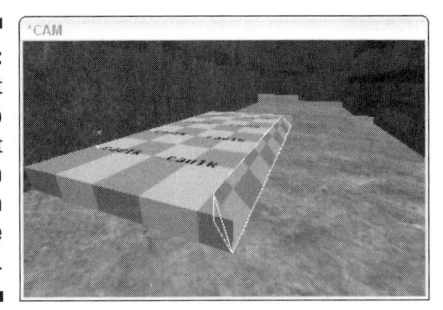

Figure 14-10: Clip the remaining two brushes around the lift's base to complete the look of the platform.

Texturing the platform

To make your structure look like a lift in the game, it needs some textures. Load the Common Floors texture set, which has a good steel texture for the top of the platform. Select the top brush face of the platform and apply the texture `common_floors/c_floor_1b`. The result is a nice, bumped-steel look for the top, as in Figure 14-11.

Figure 14-11: Texture the top of the platform with a strong metal texture that's appropriate for a lift.

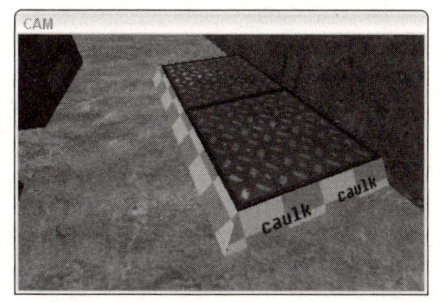

As for the beveled edges of the platform, I have a different texture in mind. Load the Core texture set. Here, locate the texture `core/sc_warning` and apply it to the tops of the beveled platform brushes.

For the texture to look correct in the game, the texture on the beveled edges is going to need to be fitted to the brush. For the two shorter beveled brush faces, open the Surface Inspector by pressing S. Change the width value next to the Fit button from 1 to 2, and then click the Fit button, as I did to get the look shown in Figure 14-12.

232 Part IV: Going Beyond the Basics

As for the longer beveled brush face, change the width to 4, and then press the Fit button. This ensures that the texture looks the same on all sides and won't look stretched.

That takes care of the top of the platform. But remember that this platform will be able to move up, meaning that the player could possibly see the bottom of it as well as the side against the wall. Therefore, you need to texture the bottom and back brush faces with something. Because it isn't overly important to have these areas look special, apply the same texture to all the remaining brush faces and use one that has already been used in your level. Here's how:

1. **Choose Materials**⇨**Show In Use to filter the textures on the Textures tab to only those in use in your map.**

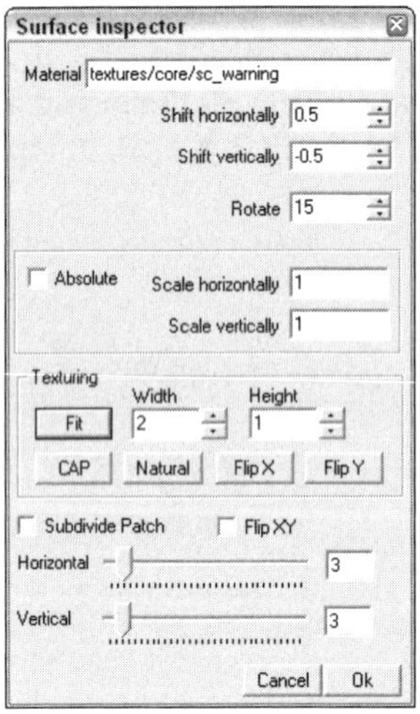

Figure 14-12: Apply a slightly different texture on the edge around the ramp to add to the detail of the structure.

2. **Before selecting your texture, select the four brushes that make up your platform and move them high enough that you can see within the CAM window the underside as well as the side currently against the wall.**
3. **Select one of these brush faces and apply the texture `terminal/t1_metal2`.**

    This texture appears on the sides of your light fixtures as well as on the door jambs.
4. **Apply this texture to the other brush faces to complete the structure, as in Figure 14-13.**

Figure 14-13:
Texturing the underside and back of the platform.

   5. **Lower the brushes back to a position on the surface of the ground.**

Creating the track

There is still another group of brushes that you need to add to your map to complete the platform. Just as you created light fixtures to make sense of the light that was shining down underneath them (see Chapter 12), you need to create something that looks like it moves the lift up and down and around. This would be a track against the wall. Follow these steps:

   1. **Select the Caulk texture and draw a brush that reaches from the ground to the top of the building. Make it stick off of the wall about 8 units, and draw it only about 16 units wide. Center it in the platform, as shown in Figure 14-14.**

Figure 14-14:
Platforms can't move on their own. So, add something to the structure that looks like it can control the platform.

2. As for the textures to apply to the track, load the Common Misc texture set.

3. For the front of the track, apply the texture `common_misc/p4_beam_5`. After it's applied, open the Surface Inspector. This texture needs to be sized a little better, so fit this texture with a width of 1 and a height of 2. Enter a value of 1 in the Width box and enter a value of 2 in the Height box. Then press the Fit button.

4. For the sides of the track, apply a texture from the same set: `common_misc/p4_beam_3`. Fit it by using the same dimensions as the front brush face. Open the Surface inspector and enter a value of 1 in the Width box and enter a value of 2 in the Height box. Then press the Fit button.

5. Texture the top brush face with the `terminal/t1_metal2` texture.

When you're done, you should have a completed track that looks like Figure 14-15.

Figure 14-15: Texture the platform's ramp appropriately.

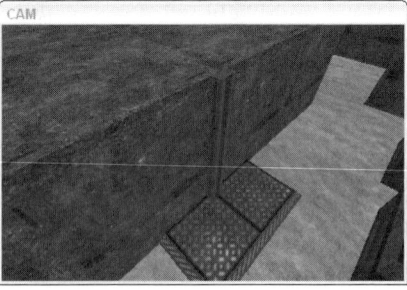

Turning the platform

When the platform reaches the top of the roof, it's going to turn so that it is resting on the top of the roof. You need another brush on top of this railing. This is where the platform will stop its upward path just above the rooftop and then twist around.

1. Add another brush on top of the track and roof. Make it a 16-unit cube and line it up flush with the track so that the rest of this brush is resting on the roof top.

2. Texture the entire brush with `terminal/t1_metal2`, as in Figure 14-16.

Chapter 14: Scripting Advanced Actions *235*

Figure 14-16: Place a brush at the top of the track that can be split and clipped into shape.

3. **Split the brush in half along the X axis.**

   While in the XY Top view of the 2D window, press X to activate the Clipper tool. Plot two clipping points down the center of the brush and press Shift+Enter to split the brush into two. The result looks like Figure 14-17.

4. **Texture the brush half that is sitting over the railing to look like a continuation of the railing itself.**

   Select the railing brush face that you want to copy the texture from, and apply it by pressing Ctrl+Shift+middle-click.

Figure 14-17: Split the brush in half by using the Clipper tool.

If you don't have a three-button mouse, you will have to apply the same texture normally, and then adjust the sizing by eye. The previously-textured railing piece was textured by using the Fit button in the Surface Inspector. Using the same method on a brush of unequal size results in different sizing. Therefore, all you can do is adjust it manually using the Surface Inspector shift and scale values until it looks good to you.

For the other half of this split brush, you are going to clip it two more times to round the corners a little bit. This will look more like something that can spin around rather than just a square block that turns.

5. **Change your grid size to one size smaller by pressing [once.**

 6. **Clip the two outer corners so that you have five outer brush faces rather than three.**

    When you're done, it should look like Figure 14-18.

Figure 14-18: Using the Clipper tool, give it some shape by cutting off two of the corners.

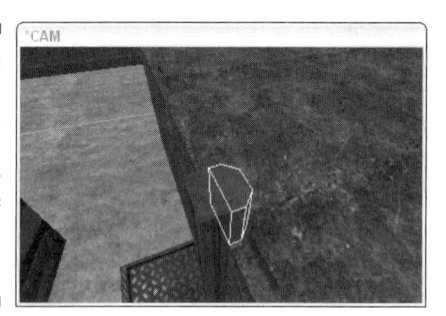

Now that you have the shape for your hinge, you need to turn it into a `func_mover` so that you can rotate it later along with the platform.

 7. **Select the two brushes at the top that will be rotating as one piece. Then select `func_mover` from the entity list.**

 8. **Open the Entity tab while this new entity is still selected. Enter a name into the text box next to Key and enter platform_hinge into the text box next to Val. Then press enter.**

    Giving this mover entity a name allows you to control it. Later, when you write your script, you will be able to call to your entity by name. This is the name that will be used.

That takes care of the hinge, the platform, and the track. Save your map so you don't lose any of the work up to this point. In the following section, you continue by turning this lift into something your script can control.

Controlling your lift

To control the lift within the game, you have to turn this lift into something that your script can call to. To call to your platform, you need to name it and in order to name it, you need to turn it into an entity. Because you want to move your entity around, not just any entity will do. You need to turn this group of brushes into a `func_mover`. As the name implies, a script can move this entity around.

Chapter 14: Scripting Advanced Actions

1. **Select the four brushes that make up your platform.**

    Don't select the track because that is going to stay right where it is.

2. **Right-click the 2D window and choose func⇨func_mover.**

    This turns your selection into a single entity.

3. **Press N to open the Entity tab.**

4. **Enter** name **in the Key field and** platform **in the Val field. Then press Enter.**

    This step gives your platform a name. Yes, it already had a name, `func_mover_1`, but that isn't an easy name to remember. Because you will need to remember this entity's name when you write your script later, giving it a better name, platform, is a good idea.

5. **Deselect your platform and select the long brush that makes up your track.**

6. **Turn your track into a `func_static`. Do this by right-clicking the selected group of brushes in the 2D window and selecting func⇨func_static.**

    As I describe in Chapter 12, to avoid the extra geometry that could slow down the speed of your game play, turning detail brushes into entities will avoid splitting the brushes in your level.

7. **Deselect the track when you're done.**

8. **Select the two brushes at the top of the track and turn them into a `func_mover` entity by right-clicking them in the 2D window and selecting func⇨func_mover.**

    This group is going to turn with the platform and will be controlled by the script. To control it, you need to name it.

9. **Open the Entity tab and rename this entity by entering** name **in the Key field and** platform_hinge **in the Val field. Then press Enter.**

Next up is creating a trigger for your platform. You need to instruct the game as to when the platform is supposed to move. Or, in this case, you instruct the script on when to run the function that moves the platform. In your the scripting exercise earlier in this chapter, you create a script that runs when the game was started. In the case of this lift, you don't want the platform to start moving when the game is loaded. Instead, you want to control it by the player's movement on top of it.

1. **Load the Common texture set and select the texture `common/trigmulti`.**

2. **Draw a brush that covers the top of the lift. This time, make the brush 8 units tall, as shown in Figure 14-19.**

    The idea here is that when your player walks onto it, the platform is triggered to lift the player to the top of the roof. When the platform reaches the top, it pauses for a few seconds before returning to the ground on its own, where the player can again activate the lift if he or she chooses to.

Figure 14-19: Add a trigger brush on top of the platform so that the player is able to activate it.

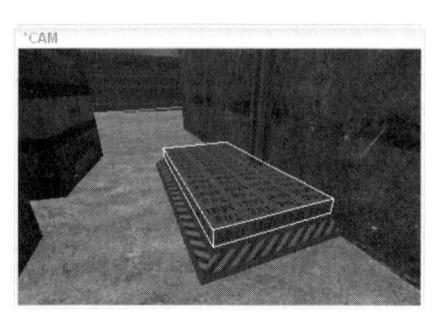

 3. **With your trigger-textured brush still selected, turn it into a `trigger_multiple` entity.**

    You do this by right-clicking the 2D window and choosing trigger⇨trigger_multiple.

    Now that it's a trigger for the player to activate, you can assign it a key and value that will call the script that runs the lift.

 4. **Open the Entity tab and give your `trigger_multiple` entity a Key of** call **and a Val of** platform_script.

    Later, when you write your script, you will name the function that controls the lift `platform_script` because this is the entity your trigger is calling.

 5. **Save your map, but this time, run it through the BSP compiling process.**

    You're going to need to test a few things before you're done with your map file; however, you won't need to do this until the script is completed. Also, don't close the editor. You still need to gather a few bits of information from it.

Scripting the action

With the map complete, all that's left to put together is the script that makes the lift work. Your script has to incorporate a number of commands that all

Chapter 14: Scripting Advanced Actions

make sense when they're put together. The idea is to control the lift and its hinge as follows:

1. When activated by the trigger, start by moving the platform upward.
2. When the platform reaches the top, combine the hinge and the platform so they can both rotate together.
3. Rotate the hinge and platform together 180 degrees on the Z axis.
4. Pause for 3 seconds to allow the player to exit the platform.
5. Perform the same actions in reverse until the platform is back to where it started.

Here's what you need to do:

1. **Open Notepad, which is where you will write the script. Start by creating your function, which was named `platform_script` when you entered that as the `call` in the `trigger_multiple` entity. You enter this into your text editor as**

   ```
   void platform_script() {
   ```

   The first process of the script is to move the platform upward. To move your `func_mover` entity, you use the scripting command `moveToPos()`. This command moves your entity to a specific position defined in X, Y, and Z coordinates. The trick is determining what those coordinates are. You could bring out the calculator, but instead here's a little trick you can do from within the mapping editor:

   a. Select your platform in the mapping editor.

   b. Raise the platform to the height where you want it to stop right on top of the roof.

   c. Open the Entity tab and take notice of the slider in the middle of the lower half of this tab.

   This slider is actually there to play the animation of a model, if animation is available. However, this slider also automatically updates the origin of your entity as it is currently placed. This origin point, now that the platform has been raised, is your destination point.

   d. Move the slider to the right and then back all the way to the left. Then scroll through your entity's information and note the origin value, as shown in Figure 14-20.

   Here you'll see that the new origin coordinates read *0 292 140*.

Figure 14-20: Move the platform to its top position, and then use the Entity tab to determine its origin for use in your script.

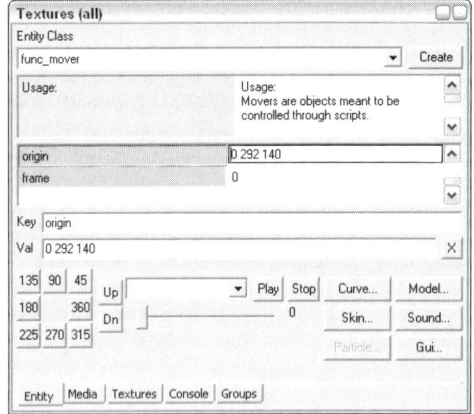

Back to the script. You now know that you want to move your platform to the position 0 292 140. The `moveToPos` script command is a `func_mover` command as opposed to a `system` command. This means that instead of running the command as `sys.println()` like you did in your first script, you need to run the movement command as `$platform.moveToPos()`. (In this command, `$platform` represents the name of the `func_mover` entity that you named as `platform` in the map editor.)

TIP

How did I know that `moveToPos` is a `func_mover` command as opposed to a `system` command? Open your scripting glossary (see "Reading the glossary," earlier in this chapter). Locate `moveToPos` in the list of functions, and then scroll up to the first group of asterisks. Between the asterisks, you see `func_mover` printed. This means that everything listed below is used in conjunction with the `func_mover` entity, and each command is called in the same manner. In this case, this means that the name of the entity is followed by the function name. If you look up the `println()` function that was used in your first script, you can see that it's preceded by `system`, meaning that it's a `system` command.

2. **Enter the second line of your script, which will be**

   ```
   $platform.moveToPos('0 292 140');
   ```

   Before you instruct your script to rotate the platform, you need to tell the script to wait until it stops moving. Scripts run each line as it is read. If you don't tell it to, the script won't stop or wait, and you'll end up rotating things while they are moving and wind up with a big mess.

3. **To instruct the game to wait for your platform to arrive at its new position, enter your third line of code as**

   ```
   sys.waitFor($platform);
   ```

This line tells the system to wait for your entity named `platform` to finish whatever instruction it is currently carrying out before moving onto the next line of code.

The next task of your script is to rotate both the platform and the hinge 90 degrees. To ensure that they both move together, you need to bind them so they act as one.

4. **To bind your two entities, enter the next line of code as**

    ```
    $platform.bind($platform_hinge);
    ```

    When you look up `bind` in your scripting glossary, you find it under the heading of `all entities`. This means that it isn't limited to just the `func_mover`, but it can be used with any entity in your map. Because you want to bind your `platform` to your `platform_hinge`, you needed to bind those two entities.

Now you need to tell your script to rotate the hinge with the attached platform 180 degrees so that it's on the top of the roof. Because the platform is bound to the hinge, it will automatically rotate with it so you don't need to write an additional line to rotate it. Also, because objects rotate around their point of origin, you want to rotate everything around the hinge.

Looking at Figure 14-21, you can see three red dots. Each red dot represents the point of origin for each of your three entities in this window. You have the platform, the hinge, and the trigger, which make up those three entities. To make your platform rotate and look proper in the game, you want it to rotate around the red dot associated with your hinge. This is why you want to rotate the hinge entity in your script as opposed to the platform entity.

1. **The `rotate` command works very much like the `move` command, so add this line as the next one in your script:**

    ```
    $platform_hinge.rotateTo('0 180 0');
    ```

    When you assigned the `moveToPos` values, you entered them in the form of X, Y, Z coordinates on the map. Rotation values can't work that way because they rotate around a single point without ever changing position. Rotation values are rather entered as Pitch, Yaw, Roll — or more plainly as nodding your head, shaking your head, and tilting your head. Therefore, by entering the values 0 180 0, you instructed the game to change only its Yaw, which turns the platform around and onto the roof top.

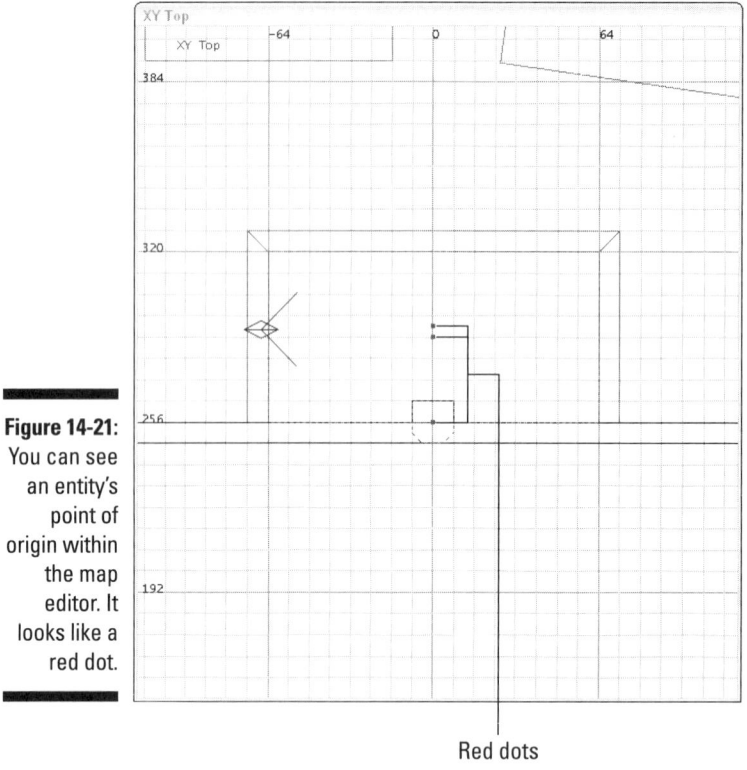

Figure 14-21: You can see an entity's point of origin within the map editor. It looks like a red dot.

Red dots

2. **Before continuing with the next step, you want to make sure that the script waits again for the rotation to complete. Because you already told your hinge to do the rotating, add the next line of code as**

    ```
    $sys.waitFor($platform_hinge);
    ```

    Now you can tell your script to pause for three seconds to let the player get off of the ramp before it reverses its pattern back to the ground. Doing so is a simple system command called wait.

3. **Add this line of code:**

    ```
    $sys.wait(3);
    ```

This is all the scripting you need to get the platform to the roof. Now you must reverse the path of the platform by entering in your code in reverse.

1. **First you need to rotate your hinge back to its original location and wait for that rotation to complete. Add these lines:**

    ```
    $platform_hinge.rotateTo('0 0 0');
        sys.waitFor($platform_hinge);
    ```

Chapter 14: Scripting Advanced Actions 243

Entering 0 0 0 as rotation values tells the game to rotate the hinge back to its original state. Previously, you rotated it 180 degrees, and that's where it stays until otherwise instructed.

 2. **Add this line of code:**

    ```
    $platform.unbind();
    ```

    This step unbinds your hinge and platform. You don't want your hinge to move to the ground with your platform while these two entities are still bound together.

 3. **Move the platform back to ground level by adding this line:**

    ```
    $platform.moveToPos('0 292 4');
    ```

    How did I arrive at the numbers 0 292 4? The same way I arrived at the previous values. I made sure the platform was in its ground position. Then I opened the Entity tab and moved the animation slider. This resets the origin position, which I was able to read and enter as 0 292 4.

Now that your script is complete, you must save it. Choose File⇨Save As and make sure you are in the same directory as your map file, which should be `C:\Program Files\id Software\Quake 4\q4base\maps\game`. Enter the same name as your map file except with the `.script` extension, `chapter14.script`.

Unfortunately, the finished lift has one more problem that needs to be smoothed out.

Adding the final touches

You need to run a test on your map before you're done. Right now, if you play this level in the game, you'll notice a minor problem: When you trigger your lift, you can jump off the lift and trigger it again while it's in motion. To solve this issue, you need to tell your `trigger_multiple` entity to wait a specified number of seconds before allowing it to be triggered again. This is where your play-testing comes into effect. You need to count the number of seconds it takes for your lift to complete its cycle.

After you have compiled your map, go ahead and load it in the game. When the game loads, open the console again. You have a few monsters in your game that are going to try to kill you. Rather than worrying about staying alive long enough to run this test, type **killMonsters** into the console and press Enter. This removes all the monsters in the game so you run your tests without distraction.

Close the console and head over to your lift. When you're ready to start counting the seconds it takes for your lift to complete its sequence, activate it by stepping on it. When I timed it, the result was seven seconds. This is the number of seconds you want your trigger to wait before it can be activated again.

Exit the game and select the lift's `trigger_multiple` entity in the editor. Open the Entity tab and enter **wait** in the Key field and **7** in the Val field, and then press Enter.

You're done. Now just save your map and run the BSP compiler again. Then load it up and have some fun.

You might want to go back later and add some attraction to the roof of your building so the player has a reason to go up there. But what you add is up to your imagination. It could be a special weapon or a secret hiding area. Just use the tips you've gathered from other chapters in this book.

Chapter 15

Creating Custom Textures

In This Chapter

▶ Understanding what goes into making a texture
▶ Taking a real-world image and making it tileable
▶ Writing a material file for the game
▶ Putting textures to good use

When I step into the gaming world, I often feel like I am taken to another place or time. I could be taken to alien stronghold in outer space, a grass hut on a paradise island, or even the homeroom of my old high school.

What makes all these scenes different is not their structures. They're all scenes that take place in a room. Instead, it's the textures. It's the difference between the cold steel of a spacecraft, the dry straw of the hut, and the white paint and chalkboards of my homeroom.

You're going to find that there is only so much you can create with the textures that were provided by the game. Eventually you'll want to do more, and that means making your own textures.

The map you've been working on up to this point could be transformed into any setting. As it is, it looks mostly like a modern military outpost. With all the steel, the sandy ground, and the fortress-like walls, your map feels very strong and foreboding. You could turn the ground into grass and the building into wood, creating a scene that feels more lush and lively. On the other hand, you could brighten the sand and make the building walls look more like clay and stack bricks around the area, making it feel like it belongs in the southwest of the United States.

When choosing a location, you need to consider what materials you have at hand.

As reality in games increases, so does the demand for quality textures. The highest quality you can achieve is with actual photographs. In some cases, depending on the type of scene you're working with, you can create your own textures with image programs such as Adobe Photoshop or modeling software such as 3D Studio Max. However, nothing can beat the look of an actual photograph for modeling something that is real.

With this in mind, you need to consider what photographs you can get your hands on — without breaking any copyright laws, of course. In my case, I can easily walk outside and find plenty of brick walls to take pictures. So, this is what I use to show you the ins and outs of creating your own textures. I take a picture of a brick wall, turn it into a texture for the game, and then apply this texture to the walls surrounding the outdoor part of the map.

Slicing Up the Texture

A texture is actually more than just an image that's been brought into a game. A texture also contains information about how a brush reacts in the 3D world — how that surface reacts to light, whether or not there are bumps and grooves in the image, and so on.

A texture most commonly consists of five separate images. Each of these images is referred to as a *map* because each maps out a single aspect of an image. These maps include

- **Diffuse map:** This is the color that will be shown in the texture. Generally, this is the actual image without any changes.
- **Specular map:** This defines the way light reacts to the texture. Parts of a texture can be more shiny than others, and this fact is important in the game world where light and shadows occur in real time.
- **Normal map:** This defines the way a texture appears to bump out or in. The bumping effect made here can actually affect the polygons upon which this texture is applied.
- **Height map:** Although very similar to the normal map, this image creates the illusion of bumps on a texture. This image should be used to create only scratches, chips, or other small bumps rather than larger, more complex ones.
- **Editor image:** This is the image that is defined for use within the mapping editor. Without this image, you won't be able to see and apply your new texture to any surfaces within the game.

To tie all these images together, you will finally create a *shader* file. This is a text file that defines the location of each of these images and which image is to be used for which purpose.

Installing Some Tools

Before you get into making your own textures, you need to install some tools for the job. The first thing you need is image-editing software. Something as simple as Windows Paint won't suffice. You need a program that can open and edit Targa (TGA) images. Targa is an image format used in *Quake 4*.

For the purpose of this chapter, I use Adobe Photoshop. This professional image-editing program, which also comes with a free trial, has been provided to you in the media located in the back of this book. If you haven't already, I recommend installing it following the instructions provided on the CD.

The second tool you need is a special filter plug-in for Photoshop called the NVIDIA Photoshop Plug-ins. This filter takes one of your images and transforms it for use with your custom texture into what is called a normal map. This is explained in more detail later in this chapter. For now, just know that you must install it to complete your texture. You'll find a copy of the installer on the CD in the back of the book.

Finally, the third tool is a conversion utility called *The Compressonator*. As the name implies, this program reads the images you create for your texture, and then compresses them into a more efficient form for the game. This, too, is explained later in the chapter. Install this tool as it is found on the CD in the back of the book.

Bricking Up the Joint

I was able to take a picture of a wall that will work well as a texture. In Figure 15-1, you can see that my picture has well-defined features. There is nice contrast between the bricks that are sticking out and the joints between the bricks that sink in. These aspects should make for a good texture.

TIP: Any image can be turned into a texture. You don't need to choose one with contrasting highs and lows. This brick picture was chosen to make it easier to illustrate the methods used in making a custom texture.

If you have your own image that you would like to use, open it in Photoshop now. Otherwise, use the same brick image titled *Brick_Image_Original.tga* that I have provided on the media located in the back of the book.

Start the Adobe Photoshop program as you would start most of your programs from within Windows — choose Start➪All Programs➪Adobe Photoshop.

Figure 15-1: If your picture is level and has a lot of detail, this will be reflected in your final texture.

After the program has finished loading, open *Brick_Image_Original.tga*. Choose File➪Open, locate the file you want to open in the File Explorer window, and then press Open.

Finding the Right Size

To begin making your custom texture, you need to determine the final size of the image. *Quake 4,* as well as most games, requires that the width and height of your image in pixels evaluates to a power of two. Basically, this means that your texture must be some combination in width and height using, but not limited to, the following numbers:

8; 16; 32; 64; 96; 128; 256; 512; 1,024

The reason for the size restriction is that the game needs to be able to resize these images while you're playing the game. The images will be scaled down to half or quarter sizes, and the game can do this only if the sizes can be divisible by two or four.

TECHNICAL STUFF: While you're playing, the game displays smaller or larger versions of the same image, based on your distance away from the textures. This is called Level of Detail (LOD) and helps to reduce the amount of computing power required to display all the imagery on the screen at once.

When determining the size of your texture, you need to consider two things. First, you don't want to take up all the computer's memory with one texture. Each texture in the game is loaded into your memory before the game starts. If the file sizes of your textures are too big, the game could run out of memory and crash. Second, there is no reason to make a texture larger than what will be used within the game. That would be like buying an 8 x 10 photo for your wallet — it's a waste of space.

Due to both of these considerations, you need to create an optimally sized image. The trick to determining the best size is to know where this texture is going to be used in the game. If you're making a texture to be placed inside your buildings in the game, take note of the height of your walls. This height in mapping units should be equal to or less than the height in pixels for your image. That's it.

The wall for which you are going to create a texture is the wall that surrounds the outside of the map, as displayed in Figure 15-2. The visible height of this wall is 128 units, and 128 units also happens to be one of sizes allowed by the game. This could be the minimum size of your texture. However, some experience plays a roll at this point.

There are a few details that you should keep in mind as you decide on the size of your texture:

- Any texture other than a sky texture should never exceed 1,024 pixels in width or height. This won't be an issue in this circumstance.

- The bigger an image, the better the details. When you shrink an image, you lose some of the details that make it look so great. The less shrinking you do, the better it will look.

- The larger the image, the more memory that is required for your computer to display it in the game. You don't want to slow down players' computers by making them load and display a texture that has a huge file size.

Knowing these facts, you need to find the balance that makes your image look great in the game and allows the game to run great with your image. This is something that you might have to experiment with at first. However, as you work more frequently with custom textures, your experience will help you to make the right choices.

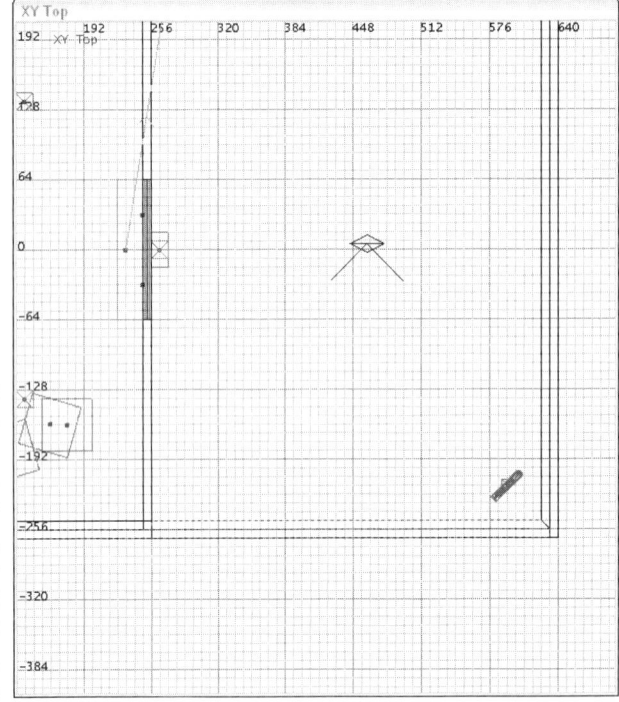

Figure 15-2: To help determine the size of your texture, consider where it will be applied in the game.

Based on my experience with textures, I recommend that you make your image 256 pixels in height. This is twice the size that is required in your map, but provides a very nice-looking and -running image in the game.

Now, it would make sense to go ahead and resize your image to the new size. However, you need to work with the image and create the five different pieces I list earlier (see the section "Slicing Up the Texture") that make up the final texture. It's much easier to work on a larger image and then to resize it to its final size just before saving it. Therefore, instead of resizing the image to 256 pixels in height, resize it to a multiple of that number closest to its original height. The image I provided, Brick_Image_Original.tga, is 2,150 pixels high. The multiple of 256 that is closest to 2,150 is 2,048 (256 × 8).

As for the width, looking at the brick texture provided, it is pretty close to being square. Therefore a width equal to the height of the image would be ideal. If the image were wider, such as 3,000 pixels wide, the image would probably look better when sized as a rectangle because there would be less distortion after the resize. Because the image is going to be square, however, the result will be an image sized to 2,048 x 2,048 pixels. After some changes are made, it can later be saved to 256 x 256 pixels.

Here's how you resize the `Brick_Image_Original.tga` image in Photoshop:

1. **Choose Image⇨Image Size.**

    This opens a dialog box, as shown in Figure 15-3.

2. **In this dialog box, make sure the Constrain Proportions check box is deselected.**

3. **Select pixels as the unit of measurement to the right of the Height and the Width fields.**

4. **Enter** 2048 **into the Height field and enter** 2048 **into the Width field.**

5. **Press OK to apply the changes.**

6. **Choose File⇨Save and save your resized image.**

Figure 15-3: When sizing your image for editing, keep it large so as not to lose details.

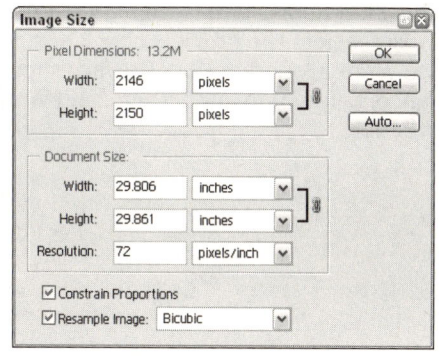

You should now have a pretty nice-looking image that's close to being ready for the game.

Tiling on Forever

In some cases, you'll use your texture only for a single application. Perhaps it's a new door, the side of a crate, or some other structure that doesn't require the image to repeat. You'll create this texture, apply it to the brush face, open the Surface Inspector, make sure the width and height values next to the Fit button are both 1 and then press Fit to properly adjust the image.

However, in most cases, you will want your texture to have the ability to repeat itself endlessly. For the case of a brick wall, it would be best to create one smaller image that can repeat itself over and over again as it goes on down the wall. Then you don't need to make a humongous texture to fit the long wall. This act of repeating is called *tiling*. Just like the tiles in your bathroom or kitchen, the tile is applied, and it repeats itself until the entire surface is covered.

Making the image tile is easy. The game can do this on its own. When you apply your texture in the mapping editor, the image will automatically repeat itself if the surface you apply the texture on is larger than the texture itself.

Making this image tile without the player being able to see where one tile starts and the other tile begins — that is the trick. So, what I want to show you now is how to create a tileable image in Photoshop.

Shifting the image to expose the seam

In Photoshop, choose Filter➪Other➪Offset. The Offset dialog box pops up, as shown in Figure 15-4. This filter allows you to adjust the image so you can see where the seams exist. Select the Preview check box, if it isn't already selected, and select the Wrap Around option. Preview shows you any changes you make in advance, before you apply them, and Wrap Around is the key to using the Offset filter.

Figure 15-4: The Offset filter in Photoshop is perfect for finding and fixing seams in tileable images.

The purpose of the Offset filter is to shift the image horizontally or vertically. It's like pushing the texture up or to the side. When you allow the image to wrap around during this process, it's like you are wrapping a package. One end starts in the middle of the package, and the other end wraps around the package until it meets up with the starting end. Thus the term *Wrap Around*.

Because the image you're working with is 2,048 pixels wide, enter a value equal to half that: 1,024. Place this value in both the Horizontal and Vertical text fields. When you do, the image adjusts itself (because you have Preview selected). The points at which the start and end of the image meet while wrapping will be right in the center of your screen — half way between 2,048

Chapter 15: Creating Custom Textures

pixels, which is why you entered an offset value that was half of the image's total size. The result before applying the change will look like Figure 15-5.

Figure 15-5: Adjust your image with the Offset filter by half it's total size both horizontally and vertically.

Press OK to apply the changes created with the Offset filter. You might have a hard time seeing the seam running through your image, but it's there. In this case, I provided you with an easy image to work with that doesn't require a lot of adjustment. However, when you zoom in really close to the middle of the picture, you see the seam. This will look even worse when tiled in the game. Figure 15-6 shows a close-up of this mismatch.

Figure 15-6: After applying the Offset filter, zooming in close shows the seam.

The goal now is to get rid of this seam in the middle of your texture. That way, when it is tiled in the game, you won't see where one begins and one ends, just like when you used the Offset filter in Photoshop.

If you haven't zoomed in to where your seams are, do so now. To zoom your image, use the Navigator window either by entering the zoom percentage or by sliding the scale rule. This window is usually in the upper-right corner of the screen and is displayed in Figure 15-7. It is often the simplest way to zoom in on your image.

Figure 15-7:
Move around a large image in Photoshop via the Navigator tab.

Stamping out your seams

Now that you can see the details of the image and where the seam lies, you are going to hide that seam by using a tool called the Rubber Stamp. You use the Rubber Stamp to copy a selected area of the image and apply it to another. Think of the selected part as the ink for your stamp; you just stamp that ink over your seam to make it disappear.

1. **Select the Rubber Stamp from the toolbar located on the left of the screen.**

    The tool's icon looks like a little rubber stamp.

    Next you need to select a brush size.

2. **On the toolbar at the top of Photoshop, you can see the word *Brush*. To the right of it is a dot, a number, and a small arrow used to open a drop-down menu. Select this arrow to open the menu, as you see in Figure 15-8. Then move the slider to the right of the curvy images until you locate the one labeled as *45*. Select it, and the window closes.**

Chapter 15: Creating Custom Textures **255**

The brush size determines how much ink the stamp selects to be applied later. A good brush size for this image is 45. It's about the same size as the grout between the bricks, which means it will be able to stamp over half the grout while overlapping the brick slightly when used. This should result in a nicely blended stamping as you will soon see.

Figure 15-8: Select an appropriate brush size for your rubber stamp.

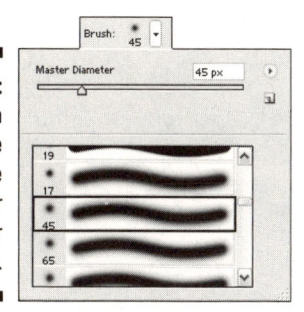

With the tool ready for use, it's time to select the ink for your stamp. This tool copies a portion of your image as if it was ink in a pad and then pastes that copy anywhere you want. After you stamp down your first copy, you can continue to stamp on down the seam and the selection of which you are copying from will move with you. If this appears confusing, it will make more sense as you use the tool. If you make a mistake, you can simply undo your last few operations.

3. **Place your mouse pointer, which now looks like a circle, exactly one brick to the right of the seam you want to cover. Use Figure 15-9 as a reference. Once positioned, press Alt+click.**

   This will be your selection that is copied before being pasted over the seam.

4. **Now, carefully move your cursor over the seam in the image in a straight, horizontal direction from your selection point to the seam. Then click to apply the stamp.**

   This hides your seam.

5. **Continue to click on the seam as you move up and down the image as I have started to do in Figure 15-10.**

   Your original selection position for the rubber stamp moves in relation to your mouse, so you don't have to reselect the part you want to copy. You can also click and drag the cursor, and the application of the stamp will follow you. This is great if you have a steady hand while dragging across the image. However, stick with individual clicks if you want to be more precise.

Part IV: Going Beyond the Basics

Figure 15-9: The rubber stamp mouse pointer looks like a circle, and the first application of this tool needs to be as precise as you can do it.

Seam — Mouse pointer

REMEMBER: As you apply the Rubber Stamp selection over the seam, you might come across areas that the application of the stamp doesn't look good. Just undo your last application, make a new rubber stamp selection, and apply that selection appropriately.

  6. **Before you move on, zoom out so that you can see the image as a whole. Inspect it for any seams that you might have missed.**

TIP: When using the rubber stamp, I constantly reset the position from which I copy. I'm somewhat of a perfectionist in my mods and would rather take the extra time making the texture as perfect as I can make it.

Take your time stamping out the seam in your image. Remember that you have seams that run both vertically and horizontally and that both need to be cleaned up. It might take some time to get it just right, but it's worth it. It will look better in the game.

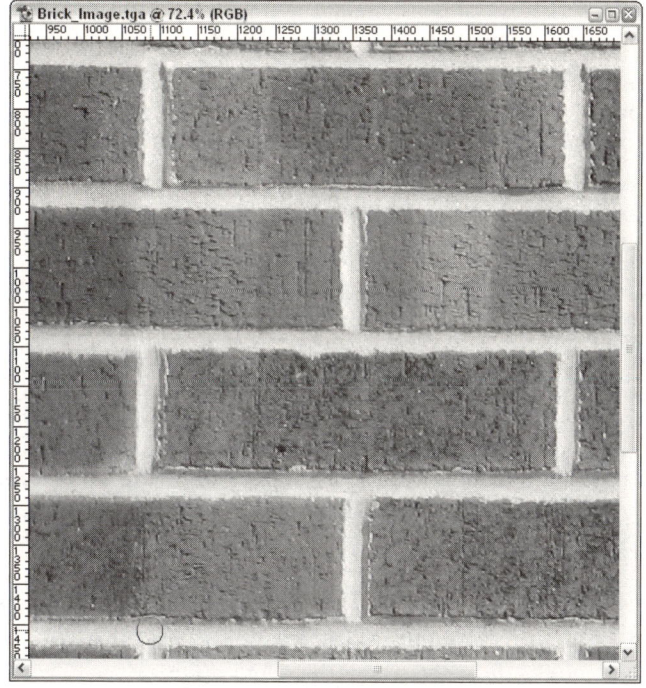

Figure 15-10: After you apply the rubber stamp to your image, the seam will disappear.

Shifting back to ground zero

When the seam has been completely stamped out, return the image to its original position. Using the Offset filter has moved the image from where it started, and you should return it to that starting point.

In the case of this image, offsetting the image back to its original position isn't required, but it is a good practice. When you return the image to the starting position, you might notice something that looks out of place and needs more touching up before you move on.

1. **Choose Filter➪Other➪Offset.**

    Because you shifted your image exactly half its width, all that's left is to shift it again that same distance.

2. **Make sure the Horizontal and the Vertical entry is** 1024 **pixels as it was before.**

3. **Press OK to apply the change.**

Part IV: Going Beyond the Basics

Now your texture can be tiled, and you won't see any seams where one tile ends and the next begins.

Before moving on, save this image someplace safe. For the texture, you are going to be transforming this image in different ways, and it's a good idea to have the original at hand in case you want to go back and make some more changes later on.

4. **Choose File➪Save As and find a good place on your hard drive to keep it.**

   The game isn't going to be using this image, so where you save it is not important.

   Before pressing the Save button, select a high-quality format for your image. JPEG and GIF file formats actually compress your image, which can lower the detail and quality. Instead, select Targa from the drop-down list located under the File Name field, as shown in Figure 15-11. This is a good-quality format and happens to be the same format that will be used for the final images used in the texture.

5. **Press Save.**

   You are prompted with a selection of Targa options.

6. **Select 24 bits/pixel and press OK.**

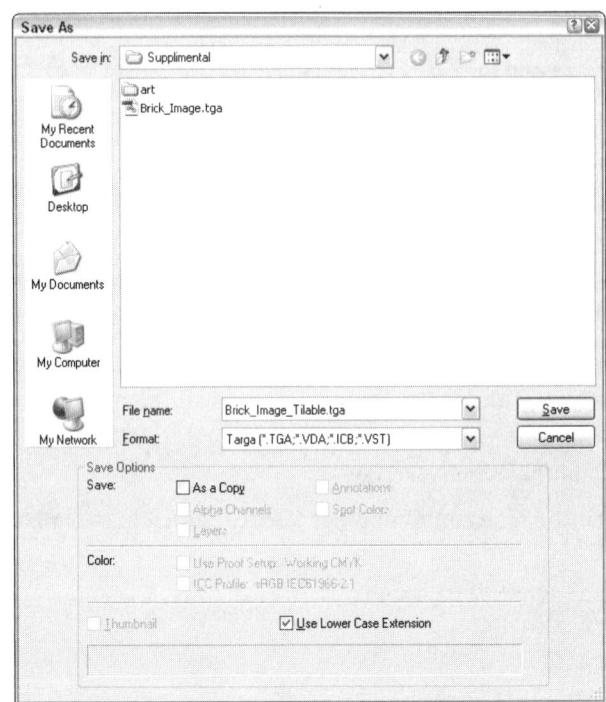

Figure 15-11: After you have the image adjusted, save it under a new name for safekeeping.

Chapter 15: Creating Custom Textures *259*

TECHNICAL STUFF. A 24-bit Targa image is the high-quality image size for this file type. Sixteen bit is low quality because it limits the number of colors used in the image, and 32 bit is reserved for images that have transparency.

Mapping Your Images

The image is now ready to be transformed into the different pieces that make up the texture. You need to make five different images from this one, each to serve its own purpose. Later, the game will combine each of these pieces and present the player with the final texture.

Splashing on some color: The diffuse map

The first image to create is the *diffuse map*. This image represents the color for your texture and is really nothing more than the image you now have displayed in Photoshop. All you have to do is resize it to its final size and save it.

1. **Choose Image**⇨**Image Size within Photoshop.**

2. **In the dialog box that pops up, as shown in Figure 15-12, select the Constrain Proportions check box.**

    This means that when you change one size value, the other changes in the same proportion.

3. **Enter a width of 256 pixels.**

    This size is the goal set forth at the beginning of the chapter. Because you have Constrain Proportions checked off in the bottom of the dialog box, the Height automatically changes to 256 pixels as well.

4. **Now press OK to apply the size change.**

Figure 15-12: Resize the image.

The image appears pretty small on your screen after you apply the above changes, but that's also because you are zoomed way out. If you entered the numbers as outlined, everything is as it should be.

5. **To save the file, choose File**➪**Save As.**

   You have to save this image and each after it in a specific location so that the game can find and use these files.

6. **At the top of this Save As dialog box, change the Save In location to** `C:\Program Files\id Software\Quake 4\q4base`**. Here, create a new folder by clicking the New Folder icon shown in the margin. Create a folder named textures. Access this folder.**

   In the textures folder that you just created, you can create your custom texture folder. This folder can have any name that you desire. However, I recommend that you name it the same as your map file. This way, when you go to distribute your map, it is less likely that this folder and the files within it are overwritten by another map with the same name. It's less likely that your map has the exact same name as someone else as opposed to using a generic folder name for your custom textures.

7. **Because the name of this map is going to be** `chapter15.map`**, name this new folder chapter15.**

   In this new texture folder, which is now `C:\Program Files\id Software\Quake 4\q4base\textures\chapter15`, you can save your diffuse map.

8. **Select the Format for your image to be Targa. This is the format used by the game. Because this texture can appropriately be called *brick* and this is the diffuse map version, enter a File Name of** brick_d.tga.

9. **Press Save to save the file. When prompted for the Targa resolution, select 24 bits/pixel, and you're done.**

Picking out the highlights: The specular map

The next image you need to create is the *specular map*. This image defines how the light reacts. Some parts of the image might be shinier than others, but some might not reflect any light at all. By making shiny parts of your image white and dull parts black, you can tell the game how to reflect the light off your texture.

Before proceeding, you need to go back to the larger version of your image. The one open in Photoshop now has been scaled down to 256 x 256 pixels.

To go back to the previous version, you have two options. You can close the one you have and open the high-quality version that you saved earlier, or you can go back in history to a point before you scaled the image down in size. I show you the latter.

Photoshop has the ability to save the history of changes made to an image. Look on the right side of the program and find a tab labeled History, as shown in Figure 15-13. If you find it, select it now; otherwise choose Window⇨History to display it. On the right side of this History tab, you can scroll through the changes that have been made to your image. Select the history item that comes just before *Image Size*. That will be the image state before you changed the size of the image.

Now that you're back to the original image, you can continue with making a new image map.

Often, brick isn't very shiny. Looking at the picture, what you can determine about how light shines on the elements in the picture is that anything that looks black is not shiny. This is where there is either to much shade or there is no shiny quality about it. The rest of the image is just flat in terms of light.

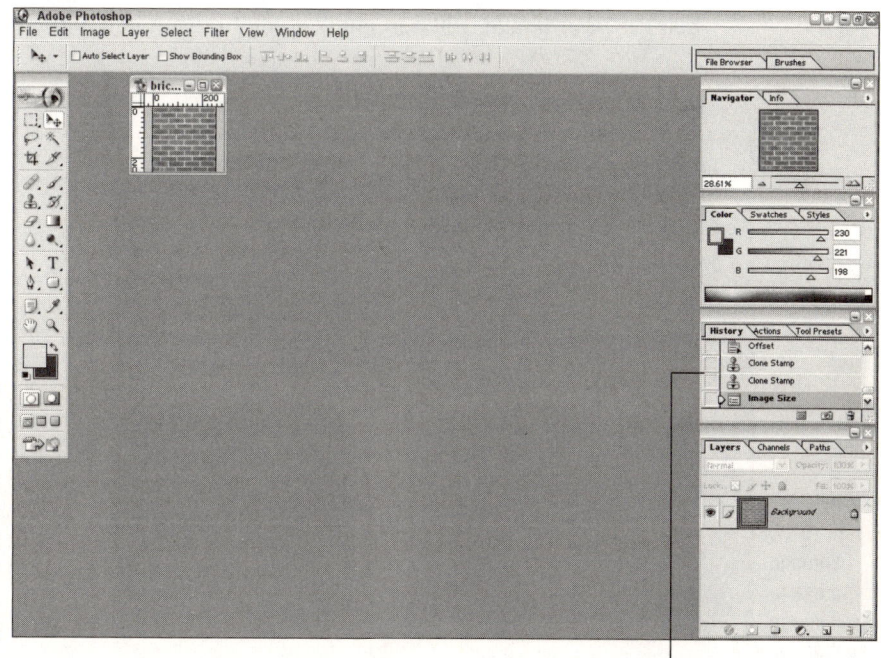

Figure 15-13: When you resize your image, it might appear pretty small.

History tab

So, you need to tell the game that all the black areas of the texture are un-shiny and that the rest of the image is neither shiny nor un-shiny, but rather flat. With Photoshop, this is easy to do.

1. **Zoom in 125 percent to the image in Photoshop.**

   The "Shifting the image to expose the seam" section offers several zooming methods.

   You can tell when you are at 125 percent by either looking at the title bar on your image's window or by looking at the Navigator window. There you will see the zoom percentage reflected, as shown in Figure 15-14.

2. **Choose Select➪Color Range.**

   A dialog box opens, and an eyedropper replaces your mouse pointer. You can use this eyedropper either in the box shown in this small dialog box or on the image you're working on in Photoshop. The idea is to select the black color in your image. This selection will then be translated to the game as the shiny area of the texture.

3. **Before selecting the black color, change the Fuzziness value to 150 by adjusting the slider near the top of the window.**

   This is the percentage of color to be selected. Because there is so little black in your image, 150 percent is going to result in a better selection.

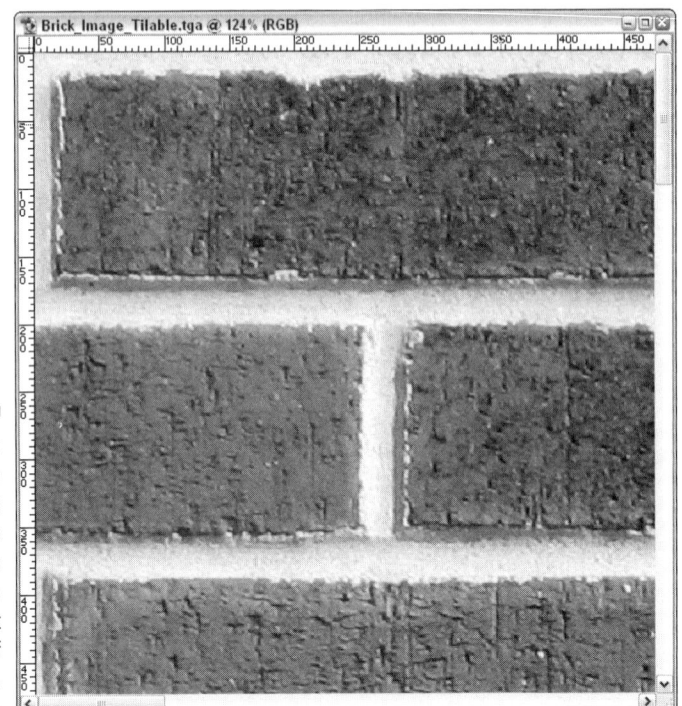

Figure 15-14: Zoom in close to your image so that you can see the distinct colors of your brick.

Chapter 15: Creating Custom Textures *263*

 4. **Use the eyedropper on the image in Photoshop behind the Color Range dialog box by pointing and clicking it with your eyedropper. Because you zoomed in, you can more easily select the black color in your image.**

    When you select the black color, what you selected should be displayed as white in the small dialog box, as it is in Figure 15-15.

 Figure 15-15: When you select black, it appears as white in the Color Range preview window.

 5. **Press OK to make your selection and close the dialog box.**

    All the black in your image has been selected. You now need to use this selection to your advantage.

 6. **Create a new layer in Photoshop.**

    In the bottom-right corner of the editor is a tab labeled Layers. (If this tab is not opened, select it now.) At the bottom of this tab is a group of icons. The second icon from the right looks like a page with the bottom corner folded over and is displayed in the margin. You can use this icon to create new layers in Photoshop. Press it once now.

    When you add a new layer, it is added to the list of available layers, as shown in Figure 15-16. The layer will be named Layer 1, but the name isn't important. What's important is that you can add more imagery to this layer that will lay over top of the existing layer. That's because it is listed over top of the other layer called *Background*.

 7. **Choose Edit⇨Fill.**

    A dialog box like the one in Figure 15-17 opens. In this dialog box, you can define which color is to fill in your selected area.

 8. **From the Use pull-down menu, select Black and then press OK.**

Figure 15-16:
Create a new layer on the Layers tab.

You might not see much of a difference yet, but it's coming.

9. **Deselect everything. You can do this either by choosing Select⇨Deselect or with the shortcut Ctrl+D.**

10. **Back to the Layers tab, select the Background layer.**

Figure 15-17:
When you go to fill your selection, you have a choice of color of which to apply.

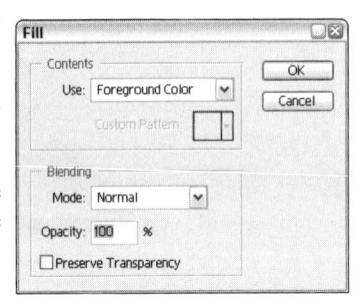

11. **Add another new layer by clicking the Create a New Layer icon.**

12. **Fill this new layer with a flat, gray color. Choose Edit⇨Fill. Select 50% gray as your fill color. Then press OK to apply the changes.**

A level of 50 percent gray is considered neutral in the game, so anything that is black won't be shiny, and anything that is white will be shiny. The result looks like Figure 15-18.

When you present this to the game as the specular map, each of these colors will tell the game something specific. Anything that is 50 percent gray is basically ignored. It is considered neither shiny nor dull. Anything that is black is considered dull. Anything that is white, if there were white in this image, would be considered shiny. That leaves all the shades of gray in between that represent different levels of shininess.

All that's left is to resize and save it for the game.

Chapter 15: Creating Custom Textures 265

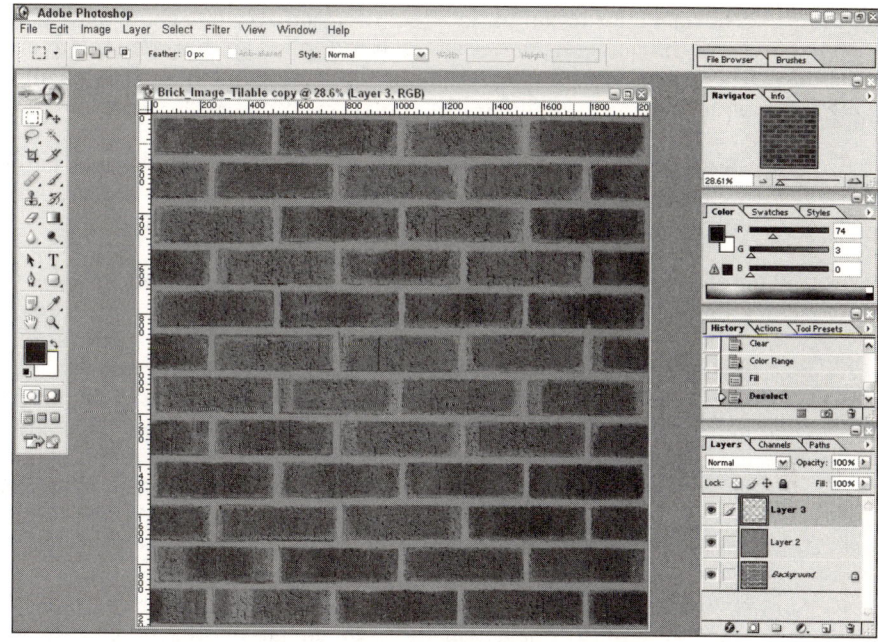

Figure 15-18: Fill the layer with a neutral color.

13. Resize the image by choosing Image⇨Size and entering a width and height of 256 pixels. Press OK to apply the change.

14. Choose Save⇨Save As and make sure that the same game folder is still selected.

    That folder was `C:\Program Files\id Software\Quake 4\q4base\textures\chapter15`.

15. Select Targa as the Format for your image and then enter brick_s.tga for the name.

16. Press Save, select 24 bits/pixel when prompted.

    You're ready to move on to the next piece of your texture.

Bumping polygons in and out: The normal map

The next image up is going to be the normal map. This image describes the surface of the map; it tells the game what parts stick out and back in. It's very similar to the height map, which comes next, except that this *normal map* also affects the way light reflects off the texture.

266 Part IV: Going Beyond the Basics

TECHNICAL STUFF A normal map actually can affect the geometry of a game map. It's meant to move the polygons under which it is applied so that they bump out or in. This is why light is affected by this texture element, because light would bounce off a curve differently than it would off a flat surface.

Before starting, use your History tab in Photoshop to go back in time before the image was altered for your specular map. Scroll up until you find the Color Range history layer and select the layer before it.

In the beginning of this chapter, I mention that you need a conversion tool found on the CD in the back of the book titled `Photoshop_Plugins_7.83.0629.1500.exe`. Well, now is the time to use it, so make sure you've installed it for use with Photoshop. If you need confirmation that it has been installed, in Photoshop, choose Filter. Near the bottom of the drop-down menu you should see a file called NVIDIA Tools. If you see this filter, you're ready to go. If you are unable to install or use the Photoshop plugin as provided, save the image you have currently open in Photoshop as `brick_local_pre.tga`. Then, skip to the end of this section where I discuss an alternative to creating a normal map.

Now that you're ready to create your normal map, it's time to tell Photoshop what parts of the image will stick out, lie flat, or stick in. Like the specular map you just created, you define these different aspects of the image by using white, black, and shades of gray. White defines the areas that stick out, such as the bricks, and black defines the areas that stick in, like the grout. You do all this by using the color-selecting tool in Photoshop.

1. **Open the color selector by choosing Select**⇨**Color Range.**
2. **In the image, select the group with your eyedropper.**

    Starting with the grout is easiest because it's mostly solid color.

3. **Turn the Fuzziness down to 100 using the slider near the top of the window because you want to select only the white and no more than that. Then, when you have what looks like Figure 15-19, press OK to make your selection.**

    This selection that you just made is going to be sticking in on the texture. Therefore it will be defined with the fill color of black.

4. **Create a new layer in the Layers tab in Photoshop. Choose Edit**⇨**Fill, select Black as the Use color, and then press OK to apply the color fill to the new layer.**

    The rest of the image is going to be sticking out, and there won't be any in-between part of the image that lies flat.

Chapter 15: Creating Custom Textures 267

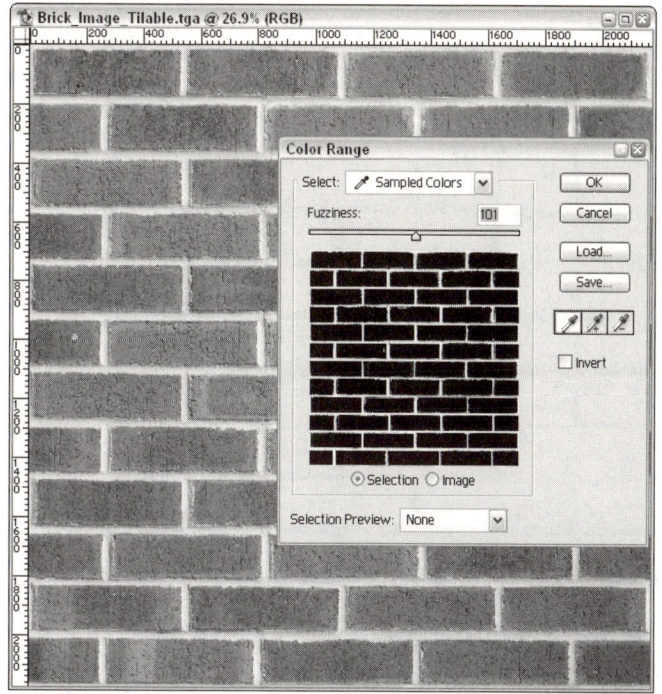

Figure 15-19: Select the white color in the grout between your bricks.

 5. **Select the Background layer in the Layers tab and create another new layer. Deselect everything by pressing Ctrl+D. Then fill the new layer with white by choosing Edit➪Fill and applying White as the Use color.**

 The result looks like Figure 15-20.

 Now for the NVIDIA filter that you installed earlier. In order to use this filter, you need to combine all of your layers into one layer. In Photoshop, this is called flattening.

 6. **Choose Layer➪Flatten Image.**

 All your layers are combined into a single layer. Now you can apply the NVIDIA filter.

 7. **Choose Filter➪NVIDIA Tools➪NormalMapFilter.**

 A dialog box opens. There are a lot of options in this tool, and for this filter to work with the game it's important that you set them correctly. As shown in Figure 15-21, there are three columns of options, and you should set them as follows.

 a. The first column of options should be left all deselected.

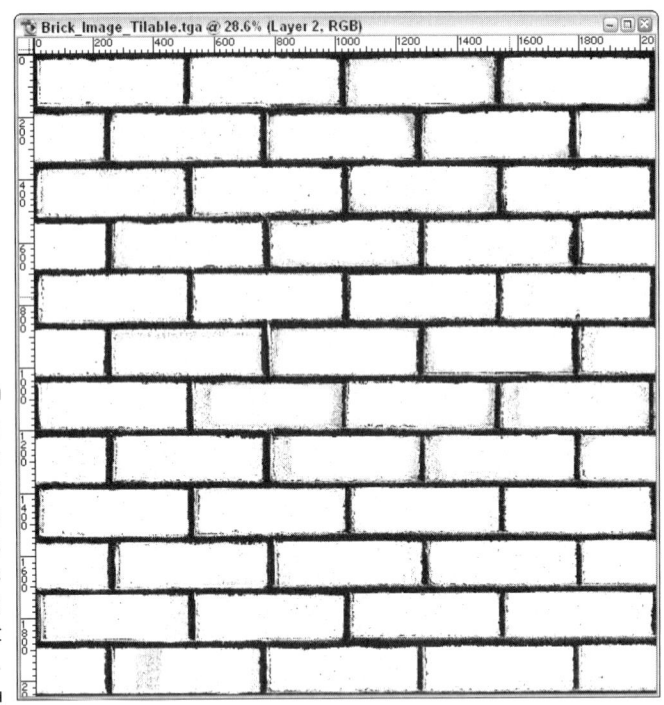

Figure 15-20: Apply color information: White represents what sticks out and black what sticks in.

- b. In the second column, select a Filter Type of 4 Sample because this is a required option for the game. Also select the Wrap check box because this image is a tileable image that can be wrapped. Your MinZ should be set to 0, indicating that your lowest height value is 0, and your Scale set to 16. (I explain the Scale in more detail shortly.) Select the check box for Animate Light because this helps display your changes in the 3D Preview.

- c. In the third column, select Average RGB, which should be the only available option. Do not select any of the Alternative Conversions. Then select an Alpha Field of Height.

You might want to experiment with the Scale option. This setting adjusts how much bumping will occur with your image. The lower the number, the less of a bumping effect your image will have. I suggested that you set this to 16, but you can try other values. Play with the number if you want, and then press the 3D Preview button to see what it might look like in the game.

8. **When you're ready, press OK to apply the filter changes to your image.**

   When you do, your image turns to a mostly blue color, something like Figure 15-22. (Trust me, it's blue.) This is typical because the normal map uses color information to create the effect of bumpiness. This is

Chapter 15: Creating Custom Textures **269**

your height map, and other than requiring a resize and save, it's ready for the game.

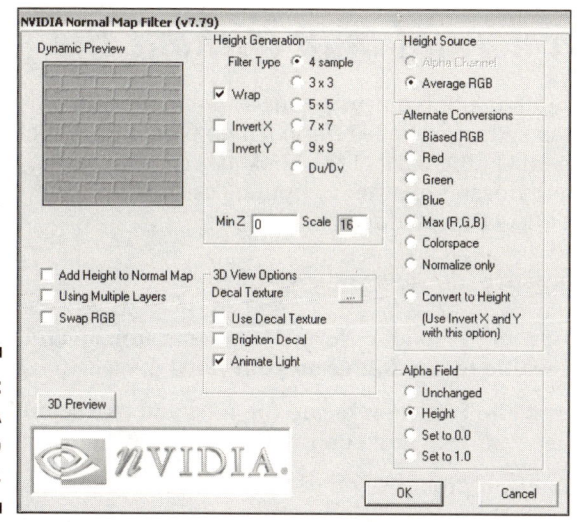

Figure 15-21: The NVIDIA Normal Map Filter.

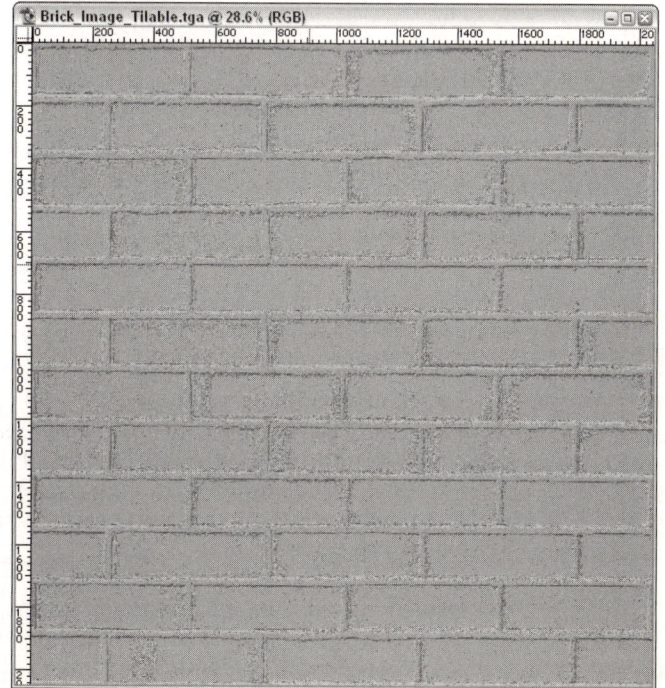

Figure 15-22: Apply the filter changes to your normal map. It will look blue in color.

Part IV: Going Beyond the Basics

9. **Resize the image to 256 pixels in height and width. Then save the image in your custom textures folder as `brick_local.tga`.**

Creating a normal map without the filter

If you can't use the Photoshop plugin detailed above, then there is another option. ATI has released a tool called *Normal Map Generator,* which I have included on the media in the back of the book as well. This image converter is not as precise and doesn't offer many options as the Photoshop plugin from NVIDIA, but it gets the job done.

To install this alternative tool, follow these steps:

1. **Open the file from the media, NormalMapGenerator.zip and extract the contents of this file to any folder on your hard drive.**

2. **Using Windows File Explorer, locate the files you extracted from** NormalMapGenerator.zip **and run the file** TGAtoDOT3.exe.

   When it's running, it prompts you to select a TGA image file.

3. **Select the file you just saved in Photoshop titled** brick_local_pre.tga **and press Open.**

   Almost instantaneously, you will see a message pop-up that reads, "Success! New TGA file: `C:\Program Files\id Software\Quake 4\ q4base\textures\chapter15\brick_local_preDOT3.tga`". Now just rename that file for use within the game.

4. **Locate** C:\Program Files\id Software\Quake 4\q4base\textures\ chapter15\brick_local_preDOT3.tga **in File Explorer, right-click the file, select Rename, and change the name to** brick_local.tga.

Defining the ups and downs: The height map

Revert your image to its colorful self using the History tab. In the History tab, there are listed in sequence the actions you performed in Photoshop. Select the action that makes your image look like it did when you saved it as the diffuse map. It should look like the nice, red brick that you expect to see in the game.

It's time to make another image for your texture. This time, the image you make will be the *height map.* The height map outlines the finer details of bumps such as cracks, pits, and other small defects in the image.

The height map is extremely similar to the normal map. The difference is how the game utilizes it. For instance, the normal map can deform the surface upon which it has been applied. The height map, on the other hand, uses light and shadows to trick the viewer into seeing depth. Also, a normal map requires use of the NVIDIA filter to define the bumps in the image. The height map uses only black-and-white shading, just like the specular map.

So, because the height map makes you see bumps in your texture only by playing tricks, it can't be used in same manner as the normal map. If you include as your height map a back-and-white version of your normal map, you'll get visual errors. That's because the two maps are trying to provide similar information and are fighting each other for dominance.

In the case of the texture you're building with the bricks, what you want is a height map that looks just like the specular map. You want to define where the pits and creases are in the bricks, but you don't want to go to the same extremes as you did with the specular map. When you selected the black color for the specular map, you selected it at 150-percent fuzziness. This time, you want to select it at a lower percentage.

1. **In Photoshop, zoom into the image at about 125 percent.**

   I give you zooming instructions in the earlier section, "Shifting the image to expose the seams."

2. **Choose Select➪Color Range and select a black spot on your image with the eyedropper. Make sure your Fuzziness level is at 100 this time by adjusting the slider near the top of the window. Then press OK to make your selection.**

3. **Create a new layer in the Layers tab by clicking the New Layer icon on the Layers tab. Choose Edit➪Fill, select Black as the color, and apply your changes.**

   This step fills your selection with black, defining the indentation caused by your height map.

4. **Select the Background layer again and create another new layer. Deselect everything in the image by pressing Ctrl+D. Then fill the layer with 50 percent gray.**

   The result looks like Figure 15-23.

Figure 15-23: Black represents what bumps in, and white represents what bumps out.

Now, the image might look ready to go, but before you proceed, there is one more thing that should be added. In real life, grout and brick tend to have tiny bumps all over them. You should include such bumps in this height map.

 5. **Create another new layer, but do so from the currently selected layer that was just filled with 50 percent gray. Fill this new layer with white.**

    Select Edit➪Fill and then choose White as the Use color and press OK to perform the action.

 6. **Select choose Filter➪Noise➪Add Noise.**

    What you are going to do is add a bunch of tiny black dots to the image that represent all the tiny bumps in the grout and bricks.

    When you select the Add Noise filter, you get a dialog box that looks like Figure 15-24.

 7. **Select Uniform as the Distribution method for the noise and, because you don't need any colors in this image, check the box for Monochromatic. Adjust the noise amount until you see a lot of little dots all over the image. This should be at about 70 percent. Then press OK to apply.**

Chapter 15: Creating Custom Textures 273

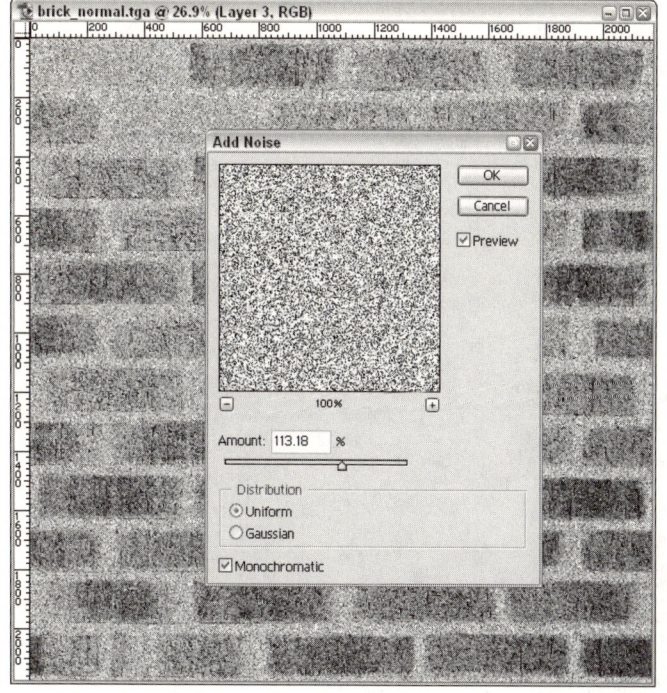

Figure 15-24: Apply a noise filter to make the tiny bumps that you often see in bricks and grout on buildings.

What's wrong with the image in its present state is that you have covered over the 50 percent gray, your noise bumps are pointing inward rather than outward, and there is way too much noise information.

First, I show you how to solve the bumping direction. This is easily fixed by inverting your image so that the black and white colors switch.

 8. **Choose Image⇨Adjustments⇨Invert and the colors switch resulting in Figure 15-25.**

    Now that you see way too much black, you need to adjust the layer properties so that only the white dots affect what you see.

 9. **Select the Screen option from the pull-down list at the top of the tab that currently reads as *Normal*.**

    You now have a much better-looking image, like the one of Figure 15-26. However, you must adjust how prominently the white bumps show up, which you can do by lowering the opacity.

10. **On the Layers tab, change the Opacity from 100% to 20%.**

    This step adjusts how prominently the white bumps show up. Remember, these are supposed to be tiny bumps that barely affect the image. However, having them in there will add a lot more to the effect of the overall texture in the game.

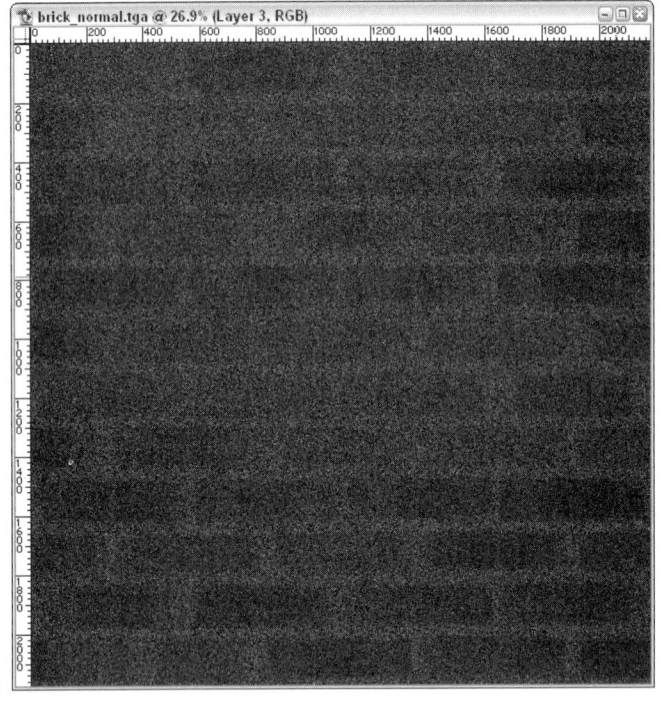

Figure 15-25: Your image may look very dark right now, but a few more changes and the effect will be complete.

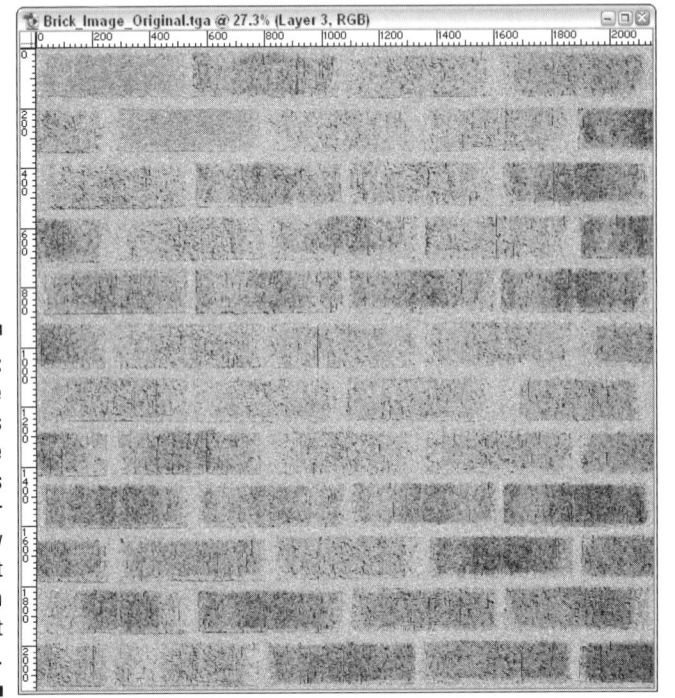

Figure 15-26: Inverting the colors has made the little bumps in your image. Now you must turn down the amount of bumping.

Now you're ready to save your image.

11. **Resize the image to 256 pixels in width and height. Then save the image in the correct textures folder as `brick_h.tga`.**

Finding the texture: The editor image

There's one last image to create before you can close Photoshop: the *editor image*. Thankfully, this is the second-easiest image to create for the game. This is the image that shows up in the mapping editor. This way you can find your texture and apply it to whatever surface you want in the game.

1. **Revert your image back to the original brick by back-tracking through the History tab.**
2. **When you have the nice brick image back, resize it to 64 pixels in height and width.**
3. **Save the image as `brick_ed.tga`.**

Generally, an editor image is never larger than 256 pixels in size. Images larger than that would use up precious memory and fill up the preview window. This is where The Compressonator comes into play. This program has been provided to you on the CD in the back of this book.

The purpose of this program is to convert the Targa images that you just created for your texture into an image format called DDS. For each image you have, a number of different size versions of this image will be created. They will all be compressed into a single file and then saved as a `.dds` file.

This is good because it creates different levels of detail called *mip-maps*. If you're in a game and you see a building far off in the distance, you can't see the tiny details of the texture applied to that building. Therefore, there is no reason why the game should display that texture in all its glory. Instead, if a `.dds` version of this image is available, a smaller version of the image will be used. You won't miss any of the details, and your computer won't have to work as hard. When you move in close to the building, the higher-quality version of image is displayed, and everything looks great.

Note that I say "if a `.dds` version of this image is available." This isn't a requirement for your image to work in the game or editor. However, it does help to make everything run smoothly, and I highly recommended creating the `.dds` file.

1. **Load The Compressonator.**

   You can find a link to this program on your Start menu. When it's loaded, you have a fairly bland-looking interface on your screen, as shown in Figure 15-27.

Part IV: Going Beyond the Basics

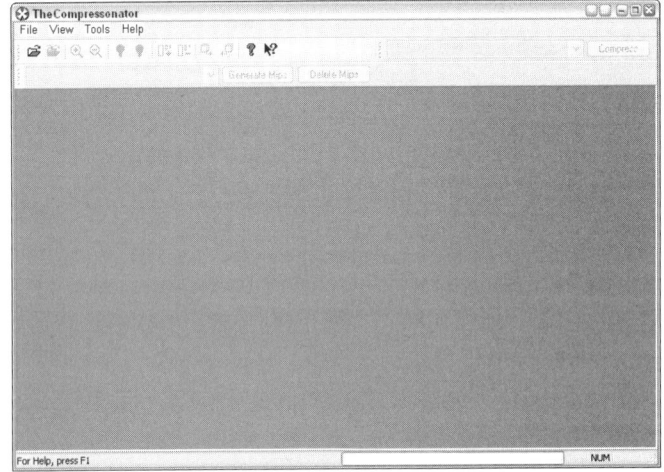

Figure 15-27: The Compressonator utility looks fairly bland, but the effect it has in the game is big.

To make things extremely easy, this program has a batch converter built in to it. This means that you can convert all your images at once without having to load and convert each one separately.

2. **Choose File⇨Batch Compress.**

   This opens a dialog box like that of Figure 15-28, where you can define all the details for your batch conversion.

3. **Navigate to the folder where your images are saved. (This should be `C:\Program Files\id Software\Quake 4\q4base\textures\chapter15`.) When you get there, select all the images except the one for `brick_ed.tga`.**

   Converting the editor image does you no good because it isn't used in the game.

   As for the other settings, here is what you want to apply:

   a. Select the Use Input Directory check box under the Output Directory heading. This saves your converted images to the same directory from which they came.

   b. For Output File Format, select the option DirectDraw Surface Textures (*.DDS).

   c. For Output Format, select the option DirectX Texture Compression. Then click the Option button next to it to bring up the option dialog box shown in Figure 15-29. Because the fact that your textures do not have an alpha channel would define part of the image as being transparent, select the DXT1 (0/1 bit Alpha) option and leave the rest of the settings in their default state. Press OK when you have made the changes.

Chapter 15: Creating Custom Textures 277

Figure 15-28: You can batch convert your images into their DDS format to save time and effort.

d. For Mipmaps, select Box-Filter. Then press the Option button next to it to bring up the window shown in Figure 15-30. Make sure the Lowest Mip-Level is set to 1 x 1 and click the Generate button to continue.

Figure 15-29: Apply these precise compression settings, or your texture won't work.

Figure 15-30:
Your lowest mip-map level should be set to 1x1.

With the settings in place and your four images selected, press the Compress button to perform the conversion. When you do, a window appears, providing you with the conversion status of each image. When the conversion is complete, your window will look like Figure 15-31. You can close this program and confirm that there are now four new files ending in `.dds` within your `textures\chapter15` folder.

Figure 15-31: While The Compressonator works on your images, a window displays the progress.

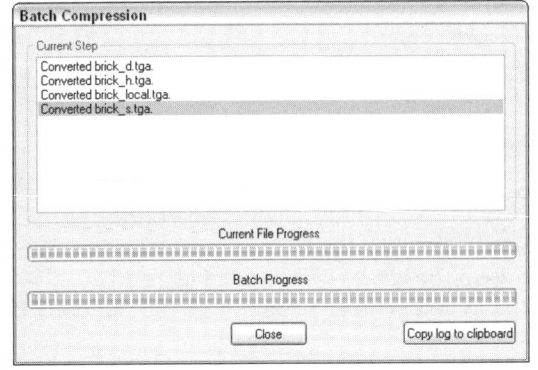

Sometimes The Compressonator will get stuck and not perform the operation you request. If you have any trouble with the program, close it and reopen it. That usually fixes any issues.

That's it. Your images are ready, and you can now instruct the game on how to use them. You may now close your image programs and proceed.

Making Everything Work Together

Now that you have all the pieces of the texture puzzle, it's time to assemble them. In a text file that looks just like a script, you need to tell the game where to find each of these images and how to assemble them. This bit of script in your text file is called a *shader*.

Building a shader

To create a shader for this new texture, follow these steps:

1. **Open NotePad.**
2. **In the text editor, type the following line of text:**

   ```
   textures/chapter15/brick {
   ```

   This line tells the game that you are defining a new texture called `chapter15/brick`. Just like when you applied the texture `common/caulk` in your map, you would apply this new texture `chapter15/brick` after this file has been completed.

3. **(Optional) To instruct the game that you want your material to behave like brick, add this line to your text files:**

   ```
   stone
   ```

   This second line defines the surface type of material you are creating. This addition isn't required, but it will affect how objects interact with your texture. For example, if you were making a metal texture, you would want to tell the game that the surface material is made of metal. This way, when someone shoots at the texture, the bullets would bounce off with sparks just like on metal. On the other hand, if this were a sand texture for the ground, you would want it to sound like sand when someone was walking on it rather than metal or wood. You wouldn't want bullets looking like they bounce off it.

   A list of possible surface types that can be assigned to a material is as follows:

cardboard	plastic
flesh	ricochet
glass	stone
liquid	wood
metal	

4. **The next line you need to type is**

   ```
   qer_editorimage textures/chapter15/brick_ed.tga
   ```

   This line instructs the mapping editor where to find the image for the texture preview tab. When you loaded your textures in the editor, there were thumbnail images of each of the textures that made it easy to browse and select a texture of choice for your application. This is the image that you will see as a thumbnail.

5. **Continue with these next two lines of code:**

   ```
   diffusemap textures/chapter15/brick_d.tga
   specularmap textures/chapter15/brick_s.tga
   ```

Here you tell the game where to find the colorful diffuse map image and the specular map that controls the shininess of the texture. So far, these lines of scripting are quite straightforward.

6. **Type in the following line to your text file:**

   ```
   bumpmap addnormals ( textures/chapter15/brick_local.tga, heightmap (
          textures/chapter15/brick_h.tga, 1 ) )
   ```

   With this line, you define is the bumpiness of your image. This line is a little more complicated because you want to not only define how your image will deform the brush face with your normal map, but you also want to define the smaller bumps created with lighting tricks via the height map.

   This one line actually contains information for both of your bumpy images. The two images together are your bump map. First the normal map is defined, and then the height map. The height map, however, has an additional instruction at the end.

   The number 1 entered at the end of your height map tells the game how much influence this image will have on the bumping of your texture. Generally, you will enter only 1. However, in some cases, when you want the bumping to be more extreme, you might consider increasing this number slightly. I haven't found a maximum number to enter here, but I highest number I have seen used by other modders is 5. You really shouldn't need to go any higher than that.

7. **To close your script, add the closing curly bracket.**

   The result, when fully assembled in your text file, will read like this:

   ```
   textures/chapter15/brick {
       stone
       qer_editorimage textures/chapter15/brick_ed.tga
       diffusemap textures/chapter15/brick_d.tga
       specularmap textures/chapter15/brick_s.tga
       bumpmap addnormals (
              textures/chapter15/brick_local.tga, heightmap
           ( textures/chapter15/brick_h.tga, 1 ) )
   }
   ```

   With your shader file written, you need to save it someplace that the game can find and read it.

8. **Choose File➪Save As in NotePad. Navigate to the folder `C:\Program Files\id Software\Quake 4\q4base`. Here, you need to create a new folder for the game called materials. Open the materials folder and save your new shader file as `chapter15.mtr`.**

> **REMEMBER:** After you save your file as `chapter15.mtr`, open the folder location by using Windows File Explorer and double-check that the file has the correct name. Sometimes when you save a file by using NotePad and you add a file extension other than `.txt`, the program will add `.txt` to the end. The result will be a file named `chapter15.mtr.txt`. Check that this hasn't happened and, if it has, correct the error by renaming the file.

The name of the file isn't crucial, but again, you don't want it to be confused with a file that might have been created by someone else. Therefore, naming it in relation to your map makes sense.

TIP

You can add as many shaders as you want in this one material file. You don't have to create a new text file for each shader. Just follow the preceding steps for creating your scripting and you can add as many of these as you want.

Now you are done and ready to show off your work.

Applying your material

Construction time is over, and now it's time to play. This is where you get to apply your texture in the editor and then see how it looks in the game.

1. **Load the editor, and then load your last map version, which should be `chapter14.map`. So as not to mess up the previous map, save this map as a new name, `chapter15.map`.**

2. **With your map loaded in the editor, move your camera in the CAM window to the outside area.**

   You are going to apply your new brick texture to the outer walls.

3. **To load your new texture, select the Media tab where your texture sets are located. You named your new texture as `chapter15/brick`, so locate and load the newly added chapter15 texture set, as shown in Figure 15-32.**

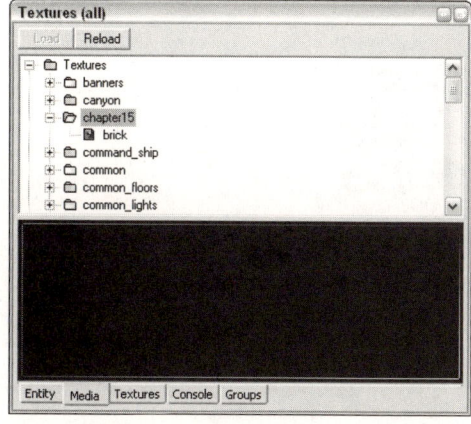

Figure 15-32: Find the texture set that you created with your material file.

4. **Switch to the Textures tab, and there you will see your new, custom texture.**

Part IV: Going Beyond the Basics

In Figure 15-33 you can see it's ready to be selected and applied to your wall.

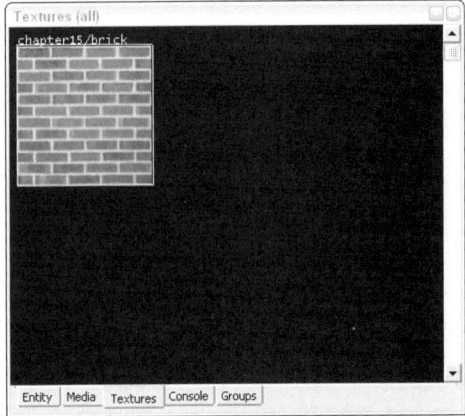

Figure 15-33: The Textures tab displays a clear picture of your texture.

  5. **Select the inner brush face of one of the walls that surrounds your outdoor area in the map. Then select and apply your new texture to it.**

  6. **Continue to apply this texture to your surrounding wall until you have covered it entirely.**

     As you do this, you will notice that you can't see where one square of the texture ends and the other begins. This means your attempt to make it tileable was successful, as shown in Figure 15-34.

Figure 15-34: When applied to the wall surrounding your map, your texture will look clean and seamless.

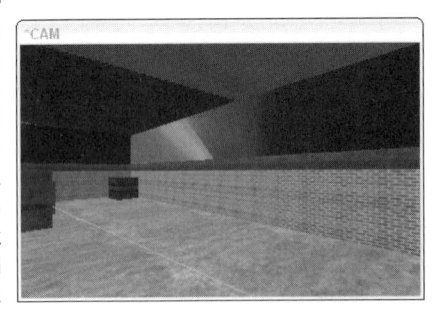

  7. **Now that you have completed applying your new texture, save your map again. Then compile it by using the BSP process.**

     Select Bsp⇨bsp and that will compile your map. Refer to Chapter 8 for details of this process.

Chapter 15: Creating Custom Textures 283

8. **When it's done compiling, start the game by pressing F2. Then load your new map through the console by typing** devmap game/chapter15.

   What you should see is a beautiful-looking brick wall like the one shown in Figure 15-35. Regardless of whether you're up close or far away, it will look good and run well in the game.

Figure 15-35: In the game, your texture will look well detailed regardless of your distance from it.

> If you're making little changes to your textures and trying to view these changes in the game, you might find that the game doesn't update them. To solve this issue, you have two options: You can close the game and restart to clear the memory, or you can open the console and type **image_use PrescompressedTextures 0** (default value is 1). Then the game will stop caching your images on load but will also take much longer to load each map.

Chapter 16

Gaming with GUIs

In This Chapter

▶ Adding an interactive entity and applying a GUI

▶ Creating your own GUI and using it in the game

▶ Finding existing GUIs that you might want to edit

The graphical user interface, or GUI, plays an important role throughout the *Quake 4* game. GUIs are used frequently to provide a means of controlling some aspect of gameplay and to provide a fancy display of graphics and sounds. For a common example, you must interact with a GUI in *Quake 4* when you want to make an elevator move.

After working with trigger brushes in your map from previous chapters, you're probably wondering why a GUI would be needed. Trigger brushes also display fancy graphics that can be animated and provide different ways for the player to interact. On a GUI, however, the player can view information as on a computer monitor, use the entire interface like a button to make something happen (such as opening a door), or use a specific area of the interface (such as a "Click Here" link) to make something else happen.

GUIs are everywhere. For example, while your map is loading, your map name appears with a dark background at the top of the screen; there is a loading bar, and there is a dark background at the bottom of the screen, too. This is all one big GUI.

To create a total modification of the game, you must know how to create your own GUIs. I show you how to add your own graphics; how to control an entity (in this case, a pair of doors); and how to make that entity usable by the player.

Opening Doors

To start, first add a simple GUI to your map. Your new GUI will be used to control the opening of the doors in place of the existing trigger brush. However, that trigger brush will need to remain in place so it can trigger the monster on the other side. This means that the player will have to walk up to this interface and use it to cause the doors to open. This effect is exactly the same as you might see in some of the single-player maps that come with the game.

> **TIP:** GUIs aren't limited to use in single-player maps. You can use GUIs in any type of map. Just be sure that when you're inserting them into your maps that you don't make them a nuisance to the player, thereby making the level less fun to play.

Looking at the wall

Before you start, open the map from the last chapter. Then save it as `chapter16.map` in the same location as the previous map. This way nothing will happen to the last map you made, and you can continue the work you've already done. Also, copy any scripts you have from the previous map version and save them under the name of the new map so that they are available in this map as well. Specifically, the `chapter15.script` needs to be copied and renamed to `chapter16.script`.

Focus the editor on the set of doors in the room at the bottom of the map. This is the blue room, and this is where you are going to add your GUI to control the doors.

1. **Load your Common texture set and select the Nodraw texture.**

   Generally you would create your brushes with the Caulk texture, but not in this case. Here, you want to make sure that your brush is invisible on all sides except the panel where the user will interact with the GUI. It also needs to be a non-solid. (The Caulk texture creates an invisible, yet solid brush.)

2. **Zoom in close to the left side of the doors on the inside of the room. Here, draw a brush with the Nodraw texture that is about 16 units away from the doors and about 16 units wide.**

3. **Move the brush so it's centered on the 64-unit Z axis and stretch it to 16 units tall.**

   The brush should look like the one shown Figure 16-1.

Figure 16-1: Create a small brush near the door for your GUI by using the Nodraw texture.

4. **Zoom in closer to your brush within the 2D window. Zoom in until the brush nearly fills the window. Then change your grid size to 1 unit by pressing 1.**

5. **Adjust the brush so that it is against the wall and is only 1 unit thick (see Figure 16-2).**

   The idea is to make your brush so thin that the player can't see that it sticks off the wall. In the game, the Nodraw texture won't be displayed, and your GUI will appear to be floating. This will hide that effect.

Figure 16-2: Make the brush 1 unit thick so that it looks like it's part of the wall.

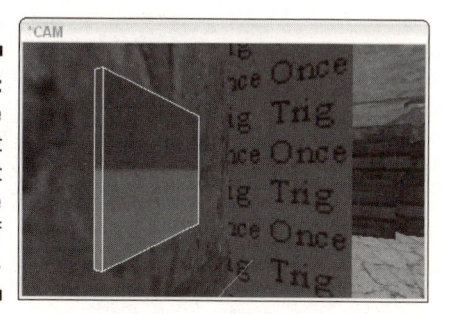

6. **When you're done stretching the brush, return your grid size to 8 units by pressing 4.**

   This way you won't accidentally make single-unit adjustments to any of your brushes later on without realizing it. Such a small unit adjustment isn't easy to see unless you're zoomed in close.

7. **Select the brush face on which you intend to apply the GUI.**

   This is the larger surface facing away from the wall and the surface that the player will interact with.

8. **Apply the texture `common/entitygui`. Open the surface inspector by pressing S. Enter a value of 1 in both the Width and Height value boxes to the right of the Fit button. Then click the Fit button, as I have done in Figure 16-3. Close the Surface Inspector.**

Figure 16-3: Apply the entitygui texture to the face of the brush and fit it to size.

Later, when you tell the game to display the GUI on this brush, the game will display it on this texture. Because the size of the texture influences the size of the GUI, you must size the entitygui texture to the size of the brush. If the texture were off-centered and too large, the GUI would also be off-centered and too large.

Interacting with an entity

Now you have to turn your brush into a GUI entity. Here's how:

1. **Select the entire brush you're working on.**

   You now must turn it into an entity so that the game can apply the GUI.

2. **Turn the brush into a `func_static` entity by right-clicking the 2D window and choosing func⇨func_static.**

3. **Open the Entity tab.**

   On the bottom-right of this tabbed window, you see a button labeled Gui. It's also shown in Figure 16-4. This button allows you to select a GUI for your entity.

4. **Press the Gui button now to launch the GUI selection window.**

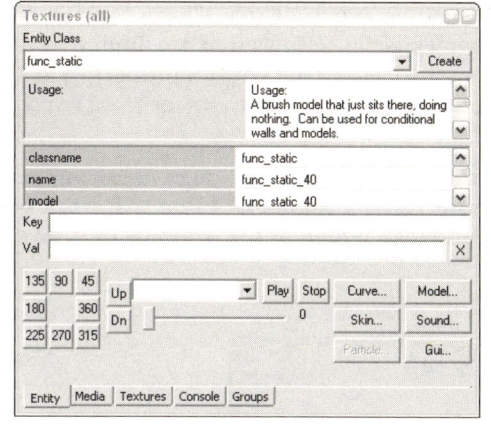

Figure 16-4: To select and apply a GUI to your entity, click the Gui button in the Entity tab.

The GUI selection dialog box looks a lot like the model select window, discussed in Chapter 12. It contains folders that better sort the different GUIs that are available. It also has a preview window on the bottom left and a comments window on the bottom-right, as shown in Figure 16-5. Feel free to explore the different GUIs that are available before continuing.

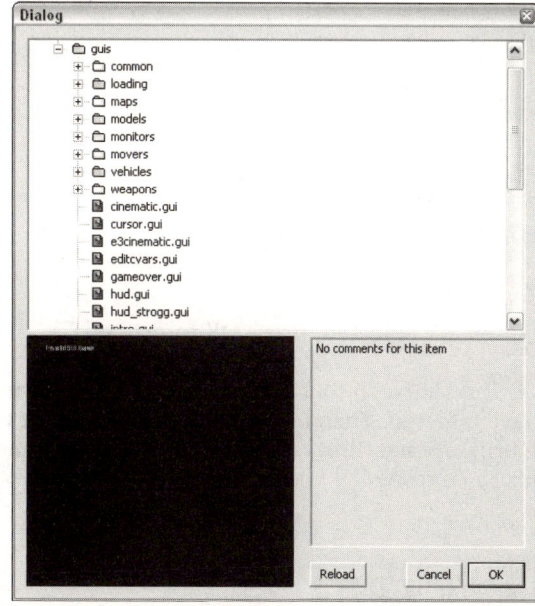

Figure 16-5: You can browse and preview GUIs just like you can with models.

TECHNICAL STUFF: Many of the GUIs have comments available. These comments are meant to assist you in applying special settings that are unique to each GUI. The settings can be applied within the entity's properties as a Val and Key or through scripting by using the `entity.setGuiParm( "Key", "Val" )` script command.

5. **For your door GUI, open the folder `base/guis/common/strogg`. Here you can find `open.gui`, a simple GUI that will work perfectly for your door. Select it and take a look at the preview of it, as shown in Figure 16-6.**

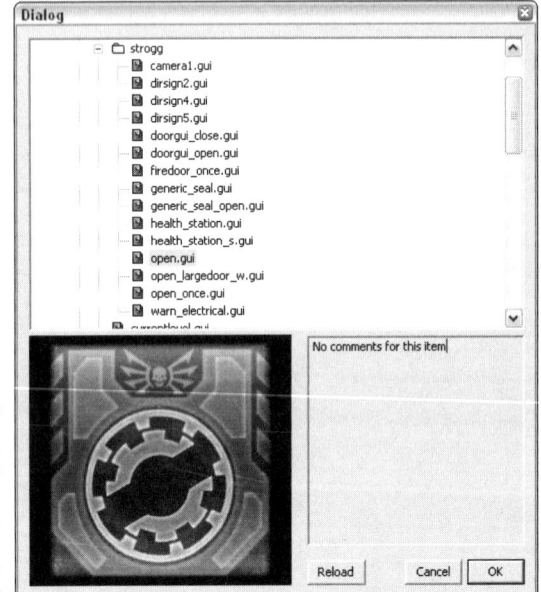

Figure 16-6: A preview of the open.gui GUI.

6. **With your GUI interface selected, press OK to proceed.**

REMEMBER: The `open.gui` GUI is simple in that when the player uses it, it triggers whatever you have targeted. Then it's ready to run again just like a trigger-multiple brush. Some GUIs can be used only once or need additional commands to be reset.

Controlling your doors

Your GUI is set for the game, but it doesn't do much other than look pretty. You still need to tell your GUI to control the doors. Follow these steps:

Chapter 16: Gaming with GUIs   291

1. **Press Esc to deselect everything, select your GUI entity first, select one of your door entities second, and then press Ctrl+K.**

    This targets your GUI to your doors in the order you selected. This targeting will be made apparent by a blue line that extends from the GUI's point of origin to the door's point of origin, as shown in Figure 16-7.

    REMEMBER

    You don't have to select both of the two doors for targeting. In Chapter 12, you used an entity Key and Val to team the doors together so that they acted in unison. So, you need to target only one of the doors to open on command, and then the other door, because it's on the same team, will open with it.

    You must do one more thing before the doors are complete. Right now, if you walk up to the doors, they open automatically. You don't want the doors to open automatically when you have an interface on the wall to perform this same function. You need to tell the doors not to open unless they have been triggered to do so.

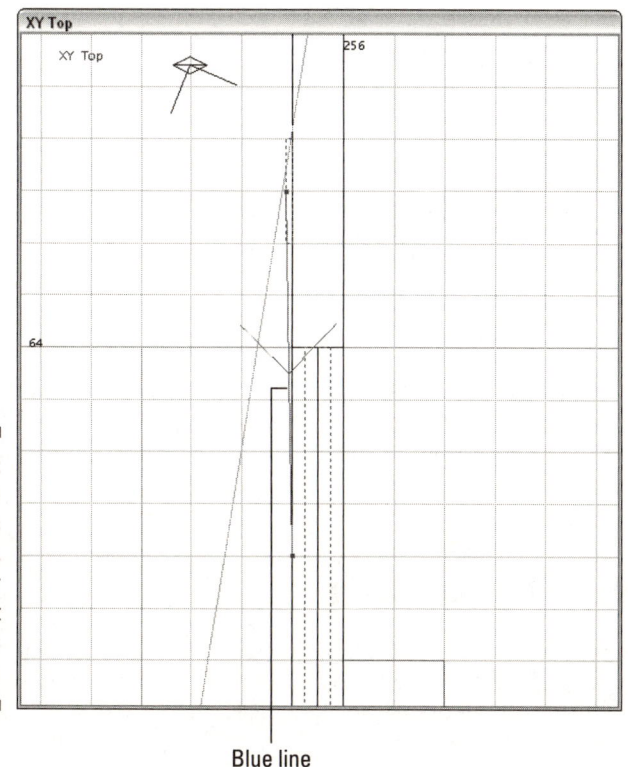

Figure 16-7: When the GUI entity is ready, remember to target your doors with it.

Blue line

Part IV: Going Beyond the Basics

2. **Press Esc to deselect everything and then select the two doors.**

   The command you're going to apply has to be applied to both doors, and you can apply the same command to all the selected entities at one time. If you look through the options available for this entity as presented in the scrollable field of the Entity tab, one of the listed options is no_touch. The description states, "the door should not be triggered by the player touching it, only by another trigger. In multiplayer, this door can't be shot to open." This is exactly what you want because the GUI is to trigger the doors to open.

3. **On the Entity tab, enter** no_touch **in the Key field and 1 in the Val field, as I have done in Figure 16-8. Then press Enter to apply the changes.**

Figure 16-8: Your doors are now controlled with a trigger and won't open automatically.

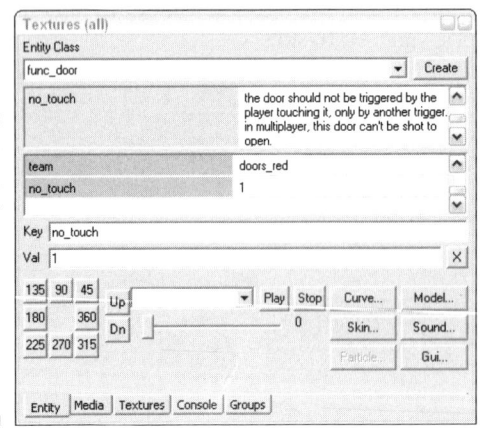

Now you can save your map, compile it, and test it in the game. The result will be a great-looking GUI to the side of the doors that the player can use to open the doors. It will look something like Figure 16-9 in the game.

Working on your own

While play-testing your map, you might notice some things that still need to be done. Depending on how you plan on using this map, you might need more interactivity with the doors. For instance, when the player gets outside of the room, how should he or she be able to get back in? Some options that you have:

Chapter 16: Gaming with GUIs

- Force the player to go around to the other side of the map and enter from the other room.
- Duplicate the GUI on the other side of the room. When doing this, you might need to retarget the duplicate.
- Add a trigger-multiple brush outside the room to trigger the doors when the player walks up to them.

Figure 16-9: In the game, your GUI looks great near the door and is ready for action.

For realism, add a structure around the GUI so that it looks like it is housed by something on the wall. Right now, the GUI is just in the middle of the wall. Adding a frame of metal would provide more logic to its existence, just like the light housings above each of your light entities in the rooms.

Creating a Custom Interface

Graphical user interfaces are not unlike map scripts. They are written in the form of functions with different commands. However, rather than calling to entities to do the actions, they call to images because this is a visual medium.

Luckily, there is an editor for building GUIs built right into the game, just like the mapping editor. This editor helps you understand the different parts of code that make up a GUI, but you won't have to write it all by hand. Instead, you can add and position the different elements of your GUI right on the screen, save them, and then use them in the game.

Starting the GUI editor

To access the GUI editor, start by launching the game. When the game has loaded, open the console, type **editguis**, and press Enter to launch the editor. When the editor loads, you should see a screen that looks like Figure 16-10.

In the next few pages, I show you how to create your own GUI. This GUI replaces the one now in the map but uses a lot of the elements that the original already has. Hopefully, you'll be able to carry this knowledge further on your own and be able to create some amazing things for the game.

Building your first GUI

To start a custom GUI, choose File⇨New. This opens a darker window on the screen, as shown in Figure 16-11. With this new GUI open in the editor, you're presented with a canvas and more options that might remind you of Photoshop. In the Navigator window, you can see your first element, called Desktop. If you explore the existing GUIs from the game, you'll notice that every GUI starts with a Desktop. This Desktop is called the *parent* because each element that you add to the GUI, be it a colored block, an image, or a line of text, is going to be a subsection (or *child*) of the Desktop.

Figure 16-10: The GUI editor.

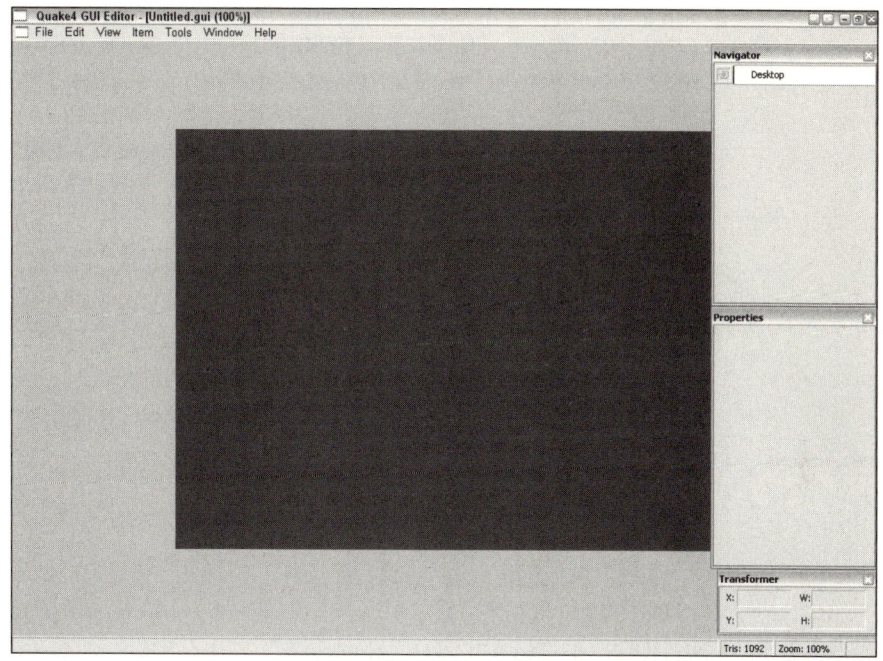

Figure 16-11: A new canvas.

Defining the background

To start off your GUI, select a background color. Here's how:

1. **Open the Desktop properties by double-clicking the Desktop layer in the Navigator window on the right. You can also access these properties by right-clicking the layer and choosing Properties from the pop-up menu.**

    You see an Item Properties dialog box pop up. The three tabs in this window are called

    - **General:** These are the basic properties of the element, including the name. In the case of the Desktop, the name should never be changed, but each child element can have any name you desire. These check boxes should remain in their default state.

    - **Image:** Here you can define for this layer a background color, a transparency, a material or texture, a border, or other visual aspects.

    - **Text:** This tab prints text on your layer. Anything you type is displayed, and you can further define how the text looks on the screen.

Part IV: Going Beyond the Basics

2. **Click the Image tab. Select the Backcolor check box and open the color drop-down selector by clicking the little down arrow to the right of the color block. Select green as your color and press OK to close the window.**

   The result should look like Figure 16-12. The smaller color block to the right of the now-green block is reserved for transparency. Ignore that for now.

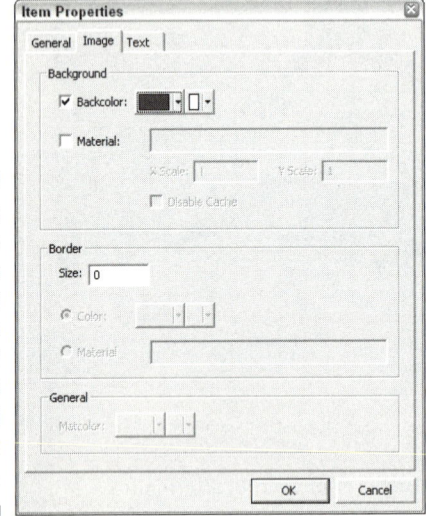

Figure 16-12: Define the properties of your Desktop layer, one of which is the background color for your GUI.

3. **Press OK to apply the background color change.**

   You should now see the color change on your screen.

Making children

Now you need to add a child layer to your Desktop. This is going to be an existing image that is already supplied with the game.

1. **Right-click the Desktop layer from within the Navigator window and choose New⇨windowDef.**

   A new layer is added. This layer is now a child of the Desktop, and it's currently named unnamed.

2. **Open the Item Properties dialog box for this new unnamed layer by double-clicking the layer from within the Navigator window. Click the General tab in the Item Properties dialog box and rename it to blue_left, as I have done in Figure 16-13.**

Chapter 16: Gaming with GUIs 297

> ### Custom GUI images
>
> If you would rather make your own GUI image, you can. The image is simply a Targa image and is easily made with Photoshop. When creating the image, size it according to how you are going to use it. In the case of this GUI, size it to 128 x 128 pixels because it's almost never going to be larger than 128 units square in your map.

Figure 16-13:
The General tab of a layer's properties.

3. **Switch to the Image tab. Select the Material check box and enter** gfx/guis/common/strogg/doorgui_bg **in the Material field (see Figure 16-14).**

4. **Press OK to apply the changes.**

    The result looks like Figure 16-15.

You can now see a familiar shape that looks like something from the GUI currently in place in your map next to the doors. However, the size and the color need to be fixed.

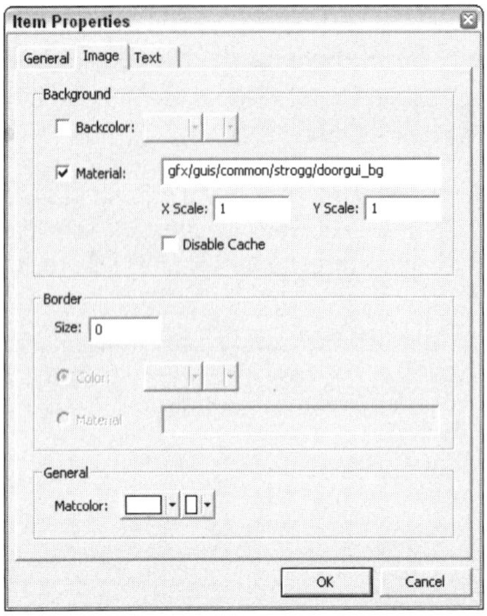

Figure 16-14: The Image tab of the layer's properties.

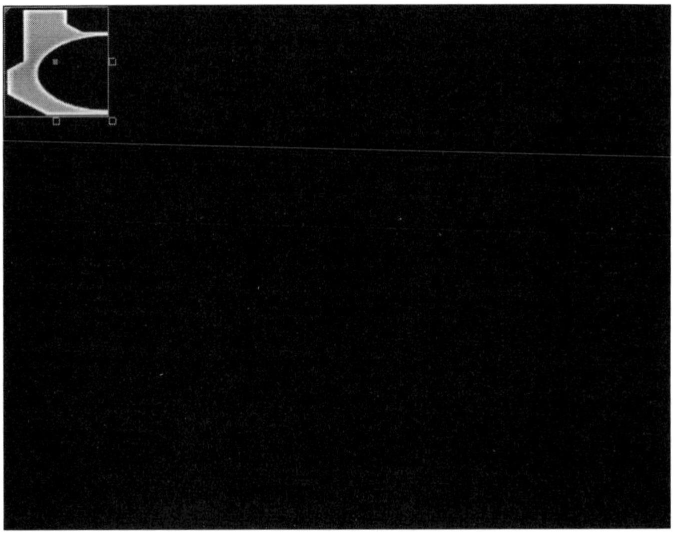

Figure 16-15: When you first apply a material to your GUI, you have to move and size it for the use you have in mind.

To fix the size, click and drag the blue boxes that surround the image. If you want to move the image, click and drag anywhere within the selected image. You can tell which one is selected by the blue outline around it. The goal is to size the image so that it covers half of the window on the left side. If you want to be more precise, here's an easy way to make it exactly half:

1. **Look over at the Properties window on the right side of the editor. The first property, rect, defines the location and the size of the image.**

   The location is the first two numbers, and they should read 0,0, which means the left, top of the window. The size is the second two numbers, and they should read 100,100. The first is the width, and the second is the height. The unit of measurement is in pixels.

   The size you want to end up with is 320,480. You want to enter 320,480 because the total size of the Desktop is 640 x 480. (You can confirm this size by clicking the Desktop and looking at the same Properties window.)

2. **Double-click the four numbers next to rect and change the numbers so they read 0,0,320,480. Press Enter when you're done.**

   The result looks like Figure 16-16.

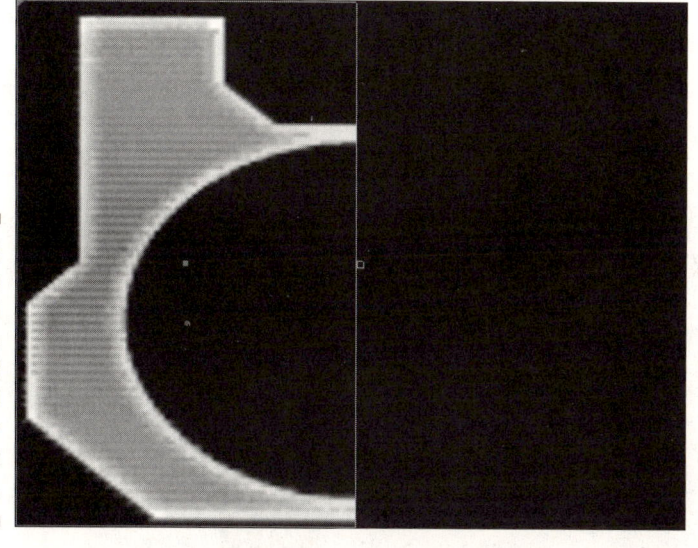

Figure 16-16: You can move and stretch the contents of your GUI layer any way that you desire.

Now that it's properly sized, you need to change the color. The image you are using was made special so that overlaying a color affects only parts of the image rather than the entire rectangle.

1. **Open the properties for your blue_left layer by double-clicking it in the Navigator window. In the dialog box that appears, select the Image tab and look at the bottom of the tab.**

   Here you see a color selector for Matcolor. This is how you define the color that is overlaid on your image. Because this is going to be for a blue room, select a bright blue color.

2. **Click the color block to the right of Matcolor, and then in the color selector click your bright blue color of choice.**

   3. **Press OK on the color selector and OK on the dialog box to apply the change.**

Duplicating layers

Next, you need to add the other half of the image that's already in place. Because the image you want to add is a mirror of what you already have, you can do this easily by making a duplicate of what you have and inverting the image.

   1. **In the Navigator window, right-click the blue_left layer. Choose Duplicate from the pop-up menu.**

      This creates an exact duplicate of the layer you already have.

   2. **Double-click this new layer to open the Item Properties dialog box for it. Click the General tab and rename the layer to blue_right.**

   3. **Switch to the Image tab and change the X Scale number from 1 to −1.**

      This causes the image to flip on the X axis (horizontally).

   4. **Press OK to apply the changes.**

      What you end up with is the second half of your image over the top of your first, as you can see in Figure 16-17.

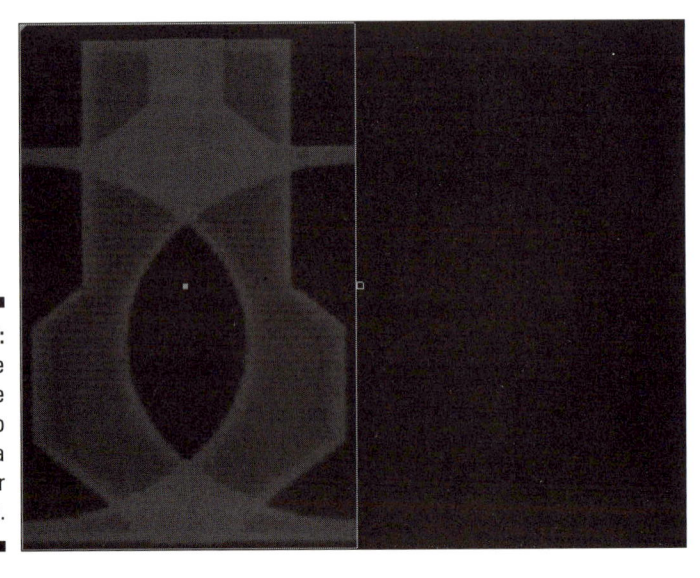

Figure 16-17: Duplicate and flip the first layer to create a mirror image.

Chapter 16: Gaming with GUIs

Because the two images are overlapping, you need to move the new one to the right side of the screen.

5. Click inside the selected image and drag it over to the right side.

You can either line it up by sight or you can enter the rect values in the Properties window located on the right side of the editor. The numbers you want to enter are 320,0,320,480. The result looks just like Figure 16-18.

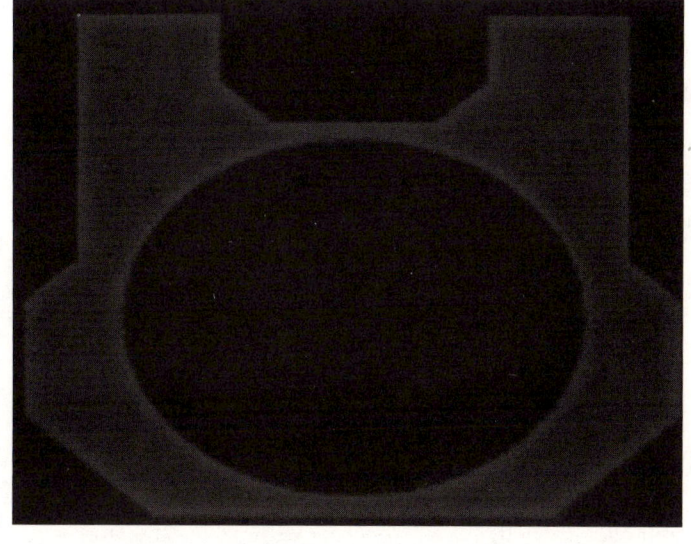

Figure 16-18: You can line up your images by sight or by entering values manually.

Now you should add a few more elements to make this interface more interesting to the player.

1. Add another layer by right-clicking the Desktop in the Navigator window and choosing New⇨windowDef.

2. Open the properties for this newly created layer by double-clicking it. Click the General tab and rename the layer to left_edge.

3. Click the Image tab and enter gfx/guis/common/strogg/doorgui_edge **in the Material field. Change your Matcolor to blue, and then click OK to apply the changes to the layer.**

The dialog box closes, and you wind up with what you see in Figure 16-19.

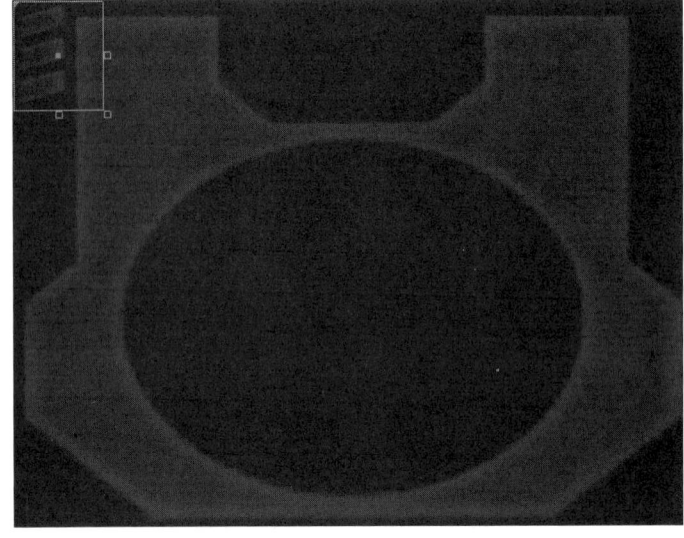

Figure 16-19: Continue to add more elements to make your GUI interesting.

   4. **Adjust the image size and position until it fills that left corner and looks good to you.**

      I explain how to adjust size and position in the earlier section, "Making children."

   5. **When the left side is done, duplicate this layer for the right side of your GUI.**

      Right-click the left_edge layer from within the Navigator window and choose Duplicate. Open the Item Properties dialog box for this layer by double-clicking it in the Navigator window, and then click the General tab and rename the layer to right_edge. Click the Image tab and change the X Scale to –1. Then press OK to apply the changes to the layer. Drag the layer over to the other side of the GUI window. You should have what looks like Figure 16-20.

      You have one more image to add before you move on, and that's something to fill the space at the top of the window.

   6. **Right-click the Desktop layer in the Navigator window and choose New➪windowDef.**

   7. **Open this new layer's Item Properties dialog box and, on the General tab, rename it to center_image. On the Image tab, enter** gfx/guis/common/strogg/decal **in the Material field. Change the Matcolor to a lighter shade of blue to make it stand out a little more. Click OK to apply the changes.**

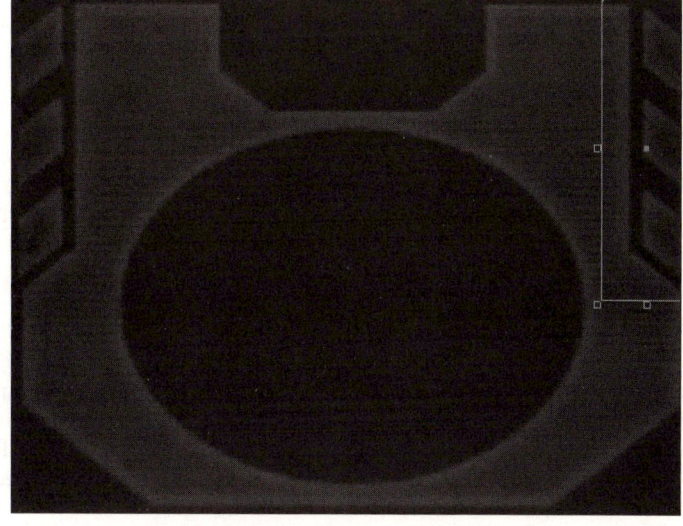

Figure 16-20:
A symmetrical layout: What you apply to one side of your GUI should be applied to the other.

8. **Adjust the size and location so that it sits in the middle of that empty space at the top of the GUI.**

   You should end up with something that looks like Figure 16-21.

Figure 16-21:
You can apply different colors or any other elements you want to the same GUI

Quake 4 developers often place an image layer that encompasses the entire GUI and makes the edges appear as if they fade out to blackness as these images reach the end of the screen. This is done by adding another image. I think it really adds to the look of the GUI.

9. **Add a new windowDef to the Desktop and open the properties dialog box for the new layer. On the General tab, change the name to edge_fade, and on the Image tab, enter** gfx/guis/common/monitor_darkedge2 **in the Material field. Change the Matcolor to black and click OK to apply the changes.**

10. **With the new layer in place, resize it to cover the entire GUI. The layer should be sized to 640,480.**

    I cover sizing in the earlier section, "Making children." You should end up with something that's a subtle yet important change to your GUI, as shown in Figure 16-22. For the *Quake 4* theme, this effect of fading at the edges makes the GUIs look old and unclean. You could expand on this theme by adding a layer with scratches, dirt, or splattered fluids.

Figure 16-22: Apply a faded-edge image to make your GUI look dirty or worn.

Typing text

Your GUI is almost complete. In the middle of the black circle is a space where you can place text to indicate the purpose of this interface. Here's how you add text:

1. **Right-click the Desktop layer and choose New**⇨**windowDef to add a new layer.**
2. **Double-click the new layer, and on the General tab, rename it to text_window.**
3. **Click the Text tab. Select the Text check box, and then add the following line of text:**

   ```
   Activate\nDoors
   ```

   Between the two words, I added `\n`. This is how you add a new line, and it results in a line break between the two words.
4. **Click the Image tab and change the Scale to 1.8 and the Alignment to Center. Then press OK to apply the changes.**

   Your GUI should now look like Figure 16-23.

Figure 16-23: You can apply not only images, but also text to your GUI.

Acting on buttons

Your GUI might look complete, but it's missing one important function. You haven't added any player interactivity to the GUI. The GUI would be finished if all you wanted to do was to create some nice eye candy. However, what you're trying to build is something the player can use to open the doors. This requires that you add a button to the GUI.

Part IV: Going Beyond the Basics

1. **Right-click the Desktop layer and choose New➪windowDef to add a new layer.**

2. **Double-click the new layer, and on the General tab, rename it button, and then click OK to close the Item Properties dialog box.**

3. **Move the new layer and resize it to cover the black circle in the middle of the GUI, as I have done in Figure 16-24.**

   This is what the player has to click to activate the doors.

Figure 16-24: Create interactive areas of your GUI.

4. **Now add some action to your GUI through the addition of a script. Right-click the button layer and choose Scripts from the pop-up menu.**

   A script window opens, as shown in Figure 16-25.

5. **Type in the following code:**

   ```
   onAction
   {
       set "cmd" "play guisound_beep2";
       set "cmd" "activate":
   }
   ```

6. **After entering this script code into the window, press the window's Close button at the top-right corner.**

   Now the button layer has a little icon on the right side that looks like a black circle with a squiggle, as shown in Figure 16-26.

Figure 16-25: Creating scripts within the GUI.

Figure 16-26: An icon tells you a script is attached to a layer.

The script that you just entered will now run when the player clicks your button. `onAction` tells the game that the enclosed lines of code should be run when the player uses the GUI. The following actions will occur:

- **Play a beep sound:** When the player uses the interface, the clicking action plays an electronic beep that indicates an action has occurred.
- **Activate the target:** The targeted door is triggered and will open.

More commands are listed in Chapter 20. Use the list there to create your own combination of actions for your custom GUI.

Saving your work

Saving your GUI requires that you place it in the proper directory.

1. Choose File➪Save As. Open the folder `C:\Program Files\id Software\Quake 4\q4base` by using the File Explorer.

2. **Create a new folder called** guis **and open it. Then create another folder that is unique to your map. In this case, name the folder** chapter16 **because this is the name of your current map.**

3. **Enter the chapter16 folder and save your GUI under the name of** open.gui.

> **TIP**
> The name of your custom GUI isn't too important. Just name it something that makes sense to you when you go to locate it in the mapping editor or wherever you plan to use it. However, naming the containing folder is very important. You must name it something that is unique to your map to avoid conflicts with other maps that already exist or are distributed online. Using the name of your map as the name of your containing folder usually ensures that the game won't confuse things.

Applying Your Custom Interface

Now that you have your custom GUI put together, you need to put it to use. The purpose of this GUI was to replace the one currently in use to control the opening of your doors. All that needs to be done is to redefine the GUI that is being used in the map.

1. **Close the GUI editor and open the mapping editor. Load your chapter16 map.**

   When you go to load your map, you might find that the editor starts you off in the wrong directory. That's because it remembers the last folder as where you saved your GUI. So, in the mapping editor's Open dialog box, navigate to the map folder, which should be C:\Program Files\id Software\Quake 4\q4base\maps\game.

2. **With your map open, locate the** func_static **where you have defined your GUI by looking for it in the CAM window. Select this entity and open the Entity tab. Click the GUI button.**

   This dialog box allows you to browse through all the available GUIs, including your custom GUI.

3. **Open** base/guis/chapter16 **folder and find your new GUI,** open.gui. **Selecting it produces a preview, as shown in Figure 16-27. Press OK to apply the new GUI to your entity.**

4. **Save your map and then recompile it. After it compiles, open the game and launch your level.**

   You should be able to walk up to your new GUI and click the area where you defined your button to open the doors, as I have in Figure 16-28.

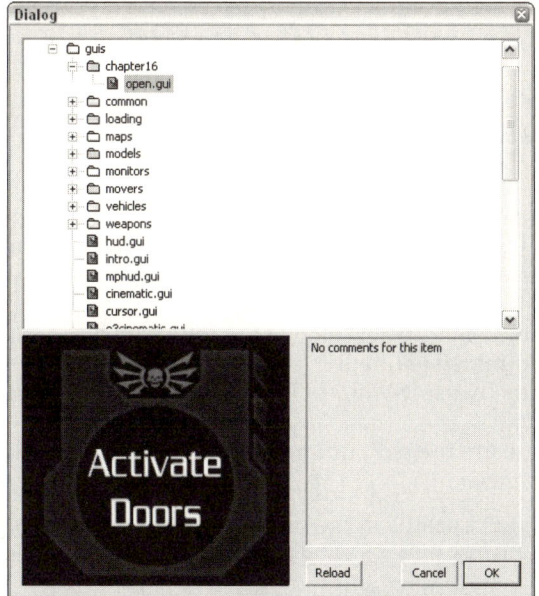

Figure 16-27: Locate and apply your custom GUI.

Figure 16-28: In the game, a custom GUI always looks great.

Exploring Deeper into the Game

You can do a lot more with your GUI other than just control doors. GUIs are used all over the game, and walking through the levels that come with it can inspire further uses in your work.

Other GUI uses that are not so obvious include loading screens, intro screens, and HUDs. If you want to create your own HUD for the game, all you have to do is use the existing GUIs as a guide and change whatever you like.

To find the original files, start by extracting the following files from the pk001.pk4 file. As outlined in Chapter 14, you can open .pk4 files and explore their contents by using WinZip. The files you want to extract are

- hud.gui: Located in the path guis/, this file defines the HUD in the single-player games.
- hug_Strogg.gui: Located in the path guis/, this file defines the HUD when the player turns into a Strogg in the single-player games.
- mplevel: Located in the path guis/loading/, this file defines the multi-player loading screen.

Although I recommend that you explore more on your own, I don't recommend that you replace the original game files that control these functions. Many people find it frustrating if you change the original files of a game and distribute them. Instead, you're better off saving it as a new mod of the game. I explore this further in Chapter 19.

Chapter 17

Separating Your Files

In This Chapter

▶ Understanding how the game finds and displays mods
▶ Discovering that the original game is a mod itself
▶ Creating a game-recognized mod

*E*verything prior to this point in the book involves creating custom pieces of a game that don't require any changes to the existing game. Rather, what you have created is in addition to what the gamer already has. You have created additional single-player and multiplayer maps, custom textures, scripts, GUIs, and much more. All these are additional elements of the game that can be added to the player's experience.

When gamers install mods, they expect to play something new, but they don't expect changes to what they already have. It isn't fun to discover that when you load your last save point in the game that everything has been changed and can't be changed back. If an installed modification caused this, you can expect the player not to come back to you looking for more mods.

In Chapter 16, I mentioned that you could change the HUD (Heads Up Display) or loading screens by altering the existing GUIs that correspond to these parts of the game. This would obviously change the original game, but there is a solution that allows you to edit existing files and leave the original game intact.

Quake 4 has the ability to load modifications to the existing game files without destroying the original game. You can see this option by loading the game and clicking the MODS button near the bottom of the screen, as shown in Figure 17-1.

Part IV: Going Beyond the Basics

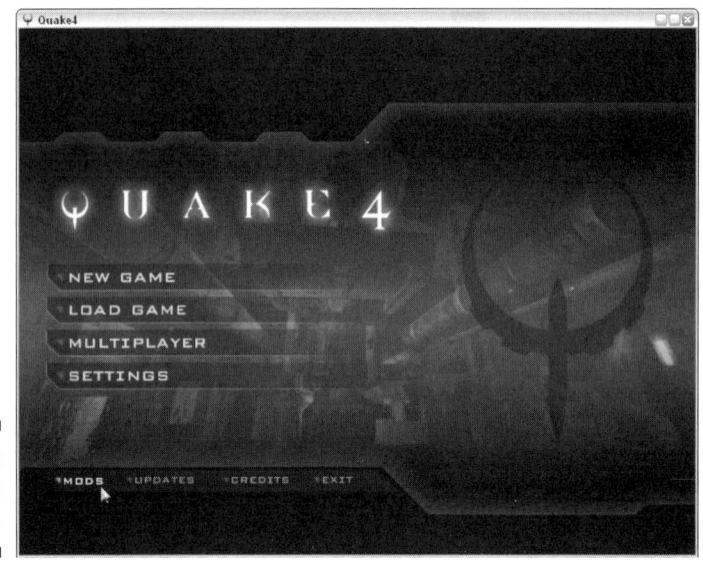

Figure 17-1:
The MODS button.

When you click the MODS button, a window appears that allows you to select a modification to load. The Modifications window looks like Figure 17-2. Although this window is probably empty right now, I show you how to add your own modification to it.

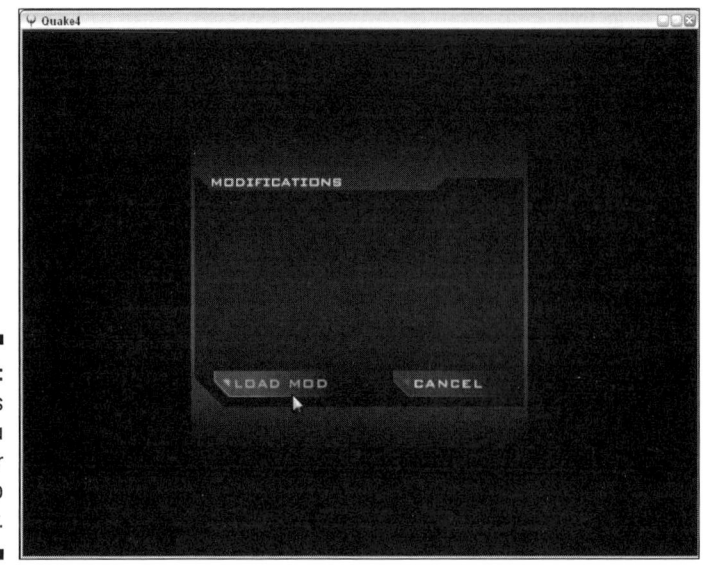

Figure 17-2:
Here is where you want your mods to appear.

Understanding Game-Defined Mods

Just because your custom maps, textures, scripts, and everything else aren't listed in the Modifications window of the game, that doesn't mean that what you have created isn't a mod. Everything that you create and add to the game is a change to the original game and therefore makes it a modification. This window is really nothing more than a way to tell the game where to find altered files.

Open your File Explorer and take look at the folder structure of the game that you currently have installed. Using Windows File Explorer, navigate to the folder `C:\Program Files\id Software\Quake 4` (see Figure 17-3). Here you can see all the files that make the game run, including the executable that starts the game, `Quake4.exe`.

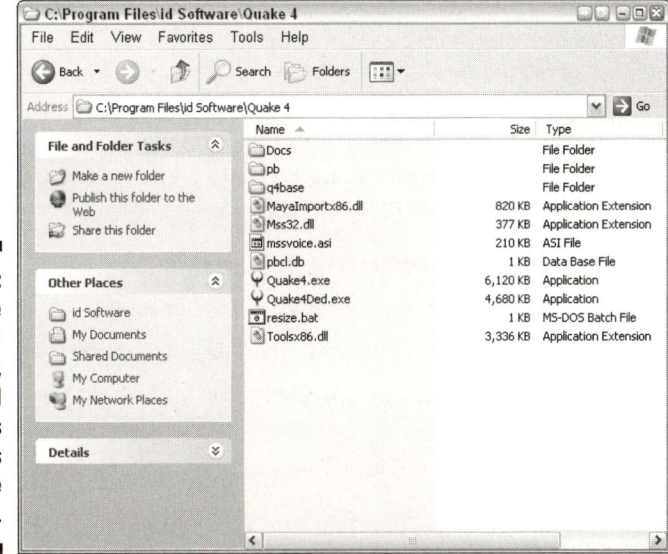

Figure 17-3: In the *Quake 4* game folder, you can find all the files and folders that make up a game.

Now open the folder q4base. In this folder are both the installed files and all the custom folders that you have created to add your content to the game. If you've been following the earlier chapters, you should see new folders such as def, guis, maps, materials, scripts, and textures.

Next, open `pak001.pk4` by using WinZip, as I showed you in Chapter 14. In the listed files in WinZip, take note of the Path column all the way on the right (see Figure 17-4). This Path column defines where the files would be located

Part IV: Going Beyond the Basics

in relation to the q4base folder. As you scroll through the list of files, the path changes. The game, when it loads these pak files, knows to read the path information as if the path were folder names on your hard drive.

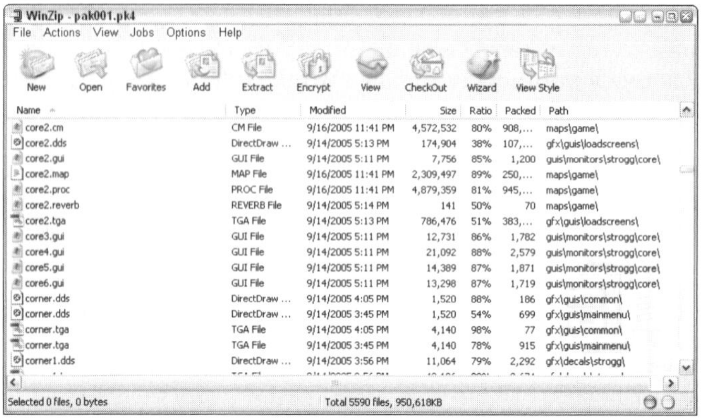

Figure 17-4:
The folder paths in the package files.

What does this all mean? It means that the q4base folder contains all the files that represent the content of the game. The files that run the game are in the folder before it, Quake 4. So, if you want to create all-new game content without altering the original, all you need to do is

1. Create a new folder next to the q4base folder.
2. Name this new folder something relative to your mod.
3. Create, copy, and save all your custom content into this new folder.
4. Make sure there is at least one pak file in this folder that you copied or created.
5. Add a description file to the folder containing the name of the mod.

That's all there is to creating a mod that doesn't alter the original game's content.

Now that you have a basic understanding of how it's done, it's time that you actually do it. This way, as you progress through the remaining chapters of the book, you can add your custom content to your mod folder. You can also save original files that have been altered here and not have to worry about altering the original game.

Naming a Mod of Your Own

The steps in the preceding section outline broadly how to add your custom mod. Here's how you do it for real:

1. **Open Windows File Explorer and navigate to the folder `C:\Program Files\id Software\Quake 4`, as I did in Figure 17-3. Create a new folder here by choosing Files⇨New⇨Folder.**

   When you do this, a new folder is created for you with the name New Folder.

2. **Rename New Folder to something relevant to your mod name.**

   When you create a new folder, you are provided with the option to give this New Folder a new name. However, if you don't have this option, right-click the folder you want to rename and choose Rename from the pop-up menu. Then type the new name of the folder and press Enter to apply the changes.

   When naming this folder, refrain from using anything other than alphanumeric characters. Quotes, slashes, spaces or other similar characters could cause the game to ignore your folder as a mod. For the sake of this book, I am going to name the folder q4mfd, which is short for *Quake 4 Mods For Dummies*. The result looks like Figure 17-5.

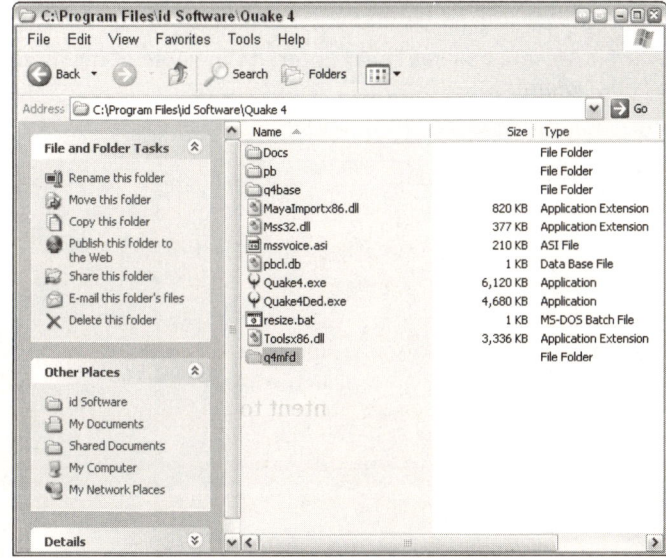

Figure 17-5: Create your own mod folder in the Quake 4 game folder.

3. **Access your new folder.**

    Here, you need to create a text file that contains the name of your mod. This will be the name that is displayed in the game when the gamer views the available mods.

    You don't have to create this text document to name your mod. If this file doesn't exist, the game will display the name of the folder you just created. However, you can include a more detailed name in the text file than you can in the folder name.

4. **Choose File⇨New⇨Text Document to create a new text file within the open Windows folder. Rename this new file `description.txt`.**

    No other filename will work. When the game loads the list of available mods, it looks for the `description.txt` file. If the file doesn't exist, the game won't use the mod title that you have entered in this file. Rather, it will default to the name of your mod's folder.

5. **Open your new text file in Notepad by double-clicking the filename. Then type out the name of your mod in Notepad, following these rules:**

    - Enter the name of the mod only as you want it displayed in the game.
    - Only the top line of text will be used as the name of the mod, so restrict yourself to that line.
    - Keep the number of characters in the name under 40. Any more characters will be ignored.

    In Figure 17-6, you can see that I entered the name of my mod, *Quake 4 Mods For Dummies*.

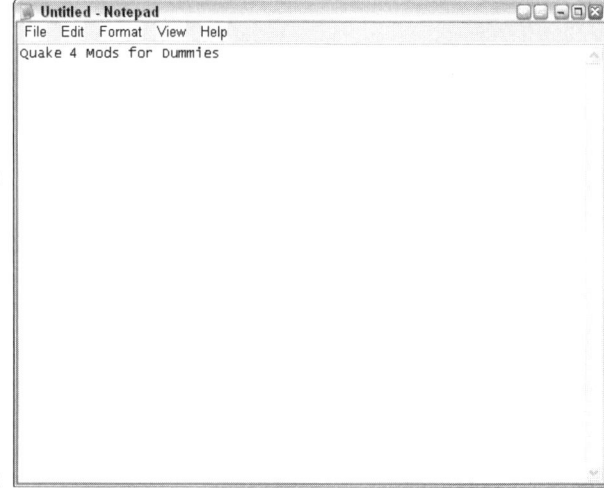

Figure 17-6: The description .txt file contains the name of your mod as viewed in game.

Chapter 17: Separating Your Files 317

6. **Save your text file by choosing File**⇨**Save.**

   Before this folder of content is recognized by the game, you need to place a pak file in here. This is the last criteria required to make this folder visible to the game as a mod. Usually, either you would be about to create custom content or you would already have your content ready to go and this would be compressed into a pak file. However, you don't have anything ready for this folder yet. Right now, you're just creating a mod location for future custom content.

   The solution: Create an empty pak file by using WinZip. There is no rule that says a pak file actually has to contain anything.

7. **Choose File**⇨**New**⇨**WinZip. This creates a Zip file in your folder named `New WinZip File.zip`. Rename your new Zip file by right-clicking it and choosing Rename from the pop-up menu. Name your new Zip file `empty.pk4`, as I've done in Figure 17-7.**

   Using this name, you won't have to worry about being confused about what's in it. You will remember that it's empty.

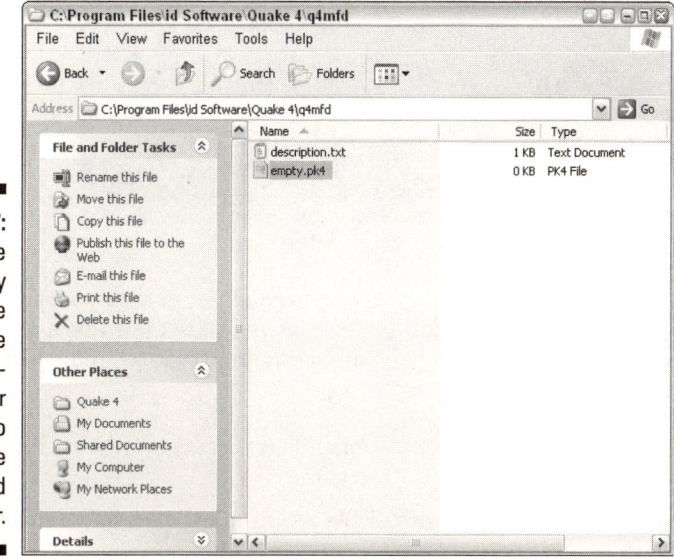

Figure 17-7: Create an empty package file to fulfill the requirements for the game to recognize your mod folder.

   Now you're done and ready to see whether it works.

8. **Load the *Quake 4* game. When it's done loading, click the MODS button at the bottom of the window.**

   When you do, you see your new mod listed, as shown in Figure 17-8. You can even select it and load it.

If you do load your new mod, nothing will be any different from the original game. How can this be? Well, the game looks in your new folder for the files necessary to make it work. These files include maps for playing, GUIs that you use to get around the game's interface, and other similar files. If these files don't exist, the game looks in the original q4base folder for what it needs. This way you don't have to duplicate what's already been done and you can focus on editing or adding your new content.

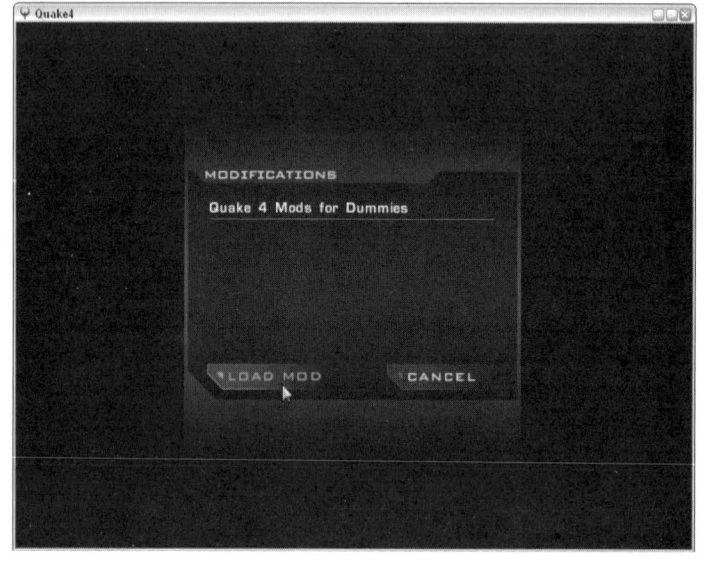

Figure 17-8: Now you can now see your mod listed in the game's Modifications window.

One last thing that you will notice if you do happen to load your new mod is the addition of files in your mod folder that you didn't put there. These additional files are created by the game and contain player-related information. They are

- `config.spec`: This specifications file is usually empty but might contain video specifications for the game.
- `gamex86.dll`: This is a driver file required by the game to make everything run.
- `Quake4Config.cfg`: This is the game and player configuration file that contains the player's key commands, such as how to move forward, backward, and so on.

Although you can decide to leave those files in there when you distribute your new mod to the public, I recommend that you remove them before distribution. This way each installation by another person can define these files as they are required.

Chapter 18

Re-Skinning the Models

In This Chapter

▶ Viewing models with ModView

▶ Following the path from skins to textures

▶ Skinning made easy; a few simple changes make all the difference

▶ Going from TGA to DDS . . . again

▶ Going from players to other entities

*H*ave you ever wanted to put yourself into the game? Or have you ever wanted to change the look of the weapons in some way? Neither of these mods requires you to know how to model, animate, or handle a separate 3D program. Instead, all you need to make these minor changes is Adobe Photoshop and an imagination.

The models in the game are textured very much like the walls in your map. In Chapter 15, you created your own texture for the game. You created a few Targa images that represented different aspects of the texture. Then you created a material file in Notepad that defined the texture name and how to put the different image files together. This then could be applied in the map editor to any brush face in the map.

Well, for a model, there is one more file involved in the texturing. That file is called the *skin* file, and it too can be opened by using Notepad.

Quake 4 has a special utility to make models easy to visualize. This utility is called *Quake 4 Model Viewer, ModView* for short. It allows you to see the model in its entirety with your new skins applied.

In this chapter, I show you how to alter a player's skin. I show you how to find the image files that need to be altered. You then edit the files in Photoshop, save them to the new mod folder that you created in the preceding chapter.

Part IV: Going Beyond the Basics

Locating the Models and Their Skins

With ModView, locating the model that you want to change couldn't be easier. This little utility was added to the game just like the mapping editor and the GUI editor. Accessing those utilities is easy, and accessing ModView is no different.

To load ModView, start by loading the game. When it's loaded, open the console and type **modview**. Then press Enter.

To load the player model that is going to be modified, select Player from the Groups drop-down list, then select player_marine_mp. The model will be visible in the preview window, as in Figure 18-1.

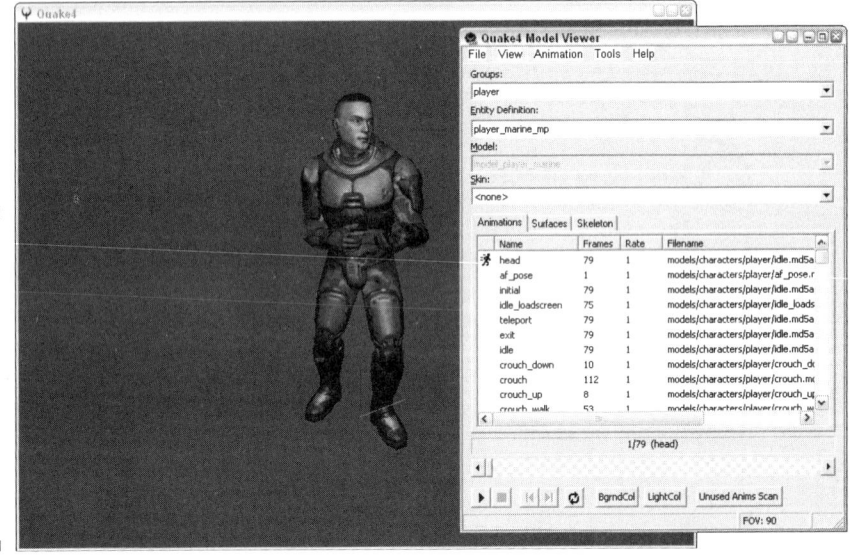

Figure 18-1: Resizing and moving windows around make viewing your model much easier.

On the Surfaces tab of the preview window, you find the different materials that are used by this model. You constructed a material file in Chapter 15 when you created your custom texture. Well, this happens to be the same thing, except in this case, it's being used by the model instead of by a map.

The materials listed on this tab should also be noted. You will be searching the game files for these material files, and knowing their paths is a great help. The list of material files is as follows:

- `models/characters/marine/body`: This material defines the torso of the model.

- `models/characters/marine/body_collision`: This defines the torso after it has received damage such as being shot in the game.
- `models/characters/marine/eye`: Even the model's eyes are separately defined.
- `models/characters/marine/hair`: This file defines the model's hair, which allows the developers to reuse materials when making different characters in the game.
- `models/characters/marine/teeth`: The teeth are separated from other files to assist in lip syncing.
- `models/characters/marine_heads/kane6`: Within the game, you play as Kane, and this file defines the face and head.
- `models/characters/marine_heads/head_collision`: Here are the face and head after they have received damage.

Hunting Down Your Mod Files

You now know what materials were used in texturing this model. You next have to locate these defined materials within the installed game files. From within them, you can find the editable images.

Searching in materials

In Chapter 15, you created your own textures and a material file with the `.mtr` file extension. From this, you know that you need to locate the material file that is associated with the materials noted earlier for the player that you're modding. You also know that material files are saved in a folder that starts with `C:\Program Files\id Software\Quake 4\q4base\materials`. This information is going to come in handy. Here's how you locate the materials associated with the model so that you can add your custom skin to the model:

1. **Open Windows File Explorer and navigate to the Quake 4 base directory. This would be `C:\Program Files\id Software\Quake 4\q4base`, where all the pak files are located.**

   As you discovered in Chapter 14, the game file you're looking for is somewhere within these pak files, and you have to locate it.

   There is actually logic to the way that the pak files are put together. If you open the pak file with WinZip and sort its contents by the Path column, you can see that they are all alphabetically listed. Each pak file is about 215M, and what doesn't fit into the first pak file is located into the next pak file. Therefore you can follow the paths alphabetically as you open the pak files numerically.

2. **Find the right material file.**

   I opened each of the pak files looking for a material file that contains the materials noted earlier (models/characters/marine/body, models/characters/marine/body collision, and so on) when the player model was open in ModView. After a little guessing and some trial and error, I found that the file that was needed was characters.mtr located right in the path materials. This file is located in pak002.pk4.

   Open pak002.pk4 with WinZip. Sort the contents of this pak file by the Path column by clicking the column name. Scroll down until you reach the path materials. Then locate the characters.mtr filename.

3. **Right-click the file characters.mtr from within WinZip. From the menu, choose View with NOTEPAD.EXE.**

   This causes the selected file to open in Notepad.

4. **Search this material file for the materials that were listed in ModView. Press Ctrl+F to open the Find dialog box. Type the first material on the list,** models/characters/marine/body, **next to Find What and click Find Next.**

   When Find has found the line exactly as entered, you have found the texture definition for this file. The result should read as follows:

```
models/characters/marine/body
{
    noSelfShadow
     unSmoothedTangents
//      materialType flesh

   renderbump   -size 1024 1024 -trace 0.07 -aa 2
        models/characters/marine/body_local.tga
        work/models/characters/marine/newbody_hi.lwo

     diffusemap   models/characters/marine/body_d.tga
     bumpmap     addnormals (
       models/characters/marine/body_local.tga,
       heightmap (
       models/characters/marine/body_h.tga, 2 ))
     specularmap
        models/characters/marine/body_s.tga
          {
     blend add
     map models/characters/marine/body_g.tga
          }
}
```

   This code segment should look very familiar. It looks a lot like the texture definition that you made in Chapter 15. From the steps in that chapter, you might have figured out that the images listed here are those that you want to modify in order to modify the player's skin. Those images are

Chapter 18: Re-Skinning the Models 323

- `models/characters/marine/body_local.tga`
- `models/characters/marine/body_d.tga`
- `models/characters/marine/body_h.tga`
- `models/characters/marine/body_s.tga`
- `models/characters/marine/body_g.tga`

Because I cover only changing the colors on the player's skin, the only image needed from those listed here is the diffuse map. This image, just like the texture you made, is named with `_d.tga`. That means you need to take note only of the image `models/characters/marine/body_d.tga` so you can remember to locate it later when you're done searching for the other materials.

5. **To continue the search for materials related to the player, open the Find dialog box if you have closed it (by pressing Ctrl+F). Then type in the next material on the list,** models/characters/marine/body_collision. **Click Find Next.**

    When located, you can see that there are no images associated with this material.

    This is normal for some of the materials used on models in the game. Not all the materials are going to refer to images that need editing. Simply ignore this one and continue the search.

6. **Search for the next material by entering** models/characters/marine/eye **and clicking Find Next.**

    When it's found, you will notice that the diffuse map associated with this material is `models/characters/marine/eye_green_d.tga`.

7. **Search for the material** models/characters/marine/hair**, which is next on the list.**

    Make sure your search starts at the beginning of the file, or you might miss it. When you do locate the material `models/characters/marine/hair`, you again find that this material has no diffuse map image associated with it. So skip it.

8. **Search for** models/characters/marine/teeth.

    This provides you with another image of which to take note. That image is `models/characters/marine/teeth_d.tga`.

9. **Search for** models/characters/marine_heads/kane6 **next.**

    You have to start at the top of the file again for this search to work correctly. When it's found, you have another image to note: `models/characters/marine_heads/kane6_d.tga`.

10. **Search for the last material on the list,** models/characters/marine_heads/head_collision.

    This material doesn't have any additional images to note.

You're now done searching through the materials file for the required images. Go ahead and close the `characters.mtr` file and then close `pak002.pk4`. Next up is locating the images in the pak files.

Because you now know the secret ordering scheme to the pak files, locating the necessary image for this player skin should be fairly easy. Because you took note of the image files that need to be edited as you worked your way through the materials file, you know that you're looking for the following images:

- `models/characters/marine/body_d.tga`
- `models/characters/marine/eye_green_d.tga`
- `models/characters/marine/teeth_d.tga`
- `models/characters/marine_heads/kane6_d.tga`

After opening a few pak files and looking at the path, you will progressively make your way to the file `pak003.pk4`. Here, the Path column starts with `models/characters/bodies_parts/`. A quick scroll through the file and you'll see the path you're looking for, `models/characters/marine/`.

As you find the image files you need, extract them to the mod folder you created in Chapter 17.

Making changes

It's now time to start changing these images for your mod. This is going to require Adobe Photoshop, so load it up. If you don't have Photoshop or don't remember where to locate it, turn to Chapter 15.

In Photoshop, open all four of the image files that you extracted. You can open them by choosing File⇨Open, or you can simply click and drag them from Windows File Explorer into Photoshop.

With your images opened in Photoshop, you should start getting an idea of what you're going to do. Figure 18-2 shows an example of all these image files open in Photoshop. You can see how the images relate to the player model in the game.

- `body_d.tga`: This image contains all the clothing on the player. Included are the body, legs, arms, and everything else that covers the model from the neck down.
- `eye_green_d.tga`: Here you have the player's eyeballs.

Chapter 18: Re-Skinning the Models *325*

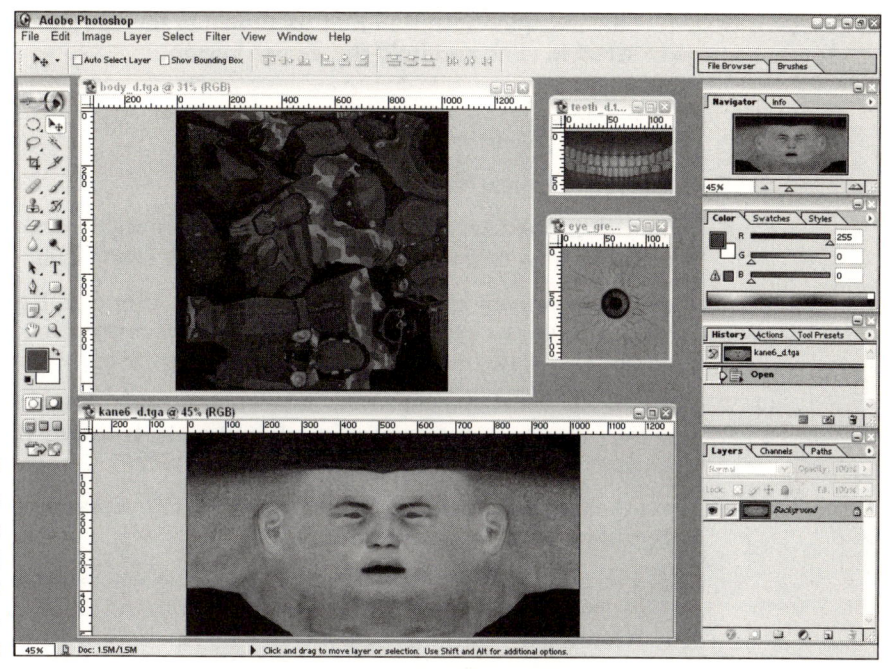

Figure 18-2: Open the skin files in Photoshop for editing.

- `kane6_d.tga`: The face and hair are reflected in this image. It has been digitally stretched out so that it can lie flat in this file and then be projected onto the model's round head in the game.
- `teeth_d.tga`: Here are the player's teeth. They might not be seen all too often, but when they are, they really add to the details of the model.

Modifying the eyeball

You can start by changing this eyeball to look more cat-like:

1. **Select the `eye_green_d.tga` image's window in Photoshop. Change your foreground color selection to black.**

   Your foreground and background color selections are found on the toolbar on the left of the program window, as shown in margin. There are two overlapping blocks, each containing a color.

2. **Click in the color block that is over the top of the other color block.**

   You are presented with the Color Picker dialog box. The over-the-top color block is called the *foreground color,* and the block behind it is called the *background color.*

3. **Select black and click OK to apply.**

Part IV: Going Beyond the Basics

4. **Select the marquee selection tool, as shown in the margin. When you go to select it, click and hold the mouse button.**

   This step pops up an options menu. Here you can select from different types of marquee selection tools.

5. **Select the Elliptical Marquee tool.**

6. **From within the Layers tab located in the lower-right corner of the screen, create a new layer by clicking the New Layer icon.**

   This was something you first did in Chapter 15. After creating the new layer, make sure you select that new layer before proceeding with any changes. This way, any changes you make are made to this layer.

7. **With the Elliptical Marquee tool, select a new pupil. Make the selection over the top of the existing pupil, but make it oblong like a cat's eye. Then fill this selection by choosing Edit⇨Fill.**

8. **From the Use pull-down menu located in the Fill dialog box, select Foreground Color and then click OK.**

   This step applies the black foreground color that you selected earlier to the selection that you made in the new layer with the Elliptical Marquee tool. It looks like Figure 18-3 when you're done.

Figure 18-3: With the marquee tool, make your selection and fill it in with the foreground color. Here I've started a cat's eye.

9. **Deselect your selection in Photoshop by pressing Ctrl+D. Then select the background layer. Create another new layer by clicking the New Layer icon at the bottom of the Layers tab.**

   Because you selected the background layer first, this new layer will be created above it and below the previous new layer.

10. **Select a new color to apply to this new layer. I suggest selecting a yellow color. Do so by clicking the foreground color block and using the Color Picker to select yellow. Click OK to apply the color change.**

11. **Choose Edit➪Fill. You are going to fill this entire layer with the yellow color. The Use selection should still read Foreground Color from your previous application, so click OK to apply the change.**

    The result will be a black, oblong pupil with a yellow background, as in Figure 18-4.

Figure 18-4: Adjust the background of the image by adding a layer underneath.

12. **Choose File➪Save because this image is complete. You want to save over the original file. Make sure that your format is Targa and that your filename reads `eye_green_d.tga`. Then click Save.**

13. **A pop-up window asks whether you want to replace the existing file. Click OK to replace it. Then you are prompted with Targa options. Select 24bits/pixel and click OK.**

    The eye image is complete, so go ahead and close this image window in Photoshop. If you're asked to save the changes, select No because you already saved your changes in the previous step. Close this window.

Modifying the body

The next image to modify is the `body_d.tga` image. You could go wild here if you want by overlaying different outfits, colors, and more. I've seen changes that overlay famous people, fancy suits, a lack of clothing, and the list goes on. For this example, you change only the color. I show you what a change to this file looks like in the game, and then you can take it further on your own.

1. **Create a new layer for the body image by clicking the New Layer icon at the bottom of the Layers tab. If you just completed the eyeball exercise, you should still have yellow as your foreground color, so fill the new layer with yellow.**

    Sticking with the yellow theme, you will just brighten up this outfit with some yellow highlighting.

2. **At the top of the Layers tab, there is a pull-down menu. (Before you make any changes, it reads Normal.) From the pull-down menu, choose Overlay.**

    That's enough changes here, so save this Targa image over the original.

Part IV: Going Beyond the Basics

3. Choose File⇨Save, and make sure the format is Targa and the filename is the same as the original. Then click Save.

4. When prompted, click OK to replace this file. Select 24 bits/pixel in the Targa Options window and click OK to continue. Finally, close this image.

Modifying the head

That leaves you with one more image, the head. In this case, I thought it would be interesting to overlay my own face. I took out my digital camera and took a photo of myself. I then imported it into Photoshop, as shown in Figure 18-5.

Figure 18-5: Don't limit your image selections. Use a digital camera to add anything you see to the game.

1. **Select the face by using the Lasso tool from the toolbar on the left.**

   The Lasso tool is represented with what looks like a lasso, as shown in the margin. When making your selection, don't include the entire face in your selection. Instead, leave some of the face outside of your selection, as I've done in Figure 18-6. This allows you to blend the image onto the original.

2. **Choose Select⇨Feather to bring up the Feather Selection window. Enter a value of 20 pixels as the Feather Radius and press OK to apply the changes.**

   This option is going to fade your selection out around the edges, allowing you to blend this image. The Feather Radius that you should enter will depend on the size of your image. In my case, 20 pixels does the trick.

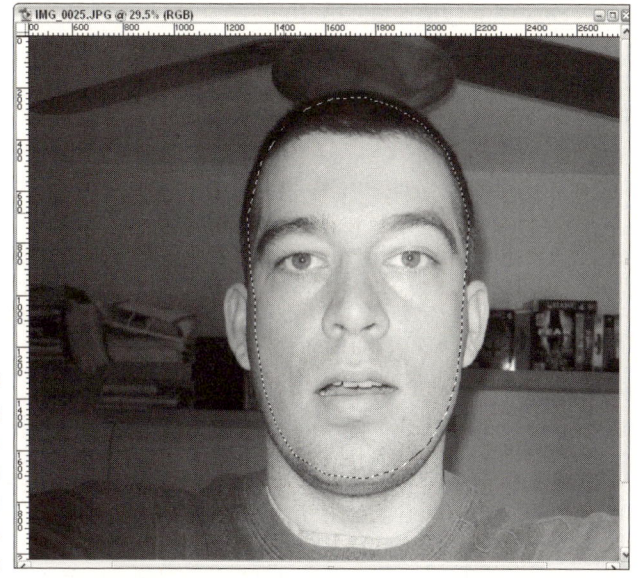

Figure 18-6: Select the face with the Lasso tool.

3. **Copy your selection. You can do this by choosing Edit➪Copy or by pressing Ctrl+C.**

4. **Switch windows to the `kane6_d.tga` image and paste your copied selection here by choosing Edit➪Paste or by pressing Ctrl+V.**

   When you paste your selection, it will be layered on your current image as a new layer, but it will probably be too large. You need to size it so that it properly fits the texture. To do this, start by changing the opacity of this newly pasted layer.

5. **At the top of the Layers tab, there is an option for Opacity. Change this from 100% to 50%.**

   This allows you to see the Background layer through the pasted layer and to size the face image more appropriately.

6. **To resize the image, choose Edit➪Transform➪Scale. Then begin to shrink the face until it fits over the original.**

   You can size it manually by entering the size changes at the top of the Photoshop window (W for width and H for height) or by dragging the corners or edges of the image.

7. **Press Enter to apply the changes.**

8. **Bring the opacity back up to 100% from with the Layers tab.**

   When you do, you will notice that the photo isn't going to match the skin tone of the original face. This mismatch will have to be fixed, or the face will look out of place. However, before changing the skin tone, the hairline needs to be faded some more to match the original.

9. **Select the Eraser tool from the toolbar.**

   This is the one that looks like a rectangular eraser, as displayed in the margin. This tool, much like the Rubber Stamp used in Chapter 15, has the option to change the brush size.

10. **At the top of the program, change your brush size to 45. Then use the eraser by clicking and dragging the cursor on the areas you want to erase.**

    The goal is to remove any dark areas around the face, such as hair (see Figure 18-7). These dark areas are not going to blend with the original image. The next step is to blend the colors between the two images and make them look like one image.

11. **Choose Image➪Adjustments➪Color Balance.**

    The Color Balance dialog box appears. This dialog box allows you to change the color balance between three different tone balances. To find the right combination for this image, you have to keep adjusting the sliders until it looks right. There is no other way to make the color match other than by sight.

Figure 18-7: Raise the opacity back up and do some more blending with the eraser tool.

After fooling with the sliders, I came up with the following values that worked for this image combination:

- **Shadows:** Color Levels: +13 +4 –12
- **Midtones:** Color Levels: +13 +6 –7
- **Highlights:** Color Levels: 0 0 0

With these new color adjustments, you can see that the left side of the face looks like it's blending quite well. However, the right side doesn't look quite as good. Luckily, there is a fairly simple solution to this problem. That is to cut the face in half and mirror the left side to the right side, which is just what you're going to do.

12. **Change your marquee selection tool from elliptical to rectangular. Click and hold the cursor over the selection icon; an option to change your selection tool appears. Select the appropriate one.**

Chapter 18: Re-Skinning the Models 331

13. Use this selection tool to select the right half of the face. Try to make your selection as close to exact as possible. Then press Delete to remove it, as I have done in Figure 18-8.

Figure 18-8: If one side of your image looks better than the other, consider mirroring the good side onto the bad.

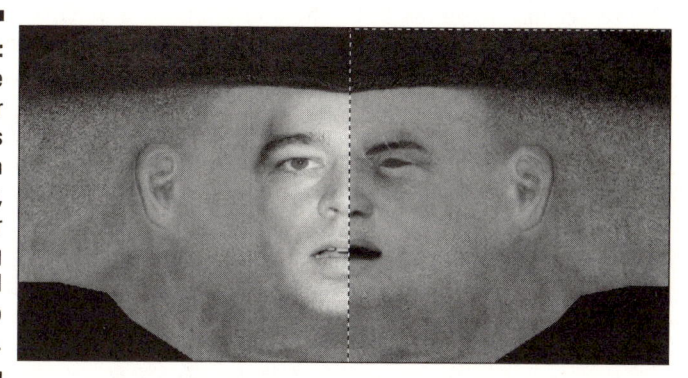

14. Select the other half of the face the same way. Press Ctrl+C to copy the selection, and then press Ctrl+V to paste the copy to a new layer.

15. Choose Edit➪Transform➪Flip Horizontal to make a mirror copy of the first half. Then line the two of them up so they look like one complete face. To move it, use the Move tool from the toolbar that looks like a mouse pointer or use your arrow keys to shift it around one.

    The result looks like a good skin for the game, as shown in Figure 18-9.

Figure 18-9: The mirrored image blends much better.

16. Save this image over the original kane6_d.tga image. Remember to make it a Targa image and to select the 24 bits/pixel Targa option when prompted.

Compressing to DDS

Just like the images used in your map texture from Chapter 15, you should create DDS image files for these new images. This helps keep the game running smoothly because it will be using the compressed mip-maps created in the DDS file format. Use The Compressonator with the Maintain Directory Structure check box selected. See Chapter 15 for details on how to use The Compressonator.

There is one more image to compress, and that's the `kane6_d.tga` image. To make things as easy as possible, just compress this one image by using the same process.

Viewing the mod

Finally, it's time to see what the new skin is going to look like in the game. The process is to start up the game and load your mod from the mod selection list. Then you will launch the ModView utility, select the marine player model, and take a look at your handiwork.

Here you can see your newly skinned player model, as shown in Figure 18-10.

Figure 18-10: There I am with my yellow cat eyes and suit to match.

Chapter 19

Showing the World

In This Chapter
▶ Putting together a single package of all your mod files
▶ Defining what's in the package and what should be done with it
▶ Dealing with added game content
▶ Handling altered game content as a separate mod
▶ Getting your mod out to the public

After you finish creating all of your custom content, you're going to want to show it off. You could just put all the files together and start handing it out, but this can lead to confusion and other problems. Practiced modders commonly use a preferred method of distribution that I outline for you here.

After you put your distribution package together, you need to get it out to the public. I show you how to find places to put your package online and get it out to the community where it can be enjoyed by all.

Creating the Package

The number of steps required to put everything together for distribution depends on the complexity of your mod. I take you through the process of putting together a full mod starting with the simple pieces such as maps and textures. Then you can expand on this simple package as if it were a total conversion modification for the game.

After you have put all of your content together and tested it to make sure it's complete, you need to write your `readme.txt`. This is a text file, also called just README, that accompanies all modifications. It tells the user who made it, what it contains, how to install it, what bugs exist if any, as well as any other information you want to include.

A good README outline supplies the users with as much information as they might need in order to know more about your map and, if necessary, to contact you for questions.

All this information would be contained within a plain text file. This way it can be easily read in Notepad or any other text editor out there because they all can read plain text.

Because I plan to show you two types of packages for distribution below, I show you the contents of each README as these packages are created.

Packaging additions to the game

The most common modification is that of maps. Sometimes they come with custom textures, sounds, and other additions. However, note that this package you are about to create contains nothing that overwrites the original game content, which means that the package contains all custom additions to the game as it exists.

With that in mind, the first package you will put together will contain

- The map and related items for that map as constructed in earlier chapters.
- The custom texture, consisting of a few images and a material file.
- The script file that controls the lift.

The last chapter that required working with your custom map and related elements was Chapter 16. The files from this chapter and its single-player level are what you will put together here. Those files include

- `guis\chapter16\open.gui`
- `maps\game\chapter16.aas32`
- `maps\game\chapter16.aas96`
- `maps\game\chapter16.aas96`
- `maps\game\chapter16.aas128`
- `maps\game\chapter16.aas250`
- `maps\game\chapter16.cm`
- `maps\game\chapter16.proc`
- `maps\game\chapter16.map`
- `maps\game\chapter16.script`
- `materials\chapter15.mtr`
- `textures\chapter15\brick_d.DDS`
- `textures\chapter15\brick_d.tga`
- `textures\chapter15\brick_ed.tga`

- ✔ `textures\chapter15\brick_h.DDS`
- ✔ `textures\chapter15\brick_h.tga`
- ✔ `textures\chapter15\brick_local.DDS`
- ✔ `textures\chapter15\brick_local.tga`
- ✔ `textures\chapter15\brick_s.DDS`
- ✔ `textures\chapter15\brick_s.tga`

Now, if this is your first mapping project, you don't have a lot of extra files in the game's base directory. However, given some time, this will change. You will have a number of different maps, textures, and other elements scattered on your hard drive that are necessary for your distribution. So, I show you how to package your file as if you had all these extra files in your base directory.

The first thing you want to do is create a temporary folder somewhere on your hard drive. Here, you will copy all the files for your project, leaving behind those that aren't needed.

1. **Open Windows File Explorer and create a temporary folder somewhere. (I like to have a folder on my `C:` drive called Temp, where I can place modified files.) To make this new folder, navigate to `C:\`. Choose File⇨New⇨Folder.**

    When you do, a new folder is created called New Folder.

2. **With New Folder still selected, choose File⇨Rename and rename this folder to Temp. Enter this folder by double-clicking it.**

3. **Open another instance of Windows File Explorer. Then navigate to the games base folder, `C:\Program Files\id Software\Quake 4\q4base`.**

    From here, you want to copy all your game files for the package. You will then paste them in your new Temp folder.

4. **Select the following folders by pressing Ctrl+click on each of these:**

    - guis
    - maps
    - materials
    - textures

    You should now have four folders selected.

5. **Press Ctrl+C to copy your selection. Switch to your other instance of Windows File Explorer, which has `C:\Temp` open. Then press Ctrl+V to paste the folders and files you selected.**

    You now have a copy in your Temp folder.

6. **Go through each of these copied folders and make sure that you have only the files that are listed at the beginning of this section.**

    You don't need to package maps and files that don't belong here. For instance, I had several other map files in my `maps\game` folder that didn't need to be there. I went in, selected them with Ctrl+click, and then deleted them by pressing Delete.

 7. **Create your README file.**

    Start by opening Notepad. For your convenience, I included an empty `readme.txt` file on the media in the back of the book. This file looks just like the README contents shown later in this chapter. Fill in the blanks with your information.

 8. **Save this file as `readme.txt` in your Temp folder.**

 9. **Create a custom image to represent your content.**

    The reason for this image is that when you submit your file to Web sites, these Web sites want to be able to post a visual of your content. If you supply the Web site administrators with that visual, you just saved them time and effort making less work for them. Less work for these Web site administrators means a better likelihood that your package will be posted without delay. Often, this means offering a screenshot from within your level. However, this image can be anything that you want.

    You don't have to go through a lot of effort in making this image. A screenshot from within the game is the most common. So, load your level in the game and create your screenshot. If you don't remember how, refer to Chapter 13 for more information on how to create one of your own.

    When you have your screenshot ready, save it in your Temp folder. Save it in the same location as your `readme.txt` file because this is where most people expect to find it. Then rename the file to the same name as your map file.

    TIP: Screenshots are often submitted in their native Targa format right out of the game. However, because the purpose of this screenshot is to provide the Web site with an image to post along with your file, you should convert this image to something appropriate for the Web. Open your file in Photoshop, change the size of the image to 640 pixels wide, and then save it as a JPEG, which is an image format that can be used online.

    Now, you're ready to create your package.

10. **Select all the files and folders in your Temp folder. Right-click your selection to open the pop-up menu and choose WinZip⇨Add to Temp.zip.**

    WinZip quickly opens and closes again, and then you are left with a new file in your folder, `Temp.zip`.

11. **Select `Temp.zip` and then choose File⇨Rename. Rename the file to `chapter16.pk4`.**

    When you press enter to rename the file, you're prompted with a warning about changing the filename extension. Click Yes to change it.

12. **Open `chapter16.pk4` and make sure all the files are in there. Also, just as important, make sure the paths to these files are correct by looking at the Path column.**

    Your paths should read as mine do in Figure 19-1. You should see that they all reflect the folder paths from which they came.

Figure 19-1: Zip it all up by using folder names so that the path in the file represents the path on your hard drive.

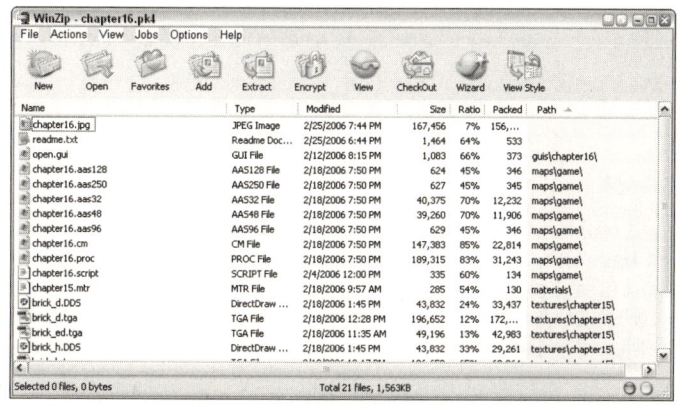

That's it. You're now ready to get your map out to the world for everyone to enjoy. Just by sending this pak file to your friends and to Web sites, you can distribute your custom game content.

Packaging mods that alter the game

Perhaps you have more than just a map with supplemental files that you want to give out. Perhaps you have custom skins or other files that alter the original game, and you now want to release your mod.

The method of packaging your content is roughly the same. You still want to create your temporary hard drive folder and then zip all the contents together with WinZip. However, the installation and use of these files are different.

Because this is a separate mod for the game, you can't just hand out a pak file. As you discovered in Chapter 17, this type of mod requires a separate folder.

Part IV: Going Beyond the Basics

For this example, I package up the same files as listed in the section "Packaging additions to the game." However, I also add the custom player skins from Chapter 18. This package will include the following files:

- models\characters\marine\body_d.DDS
- models\characters\marine\body_d.tga
- models\characters\marine\eye_green_d.DDS
- models\characters\marine\eye_green_d.tga
- models\characters\marine\teeth_d.DDS
- models\characters\marine\teeth_d.tga
- models\characters\marine_heads\kane6_d.DDS
- models\characters\marine_heads\kane6_d.tga
- description.txt
- empty.pk4

You should still have your mod folder, which contains your model skins. If you don't have this, refer to Chapters 17 and 18, where you created these folders and files. Select and copy your custom mod folder, C:\Program Files\id Software\Quake 4\q4mfd. Then paste this folder in your temporary folder, C:\Temp.

1. **From within your Temp folder, select and copy the following files:**
   - chapter16.jpg
   - chapter16.pk4
   - readme.txt

2. **Paste these files in the mod folder that you just pasted in this folder, C:\Temp\q4mfd.**

3. **Open chapter16.pk4 with WinZip. Select the files chapter16.jpg and readme.txt within this package. Then press Delete to remove them from the package. Once removed, close this pak file.**

   You won't need these files here because they will be included outside of this package. Because this is a complete game modification, you will need to change the contents of the readme.txt to reflect the additions you just made.

4. **Edit the contents of readme.txt and use this example of how it should read:**

```
============================================================
Map Title            : Chapter 16
Map Version          : v2.0
Author               : foyleman
E-mail               : foyleman@modsonline.com
Website              : http://www.modsonline.com

============================================================

Game                 : Quake 4
Supported Gametype   : single player
Map Size             : 1 player
Map Rating           : for anyone, no adult content

============================================================

Contents of this Package : This package is a complete game modification. It
                contains a map, textures, script and player skins.

============================================================

Installation Instructions: Extract the contents of this WinZip file to the
            directory C:\Program Files\id Software\Quake 4. When this mod is
            loaded within the game, the custom skins will be accessible.
            Launch the map from the console by typing 'map game/chapter16'

============================================================

Construction Date    : 04/2006
Construction Time    : 2 days
Computer Configuration : AMD 4200 X2, 2Gb Ram
Custom Content       : textures, materials, scripts, maps, skins
Known Bugs           : NA

============================================================

Credit to Authors    : NA
Special Thanks       : Quake 4 for Dummies
Additional Notes     : Check out MODSonline.com for more maps and tutorials
            for Quake 4 and more

============================================================
```

5. **Save the file and close Notepad.**

6. **Navigate to the folder** `C:\Temp`.

   You now need to zip the contents of your mod into a single file.

7. **Right-click your custom mod folder q4mfd to open the pop-up menu and choose WinZip➪Add to q4mfd.zip.**

    WinZip quickly opens and closes again, and you are left with a new file in your directory, `q4mfd.zip`.

 8. **Open this new `q4mfd.zip` file. Make sure that you have all the files in here that make up your mod. After you confirm that all the files are present, close the Zip file.**

You're now ready to distribute your custom mod. The Zip file that you just created is all you need to hand out to your friends and Web sites. With it, they can install and play with the pieces you have constructed.

Distributing the Goods

Getting your map out to the public might seem easy at first. However, when you start looking for how to get your file to the different Web sites out there that will host your file online for free, you will find it isn't so easy to figure out who to contact or where to go — unless you have a little basic direction.

The first place you want to start is with Web sites that already offer downloadable content for *Quake 4*. Because Web sites can change so frequently, I've set up a Web page where you can find a list of *Quake 4* map submission links. Please visit `www.quake4modsfordummies.com` for these links.

Part V
The Part of Tens

The 5th Wave   By Rich Tennant

"I don't know nothin' about your computer doohickey, missy. But I do know that Virgil and I just come across proof of an alien presence right here in these woods."

In this part . . .

After getting this far, you must be raring to go farther. Well, in this part, I have some tips to keep you out of trouble and help you to discover more about what modding can do.

As the book flips down to the final pages, don't be concerned: The adventure doesn't stop here. Take a look online at all the modifications you can download and enjoy. Then, explore how they were created. It's amazing what others can do with mods — and with a little creativity, you can do it, too.

Chapter 20
Ten Great Tips and Tricks

*T*o help you further your knowledge and jump over some of the beginner hurdles, I've put together the top ten tips and tricks for modding *Quake 4*. These tips answer some of the most commonly asked questions by people just starting out with mapping and modding.

Come Up with Original Ideas

You have the knowledge to get started on your own mod for *Quake 4*. Although you're ready to jump into editing, maybe you don't know what to create. This is a very common problem among modders and mappers. Either you start with an inspired idea to work or you start inspired to work without an idea of where to start. It happens to professionals and beginners alike.

To come up with ideas, use what's around you. The first place you should look is right where you're sitting. Try building a map of your house, school, work, town, or other location with which you're familiar. Most of the best maps were created around actual places. If where you live doesn't inspire you, turn toward television, books, or the Internet. With so much technology at your disposal, you can look at environments and places located on the opposite side of the world without leaving your own home.

Another way I like to start my personal projects is to think of something that hasn't been done before. I once made a map for *Soldier of Fortune* that was the first for the game series to incorporate an elevator that could stop and start at the floor of the player's choosing. The player wasn't limited to a preset path for the elevator to travel. So, ask yourself "What new thing can I add?" When you have the answer, add it.

Finally, when you have no more ideas to work on but you really have an urge to do something, try asking members of a clan (gaming group) or other gaming group if they would like a custom addition to the game. Let them know you can build it based on their requests. Clans often have a level or game type that they prefer playing over any others. However, after hours of playing the same levels, the members yearn for variety. That's where you can step in and create that spectacular add-on they've been begging for.

Plan Your Build

I don't care how experienced you are at building maps or mods — if you don't have some sort of plan for what you're constructing, you're eventually going to have to rebuild part of your map.

The solution to avoiding errors is to plan out your project before you begin. Draw a diagram of what you're trying to accomplish. Expand the diagram to include features, images, and other items that you specifically want added. If you're mapping, get yourself some graph paper and plot out the building and other structures that you plan on building. Also consider taking or finding photos of what you want to build to further illustrate what you want to accomplish.

With everything properly planned out ahead of time, you will find that your project goes together much easier and quicker. You won't have to rebuild as much, and you'll be done in no time.

Design Minimally

It's an awful thing when you construct an entire map, compile it, test it, and realize that everything is running too slowly in the game because the level contains too much detail. Although game engines have rapidly come a long way in becoming powerful delivery agents of 3D worlds, they can't yet handle everything you might want to throw at them. This is where designing minimally comes in handy.

You can have all those details that you want in your level. However, you don't have to make them into solid objects or brushes that the game has to overwork to deliver to your screen. Instead, let the textures do the work for you.

Think of the crates you constructed in Chapter 12. If you look at the crates within the game, they have dimension, indentation, and a realistic presence — things that make the crates look like they were constructed from a lot of tiny brushes. However, all you had to do for each crate was build a cube and apply a texture. This texture then did the rest of the work for you.

Where can you find textures for this purpose? You can use many different types of resources. For example, for the bricks used in Chapter 15, I took pictures of the exterior of one of my local buildings. Here are a few other good ways to acquire textures:

- **Purchase textures from the Internet.** Searching the Internet for "buy textures" turns up pages of results.
- **Buy a CD of images.** You can often find them at your local computer stores or you can look on the Internet at different places that sell individual photos. Just make sure that you read the licensing information before distributing them to your friends.
- **Use textures from other games, such as earlier versions of *Quake*, *Half-Life*, or just about any other game.** Often, I choose games that support modifications such as the Quake series because I know it will be easier to extract those textures from the game. If a game doesn't support mods, then it might not be possible to get those textures out of the game.
- **If you have experience with modeling, you can model your own scenes and render the images required for your textures.** I have, on occasion, created my own models, arranged them in a scene, rendered an image of that model, and converted it into a texture for the game.

When you don't have what you need, think outside of the box. Or, in this case, think outside of the program. Look online or outside for ways to reduce your brush count in the game while still delivering details in your level.

Avoid Errors

Although I do love the editors that came with the game, they aren't perfect. They haven't been fully bug-tested, and when errors are found, they're rarely patched. That's because game modding is the primary function of the game developers. Their purpose is to develop a game and get a playable version out for the public. If they can provide mod support to the community, they will — but only if they have the time and ambition.

Having said that, there are bugs in the mapping editor that can ruin your work. Then when it comes time to repair the damage, it's probably too late. Finding the source of the error and then fixing it can take twice as long as it would to rebuild.

So, here are some tools and operations that can create errors in your maps that you really want to avoid:

Subtracting with CSG

The CSG Subtraction tool exists to allow you to subtract the shape of one brush from another. For instance, if you want to make a doorway in the middle of a wall, you could draw a rectangular brush that is the same size as the door. You could then overlap this doorway brush with the wall and use the CSG Subtraction tool. After you delete the doorway brush you used to subtract from the wall, the result would be a hole in the wall.

The problem arises later when you go to compile your map. Sometimes, errors like "node without volume" or "leaf saw into node" come up during the compile process. To solve this, you have to delete the brush that is causing the error. However, finding that brush is like finding a needle in a haystack.

This error doesn't always occur — especially with such simple subtractions like that of a rectangle from another rectangle. When used with more complex shapes, on the other hand, the error is much more likely. However, when it comes right down to it, why would you want to run the risk of such an error when you could do the operation just as easily by using another method?

Instead of using the Subtraction tool, you have many other options. One option that comes immediately to mind is that you could build the wall with the doorway in mind. Another option is to use the Clipper tool, as in Chapter 11.

The Subtraction tool has always been a troublemaker, and it's difficult to understand why no one has just removed it from the editor. I recommend just avoiding it.

Dragging out a triangle

You will run into some instances where you need a three-sided brush rather than the usual four-sided one. The proper way to create one is either by clipping a rectangular brush or by creating a brush of arbitrary sides. (You can create an arbitrary-sided brush by choosing Brush⇨Arbitrary Sided, entering the number of sides for your brush in the text box, and pressing OK.) These are excellent ways to accomplish the task.

However, you might be tempted to try to cut some corners by manipulating the shape of a rectangular brush into a triangle. Just like when you created beveled edges in Chapter 10 by dragging the edges of the brush, you can drag the edges into a triangle shape. This method, however, only causes you errors during the compile process.

Cutting corners should be reserved for the keyboard shortcuts. When it comes to manipulating the brushes in your map, shortcuts usually lead to headaches.

Super-sizing brushes

Another error that can come up is one created by brushes that are oversized. If you make a very long wall or ground brush in the game, it can create too much work for the game compiler or game engine. Some errors that have been displayed from this are `MAX_MAP_LIGHTING`, `MAX_MAP_DRAW_SURFS`, and `WARNING: too many light styles on a face`, just to name a few.

To avoid or solve this error, just break up those long brushes. Split the brush a few times and then try compiling the map again. However, don't go crazy with your splitting. Too many splits resulting in a long string of brush faces in a straight line can cause another error, `MAX_WINDINGS_PER_CELL`.

When fixing errors, try making minor adjustments and then testing your progress. Often, you will find that a simple adjustment can make a world of difference, and you don't have to put forth so much effort in fixing your problems.

Follow Examples

You might not have realized it yet, but the game already comes with a bunch of example maps for you to look at. All the levels that you can play in the game are supplied with a map located inside the pak files.

If you're playing a level in the game, you might come across something that you would like to use or create in your own map. Take note of the level you're playing and then search it out in the pak files. Extract the map file from the pak file and open it in the editor. There, you can find exactly how it was created in the game, and you can recreate it in your own level.

The same goes for other parts of the game. Scripts, GUIs, and other things used to make a level work are included in the pak files. Even the models that are using the game can be imported into a 3D modeling program. The possibilities are staggering.

Sometimes, checking out examples can inspire you and/or drastically reduce your build time. The maps that come with the game are perfect for this. The developers of the game have put a lot of neat tricks at your fingertips.

Use Prefabs

If you're making a map or series of maps that reuse the same construction of brushes, turn it into a prefab. A *prefab* is like a tiny map that can be imported into any map that you're working on. Usually, prefabs are made up of guard towers, buildings, or other commonly used structures. This way you have to build them only once, and then you can easily duplicate them whenever you need to.

To create a prefab, select the group of brushes that you want to save. Choose Edit⇨Save Selection as Prefab. Then save the file under a name of your choosing. You can then choose Edit⇨Load Prefab to load this combination of brushes into the same or a different map as often as you like.

You can also find prefabs available online, usually at the same places you can find custom maps and mods. Sometimes, mappers like to offer their prefabs for download just like their maps. This way their great constructions can find their way into other maps. Just remember that if you do use a prefab in your map that you should give credit to the author in the README file (which I discuss in Chapter 2).

Mesh Objects

If you are trying to create a more flexible brush in your map, try looking into patch meshes. A *patch mesh* is like a brush with a lot of splits in it. You can make parts of it bump out or you can make it look cylindrical.

One use of patch meshes is for creating large terrain. If you're looking to create a ground that has hills and valleys, the patch mesh will do it for you. To use it, draw a square, thin brush roughly the size of the ground that you want to build. Choose Patch⇨Simple Patch Mesh, and then enter the number of splits you want to be created in the two axes shown in your 2D window.

However, when entering the patch density, know that adding more splits creates more polygons within the game. Too many splits, and your game could slow down due to poor optimization.

With your patch mesh created, press Y to show the vertices of your patch. Then press V to edit those vertices. Now you can click and drag the points on your patch mesh to create bumps and depressions.

As for cylinders, you can make nicely rounded pillars in your map. Create a tall, square brush in your map that you would like to turn into a pillar. Then choose Patch⇨Cylinder. The result is a pillar-like structure that you can place in your map any way that you like.

Then, if you choose Patch⇨Cap⇨Normal, you can put a top and bottom on that cylinder. This can make for a good oil can or other similar object.

Try fooling around with patch meshes some more on your own. You will find them useful in certain situations like the ones I mention in this section.

Measure the Player

A very common question in all the mapping forums is, "What are the player dimensions?" Many people want to know how the game relates to real life in order to properly plan out their maps. Perhaps they want a life-size room or building. These dimensions could help them achieve that.

The basic measurements of the player in the game are as follows:

- Player's height: 74 units
- Player's crawling height: 40 units
- Player's width: 40 units
- Player's maximum step without jumping: 16 units
- Player's maximum jumping height: 48 units
- Player's maximum jumping distance: 112 units
- Player's highest fall without damage: 136 units
- Steepest angle a player can climb: 45 degrees

The unit-to-inch conversion has been averaged out as follows: 1 unit = 1 inch. This may seem ridiculous, but keep in mind that the laws of nature do not apply in the virtual world. Therefore, you really should make your map so that it looks good — not so that it maps to real-world specifications.

Find More to Mod

If you're looking to further modify the game, you can do a lot more than what I tell you about in this book. I was able to cover only mapping, scripts, textures, and skins in the page space given to me. However, modding doesn't stop there.

- **Audio:** You can add new audio or even change the audio that already exists in the game. Weapons, background music, pickups, and several other objects in the game create sound. These are just a few places to start.

  The audio files in the game can be found in `pak010.pk4` starting in the path `sound\`. The files are in OGG format, which is a special audio format. They have been saved at 44,100 Hz, 69 Kbps mono levels, which will make sense when you go to save your custom audio file. All you need is an audio-editing program that can manage OGG files, and you are ready to go.

- **Effects:** Effects are becoming more popular to modify in games. *Effects* are text files that tell the game to make sparks, swirls, or other things that provide visual effects. You can commonly see effects around the power-ups in the game.

  You can find the definitions for the game effects in `pak001.pk4`. Take a look through there for the path `effects` to find out what is required to make the changes.

- **Modeling and animating:** You've already seen the models in the game. They include the player, weapons, and several other entities. Well, these models were created in modeling programs such as Lightwave and 3D Studio Max.

  You can create your own models and import them into the game. This might take additional time and practice on your behalf, but if you can create a model, you will be on your way to mastering games.

Look for Help

The topics I don't cover in this book might be available by way of online tutorials. My education into the world of game mods started with online tutorials. When I surpassed the tutorials that were available, I started making my own.

Chapter 20: Ten Great Tips and Tricks

Now, you can find various Web sites that offer both written and video tutorials on a variety of modding subjects. For those tasks that aren't covered by tutorials, the forums offer a wealth of information and means to ask for more.

If you're looking for more help, start with your favorite Internet search engine. You're sure to come up with a few pages of results that give you what you are looking for.

I have also created an additional source for finding Web sites that offer tutorials information for modding games. Visit `www.quake4modsfordummies.com` and follow the links provided there.

Chapter 21

Ten Great Mods

A number of great mods are already available on the Internet. They're not only great fun, but they're also a great way to gain knowledge. You can download a mod, open the contents, and explore the changes that were implemented to make what they created possible.

I've selected ten great mods and dissected them. My goal is to give you ideas on what you can do and create. In some cases, I even tell you what changes the mod authors made to the game so you can experiment. However, providing inspiration isn't all I'm trying to do. I also want to tell you what the modders could have done to further improve the mods that they released to the public. Hopefully, the result will be a lot more mods for all to enjoy.

All the mods listed in this chapter can easily be found on the Internet or at `www.quake4modsfordummies.com`. Feel free to install them as they are discussed. Play around with them to see what they can do and maybe feel inspired to create your own.

For more information on how these and other mods were created, examine their contents. Compare the files in the mod with those of the original game. This will truly help you to solve more riddles when creating your own mods.

Corpse Stay and Self Shadow

Mod Name : *Corpse Stay and Self Shadow*

Version : Unknown, released 10/22/2005

Author : Unknown

E-mail : Unknown

Web site : Unknown

Filename : `q4_corpsstay_and_selfshadow_v01.zip`

A lot of enemies come at you during the single-player game. Everywhere you turn, a monster is trying to gun you down. Obviously, your goal in the game is to stay alive, and to do so you must shoot back.

When you destroy an enemy, the body disappears with a special effect. The player model turns translucent, and a glow emanates from around the body. A couple seconds later, nothing is there to remind you of your conquest.

Another aspect of the game that you might or might not have noticed is that of shadows. Everything that has been built into the game, be it walls, hanging lights, or monsters, all cast shadows. However, your character in the game does not.

There is fair reasoning behind why this effect was left from the game. Those added shadows take up processing power in your computer. The more shadowing effect the game must request, the more demanding the game will be on your computer processor.

While playing the single-player game, there aren't any other real people to see your character cast a shadow. It's you against the computer-driven enemies. You might be able to see your own shadow on the wall when you pass in front of a light, but this isn't vital to game play. Therefore, why use up your processing power to create shadows that you might not fully appreciate?

Then again, why not make the game more realistic? Your shadow could add to the game play. Perhaps as you turn a corner in the game, you see a shadow of something moving. This causes you to jump because you think you are about to be attacked. Then it turns out to be your own shadow.

This is where the *Corpse Stay and Self Shadow* mod comes into play. This modification puts that shadow effect into the game, possibly bringing more realism to the gaming environment. It also forces those dead enemies to stick around for a while rather than disappearing a few seconds later.

This mod is a collection of weapons definition files and player material files, each one with moddable fields. Many modifications to the playability of a game require changes to these file types and will be found in almost every instance.

Basically, here's how this mod was accomplished:

- **Definitions:** The definition files specify how long to wait before a dead player is removed by using the command `removeDelay`. Rather than waiting five seconds, this mod specifies 1,201 seconds. Also defined is the command `burnaway`, which has been raised considerably.

- **Materials:** The material files define the shadowing effect. The command `noSelfShadow` has been commented out within these player and enemy material files. When used, a shadow is cast on all these characters.

Possible pitfalls

The *Corpse Stay and Self Shadow* mod is a classic modification of game play in that it alters definition and material files to accomplish its goals. However, the installation of this mod is less classic. The download is missing a README, which not only makes it nearly impossible to give credit to the author, but also means you have to figure out its installation on your own.

Another issue I have with this mod is that the files are not contained within a mod folder. This means that you must either install the files into a mod folder of your own or install them into the q4base mod of the game.

Drach-FPS-Mappack

Mod Name	: *Drach-FPS-Mappack*
Version	: released 03/11/2005
Author	: dr4ch
E-mail	: `dr4ch@web.de`
Web site	: `http://inquake.de`
Filename	: `drachfpsmappack.zip`

On the Internet, you can find not only individual maps that you can download and play in *Quake 4,* but also map packs that contain several maps. However, this particular map pack comes with more that just a few well-built maps.

Drack-FPS-Mappack actually contains maps that you've already seen. All the original *Quake 4* maps are within this package. However, they have all been enhanced with more well-defined lighting.

There is a huge market for maps that run fast and smooth with a lot of players. It takes a powerful computer to serve 12 or more players in a large map. So, rather than upgrade the hardware, it's easier to better optimize the maps for slower computers.

In this mod, all the original maps that came with the game have been modified. Specifically, the lights have been adjusted and then the maps re-compiled with these adjustments in place.

When you add lights to your map, you can adjust the detail level of those light entities. You do this by using the light editor, as I explained in Chapter 11. This detail level is used by the game in determining light's importance.

The default level for a light is 10. This means that regardless of the user's quality settings for the game, this light is going to be visible. However, if the light level is adjusted lower, toward a maximum level of –1, those lights can be filtered out of the game by the computer serving it. By entering the console command `r_lightdetaillevel` and entering a value for that level between –1 and 9, you can tell the game to use all lights that have been set with a defined level of detail between 0 and 10 respectively. The game also includes all those lights with a higher value. This means less work for those slower computers which results in a faster, smoother game for the players.

Possible pitfalls

There is a down-side to using these methods of adjusting lights. It means that there is less light available — so much less light that you might have to turn up your brightness and gamma levels to see the other players in the game. However, the other option is to use a higher level of light detail, and if you do this, you will be back to playing the level as the creator intended.

Fleischhaus

Mod Name	: *Fleischhaus*
Version	: released 10/29/2005
Author	: Major Fleischer (Moritz Reinhold)
E-mail	: `trashcan@architecs.de`
Web site	: `www.q4dev.net`
Filename	: `dm_fleischhaus.zip`

There are a lot of maps out there available for download. It's easy to find new maps when searching for new *Quake 4* content on the Internet. However, if you're a modder looking for ideas or examples of other maps, this mod is a paradise.

Fleischhaus is an example of one of these easily available maps. This map was very well built in both construction methods and originality. It's small, having only enough room for 3–6 players, but it's a great example of how you don't have to build a large map to create something fun and pretty.

This map is designed in a typical arena style. This means that it's small and forces the players into a central area for heavy battle. There is great lighting and some personal touches. On one of the walls, there is some text that looks like it belongs in this setting, but actually is an Internet address to the author's Web site.

Possible pitfalls

Although the creator used some good optimization techniques in the building of this map, further steps could have been taken. There is a lot of empty space behind the walls that the player cannot access. And although this area isn't accessible, for some reason it is still being drawn by the game. This leads me to believe that there are some leaks in the main structure of the map, and this problem was perhaps solved by simply building a big, solid box around everything. This empty space should have been avoided, and leaks into it should have been sealed.

A Web site address has been overlaid on the walls. Again, this is a great personal touch that I really like; however, the image used hasn't been optimized. This image should also be available in DDS format for games running on slow computers with the quality settings turned down.

However, even with these minor oversights in the map, I still think it's of excellent design.

Logo Crosshair

Mod Name : *Quake4logo_crosshair*

Version : Unknown, released 10/28/2005

Author : Sleepwalker

E-mail : Unknown

Web site : Unknown

Filename : `q4logo_crosshair.rar`

Not all modifications have to be difficult to be enjoyed. Sometimes simple changes make the entire game more fun. The *Logo Crosshair* modification allows you to change the crosshair used in the game to the *Quake* symbol.

To make the change, one file was modified, and another was added. The added file is that of the crosshair itself. This is a simple Targa image; however, in this image, the alpha channel defines what part of your image is visible.

The altered file is the player definition file. A couple lines were added to define the newly available selection in the game. The lines added were

```
"mtr_crosshair19""gfx/guis/crosshairs/crosshair_q4_11.tga"
"mtr_crosshair19" "gfx/guis/crosshairs/crosshair_q4_11.tga"
```

The number 19 was used because it was the next incremental number available. The Targa file listed is the new one that was created by the author. You could keep on adding more and create a mod of ten or more crosshairs.

Possible pitfalls

This modification is very simple and doesn't require much in the way of installation. The only downfall I found was that the README lacks any information to contact the author.

Q4GIB

Mod Name : *Q4GIB* - Instagib Mod
Version : 1.32, released 4/20/2006
Author : Unknown
E-mail : Unknown
Web site : `http://q4gib.dumbie.net`
Filename : `q4gib_v132.zip`

Q4GIB is short for *Quake 4* instagib. Instagib is a type of modification that means that any single shot in the game results in an instant kill. This type of modification became popular with *Quake II* and has been reintroduced in almost every game since.

Gib is a term was introduced by Adrian Carmack of id Software, Inc. It describes the pieces of a player that can sometimes fly off when they are shot or exploded. Therefore instagib equates to instant explosion of a player.

Generally, this just means that one or more weapons are redefined to inflict more damage. And although any weapon could be modified in this way, generally the more powerful weapon is selected. Then all other weapons are disabled so that everyone is fighting on equal terms.

In the case of this mod, the rail gun is the weapon that was modified. The damage was raised as high as it could go in its definition file to ensure that it instantly destroyed anyone it hit.

To make the game even more interesting, other changes were implemented. Some of those changes are as follows:

- Added unlimited ammo to the weapon
- Set the player to spawn with this weapon
- Added this modification to the single-player game
- Updated the game's main menus
- Removed all other weapons from spawning in the game
- Disabled all power-ups excluding Haste

As you can see, a lot of changes were implemented, and I didn't even list half of them. All this modding was done over time, starting with the basic change of increasing the power of the rail gun. From there, along with requests and error submissions of those who played it, improvements were made.

Possible pitfalls

This mod was built well enough that I don't foresee anything going wrong. However, I was surprised to see that although the README contained great detail on the many changes that were made with each version, there wasn't any author information. Luckily for the maker, this mod is easy to locate on the Internet.

If this is something you want to undertake, I suggest you go at it one step at a time. Don't try to implement too many new features all at once, or you might wind up with errors that you can't track down. Stick with the basics of your modification, and then work your way into more complicated ideas.

Dark Matter Mayhem

Mod Name : *Dark Matter Mayhem*
Version : 1.0, released 02/01/2006
Author : Tom "imTFG" Fragger
E-mail : `imtfgs@yahoo.com`
Web site : `http://imtfg.homeip.net/quake4`
Filename : `Dark_Matter_Mayhem.zip`

The *Dark Matter Mayhem* mod follows along the same path as the *Q4GIB* mod. This mod restricts the player to a single weapon and modifies the weapon to specific settings. However, unlike the *Q4GIB* mod, it doesn't necessarily kill in one shot.

The idea used in the making of this modification is to create a game that utilizes only the dark matter gun (DMG). This weapon is unique to *Quake*, which is possibly the inspiration.

Along with eliminating all weapons other than the DMG, changes were made to help the game flow better with this normally out-of-place weapon. Generally, this weapon fires a very slow-moving projectile. However, for this mod the projectile's speed was increased by a factor of three. The zoom from the rail gun was installed, and all ammo found in the map has been converted to DMG ammo.

All these changes were actually made simply by editing the definitions. The player definition file was modified to adjust the player's available weapons and ammo upon spawning. You can do this by changing three values and adding a fourth. The result reads

```
"weapon"            "weapon_dmg, weapon_gauntlet"
"current_weapon"    "9"
"ammo_machingun"    "0"
"ammo_dmg"          "10"
```

The weapon definition files were also changed. The DMG file raised the rate of firing, the speed of the projectile, and added the zoom option. The other weapons files are simple replacements; the DMG takes the place of each by defining the already listed command, `inherit`, found within the definition file, with a value of `weapon_dmg`.

Possible pitfalls

This modification is simple enough that errors really shouldn't arise. The README contains enough information, and the installation is straightforward.

Quake 4 WOD

Mod Name : *Quake 4 WOD - Weapons of Destruction*

Version   : 2.5 (Official release), released 12/22/2005

Author   : Multiple

E-mail   : q4wod@khalan.com

Web site : `www.khalan.com/q4wod/`

Filename : `wodv25.zip`

The *Quake 4 WOD* mod does more than just modify the weapons in the game. This mod takes things a step further by adding features that never existed. For the authors involved, what was missing from *Quake 4* were some of the weapon features from *Quake II:* specifically, a feature called *alternate fire*.

In *Quake II,* a very popular mod came out that gave most weapons two firing modes instead of just the one. The standard firing mode was what you would expect from the weapon. The alternate firing mode was a little extra that might have used more than its fair share of ammo, but also packed more punch with each shot.

I think that every weapon in the game was modified in some way in *Quake 4 WOD*. Although the primary purpose was to add the alternate firing modes termed *alt fire,* this resulted in a need to better balance the game play between these weapons. It wouldn't be fair to have a pistol that outgunned every other weapon or to provide one player with any more of an unfair advantage than the other. Therefore a lot of play-testing was involved, and a lot of tuning of the definition files occurred.

Along with the weapon changes, the authors threw in some other nice changes to the game for a more customized look.

- The gauntlet was replaced by the blaster.
- The HUD (or Heads Up Display) was replaced with a modified *Q4MAX* HUD.
- Brighter player skins were added to make it easier to spot opposing players.
- Maximum ammo limits were raised.
- Player movement was sped up.
- Many other smaller changes were added.

For all these changes to work, a lot more than just definition files had to be updated. New effects were created for the alt fire modes, and existing effects were updated for taste. GUIs had to be altered for the HUD and other visual elements. Also, new skins, materials, and other player attributes were updated partly to include firing animations of the new firing modes.

A lot of changes had to take place to put this mod together. However, the knowledge of how to implement these changes is something you can pick up on your own by searching through the work that was done. If you have the time and the will, there is a way.

Possible pitfalls

Because so many changes are involved in this mod, many things could go wrong. Luckily for the mod authors, I could find reports of only one error, one linked to using both firing modes at the same time. I'm sure even that will be fixed in a future release.

Q4 X-Battle Battlemod

Mod Name : *X-Battle* a modification for *Quake 4*
Version : 023, released 11/12/2005
Author : Multiple
E-mail : `info@xbattle.de`
Web site : `www.xbattle.de`
Filename : `xmb-v023fix.zip`

Clans are a huge market for multiplayer games. *Clans* are groups of people that play as a team against other clans. These highly competitive groups often have their own ideas of what would make a game more competitive and sporting. This is where many ideas are born and where new mods often take shape.

Some of the changes made in this mod are for easier spotting of players and pickups in the heat of battle. Player and weapon skins were made brighter so they were more easily spotted. Glow effects were added around weapons to make them stand out more.

Other changes were made to the player's HUD. To make it easier to see which weapon was selected, the visibility of the weapon's bar can be easily changed by the user. The position of the weapons bar can be moved around the screen, and the ammo count can also be more easily seen.

Because this mod is made up of mostly visual changes, there weren't a lot of files that required altering. Material files were changed for the appearance of players and weapons. GUI files were modified for the updated HUD. Then some text and sound changes were thrown into the mix.

Possible pitfalls

I describe just a few of the changes that have taken place, but many more are planned. Because the developers have released an update to the game, modders are waiting on more information on how to make their changes to this new code. New code often means more work because it could mean that a mod won't work with each update by the creators of the game.

Q4MAX

Mod Name : *Q4MAX* Competition Mod
Version : 0.74b, released 5/10/2006
Author : Multiple
E-mail : Unknown
Web site : www.q4max.com
Filename : z-q4max074b.pk4 (requires q4max074.zip)

At the time of writing, *Q4MAX* is perhaps the largest mod for *Quake 4*. It was developed by a large group of gamers who loved to play. Much like *Q4 X-Battle Battlemod,* the goal was to create a mod better suited to competition between clans.

However, unlike the *Q4 X-Battle Battlemod,* this mod has heavier modification to the game's files. New game types like *CaptureStrike* were added, referee functions like Pause were created, game launching has undergone many changes, and more.

I found one addition to be quite innovative and smart. Included with the installation files was documentation and Web code so that you could display your server's information online. With this added installation, you can let your visitors know what map is playing, who is playing, and more.

Possible pitfalls

For such a large mod, I expected it to be easier to find out more about what went into this project. However, looking at both the downloaded installation file and the team's Web site, I couldn't figure out the primary reason why this mod was created. Luckily, a log containing many of the changes that went into the modification was included, and I could deduce the rest.

SABot

Mod Name : *SABot* (Stupid Angry Bot)
Version : Alpha 9 (4/22/2006)
Author : Jarad "TinMan" Hansen
E-mail : q4wod@khalan.com
Web site : www.oakbots.co.uk/forums/viewforum.php?f=7
Filename : sabota9.zip

SABot might not be a traditional mod in that it doesn't really change the way the game looks. However, it is traditional in that with every release of the *Quake* games someone has created a mod like this.

SABot is a modification that allows you to add computer-driven players. *SABot* stands for *Stupid Angry Bot.* These bots, named for their likeness to robots, are fake players that you can add to most maps in order to increase the number of players. With them you can either play alone or you can really fill up the map.

You can do more than just add players to the game. You can also adjust each bot to perform better or worse. You can change each bot's accuracy for more challenging fights. You can also change the speed at which they are able to target you with their weapons. All the information you need is contained with the README.

> Bots are not only great for making bigger games. They can also be a great tool for modders. When I create a large map, it's sometimes difficult to determine how easy it is to get around and how well it plays with others. By adding bots, I can test out the playability of my level without requiring others to help. It's like my own private beta team.

Possible pitfalls

Although this mod works well with the original levels that come with the game, the bots won't automatically work with every level. For each map that you want available to the bot, you must create a special aas32 file. This file contains the information that the bots need to navigate your level in the game. Otherwise, they get confused and don't know what to do.

If you want to use bots in your map, all you have to do is read the instructions to compile your map for bots included in the README.

Appendix: What's on the CD-ROM?

In This Appendix
- System Requirements
- Using the CD with Windows and Mac
- What You'll Find on the CD
- Troubleshooting

System Requirements

Make sure that your computer meets the minimum system requirements shown in the following list. If your computer doesn't match up to most of these requirements, you may have problems using the software and files on the CD. For the latest and greatest information, please refer to the ReadMe file located at the root of the CD-ROM.

- A PC with a Pentium 4 2.0Ghz or Athlon XP 2000+ processor or higher
- Microsoft Windows 2000/XP or later
- At least 512MB of total RAM installed on your computer
- A CD-ROM drive
- A sound card for PCs
- A monitor capable of displaying at least 256 colors or grayscale
- A modem with a speed of at least 14,400 bps

If you need more information on the basics, check out these books published by Wiley Publishing, Inc.: *PCs For Dummies,* by Dan Gookin; *Windows 2000 Professional For Dummies, Windows XP For Dummies,* all by Andy Rathbone.

Using the CD with Microsoft Windows

To install the items from the CD to your hard drive, follow these steps.

1. **Insert the CD into your computer's CD-ROM drive. The license agreement appears.**

   Note to Windows users: The interface won't launch if you have Autorun disabled. In that case, click Start⇨Run. In the dialog box that appears, type D:\start.exe. (Replace D with the proper letter if your CD-ROM drive uses a different letter. If you don't know the letter, see how your CD-ROM drive is listed under My Computer.) Click OK.

2. **Read through the license agreement, and then click the Accept button if you want to use the CD. After you click Accept, the License Agreement window won't appear again.**

   The CD interface appears. The interface allows you to install the programs and run the demos with just a click of a button (or two).

What You'll Find on the CD

The following sections are arranged by category and provide a summary of the software and other goodies you'll find on the CD. If you need help with installing the items provided on the CD, refer back to the installation instructions in the preceding section.

Shareware programs are fully functional, free, trial versions of copyrighted programs. If you like particular programs, register with their authors for a nominal fee and receive licenses, enhanced versions, and technical support. *Freeware programs* are free, copyrighted games, applications, and utilities. You can copy them to as many PCs as you like — for free — but they offer no technical support. *GNU software* is governed by its own license, which is included inside the folder of the GNU software. There are no restrictions on distribution of GNU software. See the GNU license at the root of the CD for more details. *Trial, demo,* or *evaluation* versions of software are usually limited either by time or functionality (such as not letting you save a project after you create it).

Author-created material

Trial Version

All the examples provided in this book are located in the Author directory on the CD and work with Windows 95/98/NT and later computers. These files contain much of the sample code from the book.

WinZip

Trial Version

For Windows. This handy utility allows you to view, extract, and manipulate ZIP archives on your computer. For more information, visit www.winzip.com.

Adobe Photoshop CS 2

Trial Version

For Windows. A trial version of Adobe's powerful image manipulation software. For more information, visit www.adobe.com.

The Compressonator

For Windows. A tool for compressing textures and creating mipmap levels. For more information, visit www.ati.com.

Normal Map Generator

For Windows. A tool for converting height maps to normal maps. For more information, visit www.ati.com.

Troubleshooting

I tried my best to compile programs that work on most computers with the minimum system requirements. Alas, your computer may differ, and some programs may not work properly for some reason.

The two likeliest problems are that you don't have enough memory (RAM) for the programs you want to use, or you have other programs running that are affecting installation or running of a program. If you get an error message such as `Not enough memory` or `Setup cannot continue`, try one or more of the following suggestions and then try using the software again:

- **Turn off any antivirus software running on your computer.** Installation programs sometimes mimic virus activity and may make your computer incorrectly believe that it's being infected by a virus.

- **Close all running programs.** The more programs you have running, the less memory is available to other programs. Installation programs typically update files and programs; so if you keep other programs running, installation may not work properly.

- **Have your local computer store add more RAM to your computer.** This is, admittedly, a drastic and somewhat expensive step. However, if you have a Windows 95 PC or a Mac OS computer with a PowerPC chip, adding more memory can really help the speed of your computer and allow more programs to run at the same time. This may include closing the CD interface and running a product's installation program from Windows Explorer.

Customer Care

If you have trouble with the CD-ROM, please call the Wiley Product Technical Support phone number at (800) 762-2974. Outside the United States, call 1(317) 572-3994. You can also contact Wiley Product Technical Support at **http://support.wiley.com**. John Wiley & Sons will provide technical support only for installation and other general quality control items. For technical support on the applications themselves, consult the program's vendor or author.

To place additional orders or to request information about other Wiley products, please call (877) 762-2974.

Index

• Symbols and Numerics •

~ (tilde) key, opening/closing console with, 39–40
2D window (mapping editor)
  copying rooms, 94–95
  creating halls, 96–97
  maneuvering, 54–56
  overview, 47
  resizing brushes from, 56
  splitting brushes, 101–102
3D
  adding texture, 28
  understanding concept of, 26–27

• A •

accent lights
  adding, 155–156
  adding light entities to, 159
  adding texture to, 156–157
  copying, 160
  optimizing, 158
action. *See* multiplayer action; single-player action
Add Noise dialog box (Photoshop), creating height map with, 272–275
additions, creating distribution packages for game, 334–337
Adobe Photoshop
  altering models with, 319
  for creating custom texture, 247
  creating diffuse map in, 259–260
  creating editor image in, 275–278
  creating GUI images, 297
  creating height map in, 271–275
  creating normal map in, 265–270
  creating specular map in, 260–265
  creating thumbnail images, 211–212
  editing screenshots in, 208–209
  exposing image seams with, 252–254
  modifying model body with, 327–328
  modifying model eyeballs with, 325–327
  modifying model head with, 328–331
  modifying model images with, 324–325
  NVIDIA plug-ins, 247, 266–270
  recommended, 19
  resizing images for custom textures in, 251
  resizing screenshot images in, 209–211
  trial version, 367
alterations, creating distribution packages for game, 337–340
ambient light, simulating outdoor, 148–150
ammo, placing, 176–179
Ammo-Regen pickup, function of, 216
angle
  adjusting for armor placement, 170–172
  adjusting for gladiator entity, 193
  adjusting for health pickups, 172
  adjusting for weapon pickups, 174–175
  adjusting team spawn point, 199
antialiasing, turning off, 38–39
antivirus software, CD problems, 368
areas
  defined, 85
  dividing mapping to, 85–86
arena CTF (Capture the Flag)
  defined, 198
  special power pickups for, 216–217
armor, adding, 170–172
assets, looking for mod ideas, 11
ATI, Normal Map Generator tool, 270, 367
audio, modding, 350

• B •

background color, selecting for custom GUI, 295–296
`bfunc_mover` entity, turning platform into, 236–237

Quake 4 Mods For Dummies

Binary Space Partitioning (BSP) process, overview, 84
`bind` command, binding entities with, 241
blockades, adding for team-based play, 198–199
blocks, filling corners in with, 129–130
body
  disappearing, 353–354
  modifying model, 327–328
bottleneck, fixing, 141
boundaries
  defining with textures, 130–131
  setting maps, 25
brightness, reducing, 39–40
brush faces
  accessing difficult, 139–140
  defined, 67
  fixing textures of doorways, 137–140
  selecting/painting ceiling and floor, 71–73
  selecting/painting on walls, 68–69
brushes. *See also* brush faces
  accessing inner door, 139
  active, 29
  adding ledges to walls with, 152–153
  adding texture to ledge, 153–155
  creating climbable crates with, 164–165
  creating doorways with, 100–104
  creating error-free triangles with, 346–347
  creating GUI with, 286–288
  creating halls with, 96–97
  creating indoor light box with, 160–161
  creating outdoor environment with, 127–128
  creating platform tracks with, 233–234
  creating platforms with, 229–231
  creating portals with, 119–121
  creating triggers with, 188–189
  creating turning platform with, 234–236
  deleting unnecessary hall, 98
  drawing, 53–54
  fixing overlapping walls in, 60–63
  hollowing out, 58–59, 97–98
  making maps with, 25
  mitering, 114–117
  problems with oversized, 347
  resizing/moving, 56–57
  splitting to create doorways, 101–104
  splitting to create outside access, 136–137
  turning into detail brushes, 165
  turning into GUI entity, 288–290
  using patch meshes for, 348–349
BSP (Binary Space Partitioning) process, overview, 84
BSP command, optimizing map, 122
.bsp files, 86–87
buildings, adding texture to exterior of, 132–133. *See also* rooms
bumping effect
  creating with normal map, 265–270
  defining in script, 280
  on texture, 246
buttons
  adding player interactive to GUIs, 305–307
  in mapping editor, 47

• C •

CAM window (mapping editor)
  copying rooms in, 94–95
  light entity appearing in, 76
  maneuvering, 60
  overview, 45
  selecting brushes from, 61, 62
Canyon texture set, adding to crates, 164–165
`canyon/crate_a_front` texture, applying to crates, 164
`canyon/crate_a_top` texture, applying to crates, 165
CAP button (Surface Inspector dialog box), aligning textures with, 71
capped patches, aligning textures on, 71
Capture the Flag (CTF)
  adding crate blockades for, 198–199
  creating flags for, 201
  defined, 198
  placing flags for, 201–204
  placing team spawn points for, 199–200
Cartesian coordinate system, in gaming, 26
Catacomb 3D, FPS gaming, 10

Index

Caulk texture
  creating climbable crates with, 164–165
  creating halls with, 96–97
  creating indoor light box with, 160–161
  loading/selecting, 51–53
  overview, 50
ceiling
  option of mitering, 116–117
  selecting/painting, 71–73
child layers
  adding, 301–304
  adding to GUI Desktop, 296–297
  adjusting size of, 298–299
  changing color of, 299–300
  duplicating, 300–301
clans
  defined, 362
  getting original ideas from, 343–344
climbable crates, creating, 164–165. *See also* crates
Clipper tool
  creating doorways with, 101–104
  creating outside access with, 136–137
  creating turning platform with, 235–236
  defining boundaries with, 130–131
  splitting brushes with, 120–121
coding, versus scripting, 221
color
  adding to accent lights, 159
  changing a copied room, 95–96
  changing child layer, 299–300
  changing light entity, 78–79
  creating diffuse map for, 259–260
  modifying model body image, 327–328
  modifying model eyeball, 325–327
  selecting background for custom GUI, 295–296
  simulating ambient light, 149
  texture, 246
Color Balance dialog box (Photoshop), modifying model head image with, 330
Color Picker dialog box (Photoshop)
  changing light entity color with, 78–79
  modifying model eyeballs with, 325
Color Range dialog box (Photoshop), creating specular map with, 263

commands
  adding to shortcut's Target field, 35–36
  `bind`, 241
  BSP, 122
  `+ disconnect`, 35–36
  `g_showHud 0`, 210
  `g_showHud 1`, 210
  Move Model, 181
  `moveToPos ( )`, 239–240, 243
  `no_touch`, 292
  Rotate Model, 181
  `rotateTo( )`, 241–242
  `r_showPortals 1`, 111
  `r_showTris 2`, 110–111
  `r_useScissor 0`, 111
  `+set com_allowConsole 1`, 35–36
  to show what is being rendered within game, 110–111
  `unbind`, 243
  `vid_restart`, 39
  `waitFor`, 240–242
  Zoom Model, 181
comments, available for GUIs, 290
Common Floors texture set, adding texture to platforms from, 231
Common Lights texture set, adding to accent lights, 156–157
Common Misc texture set, adding texture to platform tracks from, 234
Common texture set
  creating GUI from, 286–288
  trigger texture, 188
Common Walls texture set
  adding texture to building exteriors with, 132–133
  adding texture to outer wall with, 134
  adding texture to roof tops with, 133
  loading, 67–68
`common/entitygui` texture, applying to brush, 288
`common_floors/c_floor_1b` texture, adding to platforms, 231
`common_floors/floor5_1` texture, applying to ceiling, 72
`common_lights/rect_light6` texture, applying to accent lights, 157

`common_lights/small_light4` texture, applying to indoor lights, 161
`common_misc/concrete05` texture, applying to floor, 72
`common_misc/p4_beam_5` texture, adding to platform tracks, 234
`common/trigonce` texture
  creating gladiator triggers with, 193
  creating Strogg triggers with, 186, 188, 190
`common_walls/ba_wall1_5c` texture, applying to walls, 68
`common_walls/c_ribwall` texture, defining outer wall with, 134
`common_walls/outdoor_wall1_1` texture, applying to building exteriors, 132
`common_walls/outdoor_wall1_1a` texture, applying to building rooftops, 133
compile process
  automatic optimization in, 117–118
  BSP process, 84
  lighting process, 86
  overview, 83–84
  starting, 87
  using after optimization, 122
  VIS process, 85–86
compressed files, accessing, 18–19
compression utilities
  accessing compressed files with, 18–19
  extracting glossary terms with, 223–226
  preparing distribution package with, 336–337
  renaming files in, 317
  trial version, 367
The Compressonator
  on CD, 367
  compressing modified model images with, 332
  converting DDS images with, 19–20
  creating custom textures, 247
  loading, 275
  performing batch conversions with, 276–278

computer memory, textures size, 249
`config.spec` file, function of, 318
console
  checking for compilation errors in, 87–89
  loading custom textured map from, 283
  showing what is being rendered within game from, 110–111
content, moddable, 12–13
copying
  accent light fixtures, 160
  child layers, 300–301
  crates, 166
  fixing ground brushes by, 128–129
  flag stand models, 202
  keyboard shortcut for, 335
  lighting to hallways, 105
  mirroring face image with, 331
  rooms, 93–95
  textures from brush face to brush face, 104
  updated information, 140
Core texture set, adding texture to platforms from, 231–232
`core/sc_warning` texture, adding to platforms, 231–232
corners
  filling in useless, 129–130
  mitering exterior, 132
  mitering floor and ceiling, 116–117
  mitering wall, 114–116
  value of mitering, 112–113
Corpse Stay and Self Shadow mod
  overview, 353–354
  problems with, 355
crates
  adding to outside structure, 168–169
  creating climbable, 164–165
  creating team-based play blockades with, 198–199
  hiding enemies behind, 186
  overview, 163–164
  placing for strategy, 166–167
  placing pickups on, 176–178
  testing, 182–183
CSG Subtraction tool, avoiding errors with, 346

Index 373

CTF (Capture the Flag)
  adding crate blockades for, 198–199
  creating flags for, 201
  defined, 198
  placing flags for, 201–204
  placing team spawn points for, 199–200
custom textures. *See also* textures
  applying, 281–282
  creating diffuse map for, 259–260
  creating editor image for, 275–278
  creating height map for, 270–275
  creating normal map for, 265–270
  creating shaders for, 279–281
  creating specular map for, 260–265
  eliminating seams in, 254–257
  exposing seams in, 252–254
  resizing images for, 248–251
  testing in game, 283
  turning images into, 247–248
  value of repeating, 251–252
cut-scenes, in loading screen, 23

• D •

Dark Matter Mayhem mod
  overview, 359–360
  problems with, 360
DDS (DirectDraw Surface) images
  converting modified model images into, 332
  converting Targa images into, 275–278
  overview, 19–20
deathmatch
  defined, 195
  defining crates presence during, 198–199
  team, 197
definition files
  creating for multiplayer levels, 205–206
  defined, 204
  determining level size, 212–215
  editing for tourney play, 216
deleting, unnecessary hall brushes, 98
`description.txt` file, 316
designing minimally, importance of, 344–345

Desktop (GUI editor)
  adding child layer to, 296–300
  overview, 294
detail brushes
  turning crate brushes into, 165
  turning light fixtures into, 158
details. *See also* pickups
  adding accent lights, 155–160
  adding crates, 163–164
  adding crates to outside structure, 168–169
  adding ledges, 152–155
  creating climbable crates, 164–165
  creating custom textures, 249
  creating mip-maps for image, 275–278
  designing minimally, 344–345
  from images to textures, 248
  pairing doors to work in tandem, 162–163
  placing crates for strategy, 166–167
  testing, 182–183
  value of adding, 151
dialog boxes
  Add Noise (Photoshop), 272–275
  Color Balance (Photoshop), 330
  Color Picker (map editor), 78–79
  Color Range (Photoshop), 263
  Fill (Photoshop), 263–264
  Find (ModView), 322–323
  GUI selection (GUI editor), 289–290
  Image Size (Photoshop), 259–260
  Item Properties (GUI editor), 295–297
  Offset (Photoshop), 252–254, 257–258
  Surface Inspector (map editor), 70–71, 288
diffuse map
  computer finding, 279–280
  creating, 259–260
  defined, 246
dimensions
  player, 349
  understanding, 26–27
DirectDraw Surface (DDS) images
  converting modified model images into, 332
  converting Targa images into, 275–278
  overview, 19–20

+disconnect command, adding to shortcut's Target field, 35–36
display mode, adjusting settings for, 36–38
distribution package
　creating custom image for, 336
　creating README file for, 336
　for game additions, 334–337
　for game alterations, 337–340
　including README files in, 333–334
distribution, tips for, 340
Doom (id Software, Inc.), FPS games, 10
doors
　adding accent lights over, 156–157
　adding GUIs to control, 286–288
　adding motion to, 142–143
　adding player interactive buttons to, 305–307
　applying texture to, 138–139
　creating appearance of sliding, 137
　creating custom GUI for, 296–305
　GUI interactivity considerations, 292–293
　pairing to work in tandem, 162–163
　setting GUIs to control, 290–292
doorways
　applying texture to, 138
　creating, 100–104
　creating with Clipper tool, 136–137
　fixing bottleneck situation, 141
　fixing textures around, 137–140
　ways of creating, 135–136
Doubler pickup, function of, 216
Drach-FPS-Mappack mod
　overview, 355–356
　problems with, 356
drawing. *See also* brushes
　creating brushes with, 53–54
　defined, 53
dr4ch (author, *Drach-FPS-Mappack* mod), 355
duplicating. *See* copying

• E •

edges, defining map, 126
editor image
　creating, 275–278
　defined, 246

effects, modding, 350
Elliptical Marquee tool (Photoshop), modifying model eyeball with, 326
end user, importance of instructing, 21
enemies
　creating triggers for Stroggs, 187–192
　inserting Stroggs for single-player game, 186
　in multiplayer versus single-player action, 185
　removing for testing, 243
entities
　adding light to maps, 76
　adding light to outdoor structure, 144
　adding portal to door, 143–144
　adding trigger entities to monster_strogg_marine, 187–192
　adding virtual sun with light, 146–148
　creating flag, 201
　creating open doors with, 142–143
　creating trigger, 187–192
　creating triggers for monster_gladiator, 193–194
　inserting monster_gladiator, 192
　inserting monster_strogg_marine, 186
　overview, 28–29
　positioning light, 78
　positioning monster_gladiator, 192–193
　simulating ambient light with, 148–150
　turning brushes into GUI, 288–290
Entity tab
　adjusting player spawn point orientation with, 81–82
　defining doors as teams in, 162–163
environment, creating with texture, 245–246
Eraser tool (Photoshop), function of, 330
errors
　creating triangles, 346–347
　CSG Subtraction tool for, 346
　oversized brushes, 347
　planning, 344
　running CD programs, 368
　ways of avoiding, 345–346
examples, re-creating from, 347–348
exiting, game, 90
eyeballs, modifying model, 325–327

• F •

faces. *See also* brushes
  accessing difficult, 139–140
  defined, 67
  fixing textures of doorways, 137–140
  selecting/painting ceiling and floor, 71–73
  selecting/painting on walls, 68–69
falloff level, creating virtual sun, 146–148
Feather tool (Photoshop), function of, 328
file corruption, using Hollow tool, 59
file extensions
  for pak files, 18
  saving files in NotePad, 280
  for script files, 227–228
  for Targa images, 19
files. *See also* specific files
  added to mods by game, 318
  avoiding overwriting game, 21
  converting Targa to DDS, 19–20, 276–278
  creating definition for multiplayer levels, 205–206
  decompressing pak, 18–19
  definition, 204
  determining level size and definition, 212–215
  editing definition for tourney play, 216
  extracting glossary terms from pak, 223–226
  importance of including all necessary, 21
  including in game additions distribution package, 334–335
  including in game alterations at distribution package, 338
  locating compiled maps, 89
  map compilation resulting in, 87
  material for models, 320–321
  modding audio, 350
  naming scripting, 280–281
  organization of pak, 321
  searching for material, 321–324
  shader, 246
  understanding game function and pak, 313–314
  viewing game, 313–314

Fill dialog box (Photoshop), creating specular map with, 263–264
final coats, texture, 50
Find dialog box (ModView), finding materials with, 322–323
first-person shooter (FPS) games, history of, 10
first-person shooter (FPS) players, competition for, 9
Fit button (Surface Inspector dialog box), adjusting texture fit with, 71
flags
  creating CTF, 201
  placing CTF, 201–204
`flag_stand_new.lwo` model, placing flags with, 202–204
Fleischer, Major (author, *Fleischhaus* mod), 356
Fleischhaus mod
  overview, 356
  problems with, 357
Flip X button (Surface Inspector dialog box), function of, 71
Flip Y button (Surface Inspector dialog box), function of, 71
floors
  option of mitering, 116–117
  selecting/painting, 71–73
flow, placing pickups, 171
folder structure, viewing game, 313
folders
  adding custom mods with, 315–316
  packaging distribution files, 335–339
  viewing game, 313–314
FPS (first-person shooter) games, history of, 10
FPS (first-person shooter) players, competition for, 9
Fragger, Tom "imTFG" (author, *Dark Matter Mayhem* mod), 359
freeware programs, overview, 366
Fullscreen mode, changing from to Windowed mode, 36–38

func_door entity
  adding portal to, 143–144
  creating opening doors with, 142
func_mover entity, turning platform hinge into, 236
func_static entities
  turning brushes into GUI, 288–290
  turning crate brushes into, 165
  turning light fixtures into, 158
  turning platform track into, 237

• G •

game modification, overview, 9
game-defined mods, understanding, 313–314
games. *See also specific games*
  development of FPS, 10
  differences among, modding, 22
gamex86.dll file, function of, 318
gaming groups, getting original ideas from, 343–344
General tab (Item Properties dialog box, GUI editor)
  adding child layer with, 296–297
  function of, 295
gladiators
  creating triggers for, 193–194
  inserting, 192
  positioning, 192–193
  removing for testing, 243
glossary
  extracting, 223–226
  of scripting terms, 222–223
GNU software, overview, 366
Gookin, Dan (*PCs For Dummies*), 365
graphical user interfaces (GUIs). *See also* GUI editor
  adding child layer to custom, 296–297, 301–304
  adding player interactive buttons to, 305–307
  adding structure around, 293
  adding text to custom, 304–305
  adding to control doors, 286–288

adjusting child layer size of custom, 298–299
applying custom, 308–309
changing child layer color of custom, 299–300
copying child layers of custom, 300–301
creating images in Photoshop, 297
exploring potential uses for, 310
interactivity considerations, 292–293
overview, 29–30
role of, 285
saving, 307–308
selecting background color for, 295–296
setting to control doors, 290–292
starting custom, 294
turning brushes into, 288–290
grid size
  changing 2D window, 55–56
  hollowing out brushes, 58
ground
  adding texture to, 132
  fixing overlapping, 128
g_showHud 0 command, hiding HUD with, 210
g_showHud 1 command, unhiding HUD with, 210
Guard pickup, function of, 216
GUI editor
  adding child layer, 296–297, 301–304
  adding text in, 304–305
  adjusting child layer size in, 298–299
  changing child layer color in, 299–300
  copying child layers in, 300–301
  overview, 293
  starting, 294
  starting custom GUI, 294
GUI selection dialog box, turning brushes into GUI entities, 289–290
GUIs (graphical user interfaces). *See also* GUI editor
  adding child layer to custom, 296–297, 301–304
  adding player interactive buttons to, 305–307
  adding structure around, 293
  adding text to custom, 304–305

Index 377

adding to control doors, 286–288
adjusting child layer size of custom, 298–299
applying custom, 308–309
changing child layer color of custom, 299–300
copying child layers of custom, 300–301
creating images in Photoshop, 297
exploring potential uses for, 310
interactivity considerations, 292–293
overview, 29–30
role of, 285
saving, 307–308
selecting background color for, 295–296
setting to control doors, 290–292
starting custom, 294
turning brushes into, 288–290
guns, placing, 173–176

• H •

halls
  creating doorways for, 100–104
  drawing connecting, 96–97
  hollowing out, 97–98
  lighting, 105–106
  resizing walls in, 98–99
  retexturing walls, 104–105
hallways, playing width, 106–107
Hansen, Jarad "TinMan" (author, *SABot* mod), 363
haste power pickups, placing, 179
head, modifying model, 328–331
Heads Up Display (HUD), hiding, 210
health pickups, placing, 172–173, 175
height
  considering sky, 126
  creating custom textures, 249
  determining hall, 96
height map
  creating, 270–275
  defined, 246
help
  finding, 350–351
  Wiley Product Technical Support, 368
hiding, doors, 138

Hollow button (mapping editor)
  hollowing halls with, 97–98
  hollowing rooms with, 59
Hovertank 3D (id Software, Inc.), FPS gaming, 10
HUD (Heads Up Display), hiding, 210

• I •

id Software, Inc.
  adding Radiant mapping tool, 33
  development of FPS games, 10
  Doom, 10
  Hovertank 3D, 10
ideas
  finding original, 343–344
  looking for mod, 11–12
Image Size dialog box (Photoshop), creating diffuse map with, 259–260
Image tab (Item Properties dialog box, GUI editor)
  function of, 295
  selecting background color from, 296
image-editing software. *See also* Adobe Photoshop
  editing screenshots in, 208–209
  selecting, 19–20
images
  antialasing and quality, 38
  compressing modified model, 332
  creating for packaging, 336
  creating screenshot for custom loading screen, 207–208
  creating thumbnail, 211–212
  editing screenshot for custom loading screen, 208–209
  eliminating seams in, 254–257
  exposing seams in, 252–254
  moddability of, 12–13
  modifying a model body in Photoshop, 327–328
  modifying model eyeball in Photoshop, 325–327
  modifying model in Photoshop, 324–325
  offsetting to original position, 257–258
  resizing for custom textures, 248–251

images *(continued)*
  resizing screenshot, 209–211
  textures consisting of, 246
  turning into custom textures, 247–248
  viewing modified model, 332
indoor lights, defining with texture, 160–162
`info_player_deathmatch` entity, creating/positioning, 195–196
instructions
  creating, 336, 338
  importance of including, 21
  missing from *Corpse Stay and Self Shadow* mod, 353–355
  preparing for distribution package, 333–334
Item Properties dialog box (GUI editor)
  adding child layer with, 296–297
  selecting background color from, 295–296

• K •

keyboard shortcuts
  copying, 335
  copying textures from brush to brush, 69
  correcting seams, 255
  deselecting items, 264
  for Find dialog box (ModView), 322
  flipping selection, 121
  maneuvering 2D window with, 55–56
  moving within CAM window, 60
  pasting, 335
  saving, 65
  screenshot, 207
  selecting brush faces, 68
  shifting texture with, 70–71
  switching among 2D Window views, 47
  targeting entities with trigger, 189
  undoing operations, 102
  using mapping editor, 48
  zooming model, 181

• L •

Lasso tool (Photoshop), function of, 328
leaks
  checking for portal, 123
  fixing around doorways, 143–144
  importance of avoiding, 64
  preventing in outdoor structures, 131
  seeing in console window, 88–89
ledges
  adding textures to, 153–155
  adding to walls, 152–153
levels
  creating definition file for, 204–206
  creating flow for, 171
  defined, 83
  determining size of, 212–215
  loading custom, 90
  moddability of, 13
  multiplayer, 204
  origin of, 24
  overview, 23
  process for creating custom, 14
light box
  adding texture to, 157–158
  defining indoor with texture, 161–162
Light Editor
  creating virtual sun with, 146–148
  simulating ambient light with, 148–150
light entities
  adding to accent lights, 159
  adding to halls, 105–106
  adding to maps, 75–77
  adding to outdoor structure, 144
  adding virtual sun with, 146–148
  changing color of, 78–79
  positioning, 78
  simulating ambient light with, 148–150
light textures, creating sun with, 146
lighting
  adding accent, 155–156
  adding light entities to ask, 159
  adding texture to accent, 156–157
  copying accent, 160
  creating specular map for, 260–265
  defining indoor with texture, 160–162
  defining reaction to texture, 246
  optimizing accent, 158
  understanding outdoor environment, 144–146
lighting process, map compilation, 86
`lights/i_nofall` texture, applying to outdoor environment, 148
limitations, creating with crates, 169

Index

loading
  adjustments for quicker, 34–36
  mods, 317–318
  ModView, 320
loading screens
  creating custom, 206
  editing screenshot for, 208–209
  moddability of, 12
  overview, 23
  taking screenshot for, 207–208
location, creating with texture, 245–246
Logo Crosshair mod
  overview, 357
  problems with, 358

• M •

Make Detail option, unavailability of, 160
mapping tool. *See* Radiant mapping editor
maps (game). *See also* Radiant mapping editor; *specific elements*
  adding light to, 75–77
  adding player spawn point to, 79
  adjusting player spawn point orientation on, 81–82
  Building blocks of, 25
  caulking, 51–53
  compiling with added hallways, 106–107
  creating outside area of, 127–128
  defining edge of, 126
  drawing brushes for, 53–54
  finding original ideas for, 343–344
  hollowing out brushes in, 58–59
  importance of designing minimally, 344–345
  importance of planning, 344
  importance of sealing, 64
  measurement units for, 27
  with multiplayer capabilities, 195
  overview, 24–25
  placing models in, 181–182
  positioning player spawn point on, 80
  re-creating from example, 347–348
  resizing/moving brushes in, 56–57
  saving, 64–65
  selecting textures for, 49
  setting boundaries, 25
  understanding dimensions of, 26–27
  using prefabs in, 348
maps (image)
  creating diffuse, 259–260
  creating editor image, 275–278
  creating height, 270–275
  creating normal, 265–270
  creating specular, 260–265
  types of, 246
Material field (Surface Inspector dialog box), overview, 70
material files
  in *Corpse Stay and Self Shadow* mod, 354–355
  creating shaders in, 279–281
  including in game package, 334
  for models, 320–321
  searching for, 321–324
Maze War, FPS gaming, 10
measuring, map units for, 27
memory, CD problems, 368
menus, in mapping editor, 47
Microsoft Windows, using CD with, 366
Microsoft Zip, accessing compressed files with, 19. *See also* WinZip
mip-maps, creating, 275–278
mitering
  exterior corners, 132
  floor and ceiling options, 116–117
  ledges, 153
  overview, 112–113
  wall corners, 114–116
modding
  additional options for, 350
  defined, 12
  differences among games, 22
  models with Photoshop, 319
  process of, 14
models
  adding for power pickups, 179–182
  altering with Photoshop, 319
  compressing modified images of, 332
  creating, 350
  loading for modification, 320–321
  material files for, 320–321
  modifying body, 327–328
  modifying eyeballs on, 325–327
  modifying head, 328–331

models *(continued)*
  modifying images in Photoshop, 324–325
  placing with flags, 202–204
  searching material files for, 321–324
  viewing modified, 332
`models/characters/marine/body` file, function of, 320
`models/characters/marine/body_collision` file, function of, 321
`models/characters/marine/body_d.tga` file
  function of, 324
  modifying, 327–328
`models/characters/marine/eye` file, function of, 321
`models/characters/marine/eye_green_d.tga` file
  function of, 324
  modifying, 325–327
`models/characters/marine/hair` file, function of, 321
`models/characters/marine_heads/head_collision` file, function of, 321
`models/characters/marine_heads/kane6` file, function of, 321
`models/characters/marine_heads/kane6_d.tga` file
  function of, 325
  modifying, 329–331
`models/characters/marine/teeth` file, function of, 321
`models/characters/marine/teeth_d.tga` file, function of, 325
Modifications window, viewing mods in, 313
mods. *See also* maps (games); models
  adding custom, 315–317
  Corpse Stay and Self Shadow, 353–355
  Dark Matter Mayhem, 359–360
  defined, 9
  Drach-FPS-Mappack, 355–356
  finding original ideas for, 343–344
  Fleischhaus, 356–357
  importance of planning, 344
  loading, 317–318
  maintaining original game with, 311–314
  naming, 315–317
  Q4GIB-Instagib Mod, 358–359
  Q4MAX Competition Mod, 363
  Quake 4 WOD-Weapons of Destruction, 360–361
  Quake4logo_crosshair, 357–358
  understanding game-defined, 313–314
  X-Battle, 362
ModView
  function of, 319
  loading, 320
  locating models/skins in, 320–321
  searching material files in, 321–324
  viewing modified model images in, 332
`monster_gladiator` entities
  creating triggers for, 193–194
  inserting, 192
  positioning, 192–193
monsters
  creating triggers for gladiators, 193–194
  creating triggers for Stroggs, 187–192
  inserting gladiators, 192
  inserting Stroggs, 186
  inserting Stroggs for single-player game, 186
  positioning gladiators, 192–193
  removing for testing, 243
  targeting the trigger entity to Stroggs, 189
`monster_strogg_marine` entity
  adding trigger entities to, 187–192
  inserting, 186
  targeting with trigger entity, 189
Move Model command, 181
`moveToPos( )` command, moving entities with, 239–240, 243
mptexture texture set, adding to ledges, 153–155
`mptextures/trim_h5` texture, applying to ledges, 153
`mptextures/vertical_5_new` texture, applying to doors, 138
multiplayer action
  playing one-on-one, 195–197
  versus single-player action, 185
  team-based play, 197–204

Index

multiplayer levels
  creating definition file for, 204–206
  determining size of, 212–215
  overview, 204
Multi-Purpose window (mapping editor), overview, 46–47

• N •

naming
  folders, 315
  following standard conventions for, 20
  GUIs, 308
  mods, 316–317
  WinZip files, 317
Natural Button (Surface Inspector dialog box), function of, 71
Nodraw texture
  creating GUI from, 286–288
  creating portals with, 119–121, 143–144
noise, adding in height map, 272
normal map
  creating with NVIDIA filter, 265–270
  creating without NVIDIA filter, 270
  defined, 246
Normal Map Generator tool (ATI)
  on CD, 367
  using, 270
Notepad
  creating definition files with, 205
  creating README files in, 336, 338
  creating script in, 227–228
  editing for tourney play in, 216
  naming mods in, 316–317
  opening script files with, 226
  saving files in, 280
  scripting, 222
  scripting platform movement in, 239–243
  scripting shaders in, 279–281
  as text editor application, 222
  updating level size information with, 213–214
`no_touch` command, triggering doors to open, 292
NVIDIA normal map filter
  example of, 269
  using, 267–268

NVIDIA Photoshop plug-ins
  creating custom textures, 247
  creating normal map with, 266–270

• O •

Offset dialog box (Photoshop)
  exposing image seams with, 252–254
  returning images to original position, 257–258
one-on-one based play, creating, 195–197
opacity, changing in Photoshop, 329
opponents
  creating triggers for Stroggs, 187–192
  inserting Stroggs for single-player game, 186
  in multiplayer versus single-player action, 185
  removing for testing, 243
optimization
  accent lights fixture, 158
  automatic during compile process, 117–118
  climbable crates, 165
  commands to show what is being rendered within game, 110–111
  creating portals, 118–121
  mitering floor and ceiling, 116–117
  mitering walls, 112–116
  need for, 109–110
  viewing after, 122–123
orientation
  correcting texture, 153–155
  of pickups, 180
original game, maintaining, 21, 311–314
outdoor environment
  adding textures for, 126
  creating with texture, 245–246
  understanding lighting of, 144–146
outdoor structures. *See also* rooms
  accessing with Clipper tool, 136–137
  adding crates to, 168–169
  adding light entities to, 144
  adding texture to building exteriors, 132–133
  adding texture to ground of, 132

outdoor structures. *See also* rooms
  (continued)
  adding texture to outer wall and sky, 134–135
  adding texture to roof tops, 133
  adding virtual sun to, 146–148
  creating, 127–128
  defining boundaries in, 130–131
  filling useless corners in, 129–130
  fixing ground problems in, 128–129
  importance of texture, 131
  overview, 125
  simulating ambient light in, 148–150
  testing, 150
overwriting, avoiding, 21, 311–314

• P •

painting
  ceiling and floor faces, 71–73
  faces, 68–69
painting a brush face, defined, 67
pak files (.pk4)
  decompressing, 18–19
  extracting glossary terms from, 223–226
  organization of, 321
  understanding game function, 313–314
parent Desktop (GUI editor), overview, 294
pasting, keyboard shortcut for, 335
patch meshes, using, 348–349
PCs For Dummies (Gookin), 365
photographs. *See also* images
  resizing for custom textures, 248–251
  turning into custom textures, 247–248
  using for custom textures, 246
Photoshop. *See* Adobe Photoshop
pickups
  adding ammo, 176–179
  adding armor, 170–172
  adding health, 172–173
  adding models for power, 179–182
  adding weapons, 173–176
  hiding, 75
  overview, 170
  placing health, 175
  placing power, 179
  testing, 182–183
pixels, measurement units for maps, 27
placing
  armor for pickup, 170–172
  crates for strategy, 166–167
  gladiator entities, 192
  health pickups, 172–173
  models, 181–182
  player interactive buttons on GUIs, 303
  Strogg entities, 186, 190–191
  weapons, 173–176
plain text. *See also* text
  defined, 18
  scripting, 222
plain text editor
  creating definition files with, 205
  creating README files in, 336, 338
  creating script in, 227–228
  editing for tourney play in, 216
  naming mods in, 316–317
  need for, 18
  opening script files with, 226
  saving files in, 280
  scripting, 222
  scripting platform movement in, 239–243
  scripting shaders in, 279–281
  as text editor application, 222
  updating level size information with, 213–214
planning, importance of, 344
platforms
  adding texture to, 231–233
  creating, 229–231
  creating track for, 233–234
  function of, 228–229
  scripting movement of, 238–243
  setting up for movement, 236–238
  testing, 243–244
  turning, 234–236
Player process, overview, 86
player spawn points
  adding, 79
  adding for one-on-one play, 195–197
  adjusting orientation of, 81–82
  placing for team play, 199–200

positioning, 80
recommended number of, 196
players. *See also* single-player action; team-based play
   creating bottleneck with, 141
   dimensions of game, 349
   maximum number allowed, 200
   one-on-one based play, 195–197
playing, before making mods, 11
plug-ins, NVIDIA Photoshop, 247, 266–270
point entities
   creating/placing armor, 170–172
   overview, 29
   placing ammo, 176–179
   placing health, 172–173
   placing power, 179
   placing weapon, 173–176
polygons
   normal map affecting, 265–266
   reducing with mitering, 112–116
   seeing after optimization, 122
   showing rendering with, 111–112
portals. *See also* areas
   adding inside doorways, 143–144
   creating for optimization, 118–121
   defined, 85
   viewing after optimization, 122
power pickups (power-ups)
   adding models with, 179–182
   for arena CTF games, 216–217
   placing, 179
prefabs, using, 348
primer, adding texture, 50
programming, versus scripting, 221

• Q •

Q4GIB-Instagib Mod
   overview, 358–359
   problems with, 359
Q4MAX Competition Mod, 363
QRAD (Quake Radiance) process, overview, 86
Quake 4 Model Viewer
  function of, 319
  loading, 320
  locating models/skins in, 320–321
  searching material files in, 321–324
  viewing modified model images in, 332
Quake 4 WOD-Weapons of Destruction mod
   overview, 360–361
   problems with, 361
Quake4Config.cfg file, function of, 318
Quake4logo_crosshair mod
   overview, 357
   problems with, 358

• R •

Radiant mapping editor. *See also* maps (game)
   adjusting screen resolution for, 42–43
   adjusting windows in, 43–44
   buttons/menus in, 47
   editor settings displayed in, 58
   fixing overlapping walls in, 60–63
   history of, 33
   image defined for use by, 246
   installing, 33–34
   launching, 41
   maneuvering CAM window in, 60
   maneuvering 2D window in, 54–56
   preparing to access, 34–40
   problems with, 48
   recommended screen resolution for, 41–42
   using keyboard shortcuts, 48
   working with textures, 50–51
railing, creating for platform, 235
RAM, CD problems, 368
Rathbone, Andy
   Windows 2000 Professional For Dummies, 365
   Windows XP For Dummies, 365
README files
   creating, 336, 338
   importance of including, 21
   missing from *Corpse Stay and Self Shadow* mod, 353–355
   preparing for distribution package, 333–334

Reinhold, Moritz (author, *Fleischhaus* mod), 356
rendering
  overview, 25
  showing, 110–112
  textures facilitating, 28
  understanding, 85
resizing
  child layer, 298–299
  head image, 329
  images for custom textures, 248–251
  screenshot images, 209–211
  specular map image, 264–265
  to thumbnail images, 211–212
resolution, resizing screenshots, 209
Rock texture set, covering ground with, 132
`rock/sand01` texture, applying to ground, 132
roof tops, adding texture to, 133
rooms. *See also* outdoor structures
  adding texture to exterior of, 132–133
  changing duplicate, 95–96
  copying, 93–95
  creating doorways for, 100–104
  drawing halls between, 96–97
  fixing overlapping walls in, 60–63
  hollowing out brushes for, 58–59
  player dimensions, 349
  positioning within outdoor environment, 127
Rotate Model command, 181
`rotateTo( )` command, causing platform rotation with, 241–242
`r_showPortals 1` command, showing what is being rendered within game, 111
`r_showTris 2` command, showing what is being rendered within game, 110–111
Rubber Stamp tool (Photoshop), eliminating image seams with, 254–257
`r_useScissor 0` command, showing what is being rendered within game, 111

• *S* •

SABot (Stupid Angry Bot) mod, 363–364
saving
  custom texture images, 258
  importance of, 22
  maps, 64–65
scale, adjusting texture, 52
Scale values (Surface Inspector dialog box), setting texture width/height with, 71
Scout pickup, function of, 216
screen resolution
  adjusting for mapping editor, 42–43
  viewing mapping editor, 41–42
screenshot images. *See also* images
  creating for custom loading screen, 207–208
  editing for custom loading screen, 208–209
  resizing, 209–211
script files, opening with Notepad, 226
scripting
  adding player interactive buttons to GUIs with, 306–307
  closing, 280
  versus coding, 221
  glossary of terms, 222–223
  necessary tools for, 221–222
  overview, 29
  platform movement, 238–243
  shaders, 278–281
  text editors, 222
  understanding, 226–228
sealing
  around doorways, 143–144
  checking for portal leaks, 123
  importance of, 64
  outdoor structures, 131
seams
  eliminating image, 254–257
  exposing image, 252–254
searching
  for material files, 321–324
  for Web sites to distribute to, 340
`+set com_allowConsole 1` command, adding to shortcut's Target field, 35–36
shader, defined, 278
shader files, texture images, 246
shadows, *Corpse Stay and Self Shadow* mod, 353–355

Index

shareware programs, overview, 366
Shift Horizontally field (Surface Inspector dialog box), using, 70
Shift Vertically field (Surface Inspector dialog box), using, 70
shortcuts. *See also* keyboard shortcuts
  creating to Quake 4, 34
  customizing, 35
single-player action
  creating triggers for Stroggs, 187–192
  inserting Stroggs, 186
  versus multiplayer action, 185
size. *See also* resizing
  determining levels, 212–215
  turning images to textures, 248–251
Skies texture set, creating open sky with, 134–135
`skies/canyonclouds_sky` texture, applying to sky, 134
skins (model)
  compressing modified images of, 332
  locating, 320–321
  modifying body, 325–327
  modifying eyeballs, 325–327
  modifying head, 328–331
  modifying in Photoshop, 324–325
  searching material files for, 321–324
  viewing modified, 332
sky, height considerations, 126
Sleepwalker (author, *Quake4logo_crosshair* mod), 357
sliding doors, creating appearance of, 137
Spasim, FPS gaming, 10
spawn points
  adding, 79
  adding for one-on-one play, 195–197
  adjusting orientation of, 81–82
  placing for team play, 199–200
  positioning, 80
  recommended number of, 196
specular map
  computer finding, 279–280
  creating, 260–265
  defined, 246
splitting. *See* Clipper tool
starting point, adding, 79
strategy, placing crates for, 166–167

`strogg_flag` entity
  creating, 201
  placing, 201–204
Stroggs
  adding trigger entities to, 187–192
  creating triggers for, 187–192
  inserting, 186
  inserting for single-player game, 186
  removing for testing, 243
  targeting the trigger entity, 189
structures. *See also* rooms
  accessing outdoor with Clipper tool, 136–137
  adding around GUI, 293
  adding crates to outdoor, 168–169
  adding light entities to outdoor, 144
  adding texture to building exteriors, 132–133
  adding texture to ground of outdoor, 132
  adding texture to light box, 157–158
  adding texture to outer wall and sky, 134–135
  adding texture to roof tops, 133
  adding virtual sun to outdoor, 146–148
  creating outdoor, 127–128
  defining boundaries in outdoor, 130–131
  defining indoor light box with texture, 161–162
  filling useless corners in outdoor, 129–130
  fixing ground problems in outdoor, 128–129
  importance of texture in outdoor, 131
  outdoor, 125
  simulating ambient light in outdoor, 148–150
  testing outdoor, 150
Stupid Angry Bot (*SABot*) mod, 363–364
Subdivide Patch option (Surface Inspector dialog box), function of, 71
sun
  adding virtual, 146–148
  reproducing effect of, 145–146
Surface Inspector dialog box
  adjusting GUI texture settings with, 288
  adjusting texture settings with, 70–71
surface type, defining for custom textures, 279
system requirements, 365

• T •

tandem, doors working in, 162–163
Targa (TGA) images
  converting into DDS format, 275–278
  creating custom texture from, 247
  image-editing software, 19
  quality levels of, 259
target, defined, 189
Target field, adding commands to shortcut's, 35–36
targeting
  enemy entity with trigger entity, 189–190
  to set GUIs to control doors, 291
team deathmatch
  defined, 197
  placing team spawn points for, 199–200
team-based play
  adding blockades for, 198–199
  placing team spawn points for, 199–200
  types of, 197–198
teams
  defining doors as, 162–163
  multiplayer games, 185
Terminal texture set, adding texture around doors with, 138
`terminal/t1_meta12` texture
  applying to bottoms of platforms, 232–233
  applying to doorways, 138, 140
  applying to light fixtures, 140, 157, 161
  applying to platform tracks, 234
text. *See also* plain text
  adding to GUIs, 304–305
  adding to screenshot, 209
  hiding, 210
text editor. *See* Notepad; plain text editor
text files, for mods naming, 316–317
Text tab (Item Properties dialog box, GUI editor), function of, 295
texture scale, adjusting, 52
texture sets
  adding Canyon to crates, 164–165
  adding Common Lights to accent lights, 156–157
  adding mptexture to ledges, 153–155
  adding texture around doors with Terminal, 138
  adding texture to platform tracks from Common Misc, 234
  adding texture to platforms from Common Floors, 231
  adding texture to platforms from Core, 231–232
  creating GUI from Common, 286–288
  creating indoor light box with, 160–162
  loading, 50–51
  loading Common, 51–52
  loading Common Walls, 67–68
  Rock, 132
  using Common Walls for building exteriors, 132–133
  using Common Walls for outer wall, 134
  using Common Walls for roof tops, 133
  using Skies, 134–135
textures. *See also* specific textures
  adding to accent lights, 156–157
  adding to building exteriors, 132–133
  adding to climbable crates, 164–165
  adding to ledges, 153–155
  adding to light, 146
  adding to light box, 157–158
  adding to outer wall and sky, 134–135
  adding to platform railing, 235
  adding to platform tracks, 234
  adding to platforms, 231–233
  adding to roof tops, 133
  adding to sky, 134–135
  adjusting settings for, 70–71
  applying custom, 281–282
  applying to hallway walls, 104
  correcting orientation of, 153–155
  creating diffuse map for custom, 259–260
  creating editor image for custom, 275–278
  creating height map for custom, 270–275
  creating location with, 245–246
  creating normal map for custom, 265–270
  creating outdoor environment, 125–126
  creating shaders for custom, 279–281
  creating specular map for custom, 260–265

defining boundaries with, 130–131
defining indoor lights with, 160–162
eliminating seams in custom, 254–257
exposing seams in custom, 252–254
fixing around doorways, 137–140
image components of, 246
importance of in outdoor structures, 131
methods of acquiring, 345
moddability of, 12–13
overview, 27–28
resizing images for custom, 248–251
selecting, 49
sizing of, 55
testing custom in game, 283
tools for creating custom, 247
trigger, 188, 193
turning images into custom, 247–248
using clipping tool, 103
value of repeating custom, 251–252
Textures folder, exploring, 51
Textures folder icon, caution about, 51
TGA (Targa) images
  converting into DDS format, 275–278
  creating custom texture from, 247
  image-editing software, 19
  quality levels of, 259
3D
  adding texture, 28
  understanding concept of, 26–27
thumbnail images
  computer finding, 279
  creating, 211–212
tilde (~) key, opening/closing console with, 39–40
tileable images, defined, 67
tiling, overview, 251–252
tools. *See also* GUI editor; ModView; plain text editor; Radiant mapping editor
  for accessing compressed files, 18–19
  ATI Normal Map Generator, 270
  Clipper, 101–104, 120–121, 130–131, 136–137, 235–236
  for converting DDS images, 20
  for creating custom texture, 247
  CSG Subtraction, 346
  Elliptical Marquee (Photoshop), 326

Eraser (Photoshop), 330
Feather (Photoshop), 328
Hollow, 59, 97–98
image-editing software, 19–20
Lasso (Photoshop), 328
necessary for scripting, 221–222
need for additional, 13
Normal Map Generator, 270
overview of necessary, 17–18
plain text editor, 18
Rubber Stamp (Photoshop), 254–257
tourney
  adding crate blockades for, 198–199
  defined, 197
  placing team spawn points for, 199–200
  playing, 215–216
triangles
  creating error-free, 346–347
  creating with Clipper tool, 119
triggers
  creating for gladiator entities, 193–194
  creating for platform, 237–238
  creating for Strogg entities, 187–192
2D window (mapping editor)
  copying rooms, 94–95
  creating halls, 96–97
  maneuvering, 54–56
  overview, 47
  resizing brushes from, 56
  splitting brushes, 101–102

• U •

`unbind` command, unbinding entities with, 243
unhiding, doors, 138
units, measuring maps, 27
user interfaces, moddability of, 12

• V •

VGA Graphics, *Wolfenstein 3D*, 10
video settings
  adjusting, 36
  adjusting display mode, 36–38

video settings *(continued)*
  reducing brightness, 39–40
  turning off antialiasing, 38–39
`vid_restart` command, reducing brightness, 39
visibility (VIS) process, overview, 85–86
Visportal texture, creating portals with, 121

• W •

`waitFor` command, instructing game to wait with, 240–241, 242
walls
  adding ledges to, 152–155
  adjusting texture settings on, 70–71
  defining map edge with, 126
  fixing outdoor structure, 128
  fixing overlapping, 60–63
  importance of mitering, 112–113
  mitering corners of, 114–116
  resizing hallway, 98–99
  retexturing hallway, 104–105
  selecting/painting faces on, 68–69
  splitting to defining boundaries, 130–131
  stretching to filling corners, 129
weapons, placing, 173–176
Web sites
  The Compressonator, 367
  for *Dark Matter Mayhem*, 359
  distributing to, 340
  for *Drach-FPS-Mappack* mod, 355
  finding help on, 365
  for *Fleischhaus* mod, 356
  Normal Map Generator, 367
  Photoshop, 367
  for *Q4GIB*-Instagib Mod, 358
  for *Q4MAX* Competition Mod, 363
  for *Quake 4 WOD-Weapons of Destruction* mod, 360
  for *Quake4logo_crosshair* mod, 357

  for *SABot* (Stupid Angry Bot) mod, 363
  WinZip, 19, 367
  for *X-Battle*, 362
width
  creating custom textures, 250
  determining hall, 96
Wiley Product Technical Support, 368
Windowed mode, changing from Fullscreen mode to, 36–38
windows
  adjusting in mapping editor, 43–44
  mapping editor, 45–47
Windows File Explorer, viewing folder structure in, 313
Windows 2000 Professional For Dummies (Rathbone), 365
Windows XP For Dummies (Rathbone), 365
WinRar, accessing compressed files with, 19
WinZip
  accessing compressed files with, 18–19
  extracting glossary terms with, 223–226
  preparing distribution package with, 336–337
  renaming files in, 317
  trial version, 367
Wolfenstein 3D, FPS gaming, 10
word processing programs
  versus plain text editor, 18
  scripting, 222

• X •

X-Battle mod, 362

• Z •

Z window (mapping editor)
  overview, 47
  resizing brushes from, 57
Zoom Model command, 181

BUSINESS, CAREERS & PERSONAL FINANCE

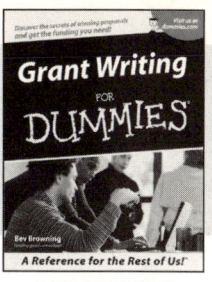

0-7645-5307-0

0-7645-5331-3 *†

Also available:
- Accounting For Dummies †
  0-7645-5314-3
- Business Plans Kit For Dummies †
  0-7645-5365-8
- Cover Letters For Dummies
  0-7645-5224-4
- Frugal Living For Dummies
  0-7645-5403-4
- Leadership For Dummies
  0-7645-5176-0
- Managing For Dummies
  0-7645-1771-6
- Marketing For Dummies
  0-7645-5600-2
- Personal Finance For Dummies *
  0-7645-2590-5
- Project Management For Dummies
  0-7645-5283-X
- Resumes For Dummies †
  0-7645-5471-9
- Selling For Dummies
  0-7645-5363-1
- Small Business Kit For Dummies *†
  0-7645-5093-4

HOME & BUSINESS COMPUTER BASICS

0-7645-4074-2

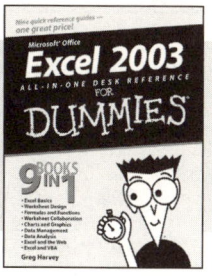

0-7645-3758-X

Also available:
- ACT! 6 For Dummies
  0-7645-2645-6
- iLife '04 All-in-One Desk Reference For Dummies
  0-7645-7347-0
- iPAQ For Dummies
  0-7645-6769-1
- Mac OS X Panther Timesaving Techniques For Dummies
  0-7645-5812-9
- Macs For Dummies
  0-7645-5656-8
- Microsoft Money 2004 For Dummies
  0-7645-4195-1
- Office 2003 All-in-One Desk Reference For Dummies
  0-7645-3883-7
- Outlook 2003 For Dummies
  0-7645-3759-8
- PCs For Dummies
  0-7645-4074-2
- TiVo For Dummies
  0-7645-6923-6
- Upgrading and Fixing PCs For Dummies
  0-7645-1665-5
- Windows XP Timesaving Techniques For Dummies
  0-7645-3748-2

FOOD, HOME, GARDEN, HOBBIES, MUSIC & PETS

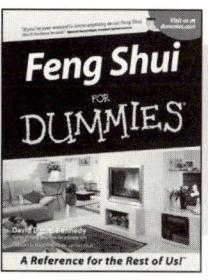

0-7645-5295-3

0-7645-5232-5

Also available:
- Bass Guitar For Dummies
  0-7645-2487-9
- Diabetes Cookbook For Dummies
  0-7645-5230-9
- Gardening For Dummies *
  0-7645-5130-2
- Guitar For Dummies
  0-7645-5106-X
- Holiday Decorating For Dummies
  0-7645-2570-0
- Home Improvement All-in-One For Dummies
  0-7645-5680-0
- Knitting For Dummies
  0-7645-5395-X
- Piano For Dummies
  0-7645-5105-1
- Puppies For Dummies
  0-7645-5255-4
- Scrapbooking For Dummies
  0-7645-7208-3
- Senior Dogs For Dummies
  0-7645-5818-8
- Singing For Dummies
  0-7645-2475-5
- 30-Minute Meals For Dummies
  0-7645-2589-1

INTERNET & DIGITAL MEDIA

0-7645-1664-7

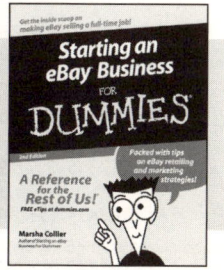

0-7645-6924-4

Also available:
- 2005 Online Shopping Directory For Dummies
  0-7645-7495-7
- CD & DVD Recording For Dummies
  0-7645-5956-7
- eBay For Dummies
  0-7645-5654-1
- Fighting Spam For Dummies
  0-7645-5965-6
- Genealogy Online For Dummies
  0-7645-5964-8
- Google For Dummies
  0-7645-4420-9
- Home Recording For Musicians For Dummies
  0-7645-1634-5
- The Internet For Dummies
  0-7645-4173-0
- iPod & iTunes For Dummies
  0-7645-7772-7
- Preventing Identity Theft For Dummies
  0-7645-7336-5
- Pro Tools All-in-One Desk Reference For Dummies
  0-7645-5714-9
- Roxio Easy Media Creator For Dummies
  0-7645-7131-1

* Separate Canadian edition also available
† Separate U.K. edition also available

Available wherever books are sold. For more information or to order direct: U.S. customers visit www.dummies.com or call 1-877-762-2974.
U.K. customers visit www.wileyeurope.com or call 0800 243407. Canadian customers visit www.wiley.ca or call 1-800-567-4797.

WILEY

SPORTS, FITNESS, PARENTING, RELIGION & SPIRITUALITY

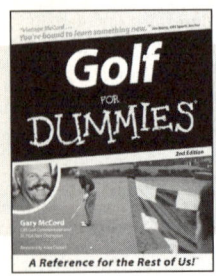

Golf For Dummies
0-7645-5146-9

Parenting For Dummies
0-7645-5418-2

Also available:
- Adoption For Dummies
  0-7645-5488-3
- Basketball For Dummies
  0-7645-5248-1
- The Bible For Dummies
  0-7645-5296-1
- Buddhism For Dummies
  0-7645-5359-3
- Catholicism For Dummies
  0-7645-5391-7
- Hockey For Dummies
  0-7645-5228-7
- Judaism For Dummies
  0-7645-5299-6
- Martial Arts For Dummies
  0-7645-5358-5
- Pilates For Dummies
  0-7645-5397-6
- Religion For Dummies
  0-7645-5264-3
- Teaching Kids to Read For Dummies
  0-7645-4043-2
- Weight Training For Dummies
  0-7645-5168-X
- Yoga For Dummies
  0-7645-5117-5

TRAVEL

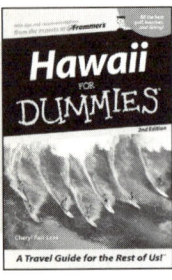

Hawaii For Dummies
0-7645-5438-7

Italy For Dummies
0-7645-5453-0

Also available:
- Alaska For Dummies
  0-7645-1761-9
- Arizona For Dummies
  0-7645-6938-4
- Cancún and the Yucatán For Dummies
  0-7645-2437-2
- Cruise Vacations For Dummies
  0-7645-6941-4
- Europe For Dummies
  0-7645-5456-5
- Ireland For Dummies
  0-7645-5455-7
- Las Vegas For Dummies
  0-7645-5448-4
- London For Dummies
  0-7645-4277-X
- New York City For Dummies
  0-7645-6945-7
- Paris For Dummies
  0-7645-5494-8
- RV Vacations For Dummies
  0-7645-5443-3
- Walt Disney World & Orlando For Dummies
  0-7645-6943-0

GRAPHICS, DESIGN & WEB DEVELOPMENT

Creating Web Pages All-in-One Desk Reference For Dummies
0-7645-4345-8

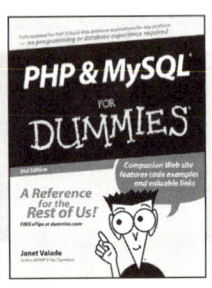

PHP & MySQL For Dummies
0-7645-5589-8

Also available:
- Adobe Acrobat 6 PDF For Dummies
  0-7645-3760-1
- Building a Web Site For Dummies
  0-7645-7144-3
- Dreamweaver MX 2004 For Dummies
  0-7645-4342-3
- FrontPage 2003 For Dummies
  0-7645-3882-9
- HTML 4 For Dummies
  0-7645-1995-6
- Illustrator CS For Dummies
  0-7645-4084-X
- Macromedia Flash MX 2004 For Dummies
  0-7645-4358-X
- Photoshop 7 All-in-One Desk Reference For Dummies
  0-7645-1667-1
- Photoshop CS Timesaving Techniques For Dummies
  0-7645-6782-9
- PHP 5 For Dummies
  0-7645-4166-8
- PowerPoint 2003 For Dummies
  0-7645-3908-6
- QuarkXPress 6 For Dummies
  0-7645-2593-X

NETWORKING, SECURITY, PROGRAMMING & DATABASES

C++ For Dummies
0-7645-6852-3

Hacking For Dummies
0-7645-5784-X

Also available:
- A+ Certification For Dummies
  0-7645-4187-0
- Access 2003 All-in-One Desk Reference For Dummies
  0-7645-3988-4
- Beginning Programming For Dummies
  0-7645-4997-9
- C For Dummies
  0-7645-7068-4
- Firewalls For Dummies
  0-7645-4048-3
- Home Networking For Dummies
  0-7645-42796
- Network Security For Dummies
  0-7645-1679-5
- Networking For Dummies
  0-7645-1677-9
- TCP/IP For Dummies
  0-7645-1760-0
- VBA For Dummies
  0-7645-3989-2
- Wireless All In-One Desk Reference For Dummies
  0-7645-7496-5
- Wireless Home Networking For Dummies
  0-7645-3910-8